Parliament Great Britain

# Report of the Commission appointed to inquire into the Methods of Oyster Culture in the United Kingdom and France

Parliament Great Britain

**Report of the Commission appointed to inquire into the Methods of Oyster Culture in the United Kingdom and France**

ISBN/EAN: 9783337273347

Printed in Europe, USA, Canada, Australia, Japan

Cover: Foto ©Suzi / pixelio.de

More available books at **www.hansebooks.com**

# REPORT OF THE COMMISSION

APPOINTED TO INQUIRE INTO

## THE METHODS

OF

# OYSTER CULTURE

IN

## THE UNITED KINGDOM AND FRANCE,

WITH A VIEW TO THE INTRODUCTION OF IMPROVED
METHODS OF CULTIVATION OF OYSTERS

INTO

## IRELAND.

*Presented to both Houses of Parliament by Command of Her Majesty.*

DUBLIN:

PRINTED BY ALEXANDER THOM, 87 & 88, ABBEY-STREET,

FOR HER MAJESTY'S STATIONERY OFFICE.

1870.

[C.—224.]  *Price 6s.*

# CONTENTS.

---

## PLATES.

WARRANT appointing JOHN A. BLAKE, Esq., M.P., FRANCIS FRANCIS, Esq., GEORGE W. HART, Esq., and THOMAS F. BRADY, Esq., to be COMMISSIONERS for INQUIRING into and REPORTING on the ARTIFICIAL CULTIVATION and PROPAGATION of OYSTERS.

---

## BY THE LORD LIEUTENANT-GENERAL AND GENERAL GOVERNOR OF IRELAND.

ABERCORN.

WHEREAS it has been represented to us that the artificial propagation of oysters, as an important article of food, is at present imperfectly understood in Ireland, and that it is desirable that inquiries should be made into the methods used in some parts of Great Britain and France, in which it has been more successfully carried on, and into the practicability of introducing improved methods of cultivation of oysters into Ireland.

We, JAMES DUKE of ABERCORN, Lord Lieutenant-General and General Governor of Ireland, do hereby nominate and appoint JOHN A. BLAKE, esq., M.P., FRANCIS FRANCIS, esq., GEORGE W. HART, esq., and THOMAS F. BRADY, esq., to be Commissioners, to make such inquiries as aforesaid, and to report fully for our information the result thereof.

Given at Her Majesty's Castle of Dublin this 2nd day of October, 1868.

By His Grace's Command,

THOMAS A. LARCOM.

# OYSTER FISHERIES.

### INSTRUCTIONS TO THE COMMISSION.

MUCH public attention having been directed to the artificial cultivation and propagation of oysters, Her Majesty's Government are very desirous that some authentic information upon this subject should be supplied to the public, with a view of encouraging this industry in Ireland.

The cultivation of oysters in this country is not in a satisfactory state, and little progress appears to have been made in consequence of recent legislation.

Out of nearly ninety licenses granted by the Board of Works for oyster planting, which embrace an area of about 15,000 acres, scarcely half a dozen can be said to be successful. This is the more surprising as Ireland is admittedly well calculated for the successful prosecution of *ostreoculture*. The favourable temperature of the sea, the large inlets and bays on the western coast, containing banks where oysters are already found in great numbers—the habits and tastes of the coast population all show that this most valuable industry might be prosecuted with great success.

With the consent of the Lords Commissioners of the Treasury, His Excellency has determined to appoint an unpaid Commission, consisting of the following gentlemen—J. A. BLAKE, esq., M.P., FRANCIS FRANCIS, esq., GEORGE W. HART, esq., T. F. BRADY, esq.

The duties they are required to perform will be as follows :— They will visit the principal places in France, England, and Ireland where oyster cultivation is, or can be carried on ; they will examine the best authorities upon the subject, and endeavour to ascertain the causes which have hitherto led to the many failures which have been experienced.

The places which should be visited in France would be the great Government Establishments at Arcachon, near Bordeaux, and the private breeding and fattening grounds at the Ile de Ré, Ile de Oleron, Marennes, and La Tremblade, all of which are within a short distance of each other. Concarneau, near Brest, where several descriptions of fish culture are carried on under Government management, it might also be desirable to visit. They will also visit those places in England where attempts, successful or otherwise, have been made to increase the supply of oysters by artificial means, and subsequently inspect certain portions of the coast of Ireland, which, in the opinion of the Commissioners, would be suitable for carrying on oyster culture.

A fortnight would probably suffice for France, the same time for England, and three weeks for Ireland.

They will report fully to His Excellency on the various matters of interest which may occur to them, and they will recommend the measures that appear to them most suitable for increasing and rendering more certain the supply of oysters.

MAYO.

DUBLIN CASTLE.

# REPORT.

MAY IT PLEASE YOUR EXCELLENCY,

We, the Commissioners appointed to inquire into the practicability of introducing improved methods of the cultivation of
oysters into Ireland, beg to report for your Excellency's information as follows :—

In compliance with our instructions, we proceeded in October,
1868, to investigate the various modes of culture employed with
respect to oysters ; the success or otherwise which has attended
such undertakings ; the condition of the natural banks in France
and the United Kingdom ; the cause of their decline in production
(if any), so far as ascertainable, and the means adopted for their
preservation.

For the purpose of carrying out these views, we visited the
following places :—

IN FRANCE :

> Arcachon, Auray, Cancale, Chattellalion, Concarneau,
> Granville, La Tremblade, La Teste, L'Orient, Marennes,
> Oleron, Ré, Rochers D'Aire, Regneville, St. Brieux.

IN THE CHANNEL ISLANDS :

> Jersey.

IN ENGLAND :

> Beaumaris, Brading, Bristol, Colchester, Cowes, Ems-
> worth, Fagborough, Faversham, Hayling, Harwich,
> Hamble, Herne Bay, Ipswich, Langston, Lymington,
> Milford, Nacton, Newtown, New Brompton, Paglesham,
> Tenby, The Solent, Whitstable.

IN IRELAND :

> Arklow, Ballyvaughan, Ballinahinch, Ballinakill, Belfast
> Lough, Baltimore, Bantry Bay, Carlingford, Cork,
> Clew Bay, Cleggan, Clifden, Clonderlaw Bay, Derreen,
> Dungarvan, Fota Island, Galway, Kenmare, Kinsale,
> Killeries, Kinvarra, Kilrush, Sligo, Lough Swilly,
> Lough Foyle, Shannon, Sneem, Queenstown, Water-
> ford, Wexford.

## NATURAL HISTORY OF THE OYSTER.

For the better elucidation of the subject with which we are charged, we deem it desirable in the first instance to give a brief account of the oyster itself.

Hanly gives the following varieties of the oyster in his catalogue of bivalves :—

| Ostrea edulis. | Ostrea rufa. | Ostrea columbiensis. |
|---|---|---|
| hippopus. | magaritaca. | laceraus. |
| adriatica. | gibbosa. | bicolor. |
| cochlear. | elliptica. | multistriata. |
| cristata. | angulata. | callichora. |
| gallina. | echinata. | glaucina. |
| lingua. | stellata. | sinensis. |
| tulipa. | prismatica. | turbinata. |
| scabra. | lamellosa. | crista galli. |
| rostralis. | uncinata. | hyotes. |
| parasitica. | raricosta. | radiata. |
| denticulata. | senegalensis. | inegadon. |
| excavata. | orientalis. | pes. tigris. |
| mytiloides. | rosacea. | lincolnii. |
| sinuata. | chemoritzii. | pyxidata. |
| trapezina. | | |

*Ostrea edulis* is the oyster of commerce in this country.

In all climates, and in all its varied species, the oyster is supposed to be hermaphrodite, and its chief characteristics appear to be the same wherever it is found.

The precise manner in which the impregnation of these molluscs is effected is yet an unsolved enigma.

There are various theories extant upon the subject, which have all been, more or less, under public consideration and discussion. One of the latest is that put forward by Dr. Kellart, which is supported by Mr. G. W. Hart, one of the members of this commission, viz., that there is a mutual fecundation partaken of by all the individuals composing an oyster-bed—a general emission of spermatozoa taking place at a period somewhat prior to the formation of ova in the ovaries.

If this view be correct, it would serve to explain much of what has hitherto been the great *casus belli* between those who hold the opinion that the present scarcity of oysters is caused by failure of spat, and those who attribute the failure to over-dredging. Viewed in this light it would appear that the aggregation of oysters into beds is a provision of nature to effectuate this mutual impregnation, and that when an oyster bank has been so greatly dredged that the component individuals upon it are at great distances from each other, the reproductive powers of the bed may be almost entirely destroyed, although dredgermen may still obtain sufficient oysters to remunerate them for their labour in seasons when prices are high. Unless the tide or current in such cases brings the spermatozoa within reach of adjacent oysters, a bank so reduced ultimately (and quickly) dies out to the great astonishment of those fishermen who can testify (and that truthfully) that there has always been oysters upon it, and that it was not in their opinion exhaustively dredged. The breeding season may be said to commence with the disappearance of the letter R from the nomen-

clature of the months; in truth, however, the development of
spermatozoa (see *a*) takes place generally in the month of April.
In two or three weeks these disappear, and the ovaries become
full of a creamy matter, causing the appearance commonly known
as milchyness.

Under a powerful microscope this is resolved into oval clusters
of globular atoms (*b*, *c*) floating in a transparent liquid, but without any apparent enclosing outline or membrane, a little later

Fig. 1.

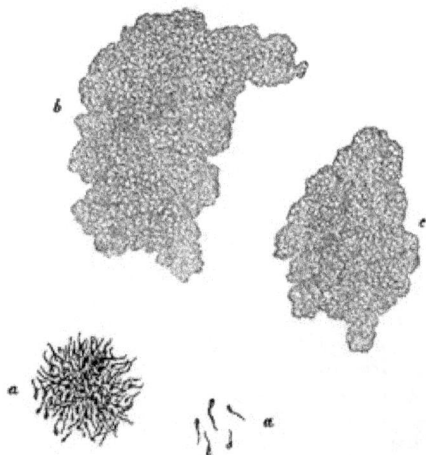

G.W.H.

*a* Spermatozoa.   *b.* Milch, early stage.   *c.* Milch, more advanced

Fig. 2.—Oyster Spat in various stages.

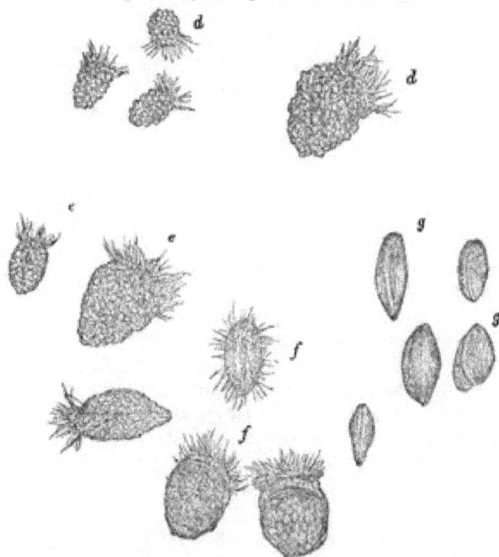

G.W.H.

*d.* White Spat, without shell.        *e.* White Spat, more advanced
      *f.* Black Spat, shell perfect.     *g.* Spat just attached.

cilia appear at the broader ends of the ovoid groups (fig. *d*), and motion commences; still no shell is visible, and at this stage the ova pass gradually from the ovaries into the mantle of the oyster.

The gills, fin, or mantle consist of four inner and two outer lobes, of which the outer are furnished with cilia, and are permeated in every direction with nerves and secretory ducts, for the exclusion of any enemy or injurious matter, and the secretion of the shell.

The cilia are in incessant motion whilst the shell is open, causing a constant flow of water over the surfaces of the branchia; these possess no nerves, but are permeated by vessels in which the blood is aerated by the contact of the water.  Between these lobes the ova are retained for some days, the mass gradually passing in tint from white through yellow, yellowish grey, and dark grey, nearly approaching black before extrusion.

When it has attained this stage, the embryos are almost perfect, and the mucous matter in which they have previously been embedded, will be found to have been absorbed.

From one to two millions of young are produced by each pregnant parent during the spatting season, and their extrusion is accomplished by a series of quick openings and shuttings of the parent shells, thereby causing a sudden outflow of water, which carries the young with it.

The emission continues until all are expelled, the process extending over a period which does not certainly exceed a week, and when emitted in the mature or black spat state, it is as perfect as when it attains its full growth.*  Artificial fecundation, such as is practised with salmonidæ, is impossible, from the fact that fecundation takes place before the extrusion of the ova from the ovaries, and therefore we must conclude that with oysters the utmost that can be done by so-called artificial breeding is *not the procuring of artificial impregnation*, but only the shepherding of the impregnated ova during infancy.

The young when in a mature state attach themselves immediately to the first clean hard substance they meet with.  It has been ascertained that the spat floating in the water for several days is that which from inability of the parent to contain it or from other causes, has been ejected, or escaped before maturity—such spat forms a large proportion of the whole, and during the time in which the spat is free and is becoming fitted for attachment, it is carried by tides and currents to great distances—is devoured by countless enemies, or is driven upon muddy or otherwise unsuitable ground, and so perishes.  Under the most favourable circumstances the proportion that never attaches is very considerable.  In a natural state the oyster remains attached, during its lifetime, to whatever object it first adheres to, but after an accidental removal it will again adhere to substances with a hard and tolerably clean surface.

To save the bulk of the spat when free is the great object of oyster culture.

It may be here stated that all descriptions of molluscs are apparently free for a longer or shorter term; of this fact the cockle, mussel, winkle, and balanus tribes afford proof.

---

* By feeding the oysters when free with coloured matter such as carmine, in the water, the interior economy is made visible, and the whole will be found to agree exactly with that of the adult oyster.

Figures 3, 4, 5, exhibit oyster spat viewed in various positions.

Fig. 3.—Black Spat, as viewed from the surface of the water when floating.

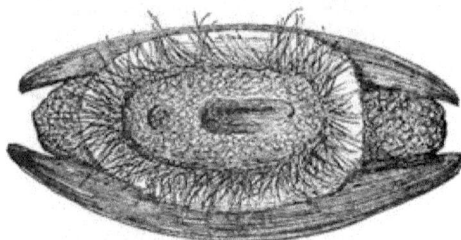

G.W.H.

Fig. 4.—Black Spat greatly magnified.

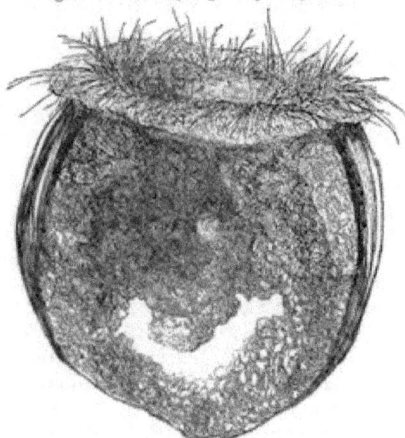

G.W.H

Fig. 5.—White Spat greatly magnified.

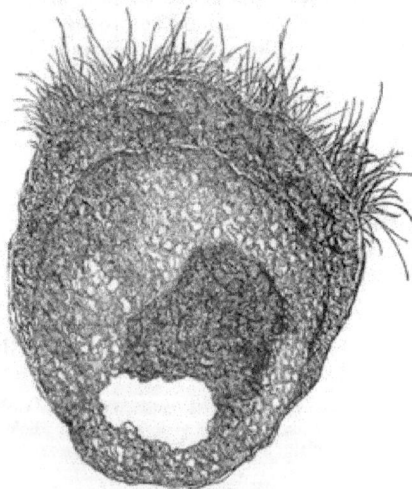

G.W.H.

In the British waters and those of France spatting usually takes
place when the parent oyster is from three to four years old,
although it is not uncommon to find oysters milchy at a much
earlier period.

It has not been clearly ascertained how often during life breeding takes place, but there is no reason to suppose that it does not
frequently occur in the lifetime of the same oyster, although it is
supposed that not more than 10 per cent. of the stock on any bed
will usually spat during any one season.

As oysters, however, from various causes, have been known to
spat very late in the year, it is impossible with accuracy to state
the proportion of full-grown oysters that breed annually.

The young oyster when perfectly mature rises immediately to
the surface upon its emission from the parent, after which it
adheres to the first clean hard substances it meets with; this
motion is effected by what has been termed a swimming pad (*see*
Figures 6, 7, 8, 9), but which is in truth but the protruded

Fig. 6.

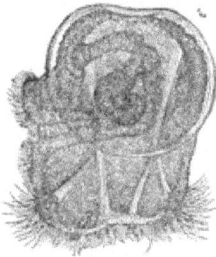

Fig. 7.

Fig. 8.

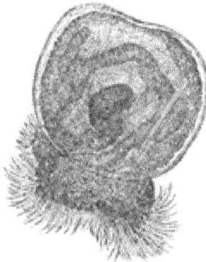

Fig. 9.

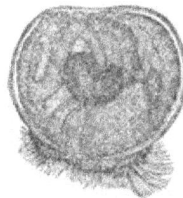

lobes of the mantle and not an organ specially formed for loco-
motion, seeing that by it the shell is secreted. It is by this
organ also that the oyster attaches itself, and this too in the
same way that it forms its shell. Swimming with open shells and
extended mantle uppermost on meeting with a clean hard surface
it remains in close contact with it and secretes over that part of
the substance which it touches a coating of the same material of
which its shell is formed—the first coating is followed by other
layers—and so the once free oyster becomes fixed, and by a repe-
tition of the process from time to time the necessary increase of

shell is made to meet the requirements of the fish; by the same means also young or adult oysters re-attach themselves to stones or other substances when removed from the places to which they first adhered.

That oyster spat invariably rises when first emitted is a fact to be appreciated in cultivation.

The nature of the bed or soil on which the oyster rests is a matter of the greatest importance, conferring as it does upon the oysters there bred or deposited special flavour or other qualities distinguishing them from all other oysters on adjacent grounds, and this influence prevails to so great extent that dredgermen can in a fog or dark night readily recognise their position by the shape, size, or colour of the oysters brought up by the dredge, and although the distance between such beds is often small they are enabled accurately to steer for the harbour from information of this peculiar kind.

The nature of the soil is important in another aspect. Many circumstances highly favourable to the growth and fattening of oysters are the reverse for successful breeding.

Growth and fattening will proceed where there may be a large amount of fresh water and a strong current; the former would prove prejudicial to spatting, and the latter tend to prevent the adhesion of spat at least in the locality at which it is voided.

Good spawning grounds have on the other hand been found less suitable for purposes of fattening—pure sea water and a clean bottom, essentials for successful spatting, not being always advantageous for the other purposes, hence it is usually found in rivers and estuaries that oysters breed better at the mouth and fatten best higher up.

There are, however, instances where the two processes are found to thrive simultaneously on the same banks.

If we refer to early English history—to the time of the invasion of our islands by the Romans—we discover that those warriors had not landed long upon our shores before they became acquainted with our oyster-beds, and British oysters soon formed an article of extensive export to Rome.

At this period oyster culture was conducted by the Romans in the Lake Avernus on precisely the same principles as that recently introduced into England.

The present diminution in the supply of oysters appears to have commenced some 10 or 12 years ago.

Since that period a greatly increased demand for oysters has resulted from the greater facilities of transport to places where previously fresh oysters had seldom reached.

Another circumstance has also added considerably to the demand, viz., the more frequent use of oysters, owing to the fashion prevalent both in England and France among the wealthier classes of consuming them at almost every meal. This materially enhances the price and has led to a vast increase in dredging.

In 1855 the price for native oysters was 41s. per bushel, and in 1879 it is £10 2s.; a similar rise has taken place in seconds, while commons in 1855, were 3s. 10d. per bushel, and in 1870, from 10s. to 18s.

Considerable difference of opinion exists as to the cause of this decrease—some authorities contending that it is altogether due to over-dredging—others to failure in the natural production of spat.

It would be tedious and confusing to enter into the various opposite theories (many of them deserving of attention) as to the cause of the decline.

Both of the above influences have doubtless adversely affected the production of oysters. If at the period when reproduction takes place a rise or fall of the temperature beyond a certain degree occurs, especially if such change be sudden, it is likely to be attended with injury to the spat—no doubt there have been years when the spatting season was cold and variable, and storms are also said to have taken place at the same period in other years. Conceding that the scarcity is in part due to the foregoing cause, it is a natural one, and one which we cannot well deal with; but the principal cause of the scarcity is attributable both in France and England to over-dredging; and this we can deal with, to a certain extent counteracting its effects by wise legislation.

No better illustration can be given than the advantageous position which Ireland occupies when compared with either of the other countries. That her natural beds have suffered much less from exhaustion may be attributed in a great measure to the enforced close time and other salutary regulations made by the Commissioners of Irish Fisheries, which are not in existence in England, and only lately came into operation in France.

### *Various branches of Oyster Fisheries.*

The oyster fisheries may be divided as follows :—

> Firstly.—Natural banks where without any action on the part of man oysters are propagated.
>
> Secondly.—Banks partly natural and partly artificial—as those in the rivers at Auray and other places in France, and of Essex and other places in England—where the production is aided by laying down fresh cultch and stock and keeping the beds clear of dirt and vermin.
>
> Thirdly.—Foreshore cultivation—where the spat from oysters on natural banks is saved or caught on collectors placed for that purpose.
>
> Fourthly.—The method of cultivation in enclosed spaces such as Lake Fusaro in Italy, at Hayling, the Isle of Wight, and other places.

### *Natural Banks.*

*France.*—To obtain information with respect to the natural banks the Commissioners visited Arcachon, La Teste, the Ile d'Oleron, the Ile de Ré, Auray, Concarneau, St. Brieux, Granville, Cancale, L'Orient.

*Channel Islands.*—Jersey.

*England.*—The Solent, Langston, Emsworth, Herne Bay, Milford, Tenby, Bristol, Beaumaris.

*Ireland.*—Arklow, Wexford, Waterford, Dungarvan, Cork, Kinsale, Baltimore, Bantry Bay, Kenmare, Tralee, Shannon, Ballyvaughan, Kinvarra, Galway, Roundstone, Cleggan, Ballinahinch, Clifden, Killery, Ballinakill, Clew Bay, Sligo, Lough Swilly, Lough Foyle, Belfast Lough, Carlingford Lough.

### For partly Natural and partly Artificial.

*France.*—Arcachon, La Teste, Ré, Chattellalion, Auray, Concarneau.

*England.*—Whitstable, Faversham, Herne Bay, Paglesham, Colchester, Ipswich, Harwich, Brading, Cowes, Newtown, Hamble.

*Ireland.*—Queenstown Island, Cork, Fota Island, Sneem, Kenmare, Kilrush, Clonderlaw Bay, Kinvarra (Burrane), Ballinahinch, Clifden, Clew Bay, Sligo, Lough Swilly, and Carlingford Lough.

### For Foreshore Cultivation.

*France.*—Ré, Oleron, Arcachon, La Tremblade, Marennes, Chatellalion, Auray.

*England.*—None.

*Ireland.*—East Ferry, Queenstown Island, Shannon.

### Enclosures.

*France.*—Regneville—for breeding. Marennes, La Tremblade, Ré, Oleron—for fattening.

*England.*—Hayling, Brading, Cowes, Newton, Lymington, Herne Bay, Nacton, Fagborough, New Brompton.

*Ireland.*—Derreen, Tramore, Shannon, Lough Swilly, Sneem, Carrig Island.

Owing to the great scarcity of oysters which had arisen, considerable efforts were made in France and England, especially the former, to promote the production of oysters by artificial means. As the earlier steps for that object were taken in France, it is deemed best in the first instance to give a sketch of the measures adopted there for the preservation and restocking of the public oyster grounds, the system of artificial cultivation, and the Government regulations with respect to this branch of the fisheries.

The chief sources of oyster supply in France are, first—the deep sea natural beds in international waters, the fishing of which is regulated by the convention between England and France (*see* Appendix A), extending with more or less perfect continuity from Nordenaye on the Hanoverian coast to Brest.

The beds which give their names to the best known varieties are those of St. Valery, Fécamp, Cape Le Héve, and Calvados; the remainder, which exist more in mid-channel, being comprised under the general name of "Channellers."

The banks exclusively French within the three-mile limit are mentioned above.

The process of collecting oyster spat on stones, &c., has been practised at the Isle of Oleron for upwards of half a century without attracting much attention, a fact which has not been previously noticed by any of the writers upon oyster culture, it having been erroneously supposed to have originated at the Ile de Ré, whereas the parc* system which Hyacinthe Bœuf introduced into that island was but a modification of the system followed at Oleron.

Bœuf's discovery is said to have been altogether accidental,

---

* For engraving of a parc see p. 24.

arising from his storing oysters within a small stone enclosure, and finding some time afterwards that a large quantity of spat had adhered to the stones.

Encouraged by this, Bœuf in the ensuing year made a larger enclosure on the foreshore and laid down more oysters and stones; the result was most successful, and many of his neighbours, seeing this, engaged in like enterprises, and were so well remunerated for their trouble and outlay that an extensive cultivation on this plan was soon in operation on various parts of the shores of the island. These layings do not extend below low-water mark, and in most places the water is retained by small embankments.

To show how extensive these enterprises are, a map of the Island, showing the various parcs, &c., is appended.—*See* map of Ile de Ré, Plate 1, Appendix.

The results were much greater the first few years than they have been latterly, as will be seen by the following figures—

RETURN of OYSTERS sold from the ISLE DE RE PARCS.

| Year. | Number of Oysters. | Value. |
|---|---|---|
| | | £ |
| 1857, | Nil. | Nil. |
| 1858, | Nil. | Nil. |
| 1859, | 157,500 | 126 |
| 1860, | 401,350 | 321 |
| 1861, | 1,615,000 | 1,315 |
| 1862, | 2,780,740 | 2,120 |
| 1863, | 5,650,250 | 4,535 |
| 1864, | 3,376,440 | 1,818 |
| 1865, | 1,919,900 | 2,020 |
| 1866, | 1,181,000 | 1,516 |
| 1867, | 879,713 | 1,245 |
| | 18,051,893 | 14,816 |

The young oysters are usually removed from the stones at one year old. They are then placed in claires* to grow and fatten, the time they remain in claires varying according to circumstances in the different localities.

The cause assigned for the recent failures was the improvidence of the concessionaires in selling off all their stock as soon as it was marketable, and leaving none from which to replenish the beds. But to a large extent it is probably also attributable to the stones, tiles, or other collectors being in a cleaner condition during the first year than they were afterwards, sufficient care not being taken to keep them free from mud and weed, without the observance of which precautions the adhesion of spat to collectors is very doubtful.

At the Ile d'Oleron, fifteen miles from the Ile de Ré, slabs of stone from one foot to two feet high by half a foot broad are placed on the shore to collect the spat which is drifted to them from the natural beds. Unlike the process at Ré, no parent or breeding oysters are placed near the collectors, the spat being altogether derived from the natural oyster grounds in deep water.

From the fact that in no instance, so far as we have ascertained, have either foreshore cultivation or enclosed breeding ponds

* For engravings of claires see plates Nos. 7 and 8.

proved successful at any considerable distance from natural banks, or where such formerly existed, it would seem that their existence forms an important desideratum in successful culture. Instances will be mentioned hereafter where under supposed favourable conditions cultivation has proved abortive, and where no apparent reason could be given beyond the fact that no oysters existed in the adjoining sea, or had ever been known to exist. It is reasonable to suppose that where oysters are absent naturally, and have always been so, some important conditions necessary for their development must be wanting in the water, soil, or temperature, &c., and this would probably also militate against artificial culture.

Considering the numerous oyster banks which have existed and still exist, the vast amount of spat annually voided, and the great distances to which it is carried by tides and currents, it is difficult to suppose that there is a square yard of our coasts that has not been visited by spawn, and it would therefore appear that in those places where oysters are not found nature protests as it were against them.

One instance of oyster breeding in France on the enclosure or tank system is that of Madame Felix, at Regneville, which will be hereafter more particularly alluded to, nearly all the other breeding operations being on the foreshores.

In some places oysters are subject to exposure of more or less duration. In most parts of Ireland this would be attended with considerable risk from frost in winter, unless provision were made for having them submerged, as is the general practice in England.

Although the cultivation is much less remunerative than it was formerly in France, still even in its present depressed condition it pays better than any other industry pursued by the same class for the labour and capital expended upon it, and possesses the advantage of interfering but little with other occupations, as the attention required to be bestowed on oysters, could be given at times when those following agriculture would be at leisure.

The most encouraging instances of successful cultivation in France are to be found at L'Orient and Auray. At the former, M. Charles, the principal cultivator, shows by his returns that during the past six years his operations have, making every allowance for indifferent years, been remunerative.

At Auray cultivation is carried on on the rivers La Trinité, Bono, and La Crach. (See Plate 2, Appendix.) Each of these possesses oysters naturally, besides which others were placed near the collectors, which consist of stones and tiles—the result has been most successful on the eighty-eight parcs—as many as 300 oysters having been found on one tile; and the instance of M. Le Rouse is a good illustration of the success which has attended the cultivation of these rivers. His parc on La Trinité, at Carnac, contains 900 square metres. The first year of his operations, 1866-1867, he sold 300,000 oysters; the succeeding year was not so good, but he was able to pay off all his outlay out of profits. He is extending his operations, and

B

expects to profit at the rate of 20,000 francs per year. On the same river there are five other large proprietors; and seventy poor peasants who have received assistance from the Government, have also commenced operations.

All these rivers have a bottom of clay similar to that of the Essex rivers, and other localities where oysters are most productive.—(See Analysis in Appendix II.)

At the parc du Forêt, three leagues from Concarneau, the Government layings have proved successful.

In proceeding to notice the Government enterprises—at St. Brieux and Arcachon—it will be desirable as well as interesting to state the circumstances under which the Imperial Government undertook oyster culture at those places.

In 1858, owing to the great scarcity of oysters which had prevailed for some time, M. Coste, a most distinguished member of the Institute of France, who had for some years devoted himself to the study and promotion of pisciculture, turned his attention, with most important results, to the promotion of oyster cultivation. By command of the Emperor he entered into an inquiry on the subject, visited what may be called the parent source of oyster culture—Lake Fusaro, in Italy, and commenced operations in France.

The result of his researches and efforts is to be found in his justly celebrated work addressed to the Emperor, which should be read by all who desire to be conversant with the subject.

It is much to be regretted that but a very brief notice of what that eminent man accomplished can be given.

One of his first undertakings was carried out at St. Brieux. This consisted of placing parent oysters at certain distances on the bottom of the bay, over an area of forty miles, and fascines or bundles of twigs were sunk attached to large stones. The result exceeded all expectation, as many as 30,000 oysters being in some instances attached to the fascines—nearly all were plentifully covered.

Fig. 10.

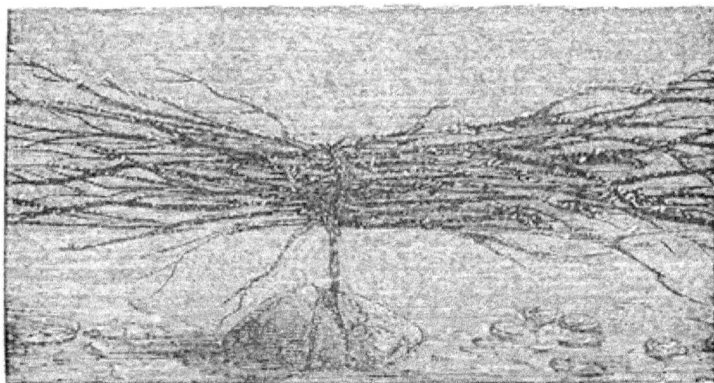

Fascine at St. Brieux (with the spat attached).

Unfortunately, however, this most promising experiment was frustrated by severe storms which covered the bottom of the bay with sand so as to completely bury the fascines.

M. Coste's next operation was at Arcachon, on the Bay of Biscay—a landlocked basin of 100 kilometres circumference, and containing 1,500 square kilometres in area, equal to about 30,000 English acres. See plate 3, Appendix.

Many years ago a very important oyster fishery had existed there, yielding annually nearly 80,000,000 of oysters, valued at £10,000. As alleged, this fishery became nearly destroyed from over-dredging. Under M. Coste's directions in 1859, two Imperial parcs, Grand Ces and Crastorbe, were constructed. The first collectors used were wood, to which shells, &c., were attached by a resinous cement; these decayed rapidly, and were replaced by tiles, shells, and stone collectors.

The first two years the proceeds were very considerable; subsequently there was a great falling off—but 1869 appears to have produced a very large crop. During six years the quantity removed from the Imperial parcs was nearly sixteen millions of oysters—this is independent of the parcs of private proprietors —many of them concessions or allotments by Government, varying from one to eight acres.

A long grass-like weed—Zostera marina—which grows in great quantity on the beds, proves very useful in protecting the oysters at low tide from the heat of the sun.

Besides the area under cultivation there are several natural beds in different parts of the basin, all subject to the Government regulations which will be hereafter more particularly described.

The great bulk of the oysters bred at Arcachon are sent to Marennes and Tremblade, where the green tint so much esteemed in France is imparted to the beard of the oyster, but against which so unjust a prejudice exists in England as regards the Essex oysters, most of which are in consequence sent to France—the cause of the greenness being probably the same in both instances— the presence of Diatomaceæ (see figures 11, 12) and not, as at Falmouth, owing to the presence of copper. Oysters impregnated with the latter are always green in the body, whilst those of Marennes and Essex are green only in the beard or " fin."

Fig. 11.—Achnanthes longipes: a Diatom found at Chattellalion.

Fig. 12.—Various Diatomaceæ found at Hayling.

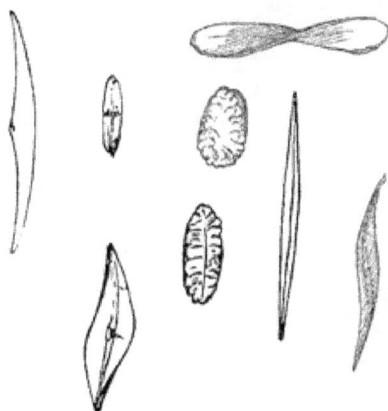

The time required for fattening depends altogether on locality. At Marennes, an oyster grows fat more rapidly than in the claires of the Ile de Ré.

The only instance of importance of enclosed or tank cultivation in France which we visited is that of Madame Felix, as already stated. Her experiments proved most successful. The enclosure is about four hectares (about ten acres) in extent; in this 11,000 oysters were placed and 11,000 tiles. The first year, 1864, the tiles were covered with spat, some of them having as many as 103 oysters, and the least of them about 20.

Madame Felix contemplated operations on a much larger scale, having only entered on the one described to ascertain what could be accomplished. Owing to private causes, as well as some local opposition offered to her enclosing a larger portion of the bay, she has suspended further action for the present.

### Natural Oyster Banks.

With respect to the natural oyster banks of France, most of them became so denuded of oysters down to 1850, as to be hardly worth fishing, and some, formerly of great importance—such as those of Cancale, Granville, &c.—have been all but destroyed.

The most important authorities on the subject in France combine in attributing the exhaustion of the natural banks mainly to over-dredging.

In 1850, the French Government became alive to the urgent necessity of adopting stringent measures to prevent the threatened destruction of the comparatively few that remained on the natural banks, as well as to endeavour to replenish them where exhaustion had taken place. The laws for this object are very effective. (See Appendix B.)

In brief, it may be stated, that the Government assume the

entire control over all the oyster banks and foreshores. As occasion may seem to require, an entire bank may, for a certain time, be altogether reserved against dredging operations, or any portion of it. The general practice seems to be to mark or buoy off a third or fourth of a bank each year; the remaining portion being dredged for a specified time by the persons permitted during the number of days allowed for the operation—the reserved portion being also dredged for a few days to clean it of weeds, mud, and vermin. The following year another part of the bank is reserved: occasionally portions are reserved for a longer period.

Everything relating to oyster fisheries is decided on by a local Commission.

This Commission is presided over by the local inspector of fisheries, or officer commanding the fishery guard, and is composed as follows:—

    The inspector of fisheries or a syndic.
    The officer commanding the fishery guard.
    Two gardes maritime.
    One fisherman, being Master of a boat.

A copy of the detailed instructions issued for the guidance of the Commission is annexed (see Ap. B.), but the following embrace the more important principles laid down:—

(Art. 2.) The beds should not be opened for fishing until the spat has acquired strength to resist the action of the dredge; until the end of January, for example.

(Art. 5.) When a bed has well established breeding capacities, a fourth or fifth part of its total area should be set apart as a reserve, and dredging over such part entirely prohibited.

(Art. 6.) A fishery guard boat should, whenever practicable, take part in the working of each bed.

(Art. 10.) When a bed is foul or encumbered with weeds or other matter noxious to the development or adherence of spat, it should be opened for dredging until cleaned.

(Art. 11.) Beds on which there is never any production of spat shall be opened all through the season.

(Art 12.) After the working of any bed is over, it should be carefully inspected, and, if necessary, replenished with proper " cultch," stones, shells, &c.

Trawling is prohibited within 525 yards of any oyster bed.

The capture of oysters is strictly forbidden between the 1st May and 31st August, within the three mile limit, and as far as French boats are concerned the close season fixed by the Convention at from 15th June to 31st August is also strictly observed in the international waters, although continually broken by English fishermen.

Grants of foreshore or concessions are made to persons desirous of cultivating oysters, the grants in most instances being much smaller than in Ireland, and not possessing the same advantages as to length of tenure.

Undoubtedly benefit accrues to the small cultivators of the soil near the sea from these grants of foreshore, either for breeding or fattening purposes, and the Government encourage such enterprises by affording facilities for obtaining stock from the Government reserves, and by occasionally making free grants both of oysters and tiles. Sailors, or the families of sailors, serving or who have served in the Imperial Marine, are allowed certain advantages over other applicants for such concessions.

The oyster and other fisheries are under the control of the Minister of Marine Department, forming a special branch under the able administration of M. de Champeaux, assisted by a permanent Commission of nine members, of which M. Coste is the head.

On the coasts the Commissaires d'Inscription Maritime are, in addition to their other duties, charged with looking after the fisheries, having under them divisional Inspectors, and occasionally other subordinate employeès. This system, as regards supervision, affording information to fishermen, enforcing regulations, and collecting statistics, appears admirable, and has been productive of vast advantage to the fisheries of France.

### Causes of Decline of Production.

It is now proposed to give somewhat more in detail an account of the various methods of cultivation existing at the places visited, and the causes which in the opinion of the Commissioners have led to the failure or decrease of the fisheries.

The wonderful increase in the yield of the natural bed of Cancale from 400,000 in 1815, to 70,000,000 in 1847, and the subsequent equally rapid decrease, is a subject which, as it bears upon the restrictions necessary for the Irish deep-sea beds, deserves attention. The return is given at length in the Appendix C. Here we have a long period of rest, and almost absolute cessation of dredging, and the fact of a vast accumulation of oysters taking place. Then follows the onset of a large fleet of boats without restrictions, which produces in a few years the destruction of the bank. Comment is needless.

Similar agreement in the main points is presented by the returns of the public beds of Arcachon; and we are happy to be able to say that the present regulations are already producing a steady improvement in the fisheries. It must be borne in mind that in certain conditions of soil, &c., the absence of dredging may be an evil instead of a benefit to the ground.

Cases of this kind are those forming the subject of a recent report by Mr. Cholmondeley Pennell to the Board of Trade.

Mr. Pennell states that the Fish and Oyster Breeding Company have cleared 100 acres of the portion of the Blackwater estuary and thirteen acres of ebb-dry foreshore. Of the state of this ground when it came into the company's hands, Mr. Pennell remarks that it was, for all practical purposes, barren of oysters, and the "cultch" covered with mud and overrun with vermin and weeds.

Fifty-six hauls of the dredge in 1867, before the company was established, resulted in nine brood and spat, and nine oysters of larger growth.

Recently (writing in 1870) Mr. Pennell states that *two* successive hauls gave—First haul, three brood and sixty-eight spat; second haul, three brood and seventy-five spat (oysters of larger growth not counted), or an increase of 450 to one as compared with 1867.

A stock of oysters to the value of £11,631 had been laid upon the ground in 1868 and 1869.

The Roach River Company have reclaimed thirty acres of similar foreshore and 270 acres of ordinary ground, and the result is equally satisfactory. In 1864, 150 hauls of the dredge gave a total of thirty-eight oysters of all ages, and in 1869, one haul gave 100 brood and 153 spat, or an increase of brood and spat above 1,000 to one as compared with 1864.

That oysters cannot be dredged too much, is the opinion of the oysterculturist from the muddy rivers of the east coast, while those who have ground in rapid and clear water, depose exactly the opposite—that rest *is all* that exhausted grounds require.

We have no hesitation in saying that all laws, to be beneficial, must consist of regulations adapted to the requirements of the locality, and not consist of a series of general rules arbitrarily adopted and enforced in despair of obtaining the truth when evidence so very conflicting is offered.

The cultivation of the foreshores at Auray we have already mentioned as a success. From the bridge to the sea, a distance of twelve miles, the shores of the rivers are the scene of oyster cultivation, such as, we trust, will in a few years be seen on many river banks both in England and Ireland. The process is of the simplest kind. Each concession, duly bounded and marked by a numbered post or stone, contains nothing more complicated than rows of tiles arranged so as to offer clean under-surfaces for the adhesion of the spat, which rises from the preserved banks in the river. To keep these clean, to remove all oysters of a year's growth, to lay them in claires to develop and grow, is all that is needful, and the result is entirely satisfactory. Upon the length of foreshore named no less than 88 parcs have been constructed.

The number of oysters at the time of our visit on some of the tiles was stated to be three hundred.

The cultivation at the other places named—Ile de Ré, Ile d'Oleron, Rochers d'Aire, Chattellalion—is the same, modified as to the nature and arrangement of the collectors as required by the conditions of the locality. The western coast of Ré is open to the full force of the Atlantic, and appears about as unpromising a place for oyster culture as one can imagine. The energy of the inhabitants, prompted, no doubt, by the success which attended the parcs at Rivedoux, on the south coast, overcame all difficulties. The commune of Ars boldly attacked the enterprise under all its apparent disadvantages. Blasting the rocks, they constructed their enclosing walls of great strength, and removed the mud, which lay to the depth of a foot on the shore. The same stones furnished

also rude but cheap collectors, and these they arranged in parallel
rows. A considerable depth of mud was removed from the shore
and utilized in the parc walls, which were thus made water-tight.

The cost of a parc of thirty yards square so constructed was
stated at £12, and the number of such increased very considerably
in a few years.

Fig. 13.—Arrangement of Collectors in a parc at the Ile de Ré.

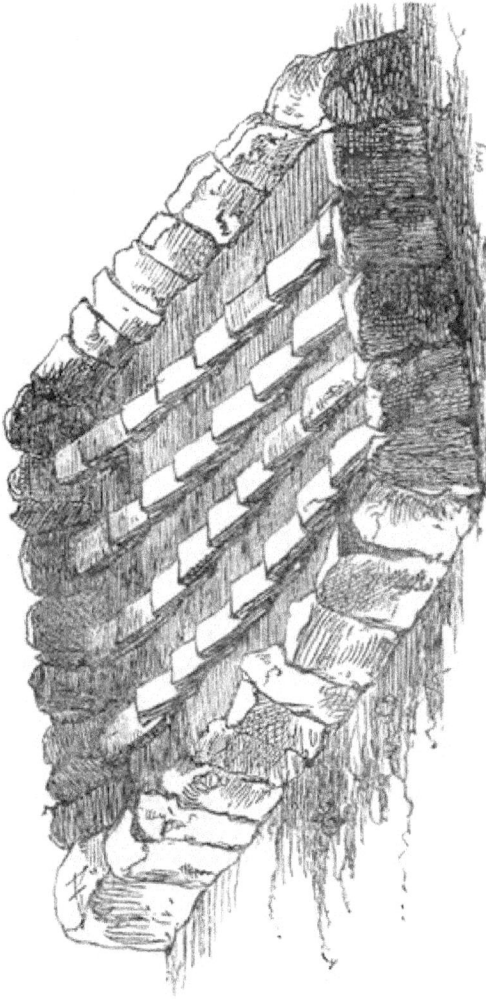

Fig. 14.—Arrangement of Stones as Collectors at Ile de Ré.

The total sale of oysters is given by the officials at 18,000,000 from 1859 to 1867 ; but by Dr. Kemmerer the correct number is stated to be 40,000,000, a discrepancy accounted for by the fact that correct returns are not made by the peasants for fear of increased taxation.

There is no reason to doubt but that the decline in production at Ré, Oleron, and other places where foreshore cultivation was so remarkably effective at the commencement is to be attributed to the dirtier state of the collectors, and also to the fact that the natural beds having been depopulated in the first instance to stock the parcs, the parent oysters were subsequently sold, and thus the source of spat was removed.

The proprietors themselves admit this to have been the case, thinking sufficient spat would settle from the young oysters attached to the stones. This expectation, however, they found to be delusive, and in the present season means are to be taken to renew the stock and collectors.

## England.

The diminution in oyster production which has taken place in England is not so great as in France—still it has been very considerable.

Great natural beds exist, or have existed in the estuaries of the Thames, Medway, Blackwater, the rivers of Essex and Suffolk, in the Solent, in Langston and Chichester harbours, Milford, Tenby, and other places.

The Royal Commissioners in their report on the sea fisheries of the United Kingdom, page 105, state—" That the supply of oysters has very greatly fallen off during the last three or four years," and this statement needs no confirmation from us. The same causes as exist in France may be assigned for it.

Besides the public beds before named, a very large number of oysters are obtained annually from private grounds in the Thames, the Blackwater, Colne, Roach rivers, in Essex, and from the rivers in Suffolk, from the Isle of Wight, from Cornwall, and elsewhere. These fisheries are held either by corporations, as at Colchester and Ipswich, or by private persons and companies as lessees or otherwise. Such private oyster beds are almost invariably well cultivated, very considerable trouble and expense being bestowed on them by the proprietors, whose efforts are mainly directed to keeping the bottom of the river free from slob and weeds, and destroying the enemies of the oyster, as starfish, crabs, the dog whelk (*purpura Lapillus*), and rough whelk (*murex erinaceus*), &c., engravings of which will be seen on the next page.

The first encloses the oyster in its grasp, and breaking off the edge of the shell contrives to devour the fish, whilst the whelks bore through the shell, and, it is supposed, abstract some fluid portion of the oyster, leaving the more solid parts to be eaten by the crabs, which follow in the wake of the whelk.

ENEMIES OF THE OYSTER.

Fig. 15.—Starfish.

Fig. 16.—Rough whelk.   Bigorneau.   (*Murex Erinaceus*).

Fig. 17.—Spawn of Dog whelk.

Besides cleaning the bed of the river for this purpose by the almost constant use of the dredge, which is in part necessitated by the large amount of mud held in suspension by the rivers on the east coast, the foreshores are carefully strewn with cultch, consisting of shells, &c., above and below low water mark. The soil is usually of the same character, blue or London clay.

In the Roach, the beard or fin of the oyster is of the green colour so much esteemed in France, where they are usually sent in consequence of the groundless prejudice against them in England, where they are wrongly confounded with the Falmouth oysters, which are green in the body, owing to the presence of copper in the water, of which the Essex rivers are altogether free, the greenness arising probably from the green weed growing on the banks resembling, in many respects, that at Marennes.*

The greenish discoloration of the body, which is an indication of copper, is not at all observable in the Essex oysters.

In England several attempts at so-called artificial culture have been made, under which misnomer all efforts to increase the means of breeding and fattening oysters must for the sake of convenience be classed. An attempt made at Southend, in Essex, to cultivate the foreshores by placing tiles as collectors of spat in 1864 was unsuccessful, but the reason is not known, nor the conditions under which the experiment was made. In the Roach the culture was attempted with fair prospects of success; but owing to the reprehensible practice of the passing barges grounding needlessly on the banks, the experiment was per force abandoned, and the cultivation now employed consists in spreading fresh cultch along the shores, just above and below low water mark, during the spatting season, and the trouble and expense gone to by the proprietors of oyster grounds to obtain fresh supplies of cultch, proves the importance they attach to the cleanliness of their spat collectors. The most important, from its magnitude, as well as the great success which attended its earlier operations, is that of Hayling Island, on the Hampshire coast. It is on the enclosure system. The collectors employed are hurdles, fascines, and twigs. Operations were commenced in 1866, and a spat obtained the same year in a pond of four acres; in 1867 the area under cultivation was increased to three ponds, containing altogether thirty-four acres, the largest of these (eighteen acres) contained in the spatting season for that year a wonderful amount of spat, of which some idea may be formed, when in addition to three millions saved, many millions perished for want of adequate provision for their reception. It comprises

---

* GREEN BEARDED OYSTERS, RIVER ROACH, ESSEX.—41, Finsbury-square, Dec. 2nd, 1863. Fredk. Wiseman, esq. Sir,—In accordance with your request I have made a very careful examination of the Green Oysters from the River Roach, or Crouch, which you left with me for analysis yesterday, and I find that the green tint which is present in the gills only of the oyster is due entirely to a natural pigment which does not contain a trace of copper or other deleterious matter. The oysters are therefore perfectly nutritious and wholesome.—I remain, sir, yours truly, HY. LETHEBY, M.A., &c., Professor of Chemistry in the College of the London Hospital, and Medical Officer of Health and Food Analyst for the City of London.

an area of eighty to ninety acres, available for breeding ponds, of which there are five, of various sizes, from four to twenty-eight acres. For plans of these beds, &c., see plate No. 9, Appendix.

The Herne Bay Oyster Company's breeding ponds were established with a view of assisting in the stocking of the extensive layings of the Company (nine square miles) in the estuary of the Thames.* Further down the bay there has been a small experimental undertaking at Reculvers.

The Brading Oyster Company in the Isle of Wight have ponds of about three acres in extent, using tiles, slates, and hurdles, &c., as collectors, and obtained a good spat in 1869.

At Lymington, ten acres of ponds produced some spat.

We are not aware how far the foregoing undertakings have been commercial successes.

The ponds of George Tomline, esq., at Nacton, on the Orwell river in Suffolk, gave a spat in 1867 and 1869, but not in 1868. The collectors were hurdles, tiles, &c.

The Medina Oyster Fisheries Company at Cowes and Newtown in the Isle of Wight was established to work two oyster fisheries at the above places. They have breeding ponds of twenty-four acres in extent in connexion with the fisheries, and have obtained a considerable amount of spat; but how far their breeding operations have answered their purpose we are not in a position to determine. They have, however, valuable fisheries independent of them on which they chiefly rely for profit. Artificial operations are carried on elsewhere, but are not of sufficient importance to call for notice.

Nearly all these ponds are similar, the chief differences being in size, and in the kind of collectors used, some consisting of tiles, others twigs, or fascines, slates, stones, and shells, attached by tar or cement to boards. The depth of water varying from two to ten feet.

### Jersey.

The seas about the Channel Islands, especially Jersey, formerly abounded in oysters—the increased demand led to a vast increase in the number of dredging vessels.

Thirty thousand pounds has been realized from the beds per annum, and employment afforded to 400 vessels, whilst now a precarious livelihood is earned by the crews of three or four. (See Appendix D.)

According to the most intelligent and reliable persons who gave evidence, this falling off must be mainly ascribed to over-dredging.†

---

* This Company has expended a large sum in laying down oysters, both for fattening and breeding, on these grounds. We dredged over a portion of them, and found spat plentifully adhering to the cultch.

† A gentleman well acquainted with the Jersey Oyster Fisheries has stated that—"The value of the Jersey fishery has several times nearly reached £30,000 a season, but for the last three or four it has been gradually getting worse and worse, and is now scarcely worth working. . . . I am informed by an owner of an oyster smack that about three or four vessels only now work the ground instead of nearly three hundred six years since, that nearly all these are now at work in mid-channel, and it would not pay even to work these three or four constantly, in consequence of which the owners fill up their time with work

## Scotland.

In Scotland the more important beds of the Forth and Lough Ryan are private property, and have been preserved by a close season and regulations against taking oysters under a certain size. In the Forth dredging is prohibited from May 1st, to September 1st.

In Lough Ryan only a limited number of boats are allowed to dredge. A licence is taken out by each boat owner, for which he is charged nine pounds.

Some years ago important beds were discovered in Wigton Bay; no restrictions were imposed; in consequence they were soon dredged out, and the oysters may now be said to be almost extinct there.

## Wales.

In Wales, particularly at Milford Haven and Tenby, a close time of four months, and restrictions with regard to the size of oysters allowed to be sold, had been enforced for some years. These regulations had a beneficial effect, but the increase of dredging boats has greatly diminished the quantity on the beds. At Milford there were only twenty-one boats dredging twenty years ago, they frequently took 2,000 oysters in a day; now there are 200 boats, the take in the day for each does not exceed from 100 to 200.

These instances go far to prove the wisdom of maintaining some regulations for the repression of indiscriminate dredging.

## Ireland.

This Commission was appointed—1st, to ascertain as far as possible the cause of the decline in the produce of Irish oyster fisheries.

2ndly, To determine the means that should be adopted to arrest further decay, and to promote their resuscitation.

3rdly, To inquire into and report on the mode of artificial culture likely to prove most efficient for the purpose in view.

More minute details will therefore be entered into in relation to Ireland than were called for with regard to France and England, as the only reason for investigating the subject in those countries was to ascertain how far the information obtained might usefully bear on the paramount object of the Commission. A large mass of information which was collected in the course of the inquiry bearing on the English oyster fisheries, as well as many recommendations which suggested themselves to the Commissioners for their improvement, they have not considered themselves warranted in putting forward, as this would considerably swell the size of this Report, and would also subject the Commissioners to the charge of travelling outside their province.

on shore, in fact, the Jersey fishing appears to be almost ' dredged to death.' This is a desperate state of things, which might have been prevented by active measures at an earlier stage, but I fear no steps will be taken to remedy the evil. . . . . All oyster fisheries should be worked under wise restrictions, and under a certain size all should be thrown overboard on the dredging ground, some breeding stock would thereby be left; but now, in many places, it is a case of *ex nihilo nihil fit*, brood and mature oysters having been alike exhausted by over dredging."

However, should the Government at any time so desire, they will be fully prepared to furnish a complete report with respect to the oyster fisheries of the other portions of the United Kingdom, and to recommend the measures which, in their opinion, should be adopted for their preservation.  Much, however, that is suggested with respect to Ireland will be equally applicable to England.

The oyster fisheries of both France and England were first investigated by the Commissioners before they proceeded to Ireland, and thus they had the advantage of knowing, before visiting the latter, every circumstance (as far as ascertainable) connected with the decline of the natural oyster fisheries of the other two countries, the success or failure which had attended attempted artificial cultivation, and the opinions of the best authorities on every point in connexion with the entire question.  There was the further advantage in reserving the visit to Ireland until the last, as it could then be determined whether the modes of oyster culture, which had proved most successful on the Continent and in England, were applicable to Ireland.

Many theories founded on the temperature of the sea in various latitudes, and the effects of the Gulf stream, &c., having been more or less discussed in connexion with the breeding of oysters, it appeared desirable that simultaneous observations of the temperature should be made in different parts of the sea coast of the United Kingdom, and these observations were also extended to France.

The Admiralty were applied to for permission to direct the Coast Guard to perform the necessary duty on being provided with thermometers, which was readily consented to, and the work most efficiently performed.  (See Professor Hennessy's report, founded on those returns, in the Appendix E.)

The First Lord of the Admiralty was also kind enough to place at the disposal of the Commissioners H. M. Steam Yacht " Vivid," which enabled them to go round the entire coast of Ireland and make the most searching investigations.

The principal oyster fisheries, taking them in the order of their magnitude, are those of Arklow, Wexford, Carlingford, Clew Bay, Cork Harbour, Achill, Belmullet, Clare, Galway Bay, Sligo Bay, Tralee, Belfast Lough, Lough Swilly, Lough Foyle, Estuary of the Shannon, Waterford Harbour, Dungarvan.

The Arklow and Wexford banks extend for forty miles along the coast at distances varying from three to fifteen miles.  Formerly, a considerable decrease in the yield had taken place, it is believed, from over-dredging, consequent upon the increased demand ; but owing to the extension of the close season, at the request of the fishermen, these beds now show an annual improvement.

Most of the oysters taken are bought for England to be laid down in fattening beds, as they are considered deficient in flavour when first taken from the banks.

The number of boats now employed, some carrying eight dredges, and a crew of six men, is 120 ; and the yield in the last season was valued at £28,000.

The Wexford banks may be said to be a continuation of those of Arklow; the number of boats, twenty-eight; the sum realized in 1869, £2,200.  A great decrease as regards former years. Here, as at Arklow, by the desire of the fishermen themselves, the close season is now fixed from 30th April to 1st September. Twenty years ago the price per thousand was only six shillings, now it sometimes reaches nearly forty shillings.

In each of the other places a considerable diminution has occurred, attributed to over-dredging and the wholesale exportation of young brood, and in some instances to failure of spat.

Cases were not wanting in Ireland where positive injury had arisen from want of sufficient dredging, as in the Estuary of the Shannon, near Scattery Island, and at Clew Bay, where the result of some dredging operations, undertaken by the Commissioners, showed that a vast amount of weeds and dirt had accumulated on the beds which judicious dredging would have removed.  The quantity of oysters procurable was, however, probably not worth the labour necessary from the unsuitable gear used in those localities.

The reasons assigned by the numerous witnesses examined as to the cause of the decrease on many beds around the coast were altogether hypothetical; nothing could well be imagined more contradictory, inconsistent, and irreconcilable than the assertions of persons, even from the same locality; each giving a different account as interest, prejudice, or opposition to what they deemed encroachments on their rights, prompted.

The only thing that could be relied on as a fact was the undoubted decrease of the oysters, but to account for it according to the evidence was simply impossible.  *Pari passu*, however, with this diminution was made evident the fact of a large increase in dredging, so that it is only fair to assume that one of the reasons for exhaustion must have proceeded from that cause.  There may also have been at the same time a certain amount of absence of spat, but whether this might or might not have been very much produced by diminution of stock, caused by over-dredging, combined with a reckless and wholesale export of the brood oysters, it is very hard to determine.

Perhaps one of the most important points for consideration is the extensive grants made by the Board of Public Works (in whom the management of the Sea Fisheries was vested up to the year 1869) of portions of foreshore and sea bottom, amounting altogether to 100 grants or licences as they are termed, and which comprise in the aggregate nearly 17,000 acres of some of the most desirable oyster ground in the country.

The smallest area so granted amounting to three acres, and the largest to 1,800 acres.

A list of these licences and the extent of the portions so allotted will be found in the Appendix F.  These licences were supposed only to be granted after a full inquiry on the spot and satisfactory proof given that not only public rights would not be interfered with to any appreciable extent, but that advantage to the public would be likely to follow from increased oyster production.

It is much to be regretted that these undertakings have as a whole fallen very far short of realizing the expectations of those who promoted legislation on the subject; hardly one of them has proved a commercial success, judging by the reports furnished by the proprietors in answer to the annual inquiries of the Board of Works, whilst most of them must be regarded as total failures so far as the production of oysters—the greatest object of all—is concerned.

In many instances the oysters laid down have fattened, and the grants have thus proved advantageous to the grantee; but this is a matter of small moment in comparison with the main object—increased production.

In giving to individuals a monopoly of what was previously a public right there is a power reserved in the later licences of withdrawing the concession at the end of three years if in the opinion of the Commissioners proper means have not been adopted to fulfil the conditions upon which it was given.

The exercise of this salutary provision is imperatively called for with regard to the great majority of the persons in possession of these grants, as the investigations made by this Commission clearly proved that, with rare exceptions, adequate means were not adopted to promote breeding, in the way of laying down a sufficiency of breeding stock, keeping the ground clean of mud and weeds, providing proper cultch or other collectors—many of the licensees contenting themselves with leaving the ground as they found it, or at best supplying an insufficient quantity of oysters for breeding purposes, laying down little or no cultch, trusting to chance for obtaining a spat and reaping what benefit they could from the oysters which were previously on the ground and the fattening of those placed there.

The Legislature never contemplated granting a monopoly of the shores or sea bottom merely for such purposes. Where the undertaking upon which such exclusive privileges were given is not fulfilled it should be withdrawn.

The Ballyvaughan, Red Bank, and Burrane beds of county Clare and that at Sneem in county Kerry are altogether used for fattening purposes. They do not appear to possess all the essentials necessary for reproduction.

The instances of tank or enclosed cultivation in Ireland are few, embracing—

1. Mr. Malcomson, at Tramore, county Waterford, about one acre and a half.

2. Mr. Power, at Kilmacleague, in the same neighbourhood, under one acre.

3. Mr. Sandes, of Carrig Island, on the Kerry side of the Shannon, under one acre.

4. Mr. Bland, at Sneem, county Kerry, consisting of about one acre.

5. Mr. Trench, at Derreen, county Kerry, comprising a space of ground twenty yards by thirty yards.

6. Mr. William Hart, at Fahan, Lough Swilly, comprising two and a half acres.

7. Mr. Henry O'Connell, at Burren, county Clare, a pond sixteen feet long by eight feet wide.

All have turned out failures, except No. 7.

Mr. Malcomson's consists of an excavated pond, extending over about half an acre, and 18 inches deep, it is situated at a place called the Back Strand, a considerable portion of which has lately been reclaimed from the sea. Arrangements were made for the admission of sea water when required; about 20,000 oysters were laid down, and fascines, oyster-shells, pebbles, and other descriptions of collectors employed; no pains or expense appears to have been spared to insure success, but during the three years the experiments have been going on not a single spat has adhered to the collectors.

It is quite possible that the pond was too shallow. That from its small size and exposed situation it was too open to heat, cold, or sudden changes of temperature; added to this, the tide, before it reaches the pond, sweeps over a wide expanse of sand and carries with it a great deal of sand, scum, and debris, which might more or less affect the well-being of the oysters.

Mr. Power's pond—about the same size as Mr. Malcomson's—is situated behind an embankment, and considerable trouble and expense have been unavailingly gone to by the proprietor to render the experiment successful. He takes much interest in oyster culture, and has visited various places in France and England to make himself acquainted with the best methods of cultivation.

The same causes disadvantageously affecting Mr. Malcomson's pond may have exercised a like influence over that of Mr. Power.

Although oysters are said to have existed in the neighbourhood formerly, none are to be found at present.

The fattening grounds of Earl Fortescue and Mr. Power, in the same locality, have answered satisfactorily, but no spat has been obtained there.

Mr. Sandes' small pond in the county Kerry, near the Shannon, was unfortunately constructed above high water-mark, thus necessitating the use of mechanical power to lift the water.

The collectors here used are boards joined together resembling doors and laid over the oysters. No spat has been obtained. From the difficulty and cost of raising the water, it is probable that it was not renewed sufficiently often.

Mr. Bland's pond at Sneem is a small enclosure of the end of a creek, but up to the present no spat has been obtained. No information as to temperature, density, &c., could be obtained with regard to these ponds.

Mr. Trench's pond was a small enclosure in Kilmacologue Harbour. No spat was ever found in the pond, the gravel on which the parent oysters were laid and the shells became partly buried in mud and covered with slime.

Mr. William Hart appears to have taken considerable trouble with his enclosure, using various descriptions of collectors; the place appears well circumstanced, but we cannot say if there has been any adhesion of spat.

Mr. Henry O'Connell used in his small pond for collectors parent oysters, old shells, stones, tiles, fascines, furze, and an old hamper. He reports that the latter was a splendid collector, and the shells, stones and oysters were very well covered with spat.

c

The locality of this pond is celebrated for its fattening properties, but hitherto hardly any production has taken place.

At Kilrush, in a small natural pond which cannot be regarded as coming within the enclosure system, Colonel Vandeleur has attempted breeding oysters without success, probably arising from the scour of the receding tide washing away the spat before it can adhere to the collectors.

Mr. Reeves' experiments in foreshore cultivation so far as production is concerned have been partially successful, a considerable quantity of spat from the natural beds in the river having attached to stone slabs placed horizontally for the purpose.

The same success has attended the experiments of Mr. John Smith on the Midleton River near Queenstown. The spat here, as at Mr. Reeves's, coming in from oysters in the river.

These are the only two instances of foreshore cultivation met with in Ireland.

Diminished as the supply of oysters is in Ireland, and suffering as this branch of fisheries is from exhaustion, there can be no doubt that the banks, both as regards stock and other conditions, are for the most part in a more satisfactory condition than those of the other portions of the kingdom or of France.

This comparatively favourable state is unquestionably due to the salutary regulations framed and enforced by the Board of Works whilst the Fisheries were under the charge of that department, the observance of close time, and the efficient service rendered by the coast-guard in carrying out these regulations. Great credit is due to the late Inspecting Commissioner of Fisheries, Mr. James Redmond Barry, for his constant and useful efforts to promote this as well as other branches of the fisheries; mainly to his representations and exertions is due the preservation of the oyster banks on the S.E. coast from being included in the conditions of the late Convention with France which would probably have proved most disastrous to the Irish oyster fisheries. Some additions to the present laws as respects the preservation and encouragement of the culture of oysters is required. (For an Epitome of these laws, compiled by Mr. Brady, Inspector of Irish Fisheries, see Appendix G.)

No circumstance is to be more regretted or calls more for interference in the interest of the seaboard population than the enormous quantity of small oysters of from one to two years old that are dredged and sold for exportation at prices as low as one shilling per hundred.

These, if kept and laid in the numerous places which might be selected for growing and fattening round the coast, would in three or four years, without trouble, and at hardly any cost, realize five or six times the amount obtained for them in an immature state.

The value of the oysters consumed in England annually is estimated at £4,000,000 sterling, and there is no doubt but that double that quantity would find ready consumption if obtainable.*

* "Suffice it to say, that such is the importance of this branch of commerce, that 700,000,000 of oysters are annually consumed in London alone, and quite as many, if not more, in the provinces. Now, supposing we value them at six-

The entire sum realized by the sale of Irish oysters is difficult to ascertain, but it does not exceed £50,000 per annum,* and assuming no increase whatever in production or capture, that amount might be greatly augmented by not allowing oysters under a certain size to be exported, and by affording the poorer classes greater facilities for obtaining portions of the foreshore for the formation of parcs and claires.

Whatever trouble and uncertainty attends breeding, there is but comparatively little with regard to fattening, and success in the latter would lead the way for experiments with regard to the former.

*The various Methods of Oyster Culture reviewed and explained.*

The most ancient method of oyster culture of which we have any record is that practised in Lake Fusaro, which has flourished more or less for about 1,900 years. This, no doubt, is the origin of all oyster culture in Europe. The following two cuts are illustrative of the methods by which oyster culture is there carried on. In the first, fascines are suspended some few feet above the bottom, to which the rising spat of the oysters becomes attached. In the second, artificial heaps of stones are thickly surrounded with stakes, and on these the oysters become fixed, and the stakes are drawn or the stones lifted for the purpose of

Fig. 18.

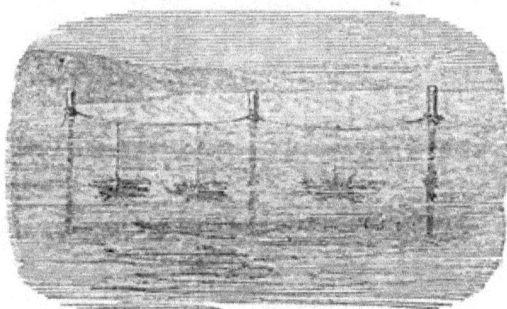

pence a dozen, which is certainly below the ordinary selling price, we shall then have an annual expenditure in England of about *three millions* sterling in oysters alone! Could any fact more powerfully attest the value of this branch of commerce?"—*From the Popular Science Review.*

"It is not easy to arrive at correct statistics of what London requires in the way of oysters; but, if we set the number down as being nearly 800,000,000 we shall not be very far wrong."—*From Bertram's Harvest of the Sea, p.* 373.

Assuming that as much oysters are consumed in the provinces as in London, and calculating the price at an average of only 5s. per 100, the result would be an expenditure of £4,000,000.

The vast proportion of these oysters are taken from the great ocean beds, far beyond the three miles limit, and from private beds also not under Government control.

* Ten years ago and even later oysters were sold at Arklow as low as 4s. per barrel; in 1869 they sold as high as 25s.—the average for the year being 17s. 9d. per barrel for all sizes. The sum realized for oysters in Ireland for some years past has, owing to the increased price, been about the same, notwithstanding the diminished production.

Fig. 19.

detaching any of the produce. The parent oysters, of course, are thickly scattered about and near these collectors. That the principles of cultivation are sound is evident from the long-continued success. If experiments in this country are not successful it is because the natural conditions are unsuitable, or because the oysterculturist lacks the skill and experience to carry his work to a satisfactory conclusion; for skill and experience are quite as requisite, if not more so, in the aquæculturist as in the agriculturist.

Oyster culture may be divided under three heads :—

1. Banks, which are always submerged.
2. Weed-beds (in France called crassats) or mud-lands, or foreshores, which are dry at low spring tides.
3. Tanks or enclosed areas of water where the in or out flow of the tides can be regulated at pleasure.

The first process is the simplest, since it consists of working over beds with the dredge at suitable seasons, in order to keep the cultch or shells on which the spat may collect clean. Another benefit derived from dredging frequently is that of preventing the oysters from running too much or too coarsely to shell; it tends to make a thinner, neater shell, and a more compact and shapeable fish. The dredge, too, removes vermin, weeds, mud, slime, &c., which, if not constantly disturbed, would overgrow the oysters and cultch, and destroy them as collectors of the spat.* The oysters also are evenly distributed, thin spots are supplied. Fattening grounds are picked for the market, and more oysters shifted to them from off the mere growing grounds. This is pretty much the *modus operandi* of the Colchester and Whitstable companies.

The Whitstable Company is the largest and wealthiest oyster corporation in the world; it is a co-operative chartered body, and the government is at once simple and effective. It cannot be said to breed largely, as it seldom obtains a spat upon its own

---

* Frequent dredging is practised in many places, but to save trouble the fishermen throw the weeds, &c., &c., overboard again after selecting the oysters, so that the frequent dredging does not produce the effect which it should.

grounds, and in former years trusted greatly to the spat from the large quantity of oysters it possessed floating on to the common ground known as "The Flats" (now the property of the Herne Bay Company), where the small oysters were dredged, and at low tide picked up, and sold to the Whitstable Company to be deposited on their grounds. The company also bought largely of the Essex dredgermen and others.

It is calculated that eight men per acre are required at Whitstable to work their grounds. Three days per week are also given to cleaning the ground, shifting oysters from one part to another, collecting the marketable-sized oysters into one place, destroying starfish and other vermin, and four hours of each other day are also devoted to this. During the other three days they dredge for the market, in which operation a certain quantity called 'a stint" is assigned to each boat, which it must complete and must not exceed. When this quantity has been obtained the day's work is over.

Each evening the amount received from the sales at Billingsgate is divided by the managers, consisting of a foreman, assisted by a jury of twelve persons, all fishermen of the Company.

The Coln river is worked in a similar way by a body of fishermen under the Corporation of Colchester.

There are in Ireland many places where such a method of oyster culture could be advantageously applied, such as the large loughs, the estuaries of rivers, and the large bays with which Ireland abounds.

The cultivation of crassats (mud lands) and ebb-dry foreshores is available for either associated bodies of fishermen or individuals; it is confined entirely to the ground above low-water at spring tides.

It is especially adapted to the wants of a poor population, on a rocky coast, partly fishermen and partly farmers, such as we find in many parts of Ireland, and where the shores are suitable for cultivation, and the requisite materials abound on every side, only requiring labour to make them available. From Cork round westward, and still onwards even to Belfast and Strangford, there is scarcely an inlet where the residents on the coast might not improve their condition by cultivating the rocks and shoals which surround them;—they possess advantages far exceeding those of the inhabitants of the Islands of Ré and Oleron in the Bay of Biscay.

The first thing necessary is in the months of April and May to clear away the weed from the rocks, to construct roughly small enclosures with the large stones at hand, placing them so as to form a low wall about a foot high; an engraving of the method on which they are constructed is given at page 24. Oysters are not yet so far destroyed at most of these places but that they are yet obtainable by dredging, and if laid in the months named in those parcs would probably deposit a valuable spat; from July to the following May no care or attention is necessary.

In the case of estuaries of rivers, bays, harbours, or loughs, when the ground consists of mud banks or weed beds, the process is somewhat different. There parcs may still be made, but it becomes necessary to attend more to the cleansing of the collectors. The collectors may be large flat stones if nothing better can be had; but tiles, as employed on the French plan, are easier to attend to, and easier to cleanse. These parcs may be simply enclosed spaces, with surrounding walls of stones so as to define each particular allotment; or in the case of a space of ground surrounded by the sea, belonging to an individual, or to two or three working in partnership, the method of placing the tiles either in rows or patches, as may be most convenient for the arresting of the spat, and as shown in figs. 20, 21, 22, and 23, may be adopted. At Arcachon the parcs are made upon this plan,

Fig. 20.

Fig. 21.

Fig. 22.

Fig. 23.

and answer admirably; a weed bed is chosen, a considerable part of which is dry at low spring tides. Upon this stacks of tiles laid crosswise, one tier above another, until they reach some three or four feet in height are erected and secured by stakes from injury by the run of the tide. About these the weed is hoed closely down, and the oysters are laid. When the spat rises it drifts under the tiles, and the under side being almost always clean, more or less spat adheres to it. If the top side of the tiles is sufficiently clean, as many will adhere to that also. Hundreds of tiles may be seen completely crusted over with oysters, as many as two or three hundred being fixed to one tile, so that hardly a portion of the tile is visible (see cuts of tiles covered with oysters, figs. 24 and 25). These stacks of tiles are erected about every twenty yards or so, the tops of the stacks being often protected by a thick planking, which is pitched on the under side, and is thickly strewn with shells of mussels, cockles, &c., which adhere to the pitch and receive a share of the spat. This cover-

Fig. 24.

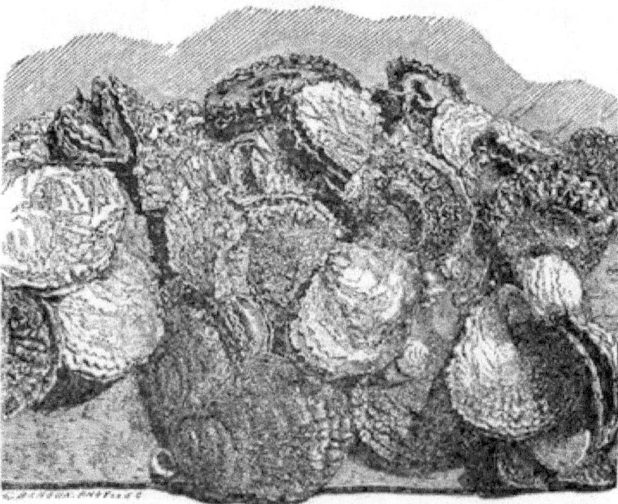

Fig. 25.

ing aids to protect the young oysters from the effects of the sun during the two or three hours daily that they are exposed at low spring tides.    Fascines, or faggots, or hurdles, are also used to arrest the spat, being pegged down in their places, and so secured from floating away; but these do not answer so well in open water as the tiles or stones.    In foreshore cultivation shells are also scattered about near the oysters to receive a share of the spat; but these also should not be cast down until immediately before the spatting season.    One great cause why collectors do not answer at times is, that they are often put down too long before the oysters commence to spat, and thus the tiles and shells, &c., become foul, and the wood gets greasy or slimy, and the oysters will not adhere to it.    Another reason for a defective spat often arises from the fact of the oysters being laid down too short a period before the spatting season.    The removal of oysters from one ground and depth of water, just before the spatting season, to another, is often found to be prejudicial.    The shorter time which elapses between the laying of the collectors and the spatting of the oysters, and the longer time between the laying of the oysters and the spatting the better.    Oysters laid on muddy ground often sink into the mud; so long as this happens gradually the oyster does not suffer, for it contrives by the flow of the water which it takes in and ejects, to keep a breathing hole open; but when this occurs from a sudden storm, so that the oysters are buried without the chance of securing an air hole, they mostly perish.    In France it is customary when the ground is very soft, and the oysters sink, to raise them every two or three months, and replace them on the surface.    In such cases, however, the oysters are usually put up for fattening, not for breeding, though oysters breed well enough either on mud lands or on weed beds.    When the oysters are only laid on weed beds to grow or fatten, it is not customary to hoe the weed.

The long wet weed is found to form an admirable protection from the sun. In fig. 20 the tiles it will be noticed are placed on a slope; this is found advantageous in a strong current. When the tide runs for a long time in one direction, as in some rivers, and when the water is more or less muddy at times, the mud deposits on the back of the tiles, and the spat attaches on the other side. Fig. 21 is more applicable where the flow is equal, and where as much mud is likely to be deposited by the ebb as the flood tide. The other methods given in figs. 22 and 23 are employed indifferently in still waters, as in creeks, &c., and in open water, mud banks, weed beds, &c., in harbours.

For sketches of one of the imperial parcs at Arcachon, see plates 4 and 5, Appendix.

The tank system of oyster culture in reality differs little from that already described, as far as the placing of collectors and oysters is concerned. The fault of many existing oyster ponds, more particularly in Ireland is, that they are too small in area, and not deep enough. The larger they are, within reasonable bounds, the better and more natural they will be for the oysters. From three or four acres to ten or twelve is the most useful and most manageable size, while they should not be less than three feet deep, and should vary to the depth of ten or twelve feet. The water should have free access every tide, save during the spatting of the oysters, when no water should be allowed to escape lest the spat escape with it. But in very hot seasons considerable evaporation takes place, more particularly in small ponds, and this causes a good deal of disturbance in the density of the water, which is prejudicial. This therefore should be carefully watched, and should it threaten to become dangerous, it will be advisable to let in a portion of fresh water if possible.

Weeds are often very troublesome in tanks or ponds, more particularly the green filmy weed " cladophera," known commonly as " blanket-weed." This is very dangerous to the oysters, and means should be taken to remove it.

It is usual in ponds to gravel large portions of the bottom in order that provision may be made to catch that portion of the spat which fails to adhere to the collectors, and the shortest time before spatting that this gravel is cast in the better for its cleanliness. Hurdles and fascines however have been found to answer well in such places, and as a large number of collectors is required, they will be found much cheaper. Engravings of hurdles, fascines, &c., are appended, and the method of fixing them is shown also (see plate 6). They are fixed in rows by means of pegs, about two or three feet above the oysters, which are scattered on the soil under them, as shown in the engraving, though of course much more plentifully than they are therein depicted. Furze bushes are also found to answer fairly, and are cheap; but fascines and bushes are scarcely so suitable in a tideway in consequence of the liability of the twigs to catch weed, break, and float away, when the spat is carried with them. In all cases when wood is employed for collectors, it should be dry, hard, and sapless, and cut at least in the preceding season.

Oysters are more easily detached from wood collectors; the

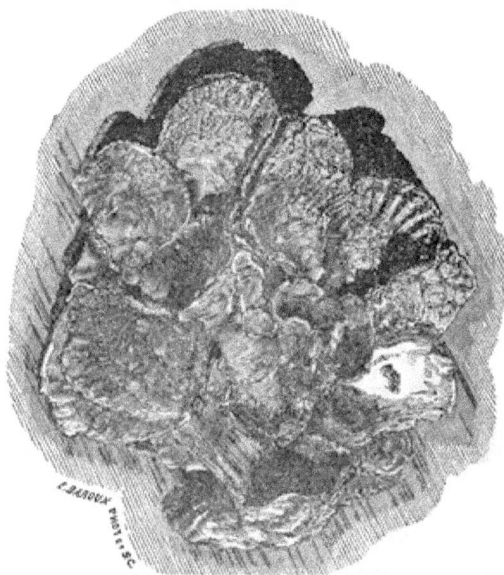

Fig. 26.—Specimen of old oyster shell covered with young oysters.

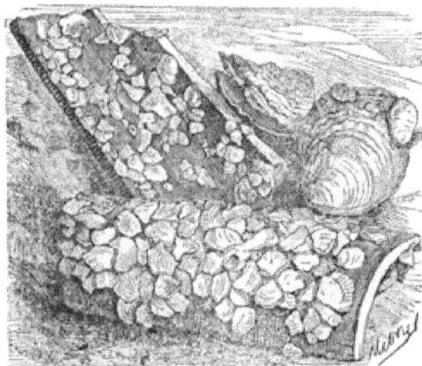

Fig. 27.—Specimen of tiles and shells covered with growing spat.

Fig. 28.—Specimen of old shell covered with *maerl*

Fig. 29.

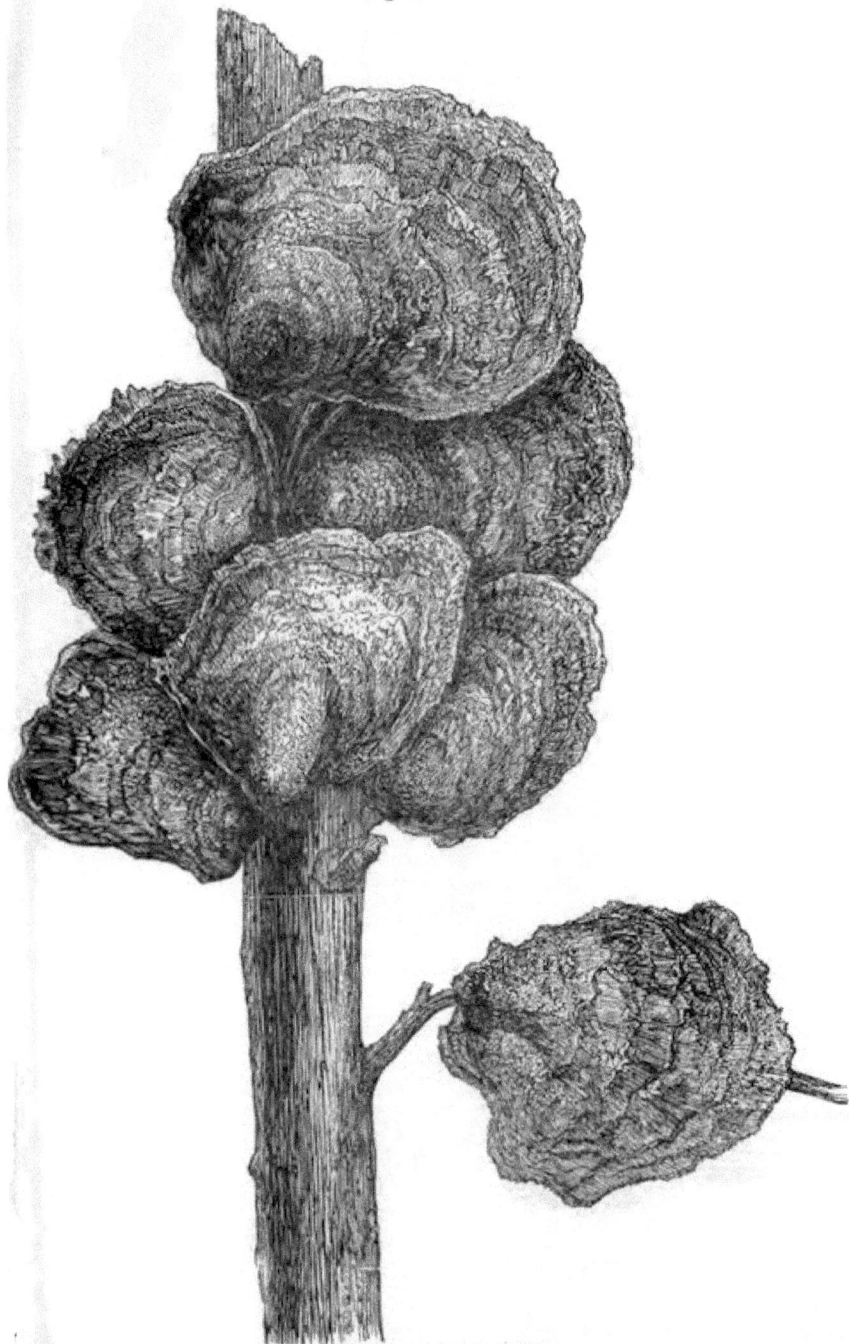

Spat on part of a fascine at Hayling, 1869.

loss by damage to the shell or fish in breaking them off is least
upon fascines, as the twigs are easily broken up.  It is greater on
hurdles, greater still on tiles, and greatest of all on stones.  The
young oyster, though somewhat malformed at times on twigs,
soon regains its shape when detached without damage.  Engravings of oysters upon a twig and a stake are shown in figures 29,
30, 31.  The latter represents oysters at various stages of their
existence.  E showing the spat at ten days, D at one month, C
three months, B six months, and A at one year.

Fig. 30.

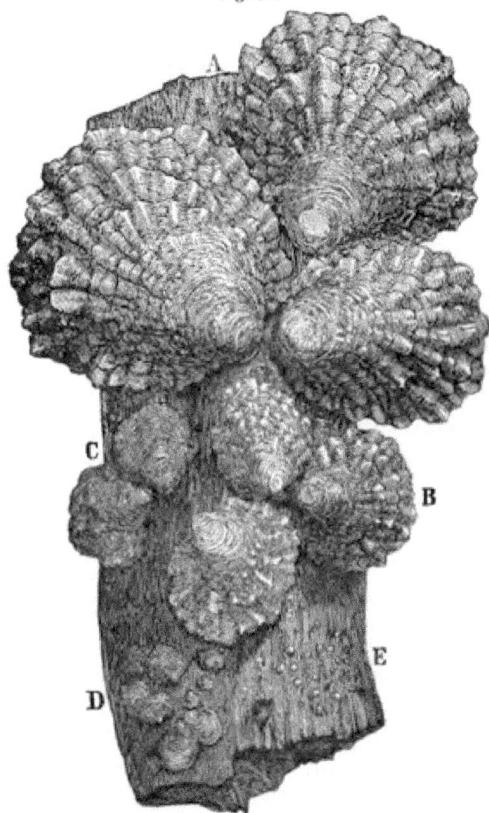

A, 1 year; B, 6 months; C, 3 months; D, 1 month; E, 10 or 14 days.

Fig. 31.

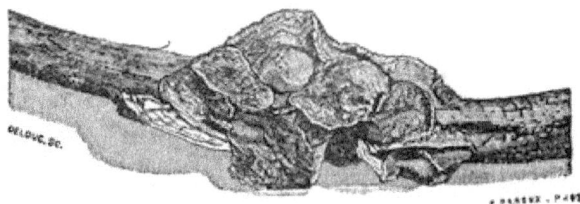

A method of coating tiles by dipping them in a thin mortar or cement so that the oysters might be more easily detached, has been invented by Dr. Kemmerer. As far as the detachment is concerned it is certainly an improvement; but collectors so coated are liable to collect the dirt more easily than others. The oysters are usually detached when they have made a suitable growth, so as not to be damaged in the operation, and this should be when they are about a year old.

The tank or enclosure method is more particularly adapted for companies, or individuals resident in the neighbourhood or the locality where such basins naturally formed exist, or where the enclosure can be rendered complete at a moderate cost. It is not adapted for the poorer class of the peasantry, but still it affords constant employment to a considerable number of persons, and it may be remarked that both for this and the foreshore cultivation the labour of women and children is available, a great portion of the duties required being of a light description.

Ireland presents from its peculiar configuration many places suitable for oyster culture in this way, which can be rendered productive to a great degree at a small cost.

With respect to the best kind of collectors to be employed on the Irish coast, these must be governed by the facilities offered by the neighbourhood, as they are very various.

Tiles are cheap in France, hence their introduction as collectors; the average cost is one sou each, or £2 per thousand. At Auray, one cultivator possesses 200,000 tiles, and upon these he obtained in 1869, six millions of oysters.

At such places, for example, as Tralee, Carlingford, Achill, Belmullet, and other localities, where the rocks naturally collect each year a large number of oysters, tiles would prove very effective. If too expensive for the class of persons who pick these oysters from the rocks, it would be worth while for some one to advance the cost, and receive it back in the following year when the harvest of oysters would enable the peasants to repay the loan; or, failing this spirit of enterprise in the inhabitants, the peasants should be instructed to break up the rocks, and place them in rows as already shown at page 24, so as to offer clean surfaces for the spat that rises from the bay.

The best arrangement of tiles in such places as Tralee and Bantry Bay, would probably be that shown in the engravings at pp. 37 and 38, Nos. 20, 21, 22, and 23; but in places where the ground admits of stakes being driven, those shown in figs. 22 and 23 are preferable. Collectors of wood are unsuitable for such places, catching passing weeds, and becoming slimy and foul, and therefore useless.

### APPROPRIATE PLACES FOR CULTIVATION.

The best places for cultivation are harbours, quiet bays, and estuaries of rivers. Exposed sea coast, though not the most desirable ground, may still be utilized where rocks or large stones abound, to which oysters can attach themselves, and from which

they obtain a certain amount of shelter. On such spots only the
rough parcs shown at p. 24 can be used.

The first named places, however, give the most favourable
chances of success. As a rule a gravelly or muddy bottom, that
is to say, with a muddy surface, is most desirable. Sand, unless
it has such a mixture of mud with it as prevents violent shifting,
being less suitable. On the gravelly bottoms the best results
will be obtained as regards breeding, the others are better for
fattening, though upon hard mud banks and weed beds in France,
parcs as already stated are formed at Arcachon and elsewhere.
The engraving of one of the Imperial parcs at Arcachon (plate 4,
Appendix), must here be again referred to. Shoals which are
dry in estuaries, harbours, or sheltered bays *only* at low spring
tides (but which are at all other times covered with water), are
often found to be favourable both for breeding and fattening, and
are utilized as noted above. Such are the shoals on which the
Imperial parcs are established.

Foreshores which are also ebb-dry at low spring tides, and which
are either gravelly or stony, can be used for parcs, more particularly if there is a bed of oysters anywhere in the neighbourhood.
For fattening, however, there are few places better than a salt
marsh, in which pools of salt water already exist. The fattening
ponds (termed claires) at Marennes and La Tremblade, of which
sketches are appended (see plates 7 and 8), are at both places
formed out of salt marshes, and are in many instances only old
disused salterns, or salt pans, in which rough salt is made. Here
oyster ponds and salterns are often mingled together in apparent
confusion. A tidal creek or canal usually runs through the marsh
which gives a fresh supply of salt-water to the ponds whenever
it may be desired. In these claires the oysters grow and fatten
rapidly. In some more rapidly than in others. The number of
oysters laid down in claires is proportioned to the time it is
intended that they should remain there. For as the food of
the oyster is only limited, of course a small number will fatten
more rapidly than a large one. The average distribution is
about two or three to the square foot. These places chiefly produce the green oyster, the prejudice against which has been
already noticed in this report—a more foolish prejudice, or one
which it is more desirable to dispel, could hardly exist. The
oysters thus gathered are of excellent flavour and quality. Indeed
they are by far the best produced in France, and by the prejudice
existing against these oysters in England, they shut out very extensive fattening grounds in the vast extent of salt marshes which
abound around the coasts, which are now of comparatively little
value, but could be most easily utilized, and which would be less
liable to plunder and danger than beds in the sea.

We have frequently referred to muddy or marly bottoms as being
most favourable to the growth of the oyster. The blue or London
clay, known as marl in Ireland, is usually the foundation of those
bottoms. An able report and analysis by Professor Sullivan,
given in the Appendix H, deals more fully with this matter, and
shows on what parts of the seaboard of Ireland soil of an analogous
nature is to be found.

With respect to the point of the density of the water, it may be stated that at Hayling Island the rate of density which was found favourable to the adherence of the spat was about 27° hydrometer.

It might be difficult perhaps to lay down any law or exact scale as to the temperature required for a satisfactory spat, but probably when the water ranges from 62° to 72° by day, within those margins, the temperature will be found to be sufficiently favourable.

It will be noticed in the foregoing report that repetitions sometimes occur. These have been found indispensable from the form in which the report has been drawn up, owing to the desire of the Commissioners that each subject should, as far as possible, be made complete in itself, so as to afford clear and definite information.

## SUMMARY.

In concluding our report we desire to remark that the limited time and resources at our command for investigating a subject of so extensive a character and on which so much difference of opinion exists, has precluded us from giving more than a general account of the state of the oyster fisheries in the different places we visited and the causes which we consider have contributed to their decadence or the reverse. In the instances of artificial culture, whether as regards breeding or fattening, we made as close an investigation as circumstances would permit into the causes which led to success or failure.

The readiest answer that could be given to the question as to what conditions are most favourable for the production and growth of oysters would be to point to any prolific natural bank, and to detail all the circumstances, so far as ascertainable, connected with it as regarded depth, temperature, and density of water, nature of the soil, &c., &c.

We have, therefore, deemed it of the greatest importance to ascertain as accurately as possible every fact in connexion with natural oyster banks as well as artificial layings, especially in Ireland. With this object, through the co-operation of the Admiralty, we caused the temperature of the sea to be ascertained simultaneously at 32 points around the coast of the United Kingdom, directing that care should be taken that this should be done in the proximity of natural or artificial oyster fisheries. These investigations were also useful in showing the effect of the Gulf Stream on different parts of the coast.

With a view of determining the soils most favourable to the production and growth of oysters, we obtained specimens of earths forming the bottoms of various fisheries in France, England, and Ireland; and with respect to the latter country we also obtained some from localities where cultivation had not proved successful, in order to ascertain how far the nature of the ground might have influenced failure.

In the Appendix will be found a special report on the temperature of the sea by Professor Hennessy, which embodies the results obtained from the voluminous returns of the coast-guard and from France, from which the following conclusions may be drawn:—

(1.) The temperature of the sea on the coast of Ireland varies within narrower limits than on the coast of Great Britain and France, or, in other words, it is more equable throughout the year, and also throughout the season of oyster breeding.

(2.) During the summer months, especially on the south and west coasts of Ireland, the temperature at noon, and, therefore, *a fortiori* between two and three in the afternoon, is generally sufficiently high to fulfil the conditions as regards temperature required for the abundant production of healthy oyster spat. This conclusion is especially true for the months of July and August, and with high water about two or three hours afternoon.

(3.) The winter temperature of the sea on the Irish coast is such as to render the destruction of oyster beds from excessive cold a contingency that may be considered as never likely to occur.

(4.) The second of these conclusions applies equally to the greater part of the coast of Great Britain, and the third to its south and west coasts.

A reference to the Abstract of the Tables of Temperature shows that latitude most powerfully influences the temperature of the sea ; next, the situation of the place according as it is on an eastern or western shore (this probably being the effect of the Gulf Stream) ; lastly, there are local conditions, such as the shelter afforded by surrounding mountains, deep bays, inlets, &c., which during the summer months tend to give to the waters of such places an exceptional degree of heat.

The general inference being that western coasts are less liable than the eastern to great variations, although there are but few places even on the eastern coasts where this variation is so great as to prevent oyster culture being successfully adopted.

However, it is to be noticed that there prevails throughout the whole series of tables a higher degree of warmth close to the shore in summer than at some distance at sea. This might be naturally expected from the greater influence of the sun upon the soil over which there is a relatively less depth of water in accordance with the remarks made by Professor Hennessy at the end of his report, p. 75.

By our desire Professor Hennessy also laid down on the map which accompanies this report (see plate 10, Appendix) various lines showing the distribution of temperature over Ireland and on the surface of the surrounding sea. We have also indicated on the same map the site of all the natural oyster banks as far as we were able to ascertain them. For this purpose the queries in Appendix I. were sent to the various coast-guard stations.

The analysis of the earths was intrusted to Professor Sullivan. His report will be found in the Appendix H.

We have arrived at the following conclusions from the important information afforded by it :—

1. As regards mineralogical constitution, the mud of oyster grounds, suitable both for reproduction and fattening, may be derived from almost any kind of rock.

2. As regards mechanical character, fruitful oyster mud may vary within very wide limits from almost pure sand to plastic clay. In the very sandy grounds there must, however, be always a suf-

ficient quantity of highly hydrated clay to render the sand adhesive and to preserve it from becoming a mere loose running mass. In the clayey grounds there must always be calcareous mud to make the clay porous and prevent it becoming too hard—clay marls with some intermixed sand being perhaps the best of all materials for oyster grounds.

Professor Sullivan also furnishes most valuable information as to the places on the seaboard where the bottom is composed of earth of an analogous character to that where oysters exist naturally, or where artificial cultivation has succeeded. He also gives an analysis of the earth in some places where failures have occurred.

The earth known as the London clay appears to be the soil peculiarly adapted for oysters. It may be well here to explain that the term "London clay" is employed in a general and in a special sense. In the former it is used as a collective name for a number of beds of the older tertiary formation, consisting of gravels and sands below and of clays above, occupying a large portion of Sussex, Essex, and Middlesex, and portions of Berks, Surrey, and Kent. In the special or more limited sense it is applied to the blueish or blackish clay, sometimes mixed with a greenish-coloured earth and white sand, which forms the upper parts of the beds just mentioned. London clay is plastic clay, not differing much in chemical composition from ordinary potters' clay. It is sometimes highly calcareous, so as to pass it into a marly clay, and, as at Harwich, into a regular calcareous rock. The river and shore muds formed from the London clay are, however, largely mingled with sand derived from the lower beds above mentioned and from the overlying sandy beds such as the silicious sands of Bagshot in Surrey and New Forest in Hampshire, &c. All fruitful oyster muds contain organic matter, always due in part to the presence of infusoriæ, and sometimes in part to small algæ or confervæ, remains of shell-fish and other marine creatures.

It will be seen in the report that this London clay is to be found in many places in the rivers and around the shores of Ireland.

We are, therefore, enabled to state that, both as regards temperature and soil, Ireland appears to be capable of a far greater amount of oyster production than is yielded at present.

There are, however, other conditions to be fulfilled the existence of which can only be ascertained by observation and experience.

We deem it incumbent on us to recommend the utmost caution with respect to all attempts at artificial cultivation, particularly as regards propagation. We have found fully ten instances of success in fattening for the one in the way of production. Experiments in the former are much more conveniently and inexpensively made than in the latter, more especially where the tank or enclosure system is attempted.

Before, therefore, enterprises of the latter kind are undertaken it should be carefully considered whether all the requirements which experience has pointed to as essential to success would be likely to be fulfilled, not the least important of which would be

D

the outlay, the extent of which is generally difficult to calculate, as considerable departures from the original plans would often be necessitated in the event of the experiment not proving at once successful of accomplishment. Foreshore cultivation such as is in satisfactory operation at Auray in Brittany, described at pages 17 and 23, would be found much less hazardous and easier of accomplishment and in other respects more desirable generally for Ireland.

There are many places bordering on rivers and also on the sea where enterprises of this kind might be profitably carried on.

As already observed, it is much to be regretted that the practice so extensively prevails of selling oysters of immature growth for exportation, there being so many places in Ireland which are suitable for growth and fattening. It is most unwise to dispose of oysters of a year or eighteen months old, often at as low a price as 10s. per thousand, when, by laying them up for a longer period, they would be vastly increased in value.

It is also to be regretted that no restrictions have been enforced against the continuous dredging of banks after they have commenced to show signs of exhaustion, as this would, in our opinion, have tended considerably to avert the great falling off in supply in several banks formerly productive.

We are far from concurring in the opinion put forward by some authorities that, owing to the wonderful productiveness of the oyster, if only a few be left upon a bank they are sufficient for its replenishment.

It must be borne in mind that not more than ten per cent breed annually, and that from the moment of its birth the oyster is subject to numerous dangers—amongst them it is liable to be killed by a sudden fall or rise of temperature, to be borne to situations where it cannot attach itself, to be devoured soon after birth by the vermin that await it at that stage, or, later on, to be smothered by mussels, or attacked by the star-fish, dog-whelk, and crab, besides suffering numerous perils from mud and sand.

The number that arrive at maturity must therefore be comparatively few. Indeed it is asserted that not a dozen on an average out of the vast quantity originally given birth to, and which is said to consist of from one to two millions, survive.

Although we have collected a large amount of information with respect to oyster produce in America and other countries, we found that there were some important points of difference as regarded the nature of the oyster, and the influences to which it was subject, as compared with those of the British Islands and France, we have therefore deemed it best to omit it.

We have already given the leading facts with regard to the best situations and circumstances for production and growth, as well as the modus operandi of artificial culture and we have now only to consider, with a view to arriving at some decision on the point, the facts and evidence already alluded to as regards the cause of the deterioration of the oyster fisheries.

A perfectly unanswerable case is that of the Bay of Granville, at one time possessed of a large accumulation of oysters, but now over-run with vermin and covered with weed and filth. Where similar cases exist in Ireland, it might perhaps be well to allow certain powers hereafter mentioned to the Inspectors of Fisheries for the revival and conservation of the beds.

Nothing can better illustrate the extreme difficulty experienced in arriving at a decision as to the cause of the enormous falling off in the productiveness of the English Oyster Fisheries than the opposite opinions expressed by those whom it might be supposed were most competent to pronounce on them.

The Royal Commission appointed in 1862 to report on the Sea Fisheries of the kingdom, declare in the most positive manner that the decline in production proceeded from a failure in spat during certain years.

In their Report, page 105, they say :—

"That this decrease has not arisen from over-fishing, nor from any causes over which man has direct control, but from the very general failure of the spat, or young of the oyster, which appears during the years in question to have been destroyed soon after it was produced. A similar failure of the spat has frequently happened before, and probably will often happen again."

The Commissioners were so impressed with the idea that oyster grounds cannot be dredged out, that their recommendation goes to the extent of having no restrictions whatever, not even a close season.

Doubtless, their opinions influenced Parliament in passing the late Act for giving effect to the Convention with France, whereby the close season in the channel has been reduced to ten weeks, and the whole of the coasts of England and Wales left open to unrestricted dredging throughout the year.

But it is evident that where the principles thus enunciated by the Commissioners have been allowed to prevail both before and since that time, the supply of oysters has so greatly fallen off as almost to have ceased in some places; while, on the other hand, in those places where proper protection has been extended, either no falling off at all has been observed, or a positive increase has been the distinct result. These are facts that cannot be disputed, and the inference from them is plain. In 1862, when the Commissioners laid down their principle, native oysters were £2 8s. per bushel. They are now (eight years after) £10. If this is the fruit of following out such principles, is it not time to try what a reverse of this system may do for us? or will it be thought advisable to wait a few years longer until oysters are worth their weight in silver? Is it reasonable to suppose that nature should fail in one of its great principles of reproduction for eight or nine years in succession? The bulk both of evidence and facts which we have been able to collect, has been overwhelming in condemnation of over and reckless dredging.

There is yet another point on which some controversy exists, upon which it may be well to touch, and that is as to the necessity for dredging over some oyster grounds to keep them clear of mud, weeds, and vermin.

D 2

The advocates for the removal of all restrictions against continuous dredging, contend that during the close season much more injury is inflicted by allowing slob and weeds to accumulate, and the enemies of the oyster to prey unrestrainedly on them than any amount of dredging would accomplish. (See Commissioners' Report, Appendix K.)

Those in favour of a close season assert in answer, that if the constant operations of the dredger were so necessary for the preservation of oyster grounds, the extensive banks, some with layers upon layers of oysters many feet deep, never could have survived so long—subject as they were to be covered with mud, overrun with weeds, bored through by the whelk, or devoured by starfish and crabs.

Both disputants are to a certain extent right.

The great ocean beds over which a dredge may never have passed until their discovery, appear to support the theory that such grounds could thrive without the aid of man; and on the other hand, the ruined state to which many natural banks have often been rapidly reduced, soon after their discovery by the dredgers, is again a strong fact in support of the evidence as to the mischief of overdredging.

But it sometimes occurs that when owing to this serious diminution of oysters, such banks have been nearly or altogether abandoned, they rapidly become ruined by the collection of mud, weeds, and vermin, proving the necessity of continuing the dredging for cleansing purposes.

The answer to both sides is plain; many banks, though not all, really require human care for their preservation. Under other circumstances, where neither weeds nor mud accumulate, vermin abound, owing to causes difficult to account for; generally where the scour is sufficient to keep the cultch in a clean state, no interference on the part of man is necessary.

It may be asked why, if at one period banks were productive without artificial aid they should afterwards require it. There are various reasons why this may be so which may carry more or less weight. The disturbance of the soil by dredging may render all around loose and more shifting, and thus weed or soil may more easily drift into the depression caused by the abstracted oysters, or the drift of mud, &c., may attract vermin in large numbers from a distance, even as the fisherman rakes the bottom to attract fish. Alterations of currents and storms may now and then occur. Indeed there *may be* many ways of accounting for it, but it may be taken for granted that the fact is so. The case of Granville, for example, is one in point.

## RECOMMENDATIONS.

As the result of our inquiry, we beg to offer the following recommendations for your Excellency's consideration :—

1. That all regulations with regard to the close time around the Irish coast should be strictly maintained.

2. That the Inspectors of Irish fisheries should have power, whenever they determine to reserve a bank or any portion thereof from public dredging for the purpose of recovery, to make such arrangements as may seem desirable for keeping the restricted part free from weeds and vermin.

3. That there should be procurable at each coastguard station, at a small cost, general information as to oyster culture, and simple instructions as to the best modes of proceeding.

4. That the Inspectors be empowered to adopt such other means as they may deem necessary to afford information and in-struction to those requiring it with respect to oyster culture.

5. That having unsizable oysters in possession in places where it is prohibited by any by-law to take oysters from any public beds under a certain size shall be *prima facie* evidence that such oysters were taken in places so prohibited ; such regulation not to apply to private oyster grounds.

6. That facilities be afforded to the coast population to acquire the use of small portions of foreshore, or sea bottom, for oyster cultivation, and to obtain loans on satisfactory security for the pre-paration of same, and for the purchase of oysters, collectors, &c.

7. That landed proprietors desirous of cultivating oysters on the shores adjoining their lands, be empowered to avail themselves of the provisions of the Irish Land Improvement Acts, for the pur-pose of oyster cultivation.

### CONCLUSION.

In conclusion we beg to state that, in addition to the personal investigation we made into the condition of the natural and artifi-cial oyster fisheries of the United Kingdom and France, we carried out the direction we received as to consulting the best authorities on the subject.

Besides perusing everything procurable that has been written on the question, we had also personal conferences with nearly all the best authorities, and correspondence with others whom we did not find it practicable to meet.

Although we do not concur in the opinion put forward by some as to the extraordinary profits to be made from oyster cultivation, still we believe, if judiciously undertaken, and prudently and per-severingly carried out, that it is profitable and that there is very much to encourage enterprises of the kind.

Ireland undoubtedly possesses many advantages for this industry especially as regards foreshore cultivation, the fattening process at least being attended with little risk, and the results being often most remunerative.

When it is recollected that the consumption of oysters in Eng-land is said to reach in value over four millions of pounds sterling, with a largely increasing demand at even the present high prices, it can be understood what great room there is for the disposal of much more than the scarcely fifty thousand pounds worth produced on the Irish coast.

Ten times that amount would find a ready market at good prices in England and France.

Comparatively insignificant as the subject may appear, yet we beg to submit to your Excellency, that the successful promotion of the oyster fisheries of Ireland would be likely to be productive of very important advantages to the coast population.

Besides affording remunerative occupation, not likely to interfere with other employment, it might also be the means in many instances of enabling them to procure the appliances for pursuing sea fishing, and thus tend to promote that important but neglected and decaying industry.

We feel bound to express our obligation to the Government of His Majesty the Emperor of the French, especially to M. De Champeaux, and the officers under his department, and to M. Coste, for the great aid rendered us during our investigation in France. To the latter our thanks are particularly due for the valuable returns and other important information forwarded to us subsequently.

We have also to acknowledge the valuable co-operation of the Admiralty for the use of Her Majesty's steam Yacht *Vivid*, for proceeding round the coast of Ireland—an expedition most satisfactorily performed, owing to the very efficient assistance of Commander Sulivan, and for the directions given to the Coastguard of the kingdom to carry out our instructions for ascertaining the temperature of the sea, an order most admirably executed.

We should also add that the scientific investigations so important in their character, entrusted to Professors Hennessy and Sullivan, have been most ably executed.

All which we respectfully certify to your Excellency under our hands.

Dated in London, June 22, 1870.

JOHN ALOYSIUS BLAKE.

FRANCIS FRANCIS.

GEORGE W. HART.

THOMAS FRANCIS BRADY.

# APPENDIX.

## APPENDIX A.

CONVENTION between HER MAJESTY and the EMPEROR OF THE FRENCH, relative to FISHERIES in the SEAS between GREAT BRITAIN and FRANCE.

### ARTICLE III.

The arrangements of the present Convention shall apply beyond the fishery limits of both countries, as defined by the preceding articles, to the seas surrounding and adjoining Great Britain and Ireland, and adjoining the coasts of France between the frontiers of Belgium and Spain. The rules respecting oyster fishery shall, however, be observed only in the seas comprised within the limits hereinafter described.

### ARTICLE X.

Fishing of all kinds, by whatever means and at all seasons, may be carried on in the seas lying beyond the fishery limits which have been fixed for the two countries, with the exception of that for oysters, as hereinafter expressed.

### ARTICLE XI.

From the 16th of June to the 31st of August inclusive, fishing for oysters is prohibited outside the fishery limits which have been fixed for the two countries, between a line drawn from the North Foreland light to Dunkirk, and a line drawn from the Land's End to Ushant.

During the same period and in the same part of the channel, no boat shall have on board any oyster dredge, unless the same be tied up and sealed by the Customs authorities of one of the two countries in such a manner as to prevent its being made use of.

### ARTICLE XXIV.

All infractions of the regulations concerning the placing of boats on the fishing ground, the distances to be observed between them, the prohibition of oyster fishing during a portion of the year, and concerning every other operation connected with the act of fishing, and more particularly concerning circumstances likely to cause damage, shall be taken cognizance of by the cruisers of either nation, whichever may be the nation to which the fishermen guilty of such infractions may belong.

### ARTICLE XXIX.

In both countries the competent court or magistrate shall be empowered to condemn to a fine of at least eight shillings (ten francs), or to imprisonment for at least two days, persons who may infringe the regulations of the Convention concerning—

1. The close season for oysters, and illegal possession of dredges on board during that season ; &c.

### ARTICLE XXX.

In all cases of assault committed or of damage or loss inflicted at sea by fishermen of either country upon fishermen of the other country, the courts of the country to which the offenders belong shall condemn the latter to a fine of at least eight shillings (10 francs), or to imprisonment for at least two days. They may, moreover, condemn the offenders to pay adequate compensation for the injury.

### ARTICLE XXXI.

Fishing boats of either of the two countries shall be admitted to sell their fish in such ports of the other country as may be designated for that purpose, on condition that they conform to the regulations mutually agreed upon. Those regulations, together with a list of the ports, are annexed to the present Convention ; but without prejudice to the opening by either country of any additional ports.

### ARTICLE XXXII.

The fishing boats of the one country shall not enter within the fishery limits fixed for the other country, except under the following circumstances :—

5. When proceeding to any of the ports of the other country open to them for the sale of fish in accordance with the preceding Article ; but in such case they shall never have oyster dredges on board.

### ARTICLE XXXIII.

When fishing boats, availing themselves of the privilege specified in Article XXXI., shall have oysters on board, they shall not carry any dredges or other implement for taking oysters.

At Paris, the 11th November, 1867.

(L.S.)    LYONS.
(L.S.)    MOUSTIER.

---

## APPENDIX B.

### DECREE.

Napoleon, by the grace of God and the national will, Emperor of the French,

To all present and to come, greeting.

Considering the law of the 9th January, 1852, on the coast fisheries ;

Considering the decrees of the 4th July, 1853, and the 19th November, 1859 ;

Considering the recommendation of the permanent commission of fisheries,

On the report of our minister, the Secretary of State for the Marine and Colonies ;

The Admiralty understood ;

We have decreed and decree as follows :—

Art. 1. Fishing for all crustaceous and shell fish, except oysters, is permitted all the year, at a distance of three miles from low-water mark. Oyster dredging is permitted from the 1st September to the 30th April, on banks outside bays, or on banks situated three miles from the shore, with every description and tonnage of vessel.

Fishermen are called upon to observe, in the seas between the coasts of France and the United Kingdom of Great Britain and Ireland, the prescriptions of the convention of the 2nd August, 1839, and of the international rules of the 23rd June, 1843.

Art. 8. The prefects maritime fix by rules the time of the close and open season for the oyster fishing on the beds within bays, and on those beds situated within three miles of the coast.

They will determine the banks that are to be dredged.

Fishing is not permitted between sunset and sunrise.

Without the express permission of the prefect maritime, in the interest of cleaning the beds, fishermen should immediately throw back into the sea, all sand, gravel, and fragments of shells, as well as all oysters under the authorized size.

Wherever any establishments exist, fit to receive small oysters, these latter may be placed there, instead of throwing them back on the beds.

Thirdly. All oysters less than five centimètres.

Art. 12. The prefects maritime determine by issuing regulations, all the police measures for order, and proper precaution to hinder all accidents, damages, robberies, collisions, &c., and to guarantee to the fishermen the free exercise of their calling.

Art. 13. All the orders of the prefects maritimes with reference to the coast fisheries are submitted to the Minister of the Marine and Colonies for his approval.

Art. 14. All, or any part of any decrees or rules, issued previous to these, which are contrary to the present decree, or any part thereof, are hereby repealed.

Given at the Palace of the Tuileries this 10th day of May, 1862.

(Signed)      NAPOLEON.

By the Emperor.

The Minister Secretary of State for the Marine and the Colonies,

(Signed)      C<sup>mte.</sup> P. DE CHASSELOUP-LAUBAT.

---

Enclosure No. 3.

4th Arrondissement Maritime.    Year 1865.

IMPERIAL MARINE.

ORDER for the closing of the oyster fishery in the quarter of La Teste.

The Vice-Admiral, Prefect Maritime,

Considering the law of the 9th January, 1852, on the coast fisheries ;

Considering the decrees of the 4th July, 1855, and the 10th May, 1862 ;

Considering the prefectoral decree of the 15th October, 1864, opening the close season for oysters in the Bay of Arcachon ;

Whereas, fishing has been carried on at the places and on the days named by the prefectoral orders herewith ;

Considering the report of the local Commission which originated with the visit to the oyster beds ;

Considering the proposition of M. le Commissioner-General, chief of the marine service at Bordeaux ;

ORDER.

Art. 1. The taking of oysters in the Bay of Arcachon is, and remains prohibited from this date.

Art. 2. The Commissioner-General, chief of the marine service at Bordeaux, is charged with publishing this order, and posting it wherever necessary.

E. LARRIEU.

Rochefort, the 2nd February, 1865.

Port of Rochefort.   4th Maritime District.

IMPERIAL MARINE.

ORDER relative to the taking of oysters in the quarter of La Teste.
(Basin of Arcachon.)

The Vice-Admiral, Maritime Prefect,

Considering the law of the 9th January, 1852, on the coast fisheries ;

Considering the decrees of the 4th July, 1853, and of the 10th May,
1862 ;

Considering the report of the Commission which originated upon the
visit to the oyster beds in the Bay of Arcachon, conformably to the 73rd
article of the decree of the 4th July, 1853 ;

ORDER.

Art. 1. The taking of oysters in the Bay of Arcachon, during the summer 1865–6, will be confined to the portions hereafter more clearly
pointed out.

*1st. Dredging for Oysters.*

From the 1st December to the 28th February :—

In the *trou du Sud* and in the channels of Eyrac, Teychan, in the current of Cousse, Andernos, Germanau, Arés, Ville Girouasse, Lanton, and
Certes.

*2nd. Fishing on the Foreshore.*

The 4th December :—

1st. On the zone of the island, with the exception of the port of the
island, and that part of Courbay comprised between la Laque and the
estuary of la Réousse.

2nd. On the sockets, Cés, the parts east and west, Jean de Guiraou
and Biaou.

3rd. On le Bouc, the point of Maubinot and Comprian.

The 20, 21, 22, and 23 December, during the whole tide :—

1st. On the zone of the foreshores, comprised between the downs of
the *grand coin*, and the channel of Lège, for the space, outside the depôts
of oysters.

2nd. On the zone of the foreshores, bounded on the west, north-
west, and North, by a right line joining the west point of Aram to the
point of Mapouchette, and continued by the channels of Cousse, of Mouch-
taletto or Girouasse, the said zone comprising, with the exception of the
point of Comprian, Gravier de Carguefond, the flats of Tés, Moussettes,
Grabudes, Garèche, and Comprian, as well as the borders of the channel
of Gujan.

Art. 2. The taking of oysters is forbidden :—

1st. In the channels of Comprian or Labrugèze and Gujan.

2nd. On the foreshores hereafter named, viz. :—

That portion of Courbay, between la Laque and la Réousse.   The
port of the island, for the part situated between the park of Crastorbe
and the depôt No. 2, Germanau, Germanau, les Argiles, Cinouères,
Hautbelle, the sand of Carguefond, and the land of Gujan.

Art. 3. Wooden rakes are permitted for the purpose of fishing on the
foreshores.

Art. 4. It is forbidden, before fishing, to visit the oyster beds, for the
purpose of work.

Nobody will be allowed on the foreshore without skates.

Art. 5. On condition of an inscription on the back of the list of embarkation á mée, the taking of oysters will be permitted—

1st. By the fishermens' wives.

2nd. By their sons, not sailors, under fifteen years of age.

3rd. By their unmarried daughters.

4th. And lastly, by the widows of sailors.

For this purpose the skippers (patrons), who intend to embark their wives and children, should, before fishing commences, make a declaration to that effect, viz. :—

To the patrons of the syndicat of la Teste—at the office of the Maritime Inscription.

The patrons of Gujan, Meyran, and La Ruade—at the residence of the *garde maritime* at Gujan.

The patrons of Mestras—at the syndicat of the sailors at Mestras.

The patrons of Audenge, Lanton, and Biganos—at the syndicat of the sailors at Arés.

Art. 6. The taking of oysters is forbidden between sunset and sunrise.

At the places where it should be exercised on the 4th December, fishing will only commence when the signal has been given either by the officers, or *agents de surveillance* ("caretakers"), (inspectors of fishing, syndics of the sailors, marine officers, and *gardes maritimes*), present on the spot, by means of the national flag hoisted to the mast of their embarkation. The fishing will cease as soon as the flag has been hauled down.

On other days and places, the duration of the fishing will be in conformity with the terms of the present order.

Art. 7. Any infraction of the present order will be made amenable to, and be punished by, articles 7, 8, and 9, of the law of the 9th January, 1852.

Art. 8. The present order will be published and posted conformably to article 77 of the decree of the 4th July, 1853, by the Commissioner General, Chief of the Marine Service at Bordeaux.

E. LARRIEU.

Rochefort, the 23rd November, 1865.

---

OFFICE OF THE MINISTER OF MARINE AND THE COLONIES.

THE MINISTER OF THE MARINE AND THE COLONIES TO THE PREFECTS MARITIMES.

(2nd Direction : Personnel, 3rd Office : Fishing and Marine domains.)

Paris, 22nd May, 1865.

*Communication of a Note with reference to the Working of Oyster Beds.*

SIR,

The information concerning the oyster fisheries, centralized for several years at the office of the minister, have enabled me to reproduce in a note at the end of the present circular, the principles which should guide the administration in the preparation of the orders to intervene in execution of the 8th article of the decree of the 10th May, 1862. This note, compiled, with the advice of the permanent commission of fisheries and maritime domains, contains suggestions which I specially recommend to your attention. They are the result of experience, and their application, by assuring a reasonable working of the oyster beds, will, in consequence favour the development of the oyster industry to the profit of the fishermen, and the public supply of food.

To-day, when it has been shown that the small oysters develop more rapidly in parks than on the beds, it is well to make the fishermen aware of the advantage that would accrue to them, by the formation of establishments, where they could place these small oysters, upon their return from fishing. These establishments, of which the utility cannot be overlooked, are, in effect, the necessary object of the means granted to the fishermen to dispose of their small oysters, instead of throwing them back on the banks.

The Administration will then, if needful, lend its aid to the fishermen, to point out places suitable for the formation of such parks. It will also assist them in the drawing up of the applications which they will have to present, and the making of the plans which must accompany these applications, in the terms of the decree of the 10th November, 1862.

I request you may be good enough to submit to me, for this end, any propositions, the adoption of which may appear useful to you. The application of the terms of the subjoined note may, doubtless, be contrary to old customs of certain localities; notably, as regards the time for the fishing to commence. Also, it is necessary for the agents of the marine, who are in daily contact with the fishermen, to impress upon them as forcibly as possible, that it is in their interest that beds that are not sufficiently stocked, are not permitted to be worked; and that in shortening the time of opening certain beds for fishing, a greater means of wealth is prepared, of which they alone will profit.

However, these rules can only be applied in a certain measure; as expedient as they are, we must manage to make them suitable to the usages of the river population, until they are entirely enlightened. It is for this motive that the words "*as far as possible*" have been introduced in section 2 of the before-mentioned note (the end of January, for example), when the young oysters have acquired consistence enough to resist the action of the drag or dredge.

Receive, sir, &c.

The Minister Secretary of State for the Marine and Colonies,

(Signed),    P. DE CHASSELOUP-LAUBAT.

---

Enclosure.

*Note on the Dredging of Oyster Beds.*

1. Classed oyster beds, namely, those capable of being cultivated (dredged) from boats, sometimes bare in the whole or in part, their limits should be entirely fixed on all sides, by straight lines, buoys, poles, or in some manner or another. The marking of these limits ought to be arranged so as to permit of an efficacious surveillance.

2. Classed oyster beds, ought only, *as far as possible*, be dredged towards the end of January, namely, when the young oysters will have attained a sufficient amount of consistency to be able to resist the action of the dredge.

3. The time for the opening of the beds ought alone be mentioned in the prefectoral orders, that of the shutting being naturally dependent on the state of the bed, with regard to the quantity of oysters

to be preserved on it, for the purpose of restocking it, and the agents appointed to watch over the beds having besides power to stop the fishing, pending the promulgation of the order for stopping the fishing.

4. The prefectoral orders ought only to contain the names of the beds where fishing is allowed, it being useless to mention those on which it is forbidden.

5. When an oyster bed is found to be very productive, a portion (either one-fourth or one-fifth of the whole area) should be reserved from fishing as a fund for reproduction. This part should be marked off with buoys, and dredging should be forbidden there.

6. A vessel, or shore-boat, for guarding the fishing *should, as far as possible*, take part in the dredging of an open oyster bed.

7. No period of intermittence should be fixed for the dredging of an open oyster bed ; the number of oysters that each fishing boat can take should not be determined ; the number of boats of the quarter that can take part in the fishing each day should only be limited for the sake of order, and the carrying out of police regulations.

8. The small oysters taken in the fishing in the territorial sea, or by fishing on foot, can be placed in the establishments on the banks, and transported from the regular parks to ponds, claires, &c. Those that possess them can, in fact, dispose of them for their own interest.

9. During the dredging of a productive bed, all shells, gravel, stones, &c., should be thrown back on the bottom. All mud, sand, or vegetable matter, and all other hurtful matters or animals, should, on the contrary, be taken up with care, and kept in the boat, to be placed on sites for that purpose on the shore.

10. The dredging of all oyster beds incumbered with any matter or thing disadvantageous to the growth, or attaching of the spat, should be allowed until the bed is clean, nothing taken up being allowed to be returned.

11. The dredging of oyster beds of *agglomeration*, that is to say, where there is never any production of spat, should be allowed from the commencement to the end of the fishing season.

12. The oyster beds, after being dredged, should be visited with care, and such means of collecting the spat, as the water cannot carry away, should be laid down, such as broken pottery, stones, clean cultch, &c.

13. Classed oyster beds should be well watched during all the time that the fishing is not allowed there. This surveillance should be exercised by the Fishery Inspectors and the fishermen themselves.

14. Whenever a classed oyster bed is wholly bare, it should be well watched, so that poaching cannot take place.

15. *Gathering* oysters is authorized at all times, on all parts of the strand, beyond the limits of classed oyster beds, as well as the reserves created on the shore, or on private beds. It is only allowed on the classed beds, when they are open to dredging.

16. Those portions of the shore situated beyond the classed beds, and which after the inquiries ordained by the decree of the 10th November, 1862, are recognised as being capable of being granted to private individuals, without any public rights, can be allotted to persons (either fishermen or others) who apply for them, for the purpose of creating parks, for the taking of spat, depots for small oysters, or claires, or ponds, with a view to bettering the fish.

17. The necessary permission can only be granted on the legal conditions of revocability and danger, attached to concessions of the sort given on the public maritime property.

18. It is especially recommended to maritime authorities called upon

to grant these applications, to take care to leave every facility to the inhabitants of the shores to have access to the sea, so that they may not be deprived of the right of reaping what the waves carry there.

The Minister Secretary of State for the Marine and Colonies.

(Signed)    P. De Chasseloup-Laubat.

---

Enclosure No. 5.

MINISTRY OF THE MARINE AND COLONIES.

*Report to the Emperor.*

Sire,

For some time past numerous applications for grants of land for the formation of oyster beds, and for other deposits for shell-fish, on the sea coast, have been made to the Department of the Marine.

Although always revocable, the authorization to create private establishments on the public maritime domain would have, in certain cases, for a consequence, if they multiplied, the prevention in some sort, of free access to the shore, by the population who find means of subsistence in gathering whatever the sea throws up; lastly, it would hinder, paralyse even, fishing on a productive and important domain. The population on the shore have thus a great interest in knowing the applications for grants made to the superior administration, and it also should wish to be informed of the rights and interests to be conciliated, since it has to call for and hear them.

It is for the attainment of this end, that having taken the advice of the permanent commission on fisheries and maritime domains, I venture to submit for the approbation of the Emperor, a draft of a decree, of which the object will be to submit all the applications to an examination, prompt, without doubt, but regular, in which all interests may present themselves.

From the date of this decree, the applications will be submitted to an open inquiry for fifteen days in the commune of the territory.

The observations to which these applications will give rise will be received by the maritime authorities, and to prevent all local interest, not only the maritime authorities, but the mayors of communes, also those persons interested, will be able to address their observations directly to the prefects maritime, who will transmit the papers of the inquiry to the minister with their own suggestions. The maritime prefects will, besides, be able to know the real state of things, either by agents placed on the spot, or by the chief of the division of the shore.

Lastly, as has taken place since the decree of the 20th March, 1861, these applications will be submitted to the commission on fisheries, who fills with so much zeal the double mission of assisting the development of the means of production placed in the hands of private industry, and to watch over and keep for the shore population and for the fishermen the enjoyment of the public maritime domain.

I hope, Sire, that the decree I have the honour to submit to Your Majesty will thus give all the guarantees desirable to the different interests that it behoves us to protect.

I am, with the most profound respect, Sire, Your Majesty's very humble obedient servant and faithful subject,

The Minister Secretary of State for the Marine and Colonies,

(Signed,)    C P. De Chasseloup-Laubat.

## DECREE.

Napoleon, by the grace of God and the national will, Emperor of the French,

To all present and to come, greeting.

On the report of the Minister of the Marine and Colonies,

Considering the advice of the Permanent Commission of Fisheries and the Maritime Domain,

Have decreed and decree as follows :

Art. 1. Every application for authority to form beds or claires for oysters, as well as for permanent depots for shell-fish, on a part of the maritime domain, should be accompanied by a plan detailing the works to be constructed and a plan of the shore, shown on the marine map of the locality, so as to make the situation of the park or depot known.

Art. 4. These applications are to be always submitted to an inquiry in the commune of the territory, during fifteen days, together with a notice of such application to be posted in the locality.

Art. 5. The posting of the notices, after being viséd by the commissioner of the quarter, is to be done at the expense of the applicant.

The mayors of communes can, in the delay of article 4, transmit to the maritime authorities the observations and objections which might be addressed to them.

Art. 6. The official report of the inquiry, containing the different evidence, to which is added the documents mentioned in article 1, as well as all the notes of the inquiry, is to be transmitted to the Maritime Prefect, who forwards it to the minister with his suggestions thereon.

The Prefect Maritime also transmits to the minister all the observations or objections that he will have received directly on the subject of the demands submitted to the inquiry.

Art. 7. All the above mentioned formalities will be dispensed with as regards the applications already granted in the substitution of grants of parks or claires which have been conceded conformably to the preceding rules.

Art. 8. The Minister of the Marine and Colonies is charged to have this decree carried out.

Given at the Palace of Compiègne, 10th November, 1862.

Signed    NAPOLEON.

By the Emperor :

The Minister Secretary of State for the Marine and Colonies,

Signed    C⁰ˢ· P. DE CHASSELOUP-LAUBAT.

---

## Enclosure No. 6.

### MINISTRY OF THE MARINE AND THE COLONIES.

The Admiral, Minister Secretary of State in the Department of the Marine and the Colonies ;

Considering the article 2 of the decree of 9th January, 1852 ;

Considering the decree of the 4th July, 1853, on the exercise of the coast fishery in the        maritime division ;

Considering the decree of 10th November, 1862 ;

Considering the application of the person interested and the plan annexed hereto ;

Considering the official report of the inquiry held conformably to the above-mentioned decree of 10th November, 1862 ;

Considering the report of the ordinary engineer of the bridges and ways at         , dated         , viséd and adopted on         by the chief engineer at

Considering, with the state of the suggestion that accompanies it, the report of the Commissioner of the Maritime Inscription at         , dated

Considering the letter of the General Commissioner of Marine at         , dated

Considering the recommendation of the Commandant-in-Chief of the Naval Division at         , dated

Considering the letter of the Prefect Maritime at         , dated

Considering the recommendation of the Permanent Commission on Fisheries and Maritime domains ;

### ORDER.

Mr.         , living at         , is authorized to establish at (quarter of         ), an oyster park of a         form, being         long, by         broad.

### Article 2.

The licensee will only employ, as far as possible, for the surveillance and working of his beds, recorded fishermen, or the wives, children, mothers, or unmarried sisters of registered sailors.

---

## APPENDIX C.

Number of parks and beds situated in the Bay of Cancale. Surface occupied by these establishments :—

24 parks, measuring  3 hectares, 48 area.
1,173 beds,   - ,,     60   ,,     0  ,,

---

STATISTICS of the production of fishing in the Bay of Cancale each year, from 1800 to 1867 inclusive—

### OYSTERS.

| | Number of oysters taken in . | | |
|---|---|---|---|
| Period of the naval war. — Fishing, on our coasts was very much neglected, on account of so many of the fishermen being required for the navy, and also on account of the trouble caused by the enemy's cruisers. During this time of forced relaxation from fishing, the beds became so thickly stocked that in some places the oysters were a yard deep. | 1800 | – | 1,200,000 |
| | 1801 | – | 1,500,000 |
| | 1802 | – | 1,300,000 |
| | 1803 | – | 900,000 |
| | 1804 | – | 1,400,000 |
| | 1805 | – | 800,000 |
| | 1806 | – | 500,000 |
| | 1807 | – | 1,090,000 |
| | 1808 | – | 1,800,000 |
| | 1809 | – | 1,200,000 |
| | 1810 | – | 700,000 |
| | 1811 | – | 1,130,000 |
| | 1812 | – | 1,100,000 |
| | 1813 | – | 600,000 |
| | 1814 | – | 400,000 |
| | 1815 | – | 800,000 |
| | 1816 | – | 2,400,000 |

The information of the production for the period from 1800 to 1816, very probably does not represent the exact quantity, as we have no statistics of that time, the figures given being derived from questions asked to the old fishermen who fished during the time of the maritime war.

| | | Year | | Number of oysters |
|---|---|---|---|---|
| Number of oysters taken in . . } | | 1817 | – | 5,600,000 |
| ,, | ,, | 1818 | – | 5,300,000 |
| ,, | ,, | 1819 | – | 6,800,000 |
| ,, | ,, | 1820 | – | 6,700,000 |
| ,, | ,, | 1821 | – | 6,000,000 |
| ,, | ,, | 1822 | – | 11,800,000 |
| ,, | ,, | 1823 | – | 18,000,000 |
| ,, | ,, | 1824 | – | 20,000,000 |
| ,, | ,, | 1825 | – | 20,000,000 |
| ,, | ,, | 1826 | – | 25,000,000 |
| ,, | ,, | 1827 | – | 28,000,000 |
| ,, | ,, | 1828 | – | 33,000,000 |
| ,, | ,, | 1829 | – | 31,000,000 |
| ,, | ,, | 1830 | – | 36,000,000 |
| ,, | ,, | 1831 | – | 42,000,000 |
| ,, | ,, | 1832 | – | 38,000,000 |
| ,, | ,, | 1833 | – | 41,000,000 |
| Time of the oyster riches. — People lived on the accumulated productions during the war. The number of dredging vessels is increasing each year. | 1834 | – | 46,000,000 |
| ,, | ,, | 1835 | – | 43,000,000 |
| ,, | ,, | 1836 | – | 40,000,000 |
| ,, | ,, | 1837 | – | 36,000,000 |
| ,, | ,, | 1838 | – | 44,000,000 |
| ,, | ,, | 1839 | – | 42,000,000 |
| ,, | ,, | 1840 | – | 52,000,000 |
| ,, | ,, | 1841 | – | 56,000,000 |
| ,, | ,, | 1842 | – | 63,000,000 |
| ,, | ,, | 1843 | – | 70,000,000 |
| ,, | ,, | 1844 | – | 67,000,000 |
| ,, | ,, | 1845 | – | 67,000,000 |
| ,, | ,, | 1846 | – | 65,000,000 |
| ,, | ,, | 1847 | – | 71,000,000 |
| ,, | ,, | 1848 | – | 60,000,000 |
| ,, | ,, | 1849 | – | 52,000,000 |
| ,, | ,, | 1850 | – | 50,000,000 |
| Decrease in the production, owing to over-dredging in the preceding years. | 1851 | – | 47,000,000 |
| ,, | ,, | 1852 | – | 20,000,000 |
| ,, | ,, | 1853 | – | 49,000,000 |
| ,, | ,, | 1854 | – | 20,000,000 |
| ,, | ,, | 1855 | – | 20,000,000 |
| ,, | ,, | 1856 | – | 18,000,000 |
| ,, | ,, | 1857 | – | 19,000,000 |
| ,, | ,, | 1858 | – | 24,000,000 |
| ,, | ,, | 1859 | – | 16,000,000 |
| Disappearance of oysters, owing to continued fishing; it is almost impossible to prevent this, as the people are in a suffering state, as they have no other resource. | 1860 | – | 8,000,000 |
| ,, | ,, | 1861 | – | 9,000,000 |
| ,, | ,, | 1862 | – | 3,100,000 |
| ,, | ,, | 1863 | – | 2,090,000 |
| ,, | ,, | 1864 | – | 1,200,000 |
| ,, | ,, | 1865 | – | 1,100,000 |
| ,, | ,, | 1866 | – | 1,960,000 |
| ,, | ,, | 1867 | – | 2,000,000 |
| ,, | ,, | 1868 | – | 1,079,000 |

An almost complete wreck of the bottom, which can only be remedied by a total prohibition of fishing during several successive years.

## APPENDIX D.

RETURNS of the JERSEY OYSTER FISHERY during the years 1855–1864.—Furnished by Captain John Amy, of Gorey, Inspector of Jersey Oyster Fishery.

| — | Smacks and boats. | Men. | Tons. | No. of tubs of oysters caught. | Average price per tub. | Amount. |
|---|---|---|---|---|---|---|
| *From September 1st, 1855, to April 30th, 1856.* | | | | | *s. d.* | *£ s. d.* |
| Number of English dredging boats, | 99 | 577 | 1,086 | | | |
| „ „ smacks employed carrying, | 35 | 166 | 1,385 | | | |
| „ Jersey dredging boats, | 86 | 457 | 1,499 | 179,194 | 3 10 | 34,345 10 4 |
| „ „ open dredging boats, | 22 | 44 | 51 | | | |
| „ „ smacks employed carrying, | 14 | 57 | 453 | | | |
| Totals, | 256 | 1,301 | 5,074 | 179,194 | – | 34,345 10 4 |
| Freightage to vessels carrying oysters from Jersey to England, at 10d. per tub, | – | – | – | – | – | 7,003 18 4 |
| | – | – | – | – | – | 41,349 8 8 |
| *From September 1st, 1856, to April 30th, 1857.* | | | | | | |
| Number of English dredging boats, | 97 | 597 | 1,554 | | | |
| „ „ smacks employed carrying, | 28 | 122 | 1,050 | | | |
| „ Jersey dredging boats, | 94 | 526 | 1,675 | 179,690 | 4 1½ | 37,248 5 0 |
| „ „ open dredging boats, | 25 | 56 | 50 | | | |
| „ „ smacks employed carrying, | 17 | 68 | 546 | | | |
| Totals, | 261 | 1,364 | 4,865 | 179,690 | – | 37,248 5 0 |
| Freightage to vessels for carrying 163,690 tubs of oysters to England, at 10d. per tub, | – | – | – | – | – | 7,161 8 9 |
| | – | – | – | – | – | 44,409 13 9 |
| *From September 1st, 1857, to April 30th, 1858.* | | | | | | |
| Number of English dredging boats, | 68 | 396 | 1,084 | | | |
| „ „ smacks employed carrying, | 24 | 114 | 1,104 | | | |
| „ Jersey dredging boats, | 97 | 598 | 1,770 | 150,990 | 3 11½ | 29,726 3 6 |
| „ „ open dredging boats, | 20 | 40 | 50 | | | |
| „ „ smacks employed carrying, | 15 | 62 | 531 | | | |
| „ French smacks „ „ | 2 | 11 | 56 | | | |
| Totals, | 226 | 1,221 | 4,595 | 150,990 | – | 29,726 3 6 |
| Freightage to vessels for carrying 129,490 tubs of oysters to England, at 10d. per tub, | – | – | – | – | – | 5,665 3 9 |
| | – | – | – | 150,990 | – | 35,391 7 3 |
| *From September 1st, 1858, to April 30th, 1859.* | | | | | | |
| Number of English dredging boats, | 54 | 317 | 814 | | | |
| „ Jersey „ | 92 | 545 | 1,691 | | | |
| „ „ open dredging boats, | 14 | 35 | 38 | 120,610 | 4 3½ | 25,755 5 2½ |
| „ English smacks employed carrying, | 18 | 82 | 778 | | | |
| „ Jersey „ „ | 11 | 50 | 378 | | | |
| Totals, | 189 | 1,029 | 3,699 | 120,610 | – | 25,755 5 2½ |
| Freightage to vessels for carrying 98,814 tubs oysters from Jersey to England, at 10d. per tub, | – | – | – | – | – | 4,322 18 9 |
| | – | – | – | – | – | 30,078 3 11½ |

RETURNS of the JERSEY OYSTER FISHERY during the years 1855–1864—*continued.*

| — | Smacks and boats. | Men. | Tons. | No. of tubs of oysters caught. | Average price per tub. | Amount. |
|---|---|---|---|---|---|---|
| *From September 1st, 1859, to April 30th, 1860.* | | | | | s. d. | £ s. d. |
| Number of English dredging boats, . . | 27 | 154 | 407 | | | |
| „ Jersey „ . . | 99 | 588 | 1,848 | | | |
| „ „ open dredging boats, . . | 14 | 38 | 35 | } 98,110 | 4 10 | 23,733 11 2 |
| „ English smacks employed carrying, | 13 | 60 | 570 | | | |
| „ Jersey „ „ | 12 | 48 | 370 | | | |
| Totals, . . . . . | 165 | 888 | 3,230 | 98,110 | — | 23,733 11 2 |
| Freightage to vessels for carrying 86,610 tubs oysters from Jersey to England, at 10d. per tub, . . . . . . . | — | — | — | — | — | 3,789 3 9 |
| | — | — | — | — | — | 27,522 14 11 |
| *From September 1st, 1860, to April 30th, 1861.* | | | | | | |
| Number of English dredging boats, . . | 18 | 102 | 256 | | | |
| „ Jersey „ | 86 | 518 | 1,580 | | | |
| „ „ open dredging boats, . . | 17 | 43 | 60 | } 76,380 | 4 9¾ | 18,371 5 0 |
| „ English smacks employed carrying, | 10 | 48 | 429 | | | |
| Jersey „ „ | 10 | 40 | 318 | | | |
| Totals, . . . . | 141 | 751 | 2,643 | 76,380 | — | 18,371 5 0 |
| Freightage to vessels for carrying 64,270 tubs oysters from Jersey to England, at 11d. per tub, . . . . . . | — | — | — | — | — | 2,945 14 2 |
| | — | — | — | — | — | 21,316 19 2 |
| *From September 1st, 1861, to April 30th, 1862.* | | | | | | |
| Number of Jersey dredging cutters, . | 25 | 150 | 450 | | | |
| „ „ open dredging boats, . | 14 | 35 | 42 | } 18,220 | 4 9¾ | 4,383 14 0 |
| „ smacks employed carrying, . | 3 | 14 | 129 | | | |
| Totals, . . | 42 | 199 | 621 | 18,220* | — | 4,383 14 0 |
| Freight of 10,920 tubs of oysters exported to England, average freight per tub, 10d., | — | — | — | — | — | 477 15 0 |
| | — | — | — | — | — | 4,861 9 0 |
| *From September 1st, 1862, to April 30th, 1863.* | | | | | | |
| Number of Jersey dredging cutters, . | 8 | 45 | 112 | | | |
| „ Colchester „ | 14 | 84 | 162 | } 9,841 | 6 1½ | 3,013 16 1½ |
| „ Jersey open dredging boats, . | 21 | 42 | 50 | | | |
| „ smacks employed carrying, . | 3 | 13 | 108 | | | |
| Totals, . . . . | 46 | 184 | 432 | 9,841† | — | 3,013 16 1½ |
| Freight of 3,120 tubs of oysters exported to England, average freight per tub, 12d., . | — | — | — | — | — | 156 0 0 |
| | — | — | — | — | — | 3,169 16 1½ |
| *From September 1st, 1863, to April 30th, 1864.* | | | | | | |
| Number of Jersey dredging cutters, . | 8 | 48 | 120 | } 6,196‡ | 6 3¾ | 1,955 12 0 |
| „ „ open dredging boats, | 15 | 45 | 35 | | | |

* About 3,300 tubs of the above were dredged in the British Channel and **brought to Jersey** by cutters dredging in the Channel. No English cutters came this season to dredge on our grounds.
† About 2,350 tubs of the above were dredged in the British Channel.
‡ About 3,280 tubs of the above were dredged in the British Channel and **brought to Jersey** by cutters working in the Channel. The oysters brought to Jersey from the Channel were for the manufactory established at Gorey for preserving oysters.

## APPENDIX E.

REPORT on the TEMPERATURE of the SURFACE of the SEA on the COASTS of GREAT BRITAIN and IRELAND, and on the WEST COAST of FRANCE, by HENRY HENNESSY, F.R.S., Vice-President of the Royal Irish Academy.

I have examined the records of the observations on the temperature of the surface of the sea in deep and shallow water surrounding the British Islands, and off the west coast of France, made for the purpose of elucidating the physical conditions of the sea with reference to oyster culture, and I beg to submit to the Royal Commissioners the following report, which embodies the results I have obtained. These observations were made partly during the last three weeks of October, 1868, and partly during the last three weeks of May, and the months of June and July, 1869. Those taken on the British and Irish coasts were made by the coast-guards, and those on the French coast by officers and men attached to the department of fisheries, observers from whose character and habits accuracy might be fairly expected.

In order to draw correct conclusions as to the comparative conditions of temperature in different localities, we must be assured that the observations have been made at the same hours of local time, with similar precautions, and with instruments accurately corresponding in their construction. I have reason to believe that the two latter conditions were attended to, though I have no means of forming an independent judgment on the question, as I was not consulted when the observations were set on foot.

The hour of observation seems to have been uniformly about noon. Why this hour should have been selected I cannot understand, unless because it is the hour of maximum sunshine though not of maximum temperature for either air or water.* For determining the mean temperature of the sea observations made between 9 and 10, A.M., and between 9 and 10, P.M., would be more efficient, and maximum and minimum thermometers would have been the most suitable for ascertaining the highest and lowest temperatures. This is of less consequence, however, regarding the sea than the air, as the diurnal range of water temperature is small, on account of its peculiar thermal properties, whereby it slowly acquires and parts with heat. From the same causes the time of greatest water temperature occurs later both in the day and the year than the time of maximum air temperature.

As the hour of the day at which most of the observations were made during the last three weeks of October, 1868, is not distinctly mentioned, and as in some cases it seems to have greatly varied, I have been able to make use of the records of only a few stations in connexion with the general subject of the distribution of heat at the surface of the sea. The observations made during the summer months being directly connected with the important question of the conditions of temperature under which

* The weight of the results of the British and Irish observations is less than that of the French on account of the suspension of the former on Sundays, a circumstance which has possibly arisen from the coincidence of the hour of observation with that of public worship in England, and this furnishes an additional objection to the selection of noon whenever only one observation during the day can be made.

the reproduction of the oyster takes place, I proceed to their immediate discussion. As I am not perfectly sure of the correctness of the mode of taking these observations, and as some of them appear to be doubtful, it has occurred to me that the mean temperatures for the months at each station would be more useful as being more free from error than separate results,* and I have accordingly reduced the observations and tabulated them in the form herewith annexed. The southern and western stations of Ireland, as forming a special climatal group, are placed together ; then the northern and eastern ; next the southern and western stations of Great Britain, and then the northern and eastern. The Jersey results are grouped with the French in a separate table, and I give the latter in degrees of the centigrade and Fahrenheit scales.

## TABLE I.

TABLE of Mean Summer Temperatures at Noon of the Sea and Air on the Coasts of Great Britain and Ireland.

| | May. | | | June. | | | July. | | |
|---|---|---|---|---|---|---|---|---|---|
| | At Sea. | Near Shore. | Air. | At Sea. | Near Shore. | Air. | At Sea. | Near Shore. | Air. |
| | ° | ° | ° | ° | ° | ° | ° | ° | ° |
| *South and West Coasts of Ireland.* | | | | | | | | | |
| Tramore, | – | 55·0 | 60·3 | – | 59·0 | 63·0 | – | 64·0 | 70·0 |
| Crosshaven, | 52·6 | 54·4 | 54·2 | 60·0 | 65·5 | 66·6 | – | – | – |
| Kenmare, | 54·0 | – | 57·0 | 57·0 | – | 61·0 | 66·0 | – | 68·3 |
| Ballyheigue, | – | 56·0 | 53·0 | – | 63·0 | 60·0 | – | 68·0 | 67·0 |
| Ballyvaughan, | – | 52·0 | 55·0 | – | 59·0 | 65·6 | – | 64·0 | 72·0 |
| Pigeonpoint,† | – | 53·0 | 54·6 | – | 60·7 | 62·0 | – | 65·0 | 67·5 |
| Innisgowla,† | 52·1 | 52·2 | 56·5 | 57·0 | 58·2 | 64·0 | 62·5 | 63·0 | 69·0 |
| Innislyre,† | – | 53·0 | 55·5 | – | 58·9 | 64·0 | – | 63·0 | 74·0 |
| Belmullet, | – | – | – | 56·5 | 57·0 | 64·0 | 60·0 | 61·0 | 68·0 |
| Pullendiva, | – | 52·6 | 52·2 | – | 57·2 | 61·5 | – | 63·2 | 71·0 |
| *North and East Coasts of Ireland.* | | | | | | | | | |
| Rathmullan, | – | 50·0 | 51·5 | – | 58·5 | 60·0 | – | 69·0 | 71·0 |
| Rutland, | – | 49·9 | 51·6 | – | 55·3 | 58·4 | – | 63·1 | 64·4 |
| Moville,‡ | 45·0 | – | 48·0 | 50·0 | – | 56·5 | 57·0 | – | 62·5 |
| Carrickfergus, | – | 50·0 | 52·0 | – | 56·0 | 59·0 | – | 62·0 | 65·0 |
| Carlingford,‡ | 56·0 | 55·5 | 59·0 | 58·5 | 61·5 | 65·5 | 65·0 | 66·5 | 75·5 |
| Howth,‡ | – | 50·0 | 51·0 | 52·5 | 52·3 | 60·0 | 55·3 | 56·5 | 68·1 |
| Arklow,‡ | – | – | – | 51·0 | 51·2 | 62·0 | 59·9 | 52·8 | 72·2 |
| *South and West Coasts of Great Britain.* | | | | | | | | | |
| Ramsgate, | 55·0 | 56·0 | 60·5 | 57·7 | 58·7 | 69·8 | 62·3 | 63·0 | 77·7 |
| Eastbourne, | 53·0 | 53·2 | 60·0 | 57·5 | 58·0 | 65·1 | 63·4 | 64·3 | 73·1 |
| St. Catherine's Point, | 52·0 | 52·9 | 57·0 | 56·0 | 57·3 | 62·7 | 60·4 | 61·8 | 69·4 |
| Goodwick, | – | 52·5 | 57·5 | – | 57·1 | 63·0 | – | 62·0 | 68·4 |
| Bangor, | – | 51·5 | 57·0 | – | 57·1 | 61·4 | – | 62·5 | 69·7 |
| Whitehaven, | 49·8 | 50·6 | 55·6 | 56·0 | 56·0 | 61·5 | 61·7 | 62·5 | 67·4 |
| Douglas (Man), | – | 48·5 | 52·7 | 53·0 | 52·1 | 60·0 | 57·6 | 59·3 | 65·8 |
| *North and East Coasts of Great Britain.* | | | | | | | | | |
| Stranraer, | – | 51·5 | 58·8 | – | 54·7 | 63·4 | – | 57·6 | 65·3 |
| Ardrossan, | – | 47·9 | 56·4 | – | 54·6 | 61·6 | – | 63·1 | 64·4 |
| Cromarty, | 48·3 | 49·1 | 51·4 | 51·2 | 53·2 | 56·5 | 55·0 | 57·5 | 61·5 |
| Lerwick, | 47·5 | 48·6 | 50·5 | 50·1 | 51·1 | 56·5 | 52·0 | 53·6 | 60·0 |
| N. Berwick, | 47·0 | 48·2 | 51·4 | 51·5 | 52·0 | 58·2 | 55·9 | 57·2 | 66·5 |
| Cromer,§ | – | 51·6 | – | – | 56·0 | – | 62·0 | 63·4 | 67·3 |

* These are given entire in Appendix N.
† These three Stations are in Clew Bay, and the results may be compared with Bunown in Table III.
‡ Doubtful.
§ During May and June the Air Temperatures are omitted, as neither Air or Water Temperatures were taken at noon.

## TABLE II.

TABLE of Mean Temperatures of the Sea and Air at Noon on the
West Coast of France.

### (1.) *In Centigrade degrees.*

|  | May. | | | June. | | | July. | | |
|---|---|---|---|---|---|---|---|---|---|
|  | At Sea | Near Shore. | Air. | At Sea. | Near Shore. | Air. | At Sea. | Near Shore. | Air. |
| St. Marc (Bay of Granville), | - | 13·6 | 16·4 | - | 15·2 | 18·2 | - | 17·4 | 23·8 |
| Gorvather (Bay of Trinité), | - | - | - | 17·2 | 19·0 | 22·3 | 18·8 | 20·3 | 25·0 |
| Arcachon, | - | 17·0 | 23·9 | - | 19·3 | 24·6 | - | 21·8 | 29·0 |
| Locqueltas (Auray River), . | 16·0 | 16·1 | 18·3 | 17·0 | 17·5 | 22·2 | 20·5 | 21·3 | 26·5 |
| On board the Congre, . | - | - | - | 17·0 | 19·0 | - | 20·5 | 22·2 | - |

The above Table, in Fahrenheit degrees, and including Jersey.

| | | | | | | | | | |
|---|---|---|---|---|---|---|---|---|---|
| St. Marc, . . . . | - | 56·4 | 61·6 | - | 59·0 | 64·7 | - | 63·4 | 74·8 |
| Gorvather, . . . . | - | - | - | 63·0 | 66·2 | 70·1 | 65·8 | 68·5 | 77·0 |
| Arcachon, . . . . | - | 62·8 | 75·0 | - | 66·7 | 78·3 | - | 71·2 | 84·2 |
| Locqueltas, . . . . | 60·8 | 61·0 | 64·9 | 62·6 | 63·5 | 72·0 | 68·9 | 70·3 | 79·7 |
| On board the Congre, . . | - | - | - | 62·6 | 66·2 | - | 68·9 | 72·0 | - |
| Jersey, . . . . . | - | - | - | 58·3 | - | 68·3 | 63·3 | - | 75·8 |

It is immediately manifest that the highest sea temperatures were observed at the stations in the French group, and the lowest in the northern and eastern group of Great Britain. The sea temperature on the coast of Ireland seems upon the whole to have been a little above that on the coasts of England and Scotland. These results assist, moreover, in pointing out the cause of the comparative superiority of the Irish coast sea temperature. The temperature of the surface of the ocean at any point is due principally to the sum of all it gains from sunshine and warm currents, minus the sum of all its losses from radiation, evaporation, and cold currents. If the heat brought by warm currents should be considerable it may cause the mean temperature of the water to surpass that of the air above it, and at those times of the day when the air temperature is in excess of the sea temperature the difference between them is reduced in value. At noon in summer the air is usually warmer than the sea; we may conclude, therefore, that whichever group of stations shows the smallest difference between air and water temperature at noon is the group in which the influence of heat-bearing currents is most decided. The following table is constructed to show the application of this principle to the results under discussion :—

### TABLE OF DIFFERENCES BETWEEN AIR AND SEA TEMPERATURES.

*South and West Coasts of Ireland.*

| | | | | May. | June. | July. |
|---|---|---|---|---|---|---|
| Tramore, | - | - | - | +5·3 | +10·0 | +6·0 |
| Crosshaven, | - | - | - | −0·2 | 1·1 | - |
| Kenmare, | - | - | - | +3·0 | 4·0 | 4·3 |
| Ballybeigue, | - | - | - | −3·0 | −3·0 | −1·0 |
| Ballyvaughan, | - | - | - | +3·0 | +6·6 | +8·0 |
| Pigeon Point, | - | - | - | 1·0 | 1·3 | 2·5 |
| Innisgowla, | - | - | - | 4·3 | 5·8 | 6·0 |
| Innislyre, | - | - | - | 2·5 | 6·0 | 11·0 |
| Belmullet, | - | - | - | - | - | 7·0 |
| Pullendiva, | - | - | - | −0·4 | 4·3 | 7·8 |
| Means, | - | - | - | 1·7 | 4·0 | 5·7 |

*North and East Coasts of Ireland.*

|  |  |  |  |  | ° | ° | ° |
|---|---|---|---|---|---|---|---|
| Rutland, | - | - | - | - | +1·7 | +3·1 | +1·3 |
| Rathmullan, | - | | | - | 1·5 | 1·5 | 3·0 |
| Carn (Moville), | - | - | | - | 3·0 | 6·5 | 5·5 |
| Carrickfergus, | | - | - | - | 2·0 | 3·0 | 3·0 |
| Carlingford, | - | | | - | 3·5 | 4·0 | 10·0 |
| Howth, | - | - | - | - | 1·0 | 7·7 | 11·6 |
| Arklow, | - | - | - | - | – | 10·8 ? | 12·3 ? |
| Means, | - | - | - | | 2·1 | 5·2 | 6·5 |
| Means without Arklow, | | - | | | 2·1 | 4·3 | 5·6 |

Where the difference is prefixed by the negative sign — it shows that the temperature of the water was superior to that of the air ; when there is no sign prefixed, or where it is positive, + it shows that the air was higher in temperature than the water.

*South and West Coasts of Great Britain.*

|  |  |  |  |  | May. | June. | July. |
|---|---|---|---|---|---|---|---|
| Ramsgate, | - | - | - | - | +4·5 | +11·1 | +11·7 |
| Eastbourne, | - | - | - | - | 6 8 | 7·1 | 8·8 |
| St. Catherine's Point, | | - | - | - | 4·1 | 5·4 | 7·6 |
| Goodwick, | - | - | - | - | 5·0 | 5·9 | 6 4 |
| Bangor, | - | - | - | - | 5·5 | 4·3 | 6·2 |
| Whitehaven, | - | - | - | - | 5 0 | 5·5 | 4·9 |
| Douglas (Man), | - | - | - | - | 4·2 | 7·9 | 6·5 |
| Means, | - | - | - | | 5·0 | 6·7 | 7·4 |

*North and East Coasts of Great Britain.*

|  |  |  |  |  |  |  |  |
|---|---|---|---|---|---|---|---|
| Stranraer, | - | - | - | - | +7·3 | 8·7 | 7·7 |
| Ardrossan, | - | - | - | - | 8·5 | 7·0 | 5·5 |
| Cromarty, | - | - | - | - | 2·3 | 2·3 | 4·0 |
| Lerwick, | - | - | - | - | 1·9 | 5·4 | 6·4 |
| N. Berwick, | - | - | - | - | 3·2 | 6·2 | 9·3 |
| Cromer, | - | - | - | - | – | – | 3·9 |
| Means, | - | - | - | | 4·4 | 5·9 | 6·1 |

*West Coast of France.*

|  |  |  |  | May. | June. | July. |
|---|---|---|---|---|---|---|
| St. Marc (Granville), | | - | - | +5·2 | +5·7 | +11 4 |
| Gorvather (Bay of Trinité), | – | | - | – | – | – |
| Arcachon, | - | - | - | 12·4 | 11·6 | 13·0 |
| Locqueltas, | - | - | - | 4·0 | 8·4 | 9·4 |
| | - | - | - | – | 10·0 | 10·5 |
| Means, | - | - | - | 7·2 | 8·0 | 10·5 |

On looking over these differences, and also the mean results for each geographical group of stations, it manifestly appears that the air and water temperatures differ least on the coasts of Ireland, and especially on its south and west coasts ; and we may conclude, therefore, that on these coasts the ratio of the warming influence of thermal currents compared to that of direct sunshine is at its maximum. On the contrary, the comparative influence of sunshine seems to be greatest for the group of stations on the west coast of France.

The general conclusions which may be drawn from the observations under discussion are in harmony with the results previously obtained. Thus, in 1851 observations on sea temperature on the coast of Ireland, in connexion with a series of tidal and meteorological observations, were made under the superintendence of the Council of the Royal Irish

Academy. The Rev. Provost H. Lloyd has given the results regarding
sea temperature in a memoir published in the Transactions of the
Academy, and from these and other facts, to be presently quoted, I
have been led to lay down the approximate annual isothermal lines for
the water around the Irish coast. The most remarkable result established by these observations is, that the mean temperature of the ocean
which washes the coast of Ireland surpasses the mean temperature of
the air over the island, and I was thus led to rigorously deduce the
general law that the representation of temperature distributing in Ireland must be made by isothermal lines, or lines of equal temperature,
many of which must be re-entrant curves within the island.   I subsequently extended the same conclusion to Great Britain, and showed
that it was verified by the results of meteorological observations.*   The
red lines on the map which accompanies this report, show the distribution of temperature over the surface of Ireland in conformity with my
deductions and with observation.

Mr. Nicholas Whitley has made a series of observations on the temperature of the sea on the coast of Cornwall, from which conclusions
similar to those deduced from the Irish observations may be drawn.
All of these results confirm the generally admitted opinion, that the
coasts of the British Isles are bathed by water which has acquired a
considerable amount of warmth from currents which are offshoots of the
Gulf Stream.   This great current splits into branches between the
Azores and Newfoundland, and these branches carry their thermal
influence to the western and northern coasts of Europe.   The maximum
temperature of the stream, as deduced from the most recent observations, is 88° within the Gulf of Mexico itself; it is 84° opposite Char-
leston, and moves with a velocity of from seventy to eighty miles per
day.   The line of demarcation between the stream and the cold water
on the shores of America is well defined, so that, for instance, in May,
1851, on board the *Nile*, between Bermuda and Halifax, the water under
the ship's stern was at 70°, while at the same moment, under the bow,
the thermometer stood at 40°.   This was on the N.N.W. edge of the
stream.   This sharpness of definition is gradually lost as the current
approaches Europe, and its temperature also falls while its surface
extends.   Nevertheless, the offshoots emanating from it retain sufficient
warmth to make its influence felt as far as the North Cape and Spitz-
bergen.   Thus, at the North Cape, in latitude 71° 11', the sea remains
open all the year round, while in the Baltic the water is frequently
frozen for many months.   The warmth possessed by the waters bathing
the coast of Ireland gives to it a representative character in physical
geography, as exhibiting one of the best defined examples of an insular
climate on the surface of the globe.   This is in part a result arising
from the superiority of water, as an agent for absorbing, retaining, and
distributing solar heat, compared to the other materials of the earth's
coating, as I pointed out several years since,† and which is now becoming very generally acknowledged by those who pay attention to the
climatology of the globe.   The effect of land under sunshine is to rapidly
throw off the heat it receives into the upper regions of the atmosphere
and the interplanetary spaces, both by day and night, and thus, although
it causes a considerable increase of temperature in the stratum of air
over it by day, it is not well adapted for storing up and retaining heat.

* "The Atlantis," vol. I., p. 396.   "Philosophical Magazine," October, 1858, and
"Proceedings of the Royal Society" for June, 1858.
† "Atlantis," vol. II., January, 1859.   "American Journal of Science," May, 1859.
"Phil. Mag.," vol. XVII., 4th Series.

Water is much more effective in this respect; the heat penetrates to a greater depth within it than on dry land, and it becomes more completely absorbed owing to the far higher capacity for heat of water, and the difference between its diathermanous action on the luminous heat rays entering it from the sun, compared with its action on the obscure rays quitting the particles in the interior of its mass. The incoming luminous rays penetrate freely to a moderate depth; the outgoing obscure rays are stopped almost altogether. These properties, combined with the mobility of water, as I have shown in the publications just quoted, fully account for the storing up of warmth in the tropical currents, and the retention of a considerable portion, which is ultimately given out for our benefit in the waters surrounding these islands.

The observations made in winter strikingly illustrate these conclusions, and they show that the occurrence of frost may be considered as impossible in the waters on the south and west coasts of Great Britain and Ireland. Mr. Whitley, in the essay already quoted, gives the results of observations on sea temperature, recorded in the logs of the Cunard mail steamers, and as their course for some distance beyond Cape Clear is nearly due west, the temperature recorded for 10° of west longitude may be considered as equivalent to that of the sea a little outside Crookhaven at the south-west extremity of Ireland. On this account, I include these facts in the annexed table with the numbers showing the sea and air temperatures determined on the coast of Ireland in 1851. As the temperature of the air was not taken at Bunown and Cushendall, the air temperatures observed at the two nearest stations respectively, namely, at Innisgort lighthouse, in Clew Bay, and at Portrush, may be referred to for comparison. It should be also borne in mind that these are not only mean temperatures (not like those taken at noon), but also that the sea temperatures in 1851 were observed in comparatively deep water, and never in shallows over banks close to the shore.

TABLE III.

TABLE of Mean Temperatures of the Sea and Air on the Coast of Ireland.

| — | | January. | February. | March. | April. | May. | June. | July. | August. | September. | October. | November. | December. | Mean for Year. |
|---|---|---|---|---|---|---|---|---|---|---|---|---|---|---|
| | | ° | ° | ° | ° | ° | ° | ° | ° | ° | ° | ° | ° | ° |
| In longitude 10° W., off Crookhaven, | Sea, | 51·0 | 50·0 | 51·0 | 52·0 | 53·0 | 57·0 | 59·0 | 59·0 | 58·0 | 55·0 | 53·0 | 52·0 | 54·2 |
| Castletownsend, | Sea, | 47·1 | 46·6 | 46·8 | 49·7 | 53·5 | 56·3 | 60·3 | 61·3 | 60·3 | 54·8 | 49·2 | 48·6 | 52·9 |
| | Air, | 45·4 | 46·0 | 46·1 | 47·9 | 53·6 | 57·0 | 60·7 | 61·8 | 59·6 | 54·1 | 45·7 | 46·9 | 52·1 |
| Bunown, . . | Sea, | 48·7 | 49·4 | 50·9 | 51·4 | 54·4 | 57·8 | 60·2 | 62·9 | 61·5 | 55·1 | 49·3 | 48·1 | 54·1 |
| Innisgort, . . | Air, | 46·3 | 45·2 | 46·2 | 47·3 | 52·1 | 56·5 | 58·3 | 60·9 | 58·4 | 53·7 | 47·2 | 47·8 | 51·7 |
| Courtown, . . | Sea, | 46·0 | 45·1 | 45·8 | 48·3 | 53·2 | 58·4 | 61·8 | 63·5 | 60·9 | 56·1 | 47·9 | 46·8 | 52·8 |
| | Air, | 43·3 | 43·8 | 44·3 | 46·6 | 52·5 | 57·3 | 59·5 | 60·7 | 56·5 | 51·8 | 41·6 | 45·1 | 50·3 |
| Donaghadee, . | Sea, | 46·5 | 45·6 | 45·6 | 48·1 | 50·3 | 52·5 | 55·8 | 57·4 | 57·5 | 54·7 | 50·1 | 49·3 | 51·1 |
| | Air, | 42·8 | 43·1 | 43·3 | 46·6 | 50·8 | 55·5 | 57·0 | 58·8 | 56·3 | 51·8 | 43·9 | 45·4 | 49·6 |
| Cushendall, . | Sea, | 46·6 | 45·7 | 45·6 | 47·2 | 49·1 | 52·1 | 55·4 | 57·0 | 58·3 | 55·6 | 51·6 | 49·1 | 51·1 |
| Portrush, . . | Air, | 42·0 | 42·3 | 42·9 | 45·7 | 50·2 | 55·3 | 56·5 | 58·8 | 55·5 | 51·3 | 44·4 | 44·7 | 49·1 |
| | Sea, | 46·9 | 45·6 | 45·7 | 47·9 | 50·6 | 54·3 | 57·5 | 58·7 | 58·7 | 54·9 | 49·6 | 47·8 | 51·5 |

Owing to the circumstance already alluded to at the commencement of this report, I have not made much use of the observations on the temperature of the sea in October, 1868, but as at the following stations the observations are stated to have been made at noon, except one, which I include on account of the air, temperature having been exceptionally observed, it appears desirable to compare the results with those contained in the foregoing table.

MEAN TEMPERATURE AT NOON IN OCTOBER, 1868.

|  | At sea. | Near shore. | Air. |
|---|---|---|---|
| Ballyglass (Belmullet), | 52·0 | 50 | 51·2 |
| Carrickfergus, | 50·0 | 48·8 | – |
| Carlingford (Cranfield Point), | 53·4 | 53·6 | – |
| Filey (Yorkshire), | – | 48·5 | – |
| Ramsgate, | 55·4 | 54·2 | – |

As these results are obtained from observations made during the last three weeks of October, they should be lower than the means derived from the whole month and intermediate between these and the results for November. Bearing this in mind, they may be considered as confirmatory of our general results, and especially of the superior temperature of the southern and western coasts of the British isles. They also show that the temperature of the sea in deep water during October is a little greater than near the shore, a circumstance that might be anticipated for the late autumn and winter months.

The blue lines on the map representing the distribution of mean annual temperature at the surface of the sea, are laid down partly from the results in Table III., and from indications in Maury's charts of ocean temperatures, published by the Government of the United States. The dotted lines along part of the coast in the same map represent the distribution of temperature at noon in July, deduced from the results in our first table.

It appears from Table III. that the mean temperature of the sea during the winter months was decidedly in excess of that of the air at the time when the observations were made, and this excess was maintained even in the mean annual temperatures, thus confirming the proposition already stated as to the important heating influence of currents derived from the Gulf Stream. The difference between the air and water temperatures, during the months of May, June, and July, in this table, may be instructively compared with the corresponding differences derived from the noon observations in 1869, as shown herewith.

TABLE OF DIFFERENCES OF MEAN TEMPERATURES OF AIR AND SEA.

|  | May. | June. | July. |
|---|---|---|---|
| Castletownsend, | +0·1 | +0·5 | +0·4 |
| Bunown, | −2·3 | −1·3 | −1·9 |
| Courtown, | −0·7 | −0·9 | −2·3 |
| Donaghadee, | +0·5 | +3·3 | +1·8 |
| Cushendall, | +1·1 | +3·2 | +1·1 |
| Portrush, | −0·2 | +1·0 | −1·0 |
| Means, | −0·25 | +1·0 | −0·3 |

As before, the + signifies that the air was warmer than the water, and the sign — that water was warmer than the air. This table shows in a remarkable manner the influence of heat-bearing currents during the months when sunshine is most powerful.

As the object of the present inquiry is, the determination of the conditions of sea-water climate in connexion with the development of a certain class of organized beings, I may be permitted to mention that the peculiarities of the climate of Ireland, which arise from its atmosphere deriving a considerable amount of warmth and moisture from the surrounding seas, have been referred to in order to explain the existence of a remarkable class of perennial plants found along the western and south-western shores of the island.* The plants in question belong chiefly to the family of heaths, and grow abundantly on the northern coast of Spain, and they are scattered along the east shores of the Bay of Biscay up to some of the localities on the west coast of France, where the observations whose results are given in Table II. had been made. A few of them have been also found very sparingly at the south-western extremity of Cornwall, but not in other portions of Great Britain. Mild and humid winters are the most important conditions required for this flora, and it would be impossible to point to a better illustration of the influence of the comparatively warm sea water beating against the western coast of Ireland, than the existence of these South European plants in a latitude so much to the north of their usual position, as that of the counties of Galway and Mayo.

The superior temperature of the sea in deep water, as compared to shallow water, in the month of October. is explained by the decrease of sunshine while the action of warm currents continues unabated. On the other hand, the superior temperature of the inshore water during the summer months, as disclosed by Tables I. and II., results from the greater influence of the sun during these months.

In summer, when the tide retires from shallow bays, a large extent of beach becomes frequently exposed to the mid-day sun, and this rapidly absorbs the solar heat. As the water of the incoming tide overflows the heated surface it becomes sensibly warmed, and it may thus exhibit an exceptionally high temperature. The conditions most favourable to this result would arise on bright days in a shallow bay, surrounded by hills on the north and east, and with high water two or three hours after noon.

The following deductions may be fairly drawn from the facts and reasonings contained in this report :

1. The temperature of the sea on the coast of Ireland varies within narrower limits than on the coast of Great Britain, or, in other words, it is more equable throughout the year and also during the summer season, when oyster breeding takes place.

2. The temperature of the sea at noon on the Irish coast, especially on the south and west coasts during the months of June and July is, upon the whole, higher than on the coast of Great Britain, and less than on the west coast of France.

3. This temperature seems to be sufficient for the requirements of oyster breeding, and therefore, *a fortiori*, the temperature about two in the afternoon under the conditions above referred to.

4. The highest temperature of the seas surrounding Ireland, and probably also of those surrounding Great Britain, is during the month of August, and the least during the month of February.

5. Any advantages as to temperature possessed by the seas which wash the Irish coast are unquestionably due to the thermal influence of currents connected with the Gulf Stream.

* Proceedings of the Royal Irish Academy for May, 1867, and British Association's Report for 1868, trans. sections, p. 98.

## OBSERVATIONS ON THE TEMPERATURE OF THE SEA.

NOTE.—The Temperature for column B to be taken on Oyster Banks, where such exist, but where there are no Oyster Beds, then the Temperature to be taken with the Thermometer 1 foot below the surface in shallow water near the shore. The Thermometer at sea to be lowered 6 feet below the surface and in not less than 3 fathom water.

### GOREY, JERSEY.

Taken by JOHN AMY, Harbour-master.

| 1869. | Temperature. | | Distance from Land. | Depth of Water. | State of Tide, &c. | Wind. | Temperature of Air. | Hour at which Temperature taken. | Observations. |
|---|---|---|---|---|---|---|---|---|---|
| | A. At Sea. | B. Near the Shore. | | | | | | | |
| **May.** | ° | ° | | Feet. | | | ° | | |
| 28 | – | 54 | Near the | 18 | Flowing | N E | 59 | 2 p.m. | The temperature has |
| 29 | – | 53 | land. | 18 | Ebb | N E | 55 | 10 a m. | been daily taken |
| 31 | – | 56 | do. | 20 | do. | N | 63 | 11 a.m. | at the pierhead, |
| | | | | | | | | | and I believe it is |
| | | | | | | | | | about two degrees |
| | | | | | | | | | less on the oyster |
| | | | | | | | | | beds. |
| **June.** | | | | | | | | | |
| 1 | – | 56 | do. | 30 | Flowing | N E | 62 | 11 a.m. | |
| 2 | – | 58 | do. | 24 | do. | NW | 65 | do. | |
| 3 | – | 59 | do. | 20 | Ebb | W | 70 | 2 p.m. | |
| 4 | – | 57 | do. | 28 | do. | W | 66 | do. | |
| 5 | – | 59 | do. | 28 | High water | SW | 69 | do. | |
| 7 | – | 59 | do. | 28 | Flowing | N E | 75 | 3 p.m. | |
| 8 | – | 61 | do. | 30 | do. | W | 82 | 2 p.m. | |
| 9 | – | 60 | do. | 28 | do. | N E | 76 | 3 p.m. | |
| 10 | – | 58 | do. | 26 | Ebb | E | 68 | 10 a.m. | |
| 11 | – | 58 | do. | 24 | do. | N E | 62 | do. | |
| 12 | – | 59 | do. | 28 | do. | S E | 64 | do. | |
| 14 | – | 58 | do. | 30 | do. | W | 67 | do. | |
| 15 | – | 56 | do. | 28 | do. | W | 63 | 11 a.m. | |
| 16 | – | 57 | do. | 30 | High water | NW | 65 | Noon | |
| 17 | 56 | 58 | do. | 30 | Flowing | W | 65 | 11 a.m. | |
| 18 | – | 58 | do. | 28 | do. | SW | 65 | Noon | |
| 19 | – | 58 | do. | 30 | do. | WSW | 66 | 1 p.m. | |
| 21 | – | 58 | do. | 25 | do. | W | 66 | 2 p.m. | |
| 22 | – | 58 | do. | 24 | do. | Calm | 68 | 3 p.m. | |
| 23 | – | 60 | do. | 30 | do. | SW | 69 | 4 p.m. | |
| 24 | – | 60 | do. | 24 | do. | N | 72 | do. | |
| 25 | – | 60 | do. | 20 | do. | E | 70 | 5 p.m. | |
| 26 | – | 60 | do. | 28 | Ebb | S E | 65 | 10 a.m. | |
| 28 | – | 60 | do. | 30 | do. | E | 69 | 11 a.m. | |
| 29 | 58 | 60 | do. | 30 | do. | E | 68 | 10 a.m. | |
| 30 | – | 58 | do. | 30 | High water | N E | 69 | do. | |

## GOREY, JERSEY—*continued.*

| 1869. | Temperature. A. At Sea. | Temperature. B. Near the Shore. | Distance from Land. | Depth of Water. | State of Tide, &c. | Wind. | Temperature of Air. | Hour at which Temperature taken. | Observations. |
|---|---|---|---|---|---|---|---|---|---|
| **July.** | ° | ° | | Feet. | | | ° | | |
| 1 | – | 59 | Near the | 28 | High water | N E | 67 | 11 a.m. | |
| 2 | – | 58 | land. | 28 | do. | N E | 65 | Noon | |
| 3 | – | 59 | do. | 26 | Flowing | E | 68 | do. | |
| 5 | – | 62 | do. | 24 | do. | Calm | 80 | 1 p.m. | |
| 6 | – | 62 | do. | 24 | do. | W | 75 | 3 p.m. | |
| 7 | – | 64 | do. | 28 | do. | SW | 72 | do. | |
| 8 | – | 62 | do. | 28 | do. | W | 70 | do. | |
| 9 | – | 63 | do. | 24 | do. | Calm | 75 | 4 p.m. | |
| 10 | – | 62 | do. | 26 | do. | W | 73 | do. | |
| 12 | – | 62 | do. | 30 | High water | N E | 71 | 9 a.m. | |
| 13 | – | 63 | do. | 30 | Ebb | N E | 72 | 10 a.m. | |
| 14 | – | 63 | do. | 30 | do. | N E | 70 | do. | |
| 15 | – | 63 | do. | 28 | do. | S | 72 | 11 a.m. | |
| 16 | – | 65 | do. | 28 | Flowing | S E | 77 | do. | |
| 17 | – | 66 | do. | 24 | do. | E | 79 | Noon | |
| 19 | – | 66 | do. | 26 | do. | N E | 77 | 1 p.m. | |
| 20 | – | 65 | do. | 28 | do. | N E | 75 | 2 p.m. | |
| 21 | – | 65 | do. | 30 | do. | E | 79 | 3 p.m. | |
| 22 | – | 66 | do. | 30 | do. | SW | 79 | do. | |
| 23 | – | 64 | do. | 30 | do. | W | 78 | do. | |
| 24 | – | 64 | do. | 28 | Ebb | SW | 70 | 9 a.m. | |
| 26 | – | 64 | do. | 30 | do. | SW | 74 | 10 a.m. | |
| 27 | – | 64 | do. | 28 | do. | W | 73 | do. | |
| 28 | – | 65 | do. | 28 | do. | S | 75 | 11 a.m. | |
| 29 | – | 65 | do. | 28 | do. | SW | 73 | do. | |
| 30 | – | 64 | do. | 26 | High water | W | 74 | do. | |
| 31 | – | 65 | do. | 24 | Ebb | W | 76 | Noon | |

## SOUTH YARMOUTH DIVISION.—ST. CATHERINE'S POINT STATION, ISLE OF WIGHT.

### Taken by JOHN PEPPER, Chief Officer.

| | A. | B. | Distance from Land. | Depth of Water. | State of Tide, &c. | Wind. | Temp. of Air. | Hour. | Observations. |
|---|---|---|---|---|---|---|---|---|---|
| **May.** | | | | | | | | | |
| 10 | 52 | 53 | ½ mile | 5 fathoms | Ebb | WSW | 58 | Noon | Ground sea. |
| 11 | 52 | 53 | ½ mile | 9 fathoms | do. | N E | 58 | do. | do. |
| 12 | 52 | 54 | do. | do. | do. | N E | 59 | do. | Smooth sea. |
| 13 | 52 | 54 | do. | do. | High water | E | 56 | do. | do. |
| 14 | 52 | 53 | do. | 8 fathoms | Flood | E | 54 | do. | Rough sea. |
| 15 | 52 | 52 | do. | do. | do. | E | 57 | do. | Smooth sea. |
| 17 | 52 | 52 | ¾ mile | 10 fathoms | do. | S | 58 | do. | Ground sea. |
| 18 | – | 52 | 5 yards | 3 feet | do. | S W | 59 | do. | Impracticable. |
| 19 | – | 52 | 3 yards | 4 feet | do. | WSW | 58 | do. | do. |
| 20 | 52 | 53 | ½ mile | 8 fathoms | do. | W | 64 | do. | Rough sea. |
| 21 | 52 | 53 | do. | 7 fathoms | do. | Var. | 60 | 12 30 p.m. | Smooth sea. |
| 22 | 53 | 53 | do. | do. | Ebb | N N E | 58 | Noon | do. |
| 24 | 46 | 47 | do. | do. | do. | E S E | 56 | do. | do. |
| 25 | 53 | 54 | do. | 8 fathoms | do. | E | 56 | do. | Ground sea. |
| 26 | 54 | 55 | do. | do. | do. | E | 60 | do. | do. |
| 27 | 53 | 55 | do. | do. | do. | E S E | 58 | do. | do. |
| 28 | 52 | 53 | do. | 7 fathoms | High water | E N E | 49 | do. | Rough sea. |
| 29 | 51 | 50 | do. | do. | Flood | E N E | 46 | do. | do. |
| 31 | 52 | 54 | do. | 8 fathoms | do. | N W | 56 | do. | Smooth sea. |

SOUTH YARMOUTH DIVISION, &c.—*continued.*

| 1869. | Temperature. A. At Sea. | Temperature. B. Near the Shore. | Distance from Land. | Depth of Water. | State of Tide, &c. | Wind. | Temperature of Air. | Hour at which Temperature taken. | Observations. |
|---|---|---|---|---|---|---|---|---|---|
| **June.** | ° | ° | | | | | ° | | |
| 1 | 53 | 55 | ½ mile | 8 fathoms | Flood | S S W | 57 | Noon | Smooth sea. |
| 2 | 53 | 55 | do. | 7 fathoms | do. | W | 60 | do. | do. |
| 3 | 53 | 55 | ¾ mile | do. | do. | W S W | 60 | do. | Ground sea. |
| 4 | 54 | 55 | do. | 9 fathoms | do. | W S W | 55 | do. | Smooth sea. |
| 5 | 54 | 54 | ½ mile | 7 fathoms | Low water | S W | 55 | do. | Thick fog; smooth sea. |
| 7 | 55 | 56 | do. | do. | Ebb | S S E | 72 | do. | Smooth sea. |
| 8 | 55 | 57 | do. | do. | do. | N N W | 70 | do. | do. |
| 9 | 55 | 57 | do. | do. | do. | W | 63 | do. | do. |
| 10 | 55 | 57 | do. | 8 fathoms | do. | N E | 64 | do. | do. |
| 11 | 56 | 57 | do. | 7 fathoms | do. | S S W | 60 | do. | do. |
| 12 | 56 | 57 | do. | do. | do. | S | 60 | do. | do. |
| 14 | 57 | 58 | do. | do. | Flood | W N W | 62 | do. | Rough sea. |
| 15 | – | 58 | 3 yards | 3 feet | do. | W S W | 63 | do. | Impracticable. |
| 16 | – | 58 | do. | 5 feet | do. | W N W | 60 | do. | do. |
| 17 | 57 | 58 | ½ mile | 7 fathoms | do. | N | 56 | do. | Smooth sea. |
| 18 | 58 | 58 | do. | do. | do. | N N W | 55 | do. | do. |
| 19 | 58 | 58 | do. | do. | do. | S S W | 57 | do. | do. |
| 21 | 58 | 58 | ¾ mile | 9 fathoms | Ebb | W | 58 | do. | Thermometer broken |
| 22 | – | – | – | – | – | – | – | do. | Smooth sea. |
| 23 | – | – | – | – | – | – | – | do. | do. |
| 24 | 58 | 59 | ¾ mile | 9 fathoms | Ebb | – | 80 | do. | do. |
| 25 | 57 | 59 | ½ mile | 7 fathoms | do. | S E | 65 | do. | do. |
| 26 | 57 | 59 | do. | do. | do. | N E | 67 | do. | do. |
| 28 | 58 | 60 | do. | do. | Flood | E S E | 72 | do. | do. |
| 29 | 58 | 60 | ¼ mile | 5 fathoms | do. | E S E | 69 | do. | do. |
| 30 | 58 | 60 | ½ mile | 7 fathoms | do. | N E | 66 | do. | do. |
| **July.** | | | | | | | | | |
| 1 | 57 | 58 | ½ mile | 7 fathoms | Flood | N E | 62 | Noon | Smooth sea. |
| 2 | 57 | 59 | do. | do. | do. | N E | 63 | do. | do. |
| 3 | 57 | 59 | do. | do. | do. | S E | 62 | do. | do. |
| 5 | 58 | 60 | do. | do. | Low water | W | 62 | do. | do. |
| 6 | 59 | 60 | ¼ mile | 5 fathoms | Ebb | W S W | 63 | do. | Rough sea. |
| 7 | 59 | 60 | ½ mile | 7 fathoms | do. | S W | 63 | do. | do. |
| 8 | 59 | 60 | do. | do. | do. | S | 65 | do. | do. |
| 9 | 60 | 61 | ¼ mile | 5 fathoms | do. | W | 65 | do. | Ground sea. |
| 10 | 60 | 62 | ½ mile | 7 fathoms | do. | Var. | 67 | do. | do. |
| 12 | 60 | 62 | do. | do. | do. | S | 74 | do. | Smooth sea. |
| 13 | 60 | 62 | do. | do. | High water | N E | 64 | do. | do. |
| 14 | 60 | 62 | do. | do. | Flood | W S W | 73 | do. | do. |
| 15 | 61 | 62 | do. | do. | do. | S W | 75 | do. | do. |
| 16 | 61 | 62 | do. | do. | do. | – | 77 | do. | do. |
| 17 | 61 | 63 | ¾ mile | 10 fathoms | do. | S S E | 77 | do. | do. |
| 19 | 62 | 64 | ½ mile | 6 fathoms | do. | S S W | 78 | do. | do. |
| 20 | 62 | 64 | ¾ mile | 10 fathoms | Ebb | E N E | 75 | do. | do. |
| 21 | 62 | 64 | ½ mile | 7 fathoms | do. | E | 68 | do. | do. |
| 22 | 62 | 64 | do. | do. | do. | S S E | 73 | do. | Ground sea. |
| 23 | 62 | 63 | do. | do. | do. | W N W | 76 | do. | do. |
| 24 | 63 | 64 | do. | 8 fathoms | do. | W | 80 | do. | do. |
| 26 | 63 | 64 | ¼ mile | 5 fathoms | High water | S W | 70 | do. | do. |
| 27 | 63 | 64 | ½ mile | 7 fathoms | Flood | W S W | 68 | do. | Rough sea. |
| 28 | 63 | 63 | do. | do. | do. | N E | 64 | do. | Smooth sea. |
| 29 | 63 | 64 | do. | do. | do. | W | 70 | do. | do. |
| 30 | – | 64 | 5 yards | 3 feet | do. | W | 67 | do. | Impracticable. |
| 31 | – | 64 | do. | do. | do. | W S W | 68 | do. | do. |

## Eastbourne Division.—Eastbourne Station, Sussex.

Taken by J. Henderson, Chief Officer.

| 1869. | Temperature. A. At Sea. | Temperature. B. Near the Shore. | Distance from Land. | Depth of Water. | State of Tide, &c. | Wind. | Temperature of Air. | Hour at which Temperature taken. | Observations. |
|---|---|---|---|---|---|---|---|---|---|
| **May.** | ° | ° | | | | | ° | | |
| 10 | 52 | 53 | ½ mile | 3½ fathoms | Ebb | W | 63 | Noon | |
| 11 | 51 | 52 | do. | do. | do. | WNW | 62 | do. | |
| 12 | 51 | 51 | do. | do. | do. | N E | 58 | do. | |
| 13 | 52 | 52 | ¼ mile | 2½ fathoms | High water | E | 57 | do. | Unable to launch a boat; taken from Eastbourne Pier. |
| 14 | 51 | 51 | 250 yards | 2 fathoms | Flood | E | 59 | do. | |
| 15 | 50 | 50 | do. | do. | do. | E | 57 | 12 50 | |
| 17 | 50 | 52 | ¾ mile | 3½ fathoms | do. | SW | 59 | Noon | |
| 18 | 53 | 54 | 250 yards | 2 fathoms | Ebb | WSW | 61 | 4 30 p.m. | |
| 19 | 53 | 53 | — | 1¾ fathoms | Flood | SW | 61 | 4 p.m. | |
| 20 | 54 | 55 | 250 yards | 2 fathoms | do. | W | 60 | 5 15 p.m. | |
| 21 | 54 | 53 | 1 mile | 3 fathoms | Ebb | E S E | 62 | 11 a.m. | |
| 22 | 51 | 51 | ¾ mile | 2¾ fathoms | do. | NW | 55 | do. | |
| 24 | 55 | 56 | ¼ mile | 3 fathoms | do. | S | 64 | Noon | |
| 25 | 56 | 56 | ¼ mile | 3¼ fathoms | High water | E | 62 | do. | |
| 26 | 57 | 57 | ½ mile | 3½ fathoms | — | SSW | 67 | do. | |
| 27 | 57 | 57 | do. | do. | — | E | 64 | do. | |
| 28 | 55 | 55 | 250 yards | 2¼ fathoms | — | E N E | 51 | do. | |
| 29 | 52 | 52 | — | 2½ fathoms | Flood | N N E | 51 | do. | |
| 31 | 53 | 54 | ¼ mile | 3½ fathoms | do. | NNW | 61 | do. | |
| **June.** | | | | | | | | | |
| 1 | 55 | 56 | ½ mile | 3½ fathoms | Ebb | S | 63 | 5 p.m. | |
| 2 | 56 | 56 | do. | do. | High water | NNW | 65 | do. | |
| 3 | 56 | 56 | do. | do. | do. | Var. | 61 | do. | |
| 4 | 55 | 57 | do. | 3 fathoms | Flood | W | 64 | do. | |
| 5 | 55 | 55 | ¾ mile | 3¼ fathoms | Ebb | SSW | 65 | Noon | |
| 7 | 57 | 59 | 1 mile | do. | do. | S | 76 | do. | |
| 8 | 59 | 58 | ¾ mile | 3½ fathoms | do. | N | 75 | 1 p.m. | |
| 9 | 59 | 61 | ½ mile | do. | do. | W | 70 | Noon | |
| 10 | 59 | 60 | do. | do. | High water | N E | 67 | do. | |
| 11 | 59 | 59 | do. | 3¼ fathoms | do. | SW | 66 | do. | |
| 12 | 58 | 59 | 1 mile | do. | do. | S | 66 | do. | |
| 14 | 58 | 58 | 250 yards | 3½ fathoms | Flood | NW | 63 | do. | |
| 15 | 58 | 59 | ¾ mile | 2¾ fathoms | High water | W | 60 | 3 p.m. | |
| 16 | 57 | 56 | 1 mile | 5½ fathoms | do. | N | 60 | 3 30 p.m | |
| 17 | 57 | 57 | ¾ mile | do. | Flood | W | 61 | 2 30 p.m. | |
| 18 | 57 | 57 | ¼ mile | 3½ fathoms | do. | NW | 63 | 4 p.m. | |
| 19 | 57 | 58 | 1 mile | 3¼ fathoms | do. | N | 67 | 5 30 p.m. | |
| 21 | 57 | 57 | do. | do. | Ebb | SW | 59 | Noon | |
| 22 | 57 | 57 | ¾ mile | do. | do. | W | 58 | do. | |
| 23 | 58 | 58 | ½ mile | do. | High water | SSW | 66 | do. | |
| 24 | 57 | 58 | do. | 3½ fathoms | do. | SSW | 71 | do. | |
| 25 | 57 | 58 | ¾ mile | do. | do. | S E | 69 | do. | |
| 26 | 58 | 59 | do. | do. | Flood | E | 71 | do. | |
| 28 | 60 | 61 | ½ mile | 3 fathoms | do. | E N E | 69 | do. | |
| 29 | 60 | 60 | 250 yards | do. | do. | E N E | 64 | do. | |
| 30 | 61 | 61 | do. | 2½ fathoms | High water | E N E | 68 | 4 p.m. | |

## Eastbourne Division, &c.—*continued.*

| 1869. | Temperature. A. At Sea. | Temperature. B. Near the Shore. | Distance from Land. | Depth of Water. | State of Tide, &c. | Wind. | Temperature of Air. | Hour at which Temperature taken. | Observations. |
|---|---|---|---|---|---|---|---|---|---|
| **July.** | ° | ° | | | | | ° | | |
| 1 | 60 | 60 | 250 yards | 2¼ fathoms | High water | N E | 66 | 4 p.m. | |
| 2 | 60 | 60 | — | — | — | N E | 65 | 5 p.m. | |
| 3 | 60 | 61 | ½ mile | 3¼ fathoms | Flood | E | 67 | 4 p.m. | |
| 5 | 61 | 62 | ⅝ mile | 3 fathoms | Ebb | SW | 75 | Noon | |
| 6 | 60 | 62 | do. | do. | Flood | WSW | 67 | 6 30 p.m. | |
| 7 | 58 | 60 | do. | 3¼ fathoms | Ebb | WSW | 71 | Noon | |
| 8 | 60 | 60 | do. | 3½ fathoms | High water | NW | 76 | do. | |
| 9 | 60 | 61 | 1 mile | 4 fathoms | do. | W | 72 | 11 30 a.m. | |
| 10 | 61 | 62 | ¾ mile | 3¼ fathoms | do. | SSW | 74 | Noon | |
| 12 | 65 | 66 | ½ mile | 3½ fathoms | do. | S E | 78 | do. | |
| 13 | 64 | 65 | do. | 3¼ fathoms | do. | N E | 68 | 1 30 p.m. | |
| 14 | 64 | 65 | 1 mile | do. | Flood | WNW | 72 | 11 30 a.m. | |
| 15 | 63 | 64 | ½ mile | 3½ fathoms | High water | NW | 76 | 4 p.m. | |
| 16 | 65 | 66 | ¼ mile | do. | do. | W | 80 | do. | |
| 17 | 67 | 68 | do. | do. | Flood | SSW | 81 | do. | |
| 19 | 67 | 68 | 1 mile | 3¼ fathoms | Ebb | S | 81 | Noon. | |
| 20 | 67 | 67 | ¾ mile | do. | . do. | E | 79 | do. | |
| 21 | 65 | 66 | do. | 3½ fathoms | do. | S E | 66 | do. | |
| 22 | 66 | 67 | do. | 3¾ fathoms | do· | S | 75 | do. | |
| 23 | 65 | 66 | ½ mile | do. | do. | W | 72 | do. | |
| 24 | 65 | 66 | 1 mile | 4½ fathoms | High water | NW | 72 | do. | |
| 26 | 65 | 65 | do. | 3¼ fathoms | Flood | E | 71 | do. | |
| 27 | 65 | 66 | ¾ mile | do. | do. | E | 74 | do. | |
| 28 | 65 | 65 | ½ mile | do. | High water | SW | 71 | 2 p.m. | |
| 29 | 66 | 67 | ½ mile | 3½ fathoms | Flood | WSW | 75 | Noon | |
| 30 | 65 | 66 | do. | 3 fathoms | do. | W | 71 | do. | |
| 31 | 65 | 66 | do. | do. | do. | W | 76 | do. | |

## Ramsgate Division.—Ramsgate Station, Kent.

Taken by the Officer of Station.

| | | | | | | | | | |
|---|---|---|---|---|---|---|---|---|---|
| **May.** | | | Yards. | Fathoms. | | | | | |
| 10 | 54 | 56 | 500 | 3½ | High water | WSW | 60 | Noon | |
| 11 | 52 | 56 | 550 | 3¼ | Flood | W | 60 | 11 55 a.m. | |
| 12 | 52 | 54 | 550 | 4 | — | E by N | 55 | 11 50 a.m. | |
| 13 | 54 | 55 | 600 | 4 | Flood | E by N | 58 | 12 5 p.m. | |
| 14 | - | 54 | — | - | — | N E | 58 | 11 55 a.m. | Heavy sea. |
| 15 | - | 56 | — | - | — | E | 58 | Noon | Impracticable. |
| 17 | 53 | 58 | 600 | 3 | Ebb | W | 62 | 12 5 p.m. | |
| 18 | - | 58 | — | - | do. | SW | 62 | Noon | Heavy sea. |
| 19 | - | 58 | — | - | do. | SW | 60 | do. | Impracticable. |
| 20 | 56 | 57 | 600 | 3 | do. | WSW | 61 | do. | |
| 21 | 56 | 57 | 600 | 3 | do. | E | 62 | 11 55 a.m. | |
| 22 | 57 | 58 | 550 | 3 | do. | N | 64 | Noon | |
| 24 | 56 | 58 | 550 | 3 | do. | S | 64 | do. | |
| 25 | 56 | 58 | 550 | 3½ | Flood | E | 65 | do. | |
| 26 | 57 | 59 | 550 | 3¼ | do. | E by S | 66 | do. | |
| 27 | 52 | 54 | 550 | 3¾ | do. | E by S | 68 | 11 55 a.m. | |
| 28 | - | 52 | — | - | — | N E | 55 | Noon | **Impracticable.** |
| 29 | - | 52 | — | - | — | N E | 54 | do. | **do.** |
| 31 | 54 | 55 | 600 | 3 | Flood | NW | 55 | 12 5 p.m. | |

## Ramsgate Division, &c.—*continued.*

| 1869. | Temperature. A. At Sea. | Temperature. B. Near the Shore. | Distance from Land. | Depth of Water. | State of Tide, &c. | Wind. | Temperature of Air. | Hour at which Temperature taken. | Observations. |
|---|---|---|---|---|---|---|---|---|---|
| **June.** | ° | ° | Yards. | Fathoms. | | | ° | | |
| 1 | 56 | 57 | 600 | 3 | Ebb | N N W | 65 | Noon | |
| 2 | 55 | 57 | 800 | 3 | do. | W S W | 70 | do. | |
| 3 | 55 | 57 | 800 | 3 | do. | W by S | 65 | 12 10 p.m. | |
| 4 | 56 | 53 | 900 | 3 | do. | W by S | 66 | 12 20 p.m. | |
| 5 | 58 | 59 | 800 | 3 | do. | W S W | 70 | Noon | |
| 7 | 61 | 63 | 600 | 3 | Flood | S | 72 | do. | |
| 8 | 60 | 61 | 550 | 3¼ | do. | N W | 73 | 12 10 p.m. | |
| 9 | 59 | 60 | 550 | 3½ | do. | S E | 67 | Noon | |
| 10 | 59 | 60 | 600 | 3 | do. | N E | 75 | 12 45 p.m. | |
| 11 | 57 | 59 | 500 | 3 | do. | N N E | 70 | Noon | |
| 12 | 58 | 59 | 500 | 3 | do. | S | 69 | do. | |
| 14 | 58 | 59 | 550 | 3 | Low water | W by N | 65 | do. | |
| 15 | – | 58 | — | – | — | S W | 62 | do. | Impracticable. |
| 16 | – | 57 | — | – | — | N W | 61 | do. | do. |
| 17 | 56 | 57 | 800 | 3 | Ebb | S W | 63 | 11 55 a.m. | |
| 18 | 57 | 59 | 900 | 3 | do. | N N W | 73 | 12 10 p.m. | |
| 19 | 57 | 59 | 800 | 3 | do. | N N E | 75 | Noon | |
| 21 | 57 | 59 | 800 | 3¼ | do. | N N W | 63 | 11 50 a.m. | |
| 22 | 57 | 59 | 750 | 3¼ | do. | N W | 75 | Noon | |
| 23 | 58 | 59 | 600 | 3¼ | do. | N N W | 72 | do. | |
| 24 | 59 | 60 | 500 | 3¼ | High water | N W by N | 74 | 11 50 a.m. | |
| 25 | 58 | 59 | 500 | 3½ | Flood | N | 74 | Noon | |
| 26 | 59 | 60 | 500 | 3 | do. | N N E | 75 | do. | |
| 28 | 59 | 60 | 500 | 3 | do. | N | 74 | do. | |
| 29 | 59 | 60 | 550 | 3 | do. | N | 74 | do. | |
| 30 | 58 | 59 | 600 | 3 | do. | N E | 69 | do. | |
| **July.** | | | | | | | | | |
| 1 | – | 59 | — | – | — | N E | 69 | Noon | Impracticable. |
| 2 | – | 59 | — | – | — | N E | 73 | do. | do. |
| 3 | 60 | 61 | 700 | 3 | Ebb | E N E | 74 | do. | |
| 5 | 61 | 62 | 700 | 3 | do. | S W | 75 | do. | |
| 6 | 61 | 62 | 650 | 3 | do. | S W | 74 | 12 10 p.m. | |
| 7 | 61 | 62 | 600 | 3¼ | do. | S W | 74 | Noon | |
| 8 | 62 | 63 | 500 | 3½ | do. | S | 75 | 11 55 a.m. | |
| 9 | 62 | 63 | 500 | – | do. | W S W | 78 | Noon | |
| 10 | 61 | 62 | 500 | 3¼ | Flood | S | 74 | do. | |
| 12 | 62 | 63 | 500 | 3½ | do. | S E | 77 | do. | |
| 13 | 61 | 62 | 500 | 3 | do. | S | 76 | 11 55 a.m. | |
| 14 | 62 | 63 | 550 | 3 | do. | E | 79 | 11 50 a.m. | |
| 15 | 62 | 63 | 600 | 3 | do. | N W | 84 | Noon | |
| 16 | 63 | 64 | 700 | 3 | Ebb | N N W | 80 | do. | |
| 17 | 63 | 65 | 700 | 3 | do. | S E | 82 | 11 55 a.m. | |
| 19 | 62 | 63 | 600 | 3 | do. | N | 78 | Noon | |
| 20 | 62 | 63 | 550 | 3½ | do. | N N E | 76 | do. | |
| 21 | 62 | 63 | 500 | 3¼ | do. | E N E | 84 | 11 50 a.m. | |
| 22 | 63 | 64 | 500 | 3½ | do. | E S E | 86 | Noon | |
| 23 | 63 | 64 | 500 | 3¼ | High water | N N W | 79 | do. | |
| 24 | 64 | 65 | 500 | 3¼ | Flood | S | 81 | do. | |
| 26 | 64 | 64 | 500 | 3¼ | do. | S S W | 79 | 11 50 a.m. | |
| 27 | 63 | 64 | 500 | 3¼ | do. | W | 74 | 11 55 a.m. | |
| 28 | 63 | 64 | 500 | 3¼ | do. | N E | 79 | Noon | |
| 29 | 64 | 65 | 550 | 3¼ | do. | W S W | 79 | do. | |
| 30 | 64 | 65 | 600 | 3¼ | do. | S W | 79 | 12 10 p.m. | |
| 31 | 64 | 65 | 600 | 3¼ | Ebb | S W | 80 | 12 20 p.m. | |

## CROMER DIVISION.—CROMER STATION, NORFOLK.

Taken by WILLIAM FREDERICK HUEULL, Chief Officer.

| 1869. | Temperature. | | Distance from Land. | Depth of Water. | State of Tide, &c. | Wind. | Temperature of Air. | Hour at which Temperature taken. | Observations. |
|---|---|---|---|---|---|---|---|---|---|
| | A. At Sea. | B. Near the Shore. | | | | | | | |
| **May.** | ° | ° | | | | | ° | | |
| 10 | –* | 53 | From jetty | 1½ fathoms | Ebb | SW | 59 | 7 45 a.m. | Thunder. |
| 11 | –* | 51 | do. | do. | High water | ESE | 52 | 6 p.m. | |
| 12 | –* | 53 | do. | do. | Flood | E | 52 | do. | |
| 13 | 51 | 52 | 1½ miles | do. | Ebb | NNE | 55 | Noon | |
| 14 | –* | 52 | From jetty | 5 fathoms | Flood | E | 49 | 6 p.m. | * Too much surf to |
| 15 | –* | 51 | do. | 1½ fathoms | High water | – | 50 | 10 a.m. | launch. |
| 17 | –* | 52 | do. | do. | do. | – | 50 | 10 45 a.m. | |
| 18 | –* | 51 | do. | do. | do. | N E | 50 | 11 15 a.m. | |
| 19 | 51 | 52 | 1½ miles | 5 fathoms | Flood | SW | 53 | Noon | Thunder. |
| 20 | 51 | 52 | do. | do. | do. | SW | 54 | do. | |
| 21 | –* | 53 | From jetty | 1½ fathoms | do. | NNE | 58 | do. | |
| 22 | –* | 53 | do. | do. | do. | N E | 54 | 12 30 p.m. | |
| 24 | –* | 52 | do. | do. | High water | ESE | 51 | 5 p.m. | |
| 25 | –* | 53 | do. | do. | do. | S E | 53 | 5 45 p.m. | |
| 26 | –* | 52 | do. | do. | do. | E | 50 | 6 15 p.m. | Fresh gales. |
| 27 | –* | 49 | do. | do. | Flood | ENE | 51 | 6 30 p.m. | |
| 28 | –* | 50 | do. | do. | do. | ENE | 47 | do. | * Too much surf to |
| 29 | –* | 49 | do. | do. | High water | ENE | 46 | 10 a.m. | launch. |
| 31 | – | 50 | do. | do. | do. | NNE | 49 | 10 30 a.m. | |
| | | | | | | | | | |
| **June.** | | | | | | | | | |
| 1 | –* | 52 | From jetty | 1½ fathoms | High water | NNW | 60 | 11 a.m. | |
| 2 | –* | 53 | do. | do. | do. | E | 63 | 11 30 a.m. | * Too much surf. |
| 3 | –* | 54 | do. | do. | do. | N | 54 | Noon | |
| 4 | 52 | 55 | 1 mile | 4 fathoms | Flood | SW | 64 | do. | |
| 5 | 53 | 55 | do. | do. | do. | WNW | 70 | do. | |
| 7 | 59 | 61 | do. | do. | do. | WSW | 78 | do. | |
| 8 | – | 54 | From jetty | 1½ fathoms | do. | NNE | 52 | 4 30 p.m. | Moderate gales. |
| 9 | – | 56 | do. | do. | do. | N E | 52 | 5 p.m. | |
| 10 | – | 55 | do. | do. | do. | NNE | 49 | 5 p.m. | |
| 11 | –* | 54 | do. | do. | do. | N | 52 | 6 p.m. | Strong wind. |
| 12 | –* | 56 | do. | do. | Ebb | SW | 61 | 10 30 a.m. | |
| 14 | –* | 54 | do. | do. | High water | N | 52 | 10 a.m. | Strong gale. |
| 15 | –* | 55 | do. | do. | do. | WSW | 57 | 11 a.m. | Fresh breeze. |
| 16 | –* | 53 | do. | do. | do. | NNE | 48 | 11 30 a m. | |
| 17 | –* | 54 | do. | do. | do. | W | 55 | Noon | |
| 18 | –* | 52 | do. | do. | Flood | N E | 49 | do. | |
| 19 | –* | 52 | do. | do. | do. | N E | 49 | do. | * Too much surf to |
| 21 | –* | 55 | do. | do. | do. | N E | 52 | 1 p.m. | launch. |
| 22 | –* | 56 | do. | do. | do. | N E | 54 | 2 p.m. | |
| 23 | –* | 57 | do. | do. | do. | N | 60 | 3 p.m. | |
| 24 | –* | 58 | do. | do. | do. | N | 54 | 4 p.m. | |
| 25 | 59 | 56 | 1 mile | 4 fathoms | Ebb | N E | 57 | Noon | |
| 26 | 59 | 56 | do. | do. | do. | N E | 56 | do. | |
| 28 | –* | 59 | From jetty | 1½ fathoms | do. | N E | 54 | do. | Strong winds. |
| 29 | –* | 58 | do. | do. | do. | N E | 54 | do. | |
| 30 | –* | 58 | do. | do. | do. | N E | 57 | do. | * Too much surf. |

## CROMER DIVISION, &c.—*continued.*

| 1869. | Temperature. A. At Sea. | Temperature. B. Near the Shore. | Distance from Land. | Depth of Water. | State of Tide, &c. | Wind. | Temperature of Air. | Hour at which Temperature taken. | Observations. |
|---|---|---|---|---|---|---|---|---|---|
| **July.** | ° | ° | | | | | ° | | |
| 1 | 56 | 58 | 1 mile | 5 fathoms | High water | E N E | 54 | Noon | |
| 2 | 56 | 58 | do. | do. | Flood | E N E | 54 | do. | |
| 3 | 56 | 58 | do. | do. | do. | E | 62 | do. | |
| 5 | – | 59 | – | 1½ fathoms | Ebb | W | 64 | do. | |
| 6 | – | 65 | – | do. | do. | W | 72 | do. | |
| 7 | – | 66 | – | do. | do. | W | 74 | do. | |
| 8 | – | 66 | – | do. | do. | S W | 74 | do. | |
| 9 | 60 | 62 | ½ mile | 4 fathoms | Low water | W | 78 | do. | |
| 10 | 60 | 62 | do. | do. | Ebb | N N E | 64 | do. | |
| 12 | 62 | 64 | do. | do. | do. | S W | 87 | do. | |
| 13 | 59 | 61 | do. | do. | do. | N N E | 57 | do. | |
| 14 | 60 | 62 | do. | do. | do. | N N W | 64 | do. | |
| 15 | 60 | 62 | do. | do. | do. | N W | 62 | do. | |
| 16 | 64 | 66 | do. | do. | High water | W N W | 68 | do. | |
| 17 | 64 | 67 | do. | do. | Flood | E by S | 66 | do. | |
| 19 | 61 | 62 | do. | do. | do. | N E | 58 | do. | |
| 20 | 62 | 64 | do. | do. | do. | E N E | 61 | do. | |
| 21 | 64 | 66 | do. | do. | do. | E N E | 62 | do. | |
| 22 | 64 | 66 | do. | do. | do. | S E | 74 | do. | |
| 23 | 64 | 66 | do. | do. | do. | S E | 76 | do. | |
| 24 | 64 | 65 | do. | do. | Low water | S W | 78 | do. | |
| 26 | 64 | 65 | do. | do. | Ebb | S W | 71 | do. | |
| 27 | 64 | 65 | do. | do. | do. | S W | 72 | do. | |
| 28 | 63 | 62 | do. | do. | do. | E S E | 64 | do. | |
| 29 | 63 | 64 | do. | do. | do. | S E | 70 | do. | |
| 30 | 64 | 65 | do. | do. | do. | W by S | 70 | do. | |
| 31 | 64 | 65 | do. | do. | do. | W S W | 72 | do. | |

## FLEETWOOD DIVISION.—WHITEHAVEN STATION, CUMBERLAND.

Taken by RICHARD JINKS, Chief Officer.

| | | | | | | | | | |
|---|---|---|---|---|---|---|---|---|---|
| **May.** | | | Miles. | Fathoms. | | | | | |
| 10 | 48 | 49 | 1¾ | 8 | Ebb | N E | 55 | Noon | |
| 11 | 49 | 49 | 2¼ | 8¾ | High water | N N W | 54 | do. | |
| 12 | 49 | 50 | 2½ | 9 | Flood | N W | 53 | do. | |
| 13 | 50 | 50 | 1¾ | 7 | do. | N | 52 | do. | |
| 14 | 50 | 50 | 2 | 7½ | do. | W N W | 58 | do. | |
| 15 | 50 | 50 | 2¼ | 7½ | do. | W N W | 58 | do. | |
| 17 | 50 | 51 | 1½ | 6 | do. | N N E | 57 | do. | |
| 18 | 49 | 50 | 2 | 6 | do. | E | 58 | do. | |
| 19 | 49 | 50 | 1¼ | 5½ | do. | N E | 52 | do. | |
| 20 | 49 | 50 | 2 | 6 | Low water | N W | 56 | do. | |
| 21 | 50 | 51 | 1½ | 5½ | Ebb | Calm. | 56 | do. | |
| 22 | 50 | 51 | 1¼ | 6½ | do. | N W | 61 | do. | |
| 24 | 50 | 50 | 1¾ | 7 | do. | N W | 56 | do. | |
| 25 | 50 | 50 | 1½ | 7 | do. | S E | 57 | do. | |
| 26 | 50 | 51 | 1 | 4 | High water | S E | 54 | do. | |
| 27 | 50 | 51 | 1 | 3½ | Flood. | S E | 55 | do. | |
| 28 | 51 | 51 | 2 | 6 | do. | W N W | 54 | do. | |
| 29 | 51 | 51 | 1¾ | 6 | do. | W N W | 52 | do. | |
| 31 | 51 | 51 | 2 | 7 | do. | W N W | 59 | do. | |

FLEETWOOD DIVISION, &c.—*continued.*

| 1869. | Temperature. | | Distance from Land. | Depth of Water. | State of Tide, &c. | Wind. | Temperature of Air. | Hour at which Temperature taken. | Observations. |
|---|---|---|---|---|---|---|---|---|---|
| | A. At Sea. | B. Near the Shore. | | | | | | | |
| **June.** | ° | ° | Miles. | Fathoms. | | | ° | | |
| 1 | 50 | 51 | 1½ | 8 | Flood | N E | 59 | Noon | |
| 2 | 51 | 52 | 2 | 7 | do. | NNW | 59 | do. | |
| 3 | 51 | 51 | 1½ | 6 | Low water | SW | 60 | do. | |
| 4 | 51 | 52 | 1 | 5 | Ebb | WSW | 58 | do. | |
| 5 | 52 | 52 | 1½ | 6 | do. | WNW | 57 | do. | |
| 7 | 52 | 53 | 2 | 6½ | do. | NNW | 63 | do. | |
| 8 | 52 | 53 | 1½ | 7 | do. | N N E | 61 | do. | |
| 9 | 53 | 54 | 1¾ | 7½ | do. | N N E | 59 | do. | |
| 10 | 54 | 55 | 1½ | 8 | High water | NNW | 58 | do. | |
| 11 | 55 | 55 | 1½ | 7½ | Flood | N N E | 59 | do. | |
| 12 | 55 | 55 | 1½ | 7¼ | do. | N N E | 60 | do. | |
| 14 | 56 | 56 | 1 | 4¾ | do. | NW | 57 | do. | |
| 15 | 56 | 56 | – | 2 | do. | NNW | 59 | do. | Taken off this pier; strong gale. |
| 16 | 56 | 56 | – | 1½ | do. | NNW | 56 | do. | |
| 17 | 55 | 56 | 2 | 5 | do. | WNW | 56 | do. | |
| 18 | 56 | 57 | 2 | 5 | Low water | NW | 59 | do. | |
| 19 | 56 | 57 | 1½ | 4½ | Ebb | NW | 60 | do. | |
| 21 | 56 | 57 | 1½ | 4½ | do. | NW | 60 | do. | |
| 22 | 57 | 57 | 2 | 6 | do. | NNW | 62 | do. | |
| 23 | 57 | 57 | 1½ | 5 | do. | NNW | 64 | do. | |
| 24 | 57 | 58 | 1½ | 6 | do. | Calm | 69 | do. | |
| 25 | 58 | 59 | 1½ | 6 | Flood | Calm | 69 | do. | |
| 26 | 58 | 59 | 2 | 7 | do. | NW | 68 | do. | |
| 28 | 59 | 59 | 1½ | 5 | do. | N E | 67 | do. | |
| 29 | 59 | 59 | 2 | 6 | do. | NNW | 66 | do. | |
| 30 | 59 | 60 | 2 | 6 | do. | WNW | 69 | do. | |
| **July.** | | | | | | | | | |
| 1 | 59 | 59 | 1½ | 6 | Flood | WNW | 70 | Noon | |
| 2 | 60 | 60 | 1 | 5 | Low water | NNW | 68 | do. | |
| 3 | 60 | 60 | 1½ | 5 | Ebb | WNW | 69 | do. | |
| 5 | 59 | 60 | 1¾ | 5 | do. | SW | 71 | do. | |
| 6 | 60 | 60 | 1 | 4½ | do. | SW | 63 | do. | |
| 7 | – | 60 | – | – | — | WSW | 67 | do. | Not fit weather to launch. Taken off the pier head. |
| 8 | 59 | 60 | 1 | 5 | Ebb | WSW | 66 | do. | |
| 9 | 60 | 60 | 1 | 5 | do. | W | 66 | do. | |
| 10 | 61 | 62 | 2 | 8 | High water | W | 65 | do. | |
| 12 | 62 | 63 | 1¾ | 8 | Flood | WNW | 67 | do. | |
| 13 | – | 61 | – | – | do. | NW | 65 | do. | Bad weather. From pier head. |
| 14 | 61 | 61 | 1 | 5 | do. | W | 61 | do. | |
| 15 | 62 | 62 | 1½ | 8 | do. | WSW | 67 | do. | |
| 16 | 62 | 62 | 1 | 6 | do. | SW | 61 | do. | |
| 17 | 63 | 64 | 2 | 6 | Low water | Calm | 65 | do. | |
| 19 | 64 | 65 | 1 | 6 | Ebb | NNW | 68 | do. | |
| 20 | 64 | 65 | 2 | 8 | do. | SSW | 68 | do. | |
| 21 | 64 | 65 | 2½ | 8 | do. | SW | 72 | do. | |
| 22 | 63 | 64 | 2 | 8 | do. | WSW | 69 | do. | |
| 23 | 63 | 64 | 3 | 9 | do. | WSW | 68 | do. | |
| 24 | 63 | 64 | 2½ | 9 | High water | WSW | 70 | do. | |
| 26 | 63 | 64 | 1 | 6 | Flood | WSW | 66 | do. | |
| 27 | 64 | 64 | 2 | 7 | do. | NW | 70 | do. | |
| 28 | 64 | 65 | 3 | 8 | do. | SW | 69 | do. | |
| 29 | – | 63 | – | – | — | SSW | 68 | do. | Bad weather. From the pier head. |
| 30 | – | 63 | – | – | Flood | WSW | 67 | do. | |
| 31 | 64 | 64 | 1½ | 5 | do. | S S | 66 | do. | |

## FLEETWOOD DIVISION.—DOUGLAS STATION, ISLE OF MAN.

Taken by GEORGE STEED, Boatman.

| 1869. | Temperature. A. At Sea. | Temperature. B. Near the Shore. | Distance from Land. | Depth of Water. | State of Tide, &c. | Wind. | Temperature of Air. | Hour at which Temperature taken. | Observations. |
|---|---|---|---|---|---|---|---|---|---|
| **May.** | o | o | | | | | o | | |
| 10 | – | 46 | — | — | Ebb | N W | 56 | Noon | |
| 11 | – | 47 | — | — | do. | N W | 54 | do. | |
| 12 | – | 48 | — | — | do. | N W | 54 | do. | |
| 13 | – | 48 | — | — | High water | E S E | 50 | do. | |
| 14 | – | 48 | — | — | Flood | S E | 53 | do. | |
| 15 | – | 48 | — | — | do. | S E | 52 | do. | |
| 17 | – | 47 | — | — | do. | S E | 50 | do. | |
| 18 | – | 48 | — | — | do. | E | 48 | do. | |
| 19 | – | 48 | — | — | do. | N N W | 51 | do. | |
| 20 | – | 49 | — | — | Low water | N W | 48 | do. | |
| 21 | – | 49 | — | — | Ebb | S S E | 58 | do. | |
| 22 | – | 50 | — | — | do. | N W | 53 | do. | |
| 24 | – | 50 | — | — | do. | S E | 56 | do. | |
| 25 | – | 49 | — | — | do. | S E | 51 | do. | |
| 26 | – | 49 | — | — | do. | E | 48 | do. | |
| 27 | – | 49 | — | — | High water | E | 47 | do. | |
| 28 | – | 49 | — | — | Flood | E | 51 | do. | |
| 29 | – | 50 | — | — | do. | S | 57 | do. | |
| 31 | – | 50 | — | — | do. | E by S | 55 | do. | |
| **June.** | | | | | | | | | |
| 1 | – | 51 | — | — | Flood | S W | 61 | Noon | |
| 2 | – | 50 | — | — | do. | S W | 60 | do. | |
| 3 | – | 51 | — | — | do. | S W | 60 | do. | |
| 4 | – | 53 | — | — | Ebb | S W | 59 | do. | |
| 5 | – | 53 | — | — | do. | S W | 61 | do. | |
| 7 | – | 52 | — | — | do. | S W | 64 | do. | |
| 8 | – | 53 | — | — | do. | N N W | 57 | do. | |
| 9 | – | 51 | — | — | do. | N N W | 53 | do. | |
| 10 | – | 52 | — | — | do. | N W | 56 | do. | |
| 11 | – | 52 | — | — | High water | E S E | 57 | do. | |
| 12 | – | 53 | — | — | Flood | S W | 58 | do. | |
| 14 | – | 52 | — | — | do. | N W | 54 | do. | |
| 15 | 51 | 52 | ¼ mile | 7 fathoms | do. | N W | 52 | do. | |
| 16 | 51 | 53 | do. | do. | do. | N W | 54 | do. | |
| 17 | 52 | 54 | do. | do. | do. | S W | 56 | do. | |
| 18 | 52 | 54 | do. | do. | do. | N | 55 | do. | |
| 19 | 53 | 55 | do. | do. | Ebb | S E | 56 | do. | |
| 21 | 53 | 55 | do. | do. | do. | S S E | 58 | do. | |
| 22 | 53 | 54 | do. | do. | do. | N N W | 56 | do. | |
| 23 | 52 | 53 | do. | do. | do. | N N W | 58 | do. | |
| 24 | 53 | 55 | do. | do. | do. | S E | 66 | do. | |
| 25 | 53 | 56 | do. | do. | High water | S E | 68 | do. | |
| 26 | 55 | 56 | do. | do. | Flood | S | 69 | do. | |
| 28 | 55 | 56 | do. | do. | do. | E | 71 | do. | |
| 29 | 55 | 56 | do. | do. | do. | E | 68 | do. | |
| 30 | 56 | 57 | do. | do. | do. | S E | 70 | do. | |

## FLEETWOOD DIVISION, &c.—*continued.*

| 1869. | Temperature. | | Distance from Land. | Depth of Water. | State of Tide, &c. | Wind. | Temperature of Air. | Hour at which Temperature taken. | Observations. |
|---|---|---|---|---|---|---|---|---|---|
| | A. At Sea. | B. Near the Shore. | | | | | | | |
| **July.** | ° | ° | | | | | ° | | |
| 1 | 55 | 56 | 400 yards | 7 fathoms | Flood | S | 69 | Noon | |
| 2 | 55 | 56 | do. | do. | do. | S E | 70 | do. | |
| 3 | 55 | 57 | do. | do. | Low water | E S E | 70 | do. | |
| 5 | 55 | 57 | do. | do. | Ebb | S W | 59 | do. | |
| 6 | 56 | 58 | do. | do. | do. | W | 66 | do. | |
| 7 | 56 | 57 | do. | do. | do. | S W | 61 | do. | |
| 8 | 56 | 58 | do. | do. | do. | S W | 61 | do. | |
| 9 | 56 | 58 | do. | do. | do. | S W | 61 | do. | |
| 10 | 56 | 58 | do. | do. | do. | S | 62 | do. | |
| 12 | 57 | 58 | do. | do. | Flood | W | 65 | do. | |
| 13 | 57 | 59 | do. | do. | do. | N W | 60 | do. | |
| 14 | 57 | 60 | do. | do. | do. | N W | 66 | do. | |
| 15 | 57 | 60 | do. | do. | do. | N W | 72 | do. | |
| 16 | 58 | 61 | do. | do. | do. | S S W | 70 | do. | |
| 17 | 59 | 61 | do. | do. | do. | S E | 72 | do. | |
| 19 | 59 | 62 | do. | do. | Ebb | S E | 71 | do. | |
| 20 | 59 | 60 | do. | do. | do. | S | 71 | do. | |
| 21 | 59 | 60 | do. | do. | do. | S W | 69 | do. | |
| 22 | 59 | 60 | do. | do. | do. | S W | 62 | do. | |
| 23 | 59 | 60 | do. | do. | do. | S W | 66 | do. | |
| 24 | 59 | 60 | do. | do. | do. | S W | 66 | do. | |
| 26 | 59 | 61 | do. | do. | Flood | S W | 64 | do. | |
| 27 | 59 | 61 | do. | do. | do. | N W | 62 | do. | |
| 28 | 59 | 61 | do. | do. | do. | S W | 66 | do. | |
| 29 | 60 | 61 | do. | do. | do. | S S W | 64 | do. | |
| 30 | 60 | 62 | do. | do. | do. | S W | 62 | do. | |
| 31 | 60 | 62 | do. | do. | do. | W S W | 64 | do. | |

### CHESTER DIVISION, CHESHIRE.—BANGOR STATION, FLINTSHIRE.

Taken by WILLIAM LAWDEN, Chief Boatman.

| May. | | | Yards. | Fathoms. | | | | | |
|---|---|---|---|---|---|---|---|---|---|
| 10 | – | 50 | 300 | 10½ | Ebb | – | 61 | 11 30 a.m. | |
| 11 | – | 50 | 400 | 6½ | do. | – | 58 | Noon | |
| 12 | – | 50 | 100 | 2 | do. | – | 58 | 1 p.m. | |
| 13 | – | 51 | 400 | 5½ | do. | – | 54 | 12 30 p.m. | |
| 14 | – | 52 | 100 | 3 | High water | – | 57 | 12 30 p.m. | |
| 15 | – | 52 | 100 | 3 | do. | – | 61 | Noon | |
| 17 | – | 52 | 500 | 5 | do. | – | 59 | 12 30 p.m. | |
| 18 | – | 53 | 400 | 4 | Flood | – | 61 | 12 30 p.m. | |
| 19 | – | 51 | 100 | 2 | do. | – | 58 | 1 p.m. | |
| 20 | – | 53 | 300 | 1½ | Low water | – | 56 | 12 50 p.m. | |
| 21 | – | 51 | 100 | 2 | do. | – | 55 | 1 30 p.m. | |
| 22 | – | 52 | 400 | 5½ | Ebb | – | 61 | Noon | |
| 24 | – | 53 | 400 | 4 | do. | – | 58 | 11 30 a.m. | |
| 25 | – | 53 | 500 | 2 | do. | – | 57 | 12 15 p.m. | |
| 26 | – | 50 | 50 | 5 | do. | – | 52 | 12 15 p.m. | |
| 27 | – | 50 | 50 | 2½ | do. | – | 52 | Noon | |
| 28 | – | 51 | 100 | 2½ | do. | – | 53 | 12 30 p.m. | |
| 29 | – | 51 | 200 | 3 | High water | – | 53 | Noon | |
| 31 | – | 52 | 400 | 9 | do. | – | 57 | 11 45 a.m. | |

CHESTER DIVISION, &c.—*continued.*

| 1869. | Temperature. A. At Sea. | Temperature. B. Near the Shore. | Distance from Land. | Depth of Water. | State of Tide, &c. | Wind. | Temperature of Air. | Hour at which Temperature taken. | Observations. |
|---|---|---|---|---|---|---|---|---|---|
| **June.** | ° | ° | Yards. | Fathoms. | | | ° | | |
| 1 | – | 56 | 350 | 2 | Flood | – | 64 | Noon | |
| 2 | – | 55 | 250 | 5 | do. | – | 60 | 12 15 p.m. | |
| 3 | – | 54 | 200 | 3 | Low water | – | 58 | Noon | |
| 4 | – | 56 | 350 | 5 | Ebb | – | 59 | do. | |
| 5 | – | 56 | 450 | 4½ | do. | – | 59 | 12 30 p.m. | |
| 7 | – | 58 | 400 | 5 | do. | – | 54 | 12 15 p.m. | |
| 8 | – | 56 | 300 | 6 | do. | – | 59 | Noon | |
| 9 | – | 58 | 200 | 1½ | do. | – | 62 | 12 30 p.m. | |
| 10 | – | 57 | 100 | 2½ | do. | – | 60 | 12 15 p.m. | |
| 11 | – | 57 | 200 | 3 | High water | – | 61 | 11 45 a.m. | |
| 12 | – | 56 | 400 | 5 | Flood | – | 60 | 12 15 p.m. | |
| 14 | – | 55 | 200 | 3 | do. | – | 58 | 1 p.m. | |
| 15 | – | 51 | 100 | 2 | do. | – | 52 | Noon | |
| 16 | – | 54 | 150 | 2 | do. | – | 56 | 12 30 p.m. | |
| 17 | – | 54 | 300 | 5 | do. | – | 55 | Noon | |
| 18 | – | 54 | 400 | 4 | Low water | – | 58 | do. | |
| 19 | – | 56 | 300 | 3½ | Ebb | – | 57 | do. | |
| 21 | – | 58 | 500 | 5 | do. | – | 62 | do. | |
| 22 | – | 61 | 400 | 5½ | do. | – | 63 | 1 p.m. | |
| 23 | – | 59 | 300 | 3½ | do. | – | 63 | 12 30 p.m. | |
| 24 | – | 59 | 400 | 5½ | do. | – | 65 | 12 15 p.m. | |
| 25 | – | 60 | 300 | 4½ | High water | – | 69 | Noon | |
| 26 | – | 60 | 400 | 5 | Flood | – | 68 | do. | |
| 28 | – | 63 | 500 | 6 | do. | – | 69 | 12 15 p.m. | |
| 29 | – | 63 | 550 | 6 | do. | – | 69 | Noon | |
| 30 | – | 62 | 300 | 2 | do. | – | 66 | 12 30 p.m. | |
| **July.** | | | | | | | | | |
| 1 | – | 62 | 300 | 3½ | Flood | – | 69 | 12 15 p.m. | Squally. |
| 2 | – | 64 | 400 | 5 | do. | – | 71 | 12 30 p.m. | Overcast. |
| 3 | – | 62 | 350 | 3 | Low water | – | 70 | 12 15 p.m. | Cloudy. |
| 5 | – | 62 | 400 | 3½ | Ebb | – | 66 | 11 45 a.m. | Showers. |
| 6 | – | 63 | 200 | 3 | do. | – | 69 | Noon | Cloudy. |
| 7 | – | 62 | 400 | 5 | do. | – | 69 | 12 15 p.m. | Overcast. |
| 8 | – | 61 | 250 | 3½ | do. | – | 66 | 12 30 p.m. | do. |
| 9 | – | 61 | 400 | 6 | do. | – | 66 | 12 20 p.m. | Cloudy. |
| 10 | – | 61 | 500 | 7 | do. | – | 65 | Noon | do. |
| 12 | – | 62 | 450 | 6½ | High water | – | 66 | 12 10 p.m. | do. |
| 13 | – | 59 | 300 | 4 | Flood | – | 63 | 12 30 p.m. | do. |
| 14 | – | 61 | 500 | 6 | do. | – | 68 | 12 15 p.m. | do. |
| 15 | – | 62 | 400 | 4 | do. | – | 70 | 12 15 p.m. | do. |
| 16 | – | 61 | 350 | 3½ | do. | – | 68 | 12 30 p.m. | do. |
| 17 | – | 65 | 200 | 3 | do. | – | 76 | 11 45 a.m. | do. |
| 19 | – | 64 | 300 | 5 | Low water | – | 74 | 12 30 p.m. | do. |
| 20 | – | 65 | 250 | 3½ | Ebb | – | 74 | Noon | do. |
| 21 | – | 64 | 450 | 4 | do. | – | 74 | 12 15 p.m. | Overcast. |
| 22 | – | 62 | 300 | 5½ | do. | – | 72 | 12 40 p.m. | do. |
| 23 | – | 63 | 450 | 6 | do. | – | 72 | 12 15 p.m. | Cloudy. |
| 24 | – | 62 | 300 | 5 | High water | – | 69 | 11 45 a.m. | do. |
| 26 | – | 61 | 400 | 6 | Flood | – | 68 | Noon | Overcast. |
| 27 | – | 62 | 500 | 7 | do. | – | 65 | do. | do. |
| 28 | – | 63 | 300 | 3½ | do. | – | 66 | 12 10 p.m. | Cloudy. |
| 29 | – | 61 | 400 | 5 | do. | – | 67 | Noon | do. |
| 30 | – | 62 | 300 | 4 | do | – | 69 | 12 15 p.m. | do. |
| 31 | – | 62 | 450 | 5 | do. | – | 67 | 11 45 a.m. | do. |

MILFORD DIVISION.—GOODWICK STATION, PEMBROKESHIRE.

Taken by JOHN G. ANNAL, Chief Officer.

| 1869. | Temperature. | | Distance from Land. | Depth of Water. | State of Tide, &c. | Wind. | Temperature of Air. | Hour at which Temperature taken. | Observations. |
|---|---|---|---|---|---|---|---|---|---|
| | A. At Sea. | B. Near the Shore. | | | | | | | |
| **May.** | ° | ° | | Feet. | | | ° | | |
| 10 | – | 50 | At the Quay | 2 | Low water | E | 56 | Noon | |
| 11 | – | 53 | do. | 2 | Ebb | N N E | 58 | do. | |
| 12 | – | 51 | do. | 3 | do. | N E | 59 | do. | |
| 13 | – | 54 | do. | 4 | do. | N E | 63 | do. | |
| 14 | – | 52 | do. | 5 | do. | E | 57 | do. | |
| 15 | – | 52 | do. | 6 | do. | E S E | 63 | do. | |
| 17 | – | 53 | do. | 7 | do. | W S W | 56 | do. | |
| 18 | – | 52 | do. | 8 | High water | W S W | 57 | do. | |
| 19 | – | 49 | do. | 7 | Flood | N | 47 | do. | |
| 20 | – | 54 | do. | 6 | do. | N W | 59 | do. | |
| 21 | – | 54 | do. | 5 | do. | N | 60 | do. | |
| 22 | – | 55 | do. | 4 | do. | N | 63 | do. | |
| 24 | – | 53 | do. | 3 | do. | S | 55 | do. | |
| 25 | – | 55 | do. | 2 | do. | S E | 61 | do. | |
| 26 | – | 55 | do. | 2 | Low water | E | 56 | do. | |
| 27 | – | 52 | do. | 2 | Ebb | E | 53 | do. | |
| 28 | – | 51 | do. | 3 | do. | E | 50 | do. | |
| 29 | – | 51 | do. | 4 | do. | N E | 60 | do. | |
| 31 | – | 53 | do. | 5 | do. | N W | 59 | do. | |
| **June.** | | | | | | | | | |
| 1 | – | 55 | At the Quay | 6 | Ebb | W S W | 64 | Noon | |
| 2 | – | 54 | do. | 7 | do. | S S W | 56 | do. | |
| 3 | – | 55 | do. | 8 | High water | W | 64 | do. | |
| 4 | – | 57 | do. | 8 | Flood | W | 63 | do. | |
| 5 | – | 60 | do. | 7 | do. | W | 64 | do. | |
| 7 | – | 59 | do. | 6 | do. | W | 66 | do. | |
| 8 | – | 55 | do. | 5 | do. | N E | 64 | do. | |
| 9 | – | 57 | do. | 4 | do. | N E | 64 | do. | |
| 10 | – | 58 | do. | 3 | do. | N E | 65 | do. | |
| 11 | – | 57 | do. | 2 | Low water | N E | 55 | do. | |
| 12 | – | 57 | do. | 2 | Ebb | W | 63 | do. | |
| 14 | – | 55 | do. | 3 | do. | N | 62 | do. | |
| 15 | – | 55 | do. | 4 | do. | N W | 62 | do. | |
| 16 | – | 57 | do. | 5 | do. | N | 62 | do. | |
| 17 | – | 57 | do. | 6 | do. | W | 64 | do. | |
| 18 | – | 55 | do. | 7 | do. | N E | 56 | do. | |
| 19 | – | 56 | do. | 8 | High water | N E | 57 | do. | |
| 21 | – | 59 | do. | 7 | Flood | N E | 66 | do. | |
| 22 | – | 55 | do. | 6 | do. | N E | 56 | do. | |
| 23 | – | 56 | do. | 5 | do. | N | 57 | do. | |
| 24 | – | 58 | do. | 4 | do. | E | 66 | do. | |
| 25 | – | 60 | do. | 3 | do. | Calm | 64 | do. | |
| 26 | – | 62 | do. | 2 | do. | E | 65 | do. | |
| 28 | – | 59 | do. | 2 | Ebb | E | 70 | do. | |
| 29 | – | 59 | do. | 3 | do. | E | 67 | do. | |
| 30 | – | 59 | do. | 4 | do. | E | 70 | do. | |

## MILFORD DIVISION, &c.—*continued.*

| 1869. | Temperature. A. At Sea. | Temperature. B. Near the Shore. | Distance from Land. | Depth of Water. | State of Tide, &c. | Wind. | Temperature of Air. | Hour at which Temperature taken. | Observations. |
|---|---|---|---|---|---|---|---|---|---|
| July. | ° | ° | | Feet. | | | ° | | |
| 1 | – | 62 | At the Quay | 5 | Ebb | E | 71 | Noon | |
| 2 | – | 60 | do. | 7 | do. | N | 72 | do. | |
| 3 | – | 62 | do. | 8 | High water | E | 69 | do. | |
| 5 | – | 60 | do. | 7 | Flood | SW | 64 | do. | |
| 6 | – | 62 | do. | 6 | do. | W | 68 | do. | |
| 7 | – | 60 | do. | 5 | do. | WSW | 64 | do. | |
| 8 | – | 60 | do. | 4 | do. | SW | 63 | do. | |
| 9 | – | 62 | do. | 2 | Low water | W | 64 | do. | |
| 10 | – | 61 | do. | 3 | Ebb | N | 73 | do. | |
| 12 | – | 61 | do. | 4 | do. | NNW | 75 | do. | |
| 13 | – | 59 | do. | 5 | do. | N E | 69 | do. | |
| 14 | – | 62 | do. | 6 | do. | W | 70 | do. | |
| 15 | – | 63 | do. | 7 | do. | N E | 73 | do. | |
| 16 | – | 62 | do. | 8 | High water | E | 70 | do. | |
| 17 | – | 63 | do. | 7 | Flood | E | 68 | do. | |
| 19 | – | 61 | do. | 6 | do. | E | 64 | do. | |
| 20 | – | 63 | do. | 5 | do. | Calm | 70 | do. | |
| 21 | – | 63 | do. | 4 | do. | S | 70 | do. | |
| 22 | – | 60 | do. | 3 | do. | SW | 66 | do. | |
| 23 | – | 63 | do. | 2 | Low water | W | 72 | do. | |
| 24 | – | 63 | do. | 3 | Ebb | W | 73 | do. | |
| 26 | – | 62 | do. | 4 | do. | W | 68 | do. | |
| 27 | – | 62 | do. | 5 | do. | NW | 70 | do. | |
| 28 | – | 60 | do. | 6 | do. | E N E | 64 | do. | |
| 29 | – | 60 | do. | 7 | do. | SW | 63 | do. | |
| 30 | – | 62 | do. | 8 | do. | SW | 68 | do. | |
| 31 | – | 62 | do. | 8 | Low water | W | 66 | do. | |

## QUEENSTOWN DIVISION.—CROSSHAVEN STATION, Co. CORK.

### Taken by M. LYNCH, Chief Boatman.

| | A. | B. | Distance from Land. | Depth of Water. | State of Tide, &c. | Wind. | Temp. of Air. | Hour. | Observations. |
|---|---|---|---|---|---|---|---|---|---|
| May. | | | | | | | | | |
| 10 | 53 | 53 | 200 yards | 4 fathoms | Ebb | NW | 53 | Noon | Flood runs west, |
| 11 | 53 | 53 | do. | 3 fathoms | do. | N | 52 | do. | and Ebb east at |
| 12 | 53 | 53 | do. | do. | do. | NW | 51 | do. | all times. |
| 13 | 53 | 55 | do. | do. | do. | W | 54 | do. | |
| 14 | 52 | 55 | do. | do. | do. | W | 53 | do. | |
| 15 | 52 | 53 | do. | do. | do. | ESE | 51 | do. | |
| 17 | 52 | 54 | do. | do. | do. | S E | 51 | do. | |
| 18 | 54 | 55 | do. | 5 fathoms | High water | S E | 54 | do. | |
| 19 | 53 | 55 | do. | 3½ fathoms | do. | S E | 51 | do. | |
| 20 | 53 | 54 | do. | 4 fathoms | do. | S | 53 | do. | |
| 21 | 53 | 56 | do. | 3½ fathoms | Flood | S W | 58 | do. | |
| 22 | 53 | 56 | do. | 3½ fathoms | do. | S | 59 | do. | |
| 24 | 53 | 56 | 300 yards | 4 fathoms | do. | S | 62 | do. | |
| 25 | 53 | 57 | do. | 3 fathoms | do. | S | 59 | 11 30 a.m. | |
| 26 | 51 | 54 | 200 yards | 3½ fathoms | do. | SW | 56 | Noon | |
| 27 | 51 | 53 | do. | 3 fathoms | do. | SW | 54 | do. | |
| 28 | 50 | 52 | do. | do. | do. | NW | 52 | do. | |
| 29 | 52 | 54 | do. | 3½ fathoms | do. | N | 52 | do. | |
| 31 | 54 | 56 | do. | 3 fathoms | do. | W | 57 | do. | |

QUEENSTOWN DIVISION, &c.—*continued.*

| 1869. | Temperature. A. At Sea. | Temperature. B. Near the Shore. | Distance from Land. | Depth of Water. | State of Tide, &c. | Wind. | Temperature of Air. | Hour at which Temperature taken. | Observations. |
|---|---|---|---|---|---|---|---|---|---|
| **June.** | ° | ° | | | | | ° | | |
| 1 | 57 | 58 | 200 yards | 3 fathoms | Ebb | W | 63 | Noon | The flood in the |
| 2 | 56 | 59 | do. | 5¼ fathoms | do. | W | 64 | do. | main channel of |
| 3 | 56 | 58 | do. | 3¼ fathoms | do. | NW | 62 | do. | this harbour runs |
| 4 | 54 | 56 | do. | 3½ fathoms | do. | SW | 68 | do. | north, and the |
| 5 | 56 | 56 | do. | do. | do. | SW | 62 | do. | Ebb south; but |
| 7 | 56 | 64 | do. | 3 fathoms | do. | SW | 69 | do. | in the Carrigaline |
| 8 | 56 | 68 | do. | do. | do. | SE | 62 | do. | River, where these |
| 9 | 59 | 62 | 300 yards | do. | Low water | SE | 72 | do. | observations were |
| 10 | 60 | 64 | do. | 4 fathoms | do. | S | 69 | do. | principally taken, |
| 11 | 62 | 64 | 200 yards | 3 fathoms | do. | S | 66 | do. | the Flood runs |
| 12 | 61 | 62 | 400 yards | 5 fathoms | Flood | SW | 63 | do. | west, and the Ebb |
| 14 | 59 | 60 | 500 yards | 4 fathoms | do. | NW | 60 | do. | east. |
| 15 | 57 | 59 | 400 yards | 3 fathoms | do. | NW | 59 | do. | |
| 16 | 59 | 60 | do. | 3½ fathoms | do. | NW | 62 | do. | |
| 17 | 61 | 63 | 300 yards | 3 fathoms | do. | NW | 64 | do. | |
| 18 | 62 | 64 | 500 yards | 6 fathoms | do. | N | 66 | do. | |
| 19 | 60 | 62 | do. | 4 fathoms | do. | NW | 64 | do. | |
| 21 | 61 | 64 | do. | 3 fathoms | do. | NW | 69 | do. | |
| 22 | 62 | 64 | 400 yards | do. | High water | N | 69 | do. | |
| 23 | 63 | 64 | 300 yards | 5 fathoms | do. | S | 70 | do. | |
| 24 | 64 | 66 | do. | 3 fathoms | do. | S | 68 | do. | |
| 25 | 63 | 66 | 400 yards | 4 fathoms | Ebb | S | 61 | do. | |
| 26 | 65 | 66 | do. | do. | do. | S | 64 | do. | |
| 28 | 68 | 70 | 300 yards | 3 fathoms | do. | S | 79 | do. | |
| 29 | 69 | 71 | do. | do. | do. | S | 76 | do. | |
| 30 | 71 | 80 | 400 yards | 4 fathoms | do. | SE | 81 | do. | |
| **July.** | | | | | | | | | |
| 1 | 71 | 79 | 300 yards | 4 fathoms | Ebb | S | 79 | Noon | |
| 2 | 71 | 80 | do. | 3 fathoms | do. | S | 84 | do. | |
| 3 | 70 | 78 | 400 yards | do. | do. | SE | 80 | do. | |
| 5 | 68 | 76 | 800 yards | 9 fathoms | do. | SW | 70 | do. | |
| 6 | 66 | 71 | 900 yards | 11 fathoms | do. | SW | 69 | do. | |
| 7 | 64 | 70 | 600 yards | 8 fathoms | Low water | SW | 66 | do. | |
| 8 | 63 | 68 | 400 yards | 4 fathoms | do. | SW | 68 | do. | |
| 9 | 64 | 67 | 500 yards | 3 fathoms | do. | SW | 70 | do. | |
| 10 | 64 | 69 | 300 yards | 4 fathoms | Flood | SW | 76 | do. | |
| 12 | 65 | 69 | do. | 5 fathoms | do. | N | 70 | do. | |
| 13 | 66 | 70 | do. | 11 fathoms | do. | N | 79 | do. | |
| 14 | 67 | 70 | 30 yards | 5 fathoms | do. | S | 76 | do. | |
| 15 | 64 | 69 | 900 yards | 3 fathoms | do. | E | 84 | do. | |
| 16 | 60 | 64 | 600 yards | do. | do. | SE | 82 | 2 p.m. | |
| 17 | 62 | 65 | 300 yards | 6 fathoms | do. | SE | 89 | Noon | |
| 19 | 61 | 65 | 400 yards | 7 fathoms | do. | SW | 86 | do. | |
| 20 | 59 | 64 | 500 yards | 6 fathoms | do. | SW | 80 | do. | |
| 21 | 56 | 66 | 800 yards | 9 fathoms | do. | SW | 70 | do. | |
| 22 | 54 | 64 | 900 yards | 4 fathoms | High water | SW | 79 | do. | |
| 23 | 53 | 61 | 300 yards | 3 fathoms | Ebb | SW | 71 | do. | |
| 24 | 51 | 60 | 400 yards | 4 fathoms | do. | SW | 73 | do. | |
| 26 | 50 | 61 | 300 yards | 3 fathoms | Low water | SW | 71 | do. | |
| 27 | 52 | 59 | do. | 4 fathoms | do. | S | 73 | do. | |
| 28 | 49 | 53 | 400 yards | 3 fathoms | do. | SW | 63 | do. | |
| 29 | 48 | 53 | 300 yards | 4 fathoms | Ebb | W | 66 | do. | |
| 30 | 45 | 49 | 400 yards | 3 fathoms | do. | W | 56 | do. | |
| 31 | 41 | 46 | 3 yards | 4 fathoms | do. | NW | 53 | do. | |

## WATERFORD DIVISION.—TRAMORE STATION, CO. WATERFORD.

Taken by RICHARD JOHNS, Chief Boatman.

| 1869. | Temperature. A. At Sea. | Temperature. B. Near the Shore. | Distance from Land. | Depth of Water. | State of Tide, &c. | Wind. | Temperature of Air. | Hour at which Temperature taken. | Observations. |
|---|---|---|---|---|---|---|---|---|---|
| **May.** | ° | ° | | | | | ° | | |
| 10 | – | 52 | Near the | 1 Foot | F $\frac{1}{4}$ F E | N E | 50 | 12 Noon | Rain. |
| 11 | – | 54 | shore. | do. | Low water | N | 58 | do. | Cloudy. |
| 12 | – | 54 | do. | do. | Low $\frac{1}{4}$ EW | N | 58 | do. | do. |
| 13 | – | – | — | — | — | – | – | — | — |
| 14 | – | – | — | — | — | – | – | — | — |
| 15 | – | – | — | — | — | – | – | — | — |
| 17 | – | 55 | Near the | 1 Foot | H $\frac{1}{2}$ EW | S E | 63 | 12 Noon | Rain. |
| 18 | – | 55 | shore. | do. | F $\frac{3}{4}$ EW | S E | 65 | do. | Cloudy. |
| 19 | – | 53 | do. | do. | F $\frac{3}{4}$ EW | N | 66 | do. | do. |
| 20 | – | 54 | do. | do. | High water | N | 65 | do. | do. |
| 21 | – | 54 | do. | do. | H $\frac{1}{4}$ F E | N | 61 | do. | do. |
| 22 | – | 54 | do. | do. | H $\frac{1}{4}$ F E | N | 66 | do. | do. |
| 24 | – | 56 | do. | do. | H $\frac{1}{2}$ F E | S S E | 60 | do. | Rain. |
| 25 | – | 57 | do. | do. | F $\frac{1}{4}$ F E | S S E | 67 | do. | Cloudy. |
| 26 | – | 55 | do. | do. | Low water | E | 57 | do. | Rain. |
| 27 | – | 56 | do. | do. | Low water | E | 58 | do. | Gloomy. |
| 28 | – | 58 | do. | do. | H $\frac{1}{4}$ EW | N E | 60 | do. | Cloudy. |
| 29 | – | 56 | do. | do. | H $\frac{1}{4}$ EW | N E | 60 | do. | do. |
| 31 | – | 57 | do. | do. | H $\frac{1}{2}$ EW | N | 62 | do. | do. |
| **June.** | | | | | | | | | |
| 1 | – | 57 | Near the | 1 Foot | — | W | 65 | Noon | Cloudy. |
| 2 | – | 57 | shore. | do. | — | S W | 67 | do. | do. |
| 3 | – | 56 | do. | do. | — | W | 65 | do. | do. |
| 4 | – | 56 | do. | do. | — | W | 65 | do. | do. |
| 5 | – | 57 | do. | do. | — | W S W | 67 | do. | do. |
| 7 | – | 57 | do. | do. | — | W | 68 | do. | do. |
| 8 | – | 58 | do. | do. | — | W | 69 | do. | Gloomy. |
| 9 | – | 61 | do. | do. | — | S W | 72 | do. | Fine. |
| 10 | – | 62 | do. | do. | — | N | 74 | do. | do. |
| 11 | – | 61 | do. | do. | — | N | 72 | do. | do. |
| 12 | – | 59 | do. | do. | — | W | 70 | do. | Cloudy. |
| 14 | – | 59 | do. | do. | — | N W | 68 | do. | do. |
| 15 | – | 59 | do. | do. | — | N W | 68 | do. | do. |
| 16 | – | 60 | do. | do. | — | N W | 69 | do. | do. |
| 17 | – | 57 | do. | do. | — | W | 65 | do. | Showery. |
| 18 | – | 57 | do. | do. | — | N W | 65 | do. | do. |
| 19 | – | 57 | do. | do. | — | N W | 65 | do. | Cloudy. |
| 21 | – | 59 | do. | do. | — | N | 68 | do. | do. |
| 22 | – | 59 | do. | do. | — | N | 69 | do. | do. |
| 23 | – | 58 | do. | do. | — | N | 68 | do. | do. |
| 24 | – | 65 | do. | do. | — | N | 74 | do. | Fine. |
| 25 | – | 64 | do. | do. | — | N | 72 | do. | do. |
| 26 | – | 63 | do. | do. | — | W | 70 | do. | do. |
| 28 | – | 64 | do. | do. | — | E | 72 | do. | do. |
| 29 | – | 63 | do. | do. | — | E | 72 | do. | do. |
| 30 | – | 63 | do. | do. | — | E | 73 | do. | do. |
| **July.** | | | | | | | | | |
| 1 | – | 63 | Near the | 1 Foot | — | N | 73 | Noon | Fine. |
| 2 | – | 64 | shore. | do. | — | N | 74 | do. | do. |
| 3 | – | 65 | do. | do. | — | W | 76 | do. | do. |
| 5 | – | 63 | do. | do. | — | S W | 68 | do. | Gloomy. |
| 6 | – | 63 | do. | do. | — | W | 69 | do. | Cloudy. |
| 7 | – | 63 | do. | do. | — | S W | 68 | do. | Fog. |

## WATERFORD DIVISION, &c.—continued.

| 1859. | Temperature. A. At Sea. | Temperature. B. Near the Shore. | Distance from Land. | Depth of Water. | State of Tide, &c. | Wind. | Temperature of Air. | Hour at which Temperature taken. | Observations. |
|---|---|---|---|---|---|---|---|---|---|
| July —con. | ° | ° | | | | | ° | | |
| 8 | – | 65 | Near the | 1 Foot | —— | S W | 68 | Noon | Cloudy. |
| 9 | – | 65 | shore. | do. | —— | W S W | 68 | do. | do. |
| 10 | – | 66 | do. | do. | —— | W | 73 | do. | Fine. |
| 12 | – | 66 | do. | do. | —— | N | 73 | do. | do. |
| 13 | – | 66 | do. | do. | —— | N W | 75 | do. | do. |
| 14 | – | 64 | do. | do. | —— | N W | 74 | do. | Cloudy. |
| 15 | – | 62 | do. | do. | —— | N W | 72 | do. | do. |
| 16 | – | 64 | do. | do. | —— | E | 74 | do. | Fine. |
| 17 | – | 66 | do. | do. | —— | W | 75 | do. | do. |
| 19 | – | 66 | do. | do. | —— | S W | 74 | do. | do. |
| 20 | – | 65 | do. | do. | —— | S E | 73 | do. | Fog. |
| 21 | – | 64 | do. | do. | —— | W S W | 73 | do. | Cloudy. |
| 22 | – | 65 | do. | do. | —— | W | 74 | do. | do. |
| 23 | – | 64 | do. | do. | —— | W N W | 73 | do. | Fine. |
| 24 | – | 64 | do. | do. | —— | W S W | 72 | do. | Cloudy. |
| 26 | – | 64 | do. | do. | —— | W N W | 69 | do. | do. |
| 27 | – | 64 | do. | do. | —— | N W | 69 | do. | do. |
| 28 | – | 64 | do. | do. | —— | W N W | 69 | do. | Fine. |
| 29 | – | 63 | do. | do. | —— | W S W | 67 | do. | Rain. |
| 30 | – | 63 | do. | do. | —— | W N W | 66 | do. | Fog. |
| 31 | – | 63 | do. | do. | —— | W N W | 66 | do. | Cloudy. |

## ARKLOW DIVISION.—ARKLOW STATION, CO. WICKLOW.

### Taken by ROBERT M'CONNELL, Chief Boatman.

**May.**—During this month the crew were on board H.M.S. *Royal George* for summer cruise.

| June. | | | Miles. | Fathoms. | | | | | |
|---|---|---|---|---|---|---|---|---|---|
| 1 | 50 | 52 | 1 | 6 | Flowing | W S W | 69 | Noon | Cloudy. |
| 2 | 50 | 56 | 1½ | 7 | Flood | S W | 58 | 12 15 p.m. | do. |
| 3 | 50 | 52 | 1¾ | 8 | do. | S W | 59 | 12 10 p.m. | do. |
| 4 | 51 | 50 | 2¼ | 8¼ | do. | S W | 54 | 12 15 p.m. | do. |
| 5 | 50 | 50 | 2 | 8 | do. | W | 56 | 12 10 p.m. | do. |
| 7 | 52 | 51 | 2½ | 8½ | do. | S S W | 74 | 12 15 p.m. | do. |
| 8 | 50 | 52 | 2¾ | 8 | Ebb | N E | 58 | Noon | Clear. |
| 9 | 52 | 54 | 2½ | 8½ | do. | S E | 60 | 12 30 p.m. | Hazy. |
| 10 | – | – | —— | – | —— | –– | –– | —— | Crew employed. |
| 11 | 51 | 50 | 2¾ | 9 | Ebb | S | 64 | 12 10 p.m. | Hazy. |
| 12 | – | – | —— | – | —— | –– | –– | —— | Crew employed. |
| 14 | 50 | 52 | 3½ | 10 | Ebb | W | 70 | 12 15 p.m. | Cloudy. |
| 15 | – | – | —— | – | —— | –– | –– | —— | Impracticable. |
| 16 | 52 | 50 | 3½ | 10 | Flood | S | 60 | 12 30 p.m. | Cloudy. |
| 17 | 50 | 50 | 4 | 9½ | do. | S W | 58 | 12 10 p.m. | do. |
| 18 | 50 | 52 | 4½ | 10½ | do. | S W | 56 | Noon | Rain. |
| 19 | 52 | 50 | 4½ | 11 | do. | N E | 54 | 12 15 p.m. | Hazy. |
| 21 | 52 | 50 | 4 | 11 | do. | S E | 72 | Noon | do. |
| 22 | 52 | 50 | 4½ | 11 | Low water | N W | 64 | 12 30 p.m. | Cloudy. |
| 23 | 52 | 50 | 4½ | 12 | Ebb | S | 76 | 12 15 p.m. | do. |
| 24 25 26 28 29 30 | } – | – | —— | – | —— | –– | –– | —— | { Thermometer broken by accident on 23rd. |

## Arklow Division, &c.—*continued.*

| 1869. | Temperature. A. At Sea. | Temperature. B. Near the Shore. | Distance from Land. | Depth of Water. | State of Tide, &c. | Wind. | Temperature of Air. | Hour at which Temperature taken. | Observations. |
|---|---|---|---|---|---|---|---|---|---|
| July. | ° | ° | Miles. | Feet. | | | ° | | |
| 1 } 2 } | – | – | — | – | — | — | — | — | Thermometer arrived on 2nd. |
| 3 | 58 | 54 | 2 | 7 | Flowing | S | 72 | 11 30 a.m. | Hazy. |
| 5 | 58 | 54 | 2½ | 8 | Flood | SSW | 68 | Noon | Cloudy. |
| 6 | – | – | — | – | — | — | — | — | Impracticable. |
| 7 | – | – | — | – | — | — | — | — | do. |
| 8 | – | – | — | – | — | — | — | — | do. |
| 9 | – | – | — | – | — | — | — | — | do. |
| 10 | 60 | 50 | 3 | 8½ | Ebb | SW | 70 | 12 30 p.m. | Cloudy. |
| 12 | 50 | 50 | 3½ | 10 | do. | NW | 66 | 12 20 p.m. | do. |
| 13 | 60 | 52 | 3½ | 10½ | High water | NW | 70 | 12 30 p.m. | do. |
| 14 | 58 | 54 | 3¼ | 10 | Flowing | WNW | 84 | 12 10 p.m. | do. |
| 15 | 58 | 54 | 3½ | 10¼ | Flood | SW | 84 | 12 15 p.m. | do. |
| 16 | 60 | 56 | 4 | 11 | do. | S | 86 | 11 40 a.m. | do. |
| 17 | 58 | 54 | 4 | 11 | do. | SW | 82 | Noon | Foggy. |
| 19 | – | – | — | – | — | — | — | — | Impracticable. |
| 20 | 60 | 56 | 4 | 11 | Ebb | S | 76 | 12 30 p.m. | Foggy. |
| 21 | 58 | 54 | 4½ | 12 | do. | S | 76 | 11 40 a.m. | do. |
| 22 | 60 | 52 | 4 | 10 | do. | SW | 72 | Noon | Cloudy. |
| 23 | 60 | 52 | 4 | 10½ | do. | SW | 70 | 11 50 a.m. | do. |
| 24 | 60 | 52 | 4 | 11 | do. | S | 72 | 12 30 p.m. | Clear. |
| 26 | 60 | 52 | 4 | 12 | Flood | NW | 72 | 12 30 p.m. | Cloudy. |
| 27 | – | – | — | – | — | — | — | — | Crew employed. |
| 28 | 60 | 52 | 4½ | 12 | Flood | SW | 68 | 11 40 a.m. | Cloudy. |
| 29 | – | – | — | – | — | — | — | — | Impracticable. |
| 30 | 60 | 50 | 1 | 7 | Flood | SW | 64 | 1 p.m. | Rain. |
| 31 | 60 | 52 | 4½ | 12 | do. | SW | 68 | 11 40 a.m. | Cloudy. |

## Dublin Division.—Howth Station, Co. Dublin.

Taken by William Horn.

| | | | | | | | | | |
|---|---|---|---|---|---|---|---|---|---|
| May. | | | | | | | | | |
| 10 | – | 49 | 300 yds. | 6 feet | ¼ flood | NNW | 50 | Noon. | Cloudy. |
| 11 | – | 49 | 330 | 4 feet | do. | NW | 50 | do. | Cloudy, rain. |
| 12 | – | 48 | 400 | 6 feet | ⅔ flood | NW | 50 | do. | Rough weather. |
| 13 | 40 | – | 600 | 3½ fathoms | High water | E | 50 | do. | Dry, harsh wind. |
| 14 | – | 50 | 400 | 7 feet | Last ¼ flood | E | 50 | do. | Overcast. |
| 15 | 50 | – | 600 | 3 fathoms | ¼ flood | E | 50 | do. | do. |
| 17 | – | 50 | 20 | 7 feet | ¾ flood | N E | 50 | do. | Thick weather. |
| 18 | – | 50 | 50 | 14 feet | ½ flood | N | 50 | do. | do. |
| 19 | – | 50 | 400 | 11 feet | ¾ flood | N | 50 | do. | Showery. |
| 20 | 40 | – | 900 | 3½ fathoms | Ebb | N E | 50 | do. | Thunder. |
| 21 | – | 50 | 700 | 6 feet | ¼ ebb | E | 50 | do. | Cloudy. |
| 22 | – | 50 | 600 | 3 fathoms | do. | E | 50 | do. | Overcast. |
| 24 | – | 50 | 300 | do. | ½ ebb | E | 50 | do. | do. |
| 25 | – | 50 | 100 | do. | ¾ ebb | E N E | 50 | do. | Very rainy. |
| 26 | 50 | – | 700 | 5 fathoms | 1st of ebb | E N E | 40 | do. | Rough weather. |
| 27 | 50 | – | 600 | 4 fathoms | High water | N E | 40 | do. | Fine. |
| 28 | – | 50 | 400 | 3 fathoms | Last ¼ flood | N | 40 | do. | Calm. |
| 29 | – | 50 | 50 | 2 fathoms | 1st ¼ ebb | S E | 50 | do. | Cloudy. |
| 31 | 50 | – | ½ mile | 3½ fathoms | ½ flood | — | 50 | do. | — |

## DUBLIN DIVISION, &c.—continued.

| 1869. | Temperature. A. At Sea. | B. Near the Shore. | Distance from Land. | Depth of Water. | State of Tide, &c. | Wind. | Temperature of Air. | Hour at which Temperature taken. | Observations. |
|---|---|---|---|---|---|---|---|---|---|
| **June.** | ° | ° | | | | | ° | | |
| 1 | — | 50 | 3 yards | 6 feet | Flood | S E | 50 | Noon | Overcast. |
| 2 | — | 50 | 600 yards | do. | do. | S E | 50 | do. | Thick weather. |
| 3 | — | 50 | 300 yards | 12 feet | do. | W | 50 | do. | Overcast. |
| 4 | — | 50 | 500 yards | 14 feet | Ebb | N W | 50 | do. | do. |
| 5 | — | 50 | 30 yards | 9 feet | do. | S W | 60 | do. | do. |
| 7 | — | 50 | 100 yards | 20 feet | do. | S | 60 | do. | Cloudy. |
| 8 | — | 50 | 900 yards | 10 feet | do. | N | 50 | do. | Fine. |
| 9 | — | 50 | 15 yards | 9 feet | do. | N | 50 | do. | On Kane's oyster bed. |
| 10 | 50 | — | 200 yards | 20 feet | do. | N | 50 | do. | Fine. |
| 11 | — | 50 | 60 yards | 10 feet | High water | N | 50 | do. | do. |
| 12 | 50 | — | 600 yards | 4½ fathoms | Flood | S W | 50 | do. | At Ireland's Eye; fine |
| 14 | — | 50 | 50 yards | 15 feet | do. | S W | 60 | do. | Cloudy. |
| 15 | — | 50 | 60 yards | 9 feet | do. | N | 60 | do. | do. |
| 16 | — | 50 | 50 yards | 10 feet | do. | — | 60 | do. | Showery. |
| 17 | 50 | — | ½ mile | 3 fathoms | do. | S | 60 | do. | Cloudy. |
| 18 | — | 50 | 500 yards | 9 feet | Ebb | S W | 60 | do. | do. |
| 19 | 50 | — | ½ mile | 6 fathoms | do. | S W | 60 | do. | Fine. |
| 21 | 50 | — | do. | do. | do. | S W | 60 | do. | do. |
| 22 | 50 | — | do. | 5 fathoms | do. | N E | 60 | do. | do. |
| 23 | — | 50 | 500 yards | 4 fathoms | do. | N E | 60 | do. | do. |
| 24 | — | 50 | 20 yards | 20 feet | do. | W | 60 | do. | On Kane's oyster bed. |
| 25 | 50 | — | 1 mile | 6 fathoms | Flood | E | 60 | do. | Fine. |
| 26 | — | 50 | 20 yards | 9 feet | do. | — | 70 | do. | Cloudy; on Kane's oyster bed. |
| 28 | — | 50 | 50 yards | 12 feet | do. | N E | 60 | do. | Fine. |
| 29 | — | 50 | 19 yards | 11 feet | do. | N | 60 | do. | do. |
| 30 | — | 50 | do. | 15 feet | do. | N | 60 | do. | do. |
| **July.** | | | | | | | | | |
| 1 | 50 | — | ¾ mile | 6 fathoms | Flood | N E | 60 | Noon | At sea, between Ireland's Eye and Lighthouse. |
| 2 | 50 | — | 1 mile | 5½ fathoms | do. | E | 60 | do. | Fine. |
| 3 | 50 | — | ½ mile | 2½ fathoms | Ebb | S E | 60 | do. | do. |
| 5 | 50 | — | ½ mile | 6 fathoms | do. | W | 70 | do. | do. |
| 6 | 50 | — | do. | do. | do. | W | 60 | do. | Cloudy. |
| 7 | — | 50 | 40 yards | 6 feet | do. | W | 60 | do. | Fine. |
| 8 | — | 50 | 300 yards | 9 feet | do. | S | 60 | do. | do. |
| 9 | — | 50 | 600 yards | 3 fathoms | do. | W | 70 | do. | do. |
| 10 | — | 50 | 500 yards | 2 fathoms | Flood | S W | 70 | do. | do. |
| 12 | — | 50 | 60 yards | 3½ fathoms | do. | E | 60 | do. | Cloudy. |
| 13 | — | 50 | 70 yards | do. | do. | N W | 70 | do. | do. |
| 14 | 50 | — | 1000 yards | do. | do. | W | 70 | do. | do. |
| 15 | 50 | — | ½ mile | 4½ fathoms | do. | W | 70 | do. | do. |
| 16 | 50 | — | do. | do. | do. | S E | 70 | do. | do. |
| 17 | 50 | — | 300 yards | 3½ fathoms | Ebb | S E | 70 | do. | do. |
| 19 | 60 | — | 400 yards | 4½ fathoms | do. | E | 70 | do. | do. |
| 20 | 50 | — | 300 yards | 2¾ fathoms | do. | S | 70 | do. | do. |
| 21 | — | 60 | 40 yards | 3½ fathoms | do. | S W | 60 | do. | Strong breeze. |
| 22 | 60 | — | 300 yards | 2 fathoms | do. | S W | 70 | do. | Light air. |
| 23 | 60 | — | do. | 2½ fathoms | do. | S W | 75 | do. | do. |
| 24 | — | 60 | 400 yards | 3 fathoms | do. | S E | 70 | do. | Light air; cloudy. |
| 26 | — | 60 | 600 yards | 2¾ fathoms | do. | N W | 70 | do. | do. |
| 27 | — | 60 | 200 yards | do. | Flood | W | 60 | do. | do. |
| 28 | — | 60 | 600 yards | 2½ fathoms | do. | W | 70 | do. | do. |
| 29 | — | 50 | do. | do. | do. | S W | 60 | do. | Stormy. |
| 30 | — | 50 | do. | 6 fathoms | do. | W | 60 | do. | Fine. |
| 31 | 50 | — | ¾ mile | do. | do. | W | 70 | do. | do. |

CARLINGFORD DIVISION.—CRANFIELD POINT STATION, CO. DOWN.

Taken by DANIEL COLLINS, Chief Officer.

| 1869. | Temperature. A. At Sea. | Temperature. B. Near the Shore. | Distance from Land. | Depth of Water. | State of Tide, &c. | Wind. | Temperature of Air. | Hour at which Temperature taken. | Observations. |
|---|---|---|---|---|---|---|---|---|---|
| | ° | ° | Miles. | | | | ° | | |
| **May.** | | | | | | | | | |
| 12 | – | 55 | – | 4 feet | High water | N | 56 | 11 30 a.m. | No Oyster Beds at |
| 13 | – | 55 | – | 5 feet | do. | S | 56 | Noon | Cranfield Station. |
| 14 | – | 54 | – | do. | do. | E | 57 | do. | Fresh wind & cloudy |
| 15 | – | 54 | – | do. | Flood | E by S | 56 | do. | do. |
| 17 | – | 56 | – | do. | do. | S E | 58 | do. | do. |
| 18 | – | 56 | – | 4 feet | do. | E | 58 | do. | do. |
| 19 | 57 | – | ½ | 4 fathoms | do. | N E | 60 | do. | do. |
| 20 | 58 | – | ½ | do. | do. | N | 60 | do. | do. |
| 21 | – | 56 | – | 5 feet | Low water | N N E | 58 | do. | do. |
| 22 | 54 | – | 1 | 6 fathoms | do. | N N W | 58 | do. | Moderate wind and cloudy. |
| 24 | – | 55 | – | 4 feet | Ebb | N W | 58 | do. | do. |
| 25 | – | 55 | – | do. | do. | N E | 60 | do. | Fresh wind & cloudy |
| 26 | – | 57 | – | do. | do. | E | 60 | do. | do. |
| 27 | – | 56 | – | do. | do. | E S E | 61 | do. | do. |
| 28 | – | 56 | – | 6 feet | High water | E S E | 61 | do. | do. |
| 29 | 57 | – | ½ | 5 fathoms | do. | S | 60 | do. | do. |
| 31 | 56 | – | ¾ | 2½ fathoms | Flood | S S E | 59 | do. | do. |
| **June.** | | | | | | | | | |
| 1 | – | 57 | – | 4 feet | Flood | N N W | 60 | Noon | |
| 2 | 55 | – | ½ | 4 fathoms | do. | S S W | 60 | do. | |
| 3 | 56 | – | 1 | 5 fathoms | do. | S W | 61 | do. | Moderate breeze and cloudy. |
| 4 | 56 | – | 1 | do. | do. | W S W | 60 | do. | do. |
| 5 | 58 | – | ¾ | do. | Low water | S W | 63 | do. | do. |
| 7 | – | 63 | – | 4 feet | Ebb | W | 64 | do. | do. |
| 8 | 62 | – | 1½ | 5½ fathoms | do. | N W | 65 | do. | Moderate breeze and clear. |
| 9 | 62 | – | 1 | 5 fathoms | do. | Var. | 65 | do. | do. |
| 10 | – | 63 | – | 5 feet | do. | Var. | 65 | do. | do. |
| 11 | 60 | – | 1½ | 6 fathoms | do. | Var. | 65 | do. | Fresh breeze and cloudy. |
| 12 | – | 62 | – | 5 feet | High water | S W | 64 | do. | Moderate breeze and cloudy. |
| 14 | – | 61 | – | do. | Flood | N | 63 | do. | do. |
| 15 | – | 60 | – | do. | do. | N | 63 | do. | Strong gales, &c. |
| 16 | – | 60 | – | do. | do. | N W | 63 | do. | Fresh breezes. |
| 17 | – | 59 | – | do. | do. | N W | 62 | do. | do. |
| 18 | – | 59 | – | do. | Low water | N W | 63 | do. | do. |
| 19 | 56 | – | 1 | 5 fathoms | Ebb | N W | 63 | do. | Moderate and cloudy |
| 21 | 57 | – | 1½ | do. | do. | N | 63 | do. | do. |
| 22 | – | 63 | – | 5 feet | do. | N | 67 | do. | Moderate and clear. |
| 23 | – | 63 | – | do. | do. | N W | 67 | do. | do. |
| 24 | – | 64 | – | do. | do. | N W | 69 | do. | do. |
| 25 | 60 | – | 1 | 5 fathoms | High water | Var. | 72 | do. | Moderate and hazy. |
| 26 | 62 | – | 1½ | 6½ fathoms | do. | S E | 75 | do. | do. |
| 28 | – | 63 | – | 5 feet | Flood | N | 70 | do. | do. |
| 29 | – | 63 | – | 6 feet | do. | N E | 73 | do. | Moderate and clear. |
| 30 | – | 65 | – | 5 feet | do. | E N E | 78 | do. | do. |

## CARLINGFORD DIVISION, &c.—*continued.*

| 1869. | Temperature. A. At Sea. | Temperature. B. Near the Shore. | Distance from Land. | Depth of Water. | State of Tide, &c. | Wind. | Temperature of Air. | Hour at which Temperature taken. | Observations. |
|---|---|---|---|---|---|---|---|---|---|
| **July.** | ° | ° | Miles. | | | | ° | | |
| 1 | – | 66 | — | 4 feet | Flood | S W | 78 | Noon | |
| 2 | – | 67 | — | do. | do. | N | 77 | do. | |
| 3 | 65 | – | 1½ | 4 fathoms | Low water | N E | 75 | do. | Fresh breezes. |
| 5 | 66 | – | 1 | 3 fathoms | do. | Var. | 77 | do. | Moderate breezes. |
| 6 | – | 66 | — | 4 feet | Ebb | N W | 75 | do. | Fresh breezes. |
| 7 | – | 66 | — | do. | do. | S E | 76 | do. | do. |
| 8 | – | 66 | — | 5 feet | do. | S S E | 76 | do. | do. |
| 9 | – | 65 | — | do. | do. | S | 70 | do. | do. |
| 10 | – | 66 | — | do. | do. | S | 74 | do. | Fresh breezes; clear. |
| 12 | 64 | – | 2 | 12 fathoms | High water | S E | 71 | do. | do. |
| 13 | – | 66 | — | 6 feet | Flood | W | 70 | do. | do. |
| 14 | – | 65 | — | do. | do. | N W | 70 | do. | do. |
| 15 | 65 | – | 1 | 4 fathoms | do. | N Wv. | 82 | do. | do. |
| 16 | 64 | – | 1½ | 6 fathoms | do. | S | 80 | do. | do. |
| 17 | – | 67 | — | 4 feet | do. | E | 82 | do. | do. |
| 19 | 67 | – | 1 | 4 fathoms | Low water | S S E | 83 | do. | do. |
| 20 | – | 70 | — | 3 feet | Ebb | S | 84 | do. | do. |
| 21 | – | 68 | — | do. | do. | S S W | 80 | do. | Fresh breezes; hazy |
| 22 | – | 72 | — | 4 feet | do. | S by W | 82 | do. | Moderate breeze; fog |
| 23 | – | 70 | — | do. | do. | Var. | 80 | do. | do. |
| 24 | 66 | – | 2 | 16 fathoms | do. | S W | 76 | do. | Moderate breeze; rain |
| 26 | 64 | – | ½ | 6 fathoms | High water | W | 76 | do. | Fresh breeze; cloudy |
| 27 | – | 67 | — | 6 feet | Flood | Var. | 80 | do. | Moderate breeze; clear. |
| 28 | – | 66 | — | do. | do. | S | 68 | do. | Fresh gales; rain. |
| 29 | – | 60 | — | 5 feet | do. | S W | 65 | do. | Fresh breezes & rain. |
| 30 | – | 60 | — | do. | do. | S S W | 65 | do. | do. |
| 31 | 65 | – | 1 | 4 fathoms | do. | W S W | 78 | do. | do. |

## CARRICKFERGUS DIVISION.—CARRICKFERGUS STATION, CO. ANTRIM.

### Taken by WILLIAM BAVAGE, Chief Boatman.

| May. | | | | | | | | | |
|---|---|---|---|---|---|---|---|---|---|
| 10 | – | 49 | 1½ miles | 4 fathoms | Ebb | N N E | 50 | Noon | Light airs and hazy. |
| 11 | – | 49 | 1 mile | 3½ fathoms | do. | W | 50 | do. | Moderate and fine. |
| 12 | – | 48 | do. | 3 fathoms | do. | N W | 49 | do. | Moderate & cloudy. |
| 13 | – | 49 | ¾ mile | do. | do. | E S E | 50 | do. | Moderate and fine. |
| 14 | – | 50 | 1 mile | do. | Flood | E S E | 51 | do. | do. |
| 15 | – | 52 | 300 yards | 1½ fathoms | do. | E S E | 51 | do | Strong winds; clear. |
| 17 | – | 51 | 1½ miles | 3½ fathoms | do. | E S E | 51 | 12 20 p.m. | Moderate & cloudy. |
| 18 | – | 47 | 300 yards | 1½ fathoms | do. | N | 48 | Noon | Light airs and rain. |
| 19 | – | 50 | 1½ miles | 3 fathoms | do. | N | 51 | do. | Fresh breeze; clear. |
| 20 | – | 48 | 1 mile | do. | Ebb | N N W | 50 | 12 20 p.m. | Fresh breeze; cloudy |
| 21 | – | 52 | 1½ miles | 3½ fathoms | do. | N E | 54 | do. | Moderate and fine. |
| 22 | – | 53 | 300 yards | 5 feet | do. | W | 56 | Noon | Light breeze; cloudy |
| 24 | – | 52 | 1 mile | 3½ feet | do. | E | 54 | do. | Moderate breeze and cloudy. |
| 25 | – | 49 | 1½ miles | 3½ feet | do. | E | 50 | do. | Moderate & overcast. |
| 26 | – | 50 | 300 yards | 8 feet | do. | N E | 51 | 12 15 p.m. | Fresh breeze; cloudy |
| 27 | – | 47 | 1 mile | 3½ feet | do. | N N E | 50 | Noon | do. |
| 28 | – | 50 | 300 yards | 10 feet | Flood | N E | 51 | do. | Fresh breeze; fine. |
| 29 | – | 55 | do. | 9 feet | do. | N N E | 53 | 12 15 p.m. | do. |
| 31 | – | 52 | do. | 7 feet | do. | N E | 55 | do. | Moderate and fine. |

## CARRICKFERGUS DIVISION, &c.—*continued.*

| 1869. | Temperature. A. At Sea. | Temperature. B. Near the Shore. | Distance from Land. | Depth of Water. | State of Tide, &c. | Wind. | Temperature of Air. | Hour at which Temperature taken. | Observations. |
|---|---|---|---|---|---|---|---|---|---|
| **June.** | ° | ° | | | | | ° | | |
| 1 | – | 59 | 1½ miles | 4½ fathoms | Flood | N N E | 60 | 12 20 p.m. | Fine. |
| 2 | – | 56 | 1¼ miles | 3½ fathoms | do. | S W | 59 | 12 15 p.m. | Hazy. |
| 3 | – | 52 | 1 mile | 3 fathoms | do. | S W | 53 | Noon | Fresh breeze; cloudy |
| 4 | – | 53 | do. | 2¾ fathoms | Ebb | W | 58 | do. | Moderate & cloudy. |
| 5 | – | 54 | 1½ miles | 3 fathoms | do. | W S W | 58 | 12 20 p.m. | Squally and rain. |
| 7 | – | 58 | 1½ miles | 3¼ fathoms | do. | W S W | 61 | Noon | Light breeze; fine. |
| 8 | – | 55 | 300 yards | 8 feet | do. | N | 57 | do. | Fresh breeze; fine. |
| 9 | – | 57 | 1¼ miles | 3 fathoms | do. | N W | 59 | 12 20 p.m. | do. |
| 10 | – | 55 | 1 mile | do. | do. | N | 57 | 12 30 p.m. | do. |
| 11 | – | 56 | 300 yards | 9 feet | do. | N | 58 | Noon | Light breeze; fine. |
| 12 | – | 55 | 1½ miles | 5 fathoms | Flood | W | 57 | do. | Moderate & cloudy. |
| 14 | – | 57 | 1 mile | 3 fathoms | do. | W S W | 58 | do. | do. |
| 15 | – | 51 | 200 yards | 7 feet | do. | N N W | 51 | do. | Strong breezes and squally. |
| 16 | – | 52 | 1¼ miles | 3½ fathoms | do. | N | 55 | 12 15 p.m. | Moderate & cloudy. |
| 17 | – | 56 | 1½ miles | do. | do. | N W | 60 | 12 20 p.m. | do. |
| 18 | – | 54 | do. | 3¼ fathoms | do. | N | 57 | 12 30 p.m. | do. |
| 19 | – | 55 | 1 mile | 2½ fathoms | Ebb | N W | 57 | 12 15 p.m. | do |
| 21 | – | 54 | 300 yards | 5 feet | do. | N N W | 56 | Noon | Light airs; cloudy. |
| 22 | – | 57 | do. | 6 feet | do. | N W | 61 | 12 30 p.m. | Fresh and cloudy. |
| 23 | – | 58 | 1½ miles | 3¾ fathoms | do. | W | 62 | Noon | Moderate & cloudy. |
| 24 | – | 58 | 1 mile | 3 fathoms | do. | N W | 62 | do. | Fresh breezes. |
| 25 | – | 57 | 1½ miles | 4 fathoms | do. | E | 62 | 12 15 p.m. | Light breezes. |
| 26 | – | 58 | 300 yards | 8 feet | Flood | N W | 64 | Noon | Moderate breezes. |
| 28 | – | 60 | 1¼ miles | 3½ fathoms | do. | N W | 62 | 12 15 p.m. | do. |
| 29 | – | 60 | 1½ miles | 3¼ fathoms | do. | E | 62 | 12 20 p.m. | Moderate breezes; fine. |
| 30 | – | 60 | 1 mile | 3 fathoms | do. | E | 62 | Noon | do. |
| **July.** | | | | | | | | | |
| 1 | – | 61 | 1¼ miles | 3¾ fathoms | Flood | E | 64 | 12 20 p.m. | Moderate and fine. |
| 2 | – | 61 | 1½ miles | do. | do. | E S E | 65 | Noon | Moderate and hazy. |
| 3 | – | 64 | 1¾ miles | 4½ fathoms | do. | E S E | 67 | 12 40 p.m. | Moderate and fine. |
| 5 | – | 63 | 300 yards | 6 feet | Ebb | S W | 67 | 12 15 p.m. | Moderate and rain. |
| 6 | – | 62 | 1 mile | 3 fathoms | do. | W S W | 67 | 12 30 p.m. | Moderate & cloudy. |
| 7 | – | 60 | 300 yards | 9 feet | do. | S | 67 | 12 20 p.m. | Fresh breeze; cloudy |
| 8 | – | 62 | do. | 9½ feet | do. | S | 64 | 12 15 p.m. | Strong breeze; rain. |
| 9 | – | 60 | 250 yards | 8 feet | do. | S W | 65 | 12 40 p.m. | Do. cloudy. |
| 10 | – | 60 | 1¼ miles | 3½ fathoms | do. | S W | 67 | Noon | Moderate breeze; cloudy. |
| 12 | – | 62 | 1 mile | 3 fathoms | Flood | W | 68 | do. | Light breeze; cloudy |
| 13 | – | 59 | 1½ miles | 4½ fathoms | do. | N W | 63 | 12 20 p.m. | Moderate & cloudy |
| 14 | – | 60 | 300 yards | 10 feet | do. | W | 67 | 12 30 p.m. | Strong breeze; do. |
| 15 | – | 64 | 1½ miles | 4 fathoms | do. | W | 69 | Noon | Light breeze; fine. |
| 16 | – | 60 | 250 yards | 7 feet | do. | E | 62 | do. | Fresh do.; thick fog |
| 17 | – | 66 | 2 miles | 6 fathoms | do. | E | 68 | 12 20 p.m. | Moderate and fine. |
| 19 | – | 60 | 1¼ miles | 3 fathoms | Ebb | E | 64 | 12 15 p.m. | do. |
| 20 | – | – | — | — | — | – | – | — | |
| 21 | – | 64 | 1 mile | 2½ fathoms | Ebb | S | 68 | Noon | Moderate and fine. |
| 22 | – | – | — | — | — | – | – | — | |
| 23 | – | 62 | 300 yards | 10 feet | Ebb | S | 66 | Noon | Fresh breezes; rain. |
| 24 | – | 60 | 1¼ miles | 3½ fathoms | do. | W | 65 | do. | do. |
| 26 | – | 62 | 1½ miles | 4½ fathoms | Flood | N W | 65 | do. | Light breeze; cloudy |
| 27 | – | 62 | 1¼ miles | 3 fathoms | do. | E by N | 64 | do. | do. |
| 28 | – | 64 | 1 mile | 2½ fathoms | do. | S E | 68 | do. | Moderate breeze and hazy. |
| 29 | – | 64 | 300 yards | 8 fathoms | do. | S | 65 | do. | Strong breeze; rain. |
| 30 | – | 61 | 1¼ miles | 3 fathoms | do. | S | 67 | do. | Moderate do. stormy |
| 31 | – | 63 | 1 mile | 2¼ fathoms | do. | S | 66 | do. | Do. fine. |

RATHMULLEN DIVISION.—SHEEPHAVEN STATION, CO. DONEGAL.

Taken by WILLIAM BOYD, Comd. Boatman.

| 1869. | Temperature. | | Distance from Land. | Depth of Water. | State of Tide, &c. | Wind. | Temperature of Air. | Hour at which Temperature taken. | Observations. |
|---|---|---|---|---|---|---|---|---|---|
| | A. At Sea. | B. Near the Shore. | | | | | | | |
| **May.** | ° | ° | | Feet. | | | ° | | |
| 10 | – | 49 | — | 2 | Flood | N | 52 | Noon | Frost in the morn- |
| 11 | – | 49 | — | 2½ | do. | N W | 52 | 11 45 a.m. | ings. |
| 12 | – | 50 | — | 2 | Low water | N W | 53 | Noon | |
| 13 | – | 50 | — | 3 | Ebb | N W | 52 | do. | |
| 14 | – | 49 | — | 2 | do. | E | 48 | do. | |
| 15 | – | 48 | — | 3 | do. | E | 46 | do. | |
| 17 | – | 48 | — | 3 | do. | S E | 50 | do. | |
| 18 | – | 49 | — | 2½ | do. | N E | 52 | 11 40 a.m. | |
| 19 | – | 49 | — | 3 | do. | N E | 51 | Noon | |
| 20 | – | 49 | — | 2 | Flood | N | 51 | 12 20 p.m. | |
| 21 | – | 50 | — | 3 | do. | N E | 52 | Noon | |
| 22 | – | 50 | — | 3 | do. | N E | 52 | do. | |
| 24 | – | 53 | — | 2 | do. | S | 56 | 11 40 a.m. | |
| 25 | – | 51 | — | 3 | do. | S E | 52 | Noon | |
| 26 | – | 50 | — | 2 | Low water | S E | 51 | do. | |
| 27 | – | 48 | — | 2 | Ebb | S E | 50 | do. | |
| 28 | – | 49 | — | 3 | do. | S E | 51 | 11 30 a.m. | |
| 29 | – | 51 | — | 2 | do. | N | 52 | do. | |
| 31 | – | 52 | — | 2 | do. | N W | 53 | Noon | |
| **June.** | | | | | | | | | |
| 1 | – | 52 | — | 2 | Ebb | W | 54 | Noon | |
| 2 | – | 52 | — | 2 | do. | N W | 55 | do. | |
| 3 | – | 53 | — | 2 | High water | W N W | 55 | do. | |
| 4 | – | 54 | — | 2 | Flood | W | 55 | do. | |
| 5 | – | 54 | — | 2 | do. | W | 55 | do. | |
| 7 | – | 55 | — | 2 | do. | W | 56 | do. | |
| 8 | – | 55 | — | 2 | do. | W | 56 | do. | |
| 9 | – | 57 | — | 2 | do. | W | 58 | do. | |
| 10 | – | 56 | — | 3 | do. | N N E | 57 | do. | |
| 11 | – | 56 | — | 2 | Low water | N N E | 57 | do. | |
| 12 | – | 54 | — | 2 | Ebb | N E | 56 | do. | |
| 14 | – | 54 | — | 3 | do. | W | 56 | do. | |
| 15 | – | 53 | — | 2½ | do. | N N E | 56 | do. | |
| 16 | – | 56 | — | 2 | do. | W | 58 | do. | |
| 17 | – | 58 | — | 3 | do. | W | 58 | do. | |
| 18 | – | 55 | — | 2 | High water | N W | 60 | do. | |
| 19 | – | 58 | — | 2 | Flood | N | 60 | do. | |
| 21 | – | 59 | — | 2 | do. | N N W | 60 | do. | |
| 22 | – | 61 | — | 2 | do. | N N W | 62 | do. | |
| 23 | – | 62 | — | 2 | do. | N N W | 64 | do. | |
| 24 | – | 64 | — | 3 | do. | N W | 66 | do. | |
| 25 | – | 66 | — | 2 | Low water | E N E | 68 | do. | |
| 26 | – | 66 | — | 2 | Ebb | N E | 68 | do. | |
| 28 | – | 67 | — | 2 | do. | N E | 70 | do. | |
| 29 | – | 68 | — | 3 | do. | N E | 70 | do. | |
| 30 | – | 68 | — | 2 | do. | E N E | 71 | do. | |

RATHMULLEN DIVISION, &c.—*continued.*

| 1869. | Temperature. A. At Sea. | B. Near the Shore. | Distance from Land. | Depth of Water. | State of Tide, &c. | Wind. | Temperature of Air. | Hour at which Temperature taken. | Observations. |
|---|---|---|---|---|---|---|---|---|---|
| July. | ° | ° | | Feet. | | | ° | | |
| 1 | — | 68 | — | 2 | Ebb | E | 70 | Noon | |
| 2 | — | 69 | — | 3 | do. | N E | 70 | do. | |
| 3 | — | 69 | — | 2 | High water | E | 70 | do. | |
| 5 | — | 66 | — | 3 | Flood | SW | 68 | do. | Rain. |
| 6 | — | 67 | — | 2 | do. | W | 69 | do. | |
| 7 | — | 68 | — | 2 | do. | S | 70 | do. | |
| 8 | — | 70 | — | 2 | do. | SW | 72 | do. | |
| 9 | — | 70 | — | 2 | do. | W | 73 | do. | [rain. |
| 10 | — | 68 | — | 2 | Low water | W | 70 | do. | Strong breezes and |
| 12 | — | 67 | — | 2 | Ebb | WNW | 69 | do. | do. |
| 13 | — | 66 | — | 2 | do. | WNW | 66 | do. | do. |
| 14 | — | 65 | — | 2 | do. | WNW | 66 | do. | |
| 15 | — | 67 | — | 2 | do. | WNW | 68 | do. | |
| 16 | — | 68 | — | 2 | do. | N E | 70 | do. | |
| 17 | — | 70 | — | 2 | High water | W | 74 | 11 40 a.m. | |
| 19 | — | 70 | — | 2 | Flood | N E | 73 | 11 30 a.m. | |
| 20 | — | 71 | — | 2 | do. | N E | 74 | Noon | |
| 21 | — | 72 | — | 2 | do. | S | 75 | do. | [showery. |
| 22 | — | 70 | — | 2 | do. | SW | 73 | do. | Strong breezes and |
| 23 | — | 69 | — | 2 | do. | WSW | 71 | do. | do. |
| 24 | — | 71 | — | 2 | Low water | SW | 73 | do. | |
| 26 | — | 73 | — | 2 | Ebb | NW | 76 | do. | |
| 27 | — | 73 | — | 2 | do. | W | 75 | do. | Rain. |
| 28 | — | 72 | — | 2 | do. | WNW | 74 | do. | do. |
| 29 | — | 70 | — | 2 | do. | SW | 72 | do. | do. |
| 30 | — | 68 | — | 2 | do. | W | 70 | do. | [showery. |
| 31 | — | 66 | — | 2 | do. | W | 68 | do. | Strong breezes and |

CARN DIVISION.—WATCH VESSEL, No. 39, OFF MOVILLE STATION, CO. DONEGAL.

Taken by DAVID WALLIS, Chief Boatman.

| May. | A. At Sea. | B. Near the Shore. | Distance from Land. | Depth of Water. | State of Tide, &c. | Wind. | Temperature of Air. | Hour at which Temperature taken. | Observations. |
|---|---|---|---|---|---|---|---|---|---|
| | | | | Fathoms. | | | | | |
| 10 | — | 43 | 300 yards | 3 | Ebb | N | 41 | Noon | |
| 11 | — | 49 | do. | $2\frac{3}{4}$ | do. | NW | 48 | 12 30 p.m. | |
| 12 | — | 43 | do. | 3 | do. | NW | 56 | Noon | |
| 13 | — | 44 | do. | 3 | do. | S E | 56 | do. | |
| 14 | — | 44 | do. | $3\frac{1}{4}$ | do. | S S E | 53 | do. | |
| 15 | — | 44 | do. | 4 | do. | S S E | 44 | do. | |
| 17 | — | 44 | do. | $3\frac{3}{4}$ | do. | S S E | 47 | do. | |
| 18 | — | 44 | do. | $3\frac{1}{2}$ | Flood | E | 46 | do. | |
| 19 | — | 44 | do. | $3\frac{1}{4}$ | do. | N | 45 | do. | |
| 20 | — | 44 | do. | $3\frac{1}{4}$ | do. | N | 44 | do. | |
| 21 | — | 46 | do. | $3\frac{1}{2}$ | do. | N N E | 48 | do. | |
| 22 | — | 46 | do. | 3 | do. | N N E | 47 | do. | |
| 24 | — | 46 | do. | $2\frac{1}{2}$ | Low water | E S E | 48 | do. | |
| 25 | — | 41 | do. | 3 | Ebb | E S E | 43 | do. | |
| 26 | — | 45 | do. | 3 | do. | E S E | 47 | do. | |
| 27 | — | 39 | do. | 3 | do. | E by N | 40 | do. | |
| 28 | — | 44 | do. | $3\frac{1}{2}$ | do. | N E | 51 | do. | |
| 29 | — | 45 | do. | $3\frac{1}{2}$ | do. | N by E | 48 | do. | |
| 31 | — | 45 | do. | $3\frac{1}{2}$ | do. | N N E | 59 | do. | |

CARN DIVISION, &c.—*continued.*

| 1869. | Temperature. A. At Sea. | Temperature. B. Near the Shore. | Distance from Land. | Depth of Water. | State of Tide, &c. | Wind. | Temperature of Air. | Hour at which Temperature taken. | Observations. |
|---|---|---|---|---|---|---|---|---|---|
| **June.** | ° | ° | | Fathoms. | | | ° | | |
| 1 | – | 45 | 300 yards | $3\frac{1}{2}$ | Ebb | WSW | 59 | Noon | |
| 2 | – | 47 | do. | $3\frac{1}{2}$ | do. | W | 52 | do. | |
| 3 | – | 46 | do. | $3\frac{1}{4}$ | do. | WNW | 46 | do. | |
| 4 | – | 47 | do. | $3\frac{1}{2}$ | do. | NNW | 52 | do. | |
| 5 | – | 48 | do. | $3\frac{1}{2}$ | do. | W | 54 | do. | |
| 7 | – | 49 | do. | $3\frac{1}{4}$ | do. | W | 55 | do. | |
| 8 | – | 49 | do. | $3\frac{1}{4}$ | do. | N | 50 | do. | |
| 9 | – | 49 | do. | 3 | Low water | NW | 50 | do. | |
| 10 | – | 41 | do. | $2\frac{3}{4}$ | Ebb | N | 48 | do. | |
| 11 | – | 50 | do. | 3 | do. | N | 56 | do. | |
| 12 | – | 50 | do. | $3\frac{1}{4}$ | do. | W | 48 | do. | |
| 14 | – | 50 | do. | $3\frac{1}{4}$ | do. | SW | 56 | do. | |
| 15 | – | 50 | do. | $3\frac{1}{2}$ | do. | N | 53 | do. | |
| 16 | – | 48 | do. | $3\frac{3}{4}$ | do. | N | 59 | 1 p.m. | |
| 17 | – | 50 | do. | $3\frac{1}{4}$ | Flood | Calm | 67 | Noon | |
| 18 | – | 50 | do. | $3\frac{1}{4}$ | do. | N | 55 | do. | |
| 19 | – | 50 | do. | $3\frac{1}{2}$ | do. | N | 53 | do. | |
| 21 | – | 51 | do. | 3 | do. | N | 57 | do. | |
| 22 | – | 51 | do. | $2\frac{3}{4}$ | do. | N | 54 | do. | |
| 23 | – | 52 | do. | 3 | do. | NNW | 59 | do. | |
| 24 | – | 52 | do. | 3 | Ebb | S E | 66 | do. | |
| 25 | – | 52 | do. | 3 | do. | E | 77 | do. | |
| 26 | – | 59 | do. | 3 | do. | E S E | 66 | do. | |
| 28 | – | 53 | do. | $3\frac{1}{4}$ | do. | N | 64 | do. | |
| 29 | – | 58 | do. | $3\frac{1}{2}$ | do. | N N E | 63 | do. | |
| 30 | – | 58 | do. | $3\frac{1}{2}$ | do. | N | 61 | do. | |
| **July.** | | | | | | | | | |
| 1 | – | 54 | 300 yards | $3\frac{3}{4}$ | High water | S E | 60 | Noon | |
| 2 | – | 56 | do. | $3\frac{3}{4}$ | Flood | S E | 65 | do. | |
| 3 | – | 56 | do. | $3\frac{1}{4}$ | do. | S E | 59 | do. | |
| 5 | – | 57 | do. | $3\frac{1}{4}$ | do. | WSW | 60 | do. | |
| 6 | – | 61 | do. | 3 | do. | WNW | 64 | do. | |
| 7 | – | 57 | do. | 3 | do. | SW | 63 | do. | |
| 8 | – | 63 | do. | 3 | Ebb | WSW | 63 | do. | |
| 9 | – | 54 | do. | 3 | do. | W | 59 | do. | |
| 10 | – | 56 | do. | 3 | do. | WNW | 60 | do. | |
| 12 | – | 59 | do. | 3 | do. | WNW | 64 | do. | |
| 13 | – | 52 | do. | $3\frac{1}{4}$ | do. | NW | 57 | do. | |
| 14 | – | 52 | do. | $3\frac{1}{2}$ | do. | WNW | 55 | do. | |
| 15 | – | 54 | do. | $3\frac{3}{4}$ | do. | W | 64 | do. | |
| 16 | – | 57 | do. | $3\frac{3}{4}$ | Flood | E S E | 69 | do. | |
| 17 | – | 57 | do. | $3\frac{1}{2}$ | do. | E | 72 | do. | |
| 19 | – | 58 | do. | $3\frac{1}{4}$ | do. | N E | 68 | do. | |
| 20 | – | 65 | do. | 3 | do. | Calm | 86 | do. | |
| 21 | – | 59 | do. | $2\frac{3}{4}$ | Low water | WSW | 63 | do. | |
| 22 | – | 58 | do. | $2\frac{1}{2}$ | Ebb | SW | 63 | do. | |
| 23 | – | 59 | do. | 3 | do. | WSW | 68 | do. | |
| 24 | – | 57 | do. | 3 | do. | W | 58 | do. | |
| 26 | – | 57 | do. | 3 | do. | NW | 62 | do. | |
| 27 | – | 55 | do. | $3\frac{1}{2}$ | do. | WSW | 52 | do. | |
| 28 | – | 56 | do. | 3 | do. | N | 67 | do. | |
| 29 | – | 61 | do. | $3\frac{1}{2}$ | do. | S | 51 | do. | |
| 30 | – | 55 | do. | $3\frac{1}{2}$ | do. | W | 59 | do. | |
| 31 | – | 54 | do. | $3\frac{1}{2}$ | High water | SW | 54 | do. | |

## RUTLAND DIVISION.—RUTLAND STATION, Co. DONEGAL.

Taken by E. CODRINGTON BALL, Divisional Officer, and M. M'CARTHY, Chief Boatman.

| 1869. | Temperature. | | Distance from Land. | Depth of Water. | State of Tide, &c. | Wind. | Temperature of Air. | Hour at which Temperature taken. | Observations. |
|---|---|---|---|---|---|---|---|---|---|
| | A. At Sea. | B. Near the Shore. | | | | | | | |
| **May.** | ° | ° | | Feet. | | | ° | | |
| 10 | – | 48 | — | 4 | Low water | N N W | 50 | 11 45 a.m. | |
| 11 | – | 48 | — | 5 | do. | N W | 50 | 12 15 p.m. | |
| 12 | – | 49 | — | 6 | Flood | N W | 50 | 11 30 a.m. | |
| 13 | – | 51 | — | 6 | do. | N | 56 | Noon | |
| 14 | – | 52 | — | 5 | do. | S E | 56 | do. | |
| 15 | – | 49 | — | 7 | do. | S S E | 47 | do. | |
| 17 | – | 48 | — | 7 | do. | S E | 50 | 12 30 p.m. | |
| 18 | – | 49 | — | 5 | High water | S E | 50 | 12 45 p.m. | |
| 19 | – | 49 | — | 8 | Flood | N E | 50 | 11 45 a.m. | |
| 20 | – | 50 | — | 8 | do. | N | 52 | Noon | |
| 21 | – | 50 | — | 6 | do. | N E | 50 | do. | |
| 22 | – | 49 | — | 6 | do. | N E | 51 | 12 45 p.m. | |
| 24 | – | 50 | — | 5 | do. | E N E | 51 | 1 p.m. | |
| 25 | – | 51 | — | 4 | Low water | E | 52 | 12 45 p.m. | |
| 26 | – | 50 | — | 4 | Ebb | E | 52 | Noon | |
| 27 | – | 49 | — | 5 | do. | E N E | 48 | 12 30 p.m. | |
| 28 | – | 50 | — | 6 | do. | E | 56 | 1 p.m. | |
| 29 | – | 50 | — | 4 | do. | E | 54 | 12 45 p.m. | |
| 31 | – | 49 | — | 6 | do. | N E | 56 | 1 p.m. | |
| **June.** | | | | | | | | | |
| 1 | – | 51 | — | 6 | Ebb | S E | 56 | Noon | |
| 2 | – | 52 | — | 6 | High water | N W | 56 | do. | |
| 3 | – | 52 | — | 6 | do. | N W | 54 | 1 p.m. | |
| 4 | – | 54 | — | 4 | Flood | N | 56 | 12 30 p.m. | |
| 5 | – | 54 | — | 6 | do. | S W | 58 | Noon | |
| 7 | – | 54 | — | 5 | do. | S W | 57 | 12 15 p.m. | |
| 8 | – | 55 | — | 6 | do. | S E | 58 | Noon | |
| 9 | – | 55 | — | 5 | do. | N N W | 57 | 12 15 p.m. | |
| 10 | – | 54 | — | 4 | Low water | N W | 54 | Noon | |
| 11 | – | 56 | — | 5 | do. | N | 60 | 1 p.m. | |
| 12 | – | 54 | — | 6 | Ebb | W S W | 52 | Noon | |
| 14 | – | 53 | — | 6 | do. | N W | 54 | do. | |
| 15 | – | 53 | — | 6 | do. | N | 56 | do. | |
| 16 | – | 54 | — | 7 | do. | W S W | 57 | 1 p.m. | |
| 17 | – | 54 | — | 6 | do. | W S W | 58 | Noon | |
| 18 | – | 55 | — | 7 | High water | N W | 58 | do. | |
| 19 | – | 56 | — | 6 | do. | N | 58 | 1 p.m. | |
| 21 | – | 56 | — | 6 | Flood | N | 59 | 12 30 p.m. | |
| 22 | – | 57 | — | 6 | do. | N | 59 | do. | |
| 23 | – | 57 | — | 7 | do. | N | 58 | Noon | |
| 24 | – | 58 | — | 7 | Low water | N | 60 | do. | |
| 25 | – | 59 | — | 5 | do. | N W | 64 | do. | |
| 26 | – | 59 | — | 4 | Flood | N | 65 | 1 p.m. | |
| 28 | – | 59 | — | 6 | do. | N E | 65 | Noon | |
| 29 | – | 59 | — | 6 | do. | N E | 65 | 12 30 p.m. | |
| 30 | – | 60 | — | 7 | do. | N E | 65 | 1 p.m. | |

## Rutland Division, &c.—*continued.*

| 1809. | Temperature. | | Distance from Land. | Depth of Water. | State of Tide, &c. | Wind. | Temperature of Air. | Hour at which Temperature taken. | Observations. |
|---|---|---|---|---|---|---|---|---|---|
| | A. At Sea. | B. Near the Shore. | | | | | | | |
| **July.** | ° | ° | | Feet. | | | ° | | |
| 1 | – | 60 | — | 7 | High water | N E | 64 | Noon | |
| 2 | – | 61 | — | 7 | do. | N | 64 | 12 30 p.m. | |
| 3 | – | 61 | — | 6 | Flood | S W | 63 | Noon | |
| 5 | – | 62 | — | 6 | do. | N | 64 | 1 p.m. | |
| 6 | – | 61 | — | 6 | do. | S W | 63 | 1 p.m. | |
| 7 | – | 62 | — | 5 | do. | S W | 64 | 12 30 p.m. | |
| 8 | – | 61 | — | 6 | Ebb | S W | 64 | Noon | |
| 9 | – | 61 | — | 4 | Low water | S W | 64 | 12 30 p.m. | |
| 10 | – | 64 | — | 5 | do. | S W | 66 | 1 p.m. | |
| 12 | – | 64 | — | 5 | Ebb | S W | 64 | Noon | |
| 13 | – | 60 | — | 4 | do. | N W | 64 | 1 p.m. | |
| 14 | – | 59 | — | 6 | do. | W | 62 | Noon | |
| 15 | – | 59 | — | 7 | do. | N W | 61 | 1 30 p.m. | |
| 16 | – | 62 | — | 8 | Flood | W | 64 | Noon | |
| 17 | – | 64 | — | 8 | High water | S W | 65 | 12 30 p.m. | |
| 19 | – | 65 | — | 7 | Flood | N E | 66 | 11 a.m. | |
| 20 | – | 65 | — | 6 | do. | N E | 66 | Noon | |
| 21 | – | 64 | — | 5 | do. | N | 65 | do. | |
| 22 | – | 65 | — | 4 | do. | S W | 66 | 1 p.m. | |
| 23 | – | 64 | — | 4 | Low water | W | 66 | Noon | |
| 24 | – | 64 | — | 5 | do. | W | 65 | 1 p.m. | |
| 26 | – | 65 | — | 6 | Ebb | S W | 66 | 12 15 p.m. | |
| 27 | – | 65 | — | 7 | do. | S W | 66 | 1 15 p.m. | |
| 28 | – | 64 | — | 7 | do. | W | 65 | Noon | |
| 29 | – | 64 | — | 6 | do. | S S W | 64 | 12 30 p.m. | |
| 30 | – | 65 | — | 7 | High water | W | 64 | Noon | |
| 31 | – | 64 | — | 7 | do. | W | 65 | 1 p.m. | |

## Belmullet Division.—Ballyglass Station, Co. Mayo.

Taken by James Morgan, Chief Boatman.

| June. | A. | B. | Distance from Land | Depth of Water | State of Tide, &c. | Wind. | Temperature of Air. | Hour | Observations. |
|---|---|---|---|---|---|---|---|---|---|
| | | | | Fathoms. | | | | | |
| 8 | 55 | 58 | 440 yards. | 6 and 1 | Flood | N E | 76 | 11 45 a.m. | Moderate breezes and cloudy. |
| 9 | 58 | 58 | do. | 6 ,, 1 | do. | N E | 62 | 11 50 a.m. | do. |
| 10 | 58 | 58 | do. | 5½ ,, 1 | do. | N E | 62 | Noon | do. |
| 11 | 55 | 56 | do. | 6 ,, 1 | do. | N | 60 | 11 45 a.m. | do. |
| 12 | 55 | 56 | do. | 6 ,, 1 | do. | W | 60 | do. | Do. and hazy. |
| 14 | 54 | 56 | do. | 6 ,, 1 | Ebb | N W | 61 | 11 35 a.m. | Strong do. |
| 15 | 56 | 56 | do. | 7 ,, 2½ | do. | N W | 59 | 11 40 a.m. | Do. do. |
| 16 | 56 | 56 | do. | 6 ,, 2 | do. | N | 66 | do. | Moderate breezes and cloudy. |
| 17 | 55 | 58 | do. | 7 ,, 1 | do. | N W | 63 | do. | Do. and rain. |
| 18 | 54 | 57 | do. | 6 ,, 1 | Flood | N W | 62 | do. | Do. and hazy. |
| 19 | 55 | 56 | do. | 5 ,, 1 | do. | N | 60 | 11 50 a.m. | Do. do. |
| 21 | 58 | 57 | do. | 5 ,, 1 | do. | N E | 62 | 11 45 a.m. | Do. do. |
| 22 | 55 | 57 | do. | 6 ,, 1 | do. | N W | 63 | 11 50 a.m. | Do. and cloudy. |
| 23 | 55 | 55 | do. | 5 ,, 1 | do. | W by N | 62 | 11 45 a.m. | Do. do. |
| 24 | 58 | 59 | do. | 6 ,, 1 | Low water | S W | 64 | 11 40 a.m. | Do. do. |
| 25 | 59 | 59 | do. | 6 ,, 1 | Flood | S W | 72 | Noon | Do. do. |
| 26 | 58 | 61 | do. | 5 ,, 1 | do. | N | 67 | do. | Do. do. |
| 28 | 58 | 55 | do. | 6 ,, 1 | Ebb | N E | 64 | 11 50 a.m. | Do. do. |
| 29 | 58 | 60 | do. | 6 ,, 1 | do. | N E | 66 | 11 50 a.m. | Do. and clear. |
| 30 | 58 | 61 | do. | 5 ,, 1 | do. | N E | 71 | 11 45 a.m. | Do. do. |

## BELMULLET DIVISION, &c.—*continued*.

| 1869. | Temperature. A. At Sea. | Temperature. B. Near the Shore. | Distance from Land. | Depth of Water. | State of Tide, &c. | Wind. | Temperature of Air. | Hour at which Temperature taken. | Observations. |
|---|---|---|---|---|---|---|---|---|---|
| July. | ° | ° | | Fathoms. | | | ° | | |
| 1 | 58 | 57 | ¼ of a mile. | 6 and 1 | Ebb | N E | 72 | 11 50 a.m. | Light breezes & clear |
| 2 | 58 | 57 | do. | 5½ „ 1 | do. | N | 84 | 11 45 a.m. | Do. do. |
| 3 | 63 | 62 | do. | 5 „ 1 | Flood | N | 78 | do. | Do. do. |
| 5 | 61 | 60 | do. | 5 „ 1 | do. | SW | 65 | do. | Fresh do. cloudy. |
| 6 | 58 | 65 | do | 5½ „ 1 | do. | SW | 72 | 11 50 a.m. | Do. do. |
| 7 | ⎫ | | | | | SSW | 63 | Noon | ⎫ |
| 8 | ⎬ — | — | — | — | — | SW | 64 | do. | ⎬ Fresh gales and squally. |
| 9 | ⎭ | | | | | WSW | 63 | do. | ⎭ |
| 10 | 56 | 58 | ¼ of a mile. | 5½ „ 1 | Low water | WSW | 66 | 11 50 a.m. | Fresh breezes, &c. |
| 12 | 60 | 58 | do. | 6 „ 1 | do. | W by N | 67 | Noon | Moderate do. |
| 13 | 59 | 60 | do. | 6 „ 1 | Last qr. ebb | W | 66 | do. | Do. do. |
| 14 | 58 | 60 | do. | 5½ „ 1 | do. | W | 64 | do. | Fresh breezes & hazy. |
| 15 | 62 | 61 | do. | 5 „ 1 | do. | W | 63 | 11 50 a.m. | Light do. |
| 16 | 63 | 64 | do. | 5½ „ 1 | High water | W | 74 | 11 45 a.m. | Do. do. |
| 17 | 61 | 62 | do. | 6 „ 1 | do. | W | 70 | Noon | Do. do. |
| 19 | 60 | 62 | do. | 6 „ 1 | Ebb | N E | 70 | do. | Do. do. |
| 20 | 60 | 62 | do. | 5½ „ 1 | do. | W | 71 | do. | Fresh breezes and cloudy |
| 21 | 61 | 63 | do. | 5 „ 1 | do. | S | 70 | do. | Strong winds and squally. |
| 22 | 60 | 62 | do. | 5½ „ 1 | Low water | SW | 66 | do. | Fresh winds & rain. |
| 23 | 60 | 62 | do. | 6 „ 1 | do. | SW | 68 | do. | Do. cloudy. |
| 24 | 60 | 62 | do. | 5 „ 1 | do. | W | 68 | do. | Do. do. |
| 26 | 62 | 62 | do. | 5 „ 1 | do. | W | 68 | do. | Light do. |
| 27 | 60 | 62 | do. | 5 „ 1 | Ebb | W | 64 | do. | Do. do. |
| 28 | 60 | 61 | do. | 6 „ 1 | do. | SW | 71 | do. | Do. do. |
| 29 | 60 | 61 | do. | 6 „ 1 | do. | SW | 71 | do. | Strong winds & hazy |
| 30 | 60 | 60 | do. | 6 „ 1 | do. | SW | 63 | do. | Light do. |
| 31 | 60 | 60 | do. | 6 „ 1 | do. | W | 64 | do. | Strong winds and squally. |

## WESTPORT DIVISION.—PIGEON POINT STATION, Co. MAYO.

Taken by WILLIAM JOHN, Chief Boatman.

| May. | | | | Fathoms. | | | | | |
|---|---|---|---|---|---|---|---|---|---|
| 10 | - | 52 | 1 mile | 3 | Flood | N N E | 55 | Noon | Fresh and cloudy. |
| 11 | - | 53 | ½ mile | 2½ | do. | N | 53 | 1 p.m. | Fresh and squally. |
| 12 | - | 52 | 300 yards | 2 | do. | N N W | 51 | 12 20 p.m. | do. |
| 13 | - | 53 | 400 yards | 2½ | do. | E S E | 60 | 2 p.m. | Moderate and clear. |
| 14 | - | 52 | 880 yards | 2 | Ebb | S E | 56 | Noon. | Fresh and clear. |
| 15 | - | 51 | 200 yards | 2½ | do. | S E | 52 | 12 35 p.m. | Fresh with rain. |
| 17 | - | 52 | 1 mile | 17 | do. | E | 53 | 1 15 p.m. | do. |
| 18 | - | 52 | 300 yards | 2 | do. | E | 54 | 12 10 p.m. | Moderate and cloudy |
| 19 | - | 52 | 200 yards | 2 | do. | N | 50 | 1 p.m. | Fresh and squally. |
| 20 | - | 52 | 100 yards | 1½ | do. | N | 57 | 1 p.m. | Moderate and fine. |
| 21 | - | 53 | 400 yards | 3 | High water | N | 56 | Noon. | Moderate and cloudy |
| 22 | - | 53 | 1 mile | 4 | Flood | W | 56 | 1 40 p.m. | Light and fine. |
| 24 | - | 55 | 100 yards | 1 | do. | S E | 56 | 2 30 p.m. | Fresh and cloudy. |
| 25 | - | 54 | 300 yards | 2 | do. | S E | 55 | 12 15 p.m. | Fresh with rain. |
| 26 | - | 53 | 200 yards | 1½ | do. | E | 51 | Noon. | do. |
| 27 | - | 50 | 400 yards | 2½ | do. | E | 46 | 1 p.m. | Fresh and cloudy. |
| 28 | - | 53 | 100 yards | 1½ | do. | E | 51 | 2 15 p.m. | do. |
| 29 | - | 54 | 880 yards | 2½ | Ebb | W | 59 | 12 30 p.m. | Light blue, clear. |
| 31 | - | 55 | 200 yards | 2 | do. | N W | 56 | Noon. | Moderate and cloudy |

## Westport Division, &c.—continued.

| 1869. | Temperature. A. At Sea. | Temperature. B. Near the Shore. | Distance from Land. | Depth of Water. | State of Tide, &c. | Wind. | Temperature of Air. | Hour at which Temperature taken. | Observations. |
|---|---|---|---|---|---|---|---|---|---|
| **June.** | ° | ° | | Fathoms | | | ° | | |
| 1 | – | 56 | 400 yards | 3 | Ebb | W | 58 | 1 p.m. | Fresh and showers. |
| 2 | – | 56 | 1 mile | 3½ | do. | NW | 56 | Noon. | do. |
| 3 | – | 56 | 100 yards | 1 | do. | W | 57 | 12 40 p.m. | Fresh and cloudy. |
| 4 | – | 56 | 200 yards | 2 | do | WNW | 59 | 2 30 p.m. | Moderate and fine. |
| 5 | – | 57 | 250 yards | 2½ | do. | W | 59 | 1 15 p.m. | Fresh and hazy. |
| 7 | – | 59 | 1 mile | 3½ | Flood | NW | 61 | 12 10 p.m. | Moderate and fine. |
| 8 | – | 63 | 300 yards | 2 | High water | E | 60 | 4 p.m. | do. |
| 9 | – | 63 | 400 yards | 3 | Flood | N E | 62 | Noon. | Light and clear. |
| 10 | – | 62 | 120 yards | 1½ | Low water | N N E | 58 | 12 25 p.m. | Moderate and fine. |
| 11 | – | 64 | ½ mile | 2 | do. | N E | 57 | 1 p.m. | Light and cloudy. |
| 12 | – | 63 | 200 yards | 2½ | Flood | W | 62 | 2 p.m. | do. |
| 14 | – | 59 | 1 mile | 4 | Ebb | W | 59 | 12 30 p.m. | Stormy and showers. |
| 15 | – | 63 | 400 yards | 2½ | Flood | NW | 60 | 2 30 p.m. | Moderate and clear. |
| 16 | – | 63 | 100 yards | 1½ | Ebb | N | 59 | 12 10 p.m. | Light and cloudy. |
| 17 | – | 63 | ½ mile | 2½ | do. | N | 60 | Noon. | Light and hazy. |
| 18 | – | 58 | 300 yards | 3 | do. | WNW | 62 | 1 15 p.m. | Moderate and cloudy |
| 19 | – | 60 | 120 yards | 4 | High water | NNW | 59 | Noon. | Light and hazy. |
| 21 | – | 58 | 420 yards | 3 | Flood | N | 60 | 2 p.m. | do. |
| 22 | – | 57 | 90 yards | 1½ | do. | N | 59 | 12 30 p.m. | Moderate and cloudy |
| 23 | – | 59 | 1 mile | 4 | do. | W | 61 | 1 p.m. | Moderate and fine. |
| 24 | – | 60 | 100 yards | 2 | do. | NW | 63 | 1 15 p.m. | do. |
| 25 | – | 61 | 200 yards | 2½ | Low water | WNW | 64 | Noon. | do. |
| 26 | – | 67 | ½ mile | 3 | Flood | WNW | 68 | 1 40 p.m. | Light and fine. |
| 28 | – | 65 | 300 yards | 2 | Ebb | N E | 72 | 12 30 p.m. | do. |
| 29 | – | 66 | 60 yards | 1½ | Flood | N E | 70 | 2 p.m. | do. |
| 30 | – | 66 | 130 yards | 3 | Ebb | N E | 72 | Noon. | do. |
| **July.** | | | | | | | | | |
| 1 | – | 65 | 200 yards | 2½ | Ebb | N E | 73 | 12 20 p.m. | Light and fine. |
| 2 | – | 66 | 880 yards | 3 | do. | WNW | 72 | 1 15 p.m. | do. |
| 3 | – | 66 | 90 yards | 1½ | do. | WNW | 71 | Noon. | do. |
| 5 | – | 65 | 400 yards | 3½ | do. | NW | 66 | 1 p.m. | Fresh and squally. |
| 6 | – | 65 | 100 yards | 1½ | do. | WNW | 66 | 2 p.m. | Moderate and cloudy |
| 7 | – | 65 | 1 mile | 4 | Flood | W | 67 | Noon. | Strong and squally. |
| 8 | – | 65 | 300 yards | 3 | do. | W | 65 | 1 p.m. | do. |
| 9 | – | 63 | 120 yards | 2½ | do. | WNW | 67 | 1 30 p.m. | do. |
| 10 | – | 63 | 880 yards | 3½ | do. | W | 66 | 12 30 p.m. | Moderate and fine. |
| 12 | – | 65 | 80 yards | 1½ | do. | W | 64 | 2 p.m. | Fresh and cloudy. |
| 13 | – | 63 | 400 yards | 1 | Low water | NW | 64 | 1 p.m. | Moderate and hazy. |
| 14 | – | 62 | 230 yards | 3 | Ebb | WNW | 63 | Noon. | Fresh and hazy. |
| 15 | – | 62 | 1 mile | 4½ | do. | WNW | 67 | 12 10 p.m. | Light and fine. |
| 16 | – | 64 | 100 yards | 2½ | do. | N | 78 | Noon. | do. |
| 17 | – | 64 | 400 yards | 3½ | do. | NNW | 66 | do. | Light and hazy. |
| 19 | – | 67 | 880 yards | 3 | Flood | S E | 75 | 12 20 p.m. | Light and fine. |
| 20 | – | 67 | 300 yards | 2 | High water | S | 77 | Noon. | do. |
| 21 | – | 68 | 130 yards | 2½ | Flood | SSW | 72 | 2 p.m. | Fresh and squally. |
| 22 | – | 66 | 1 mile | 4½ | do. | S | 65 | Noon. | Moderate & showers. |
| 23 | – | 65 | 220 yards | 3 | do. | NW | 66 | do. | Fresh and cloudy. |
| 24 | – | 64 | 400 yards | 3½ | do. | W | 65 | 12 20 p.m. | do. |
| 26 | – | 64 | 200 yards | 1½ | Low water | NW | 63 | 12 30 p.m. | do. |
| 27 | – | 64 | 90 yards | 1½ | Ebb | NW | 66 | Noon. | do. |
| 28 | – | 64 | 880 yards | 2½ | Low water | NW | 66 | 1 p.m. | do. |
| 29 | – | 62 | 300 yards | 3 | Ebb | NW | 62 | 12 15 p.m. | Strong and squally. |
| 30 | – | 62 | 100 yards | 2 | do. | W | 64 | 12 30 p.m. | Strong and rain. |
| 31 | – | 63 | 200 yards | 3 | do. | W | 65 | 2 p.m. | Strong and squally. |

WESTPORT DIVISION.—INNISLYRE STATION, CO. MAYO.

Taken by CHARLES THOMAS, Chief Boatman.

| 1869. | Temperature. | | Distance from Land. | Depth of Water. | State of Tide, &c. | Wind. | Temperature of Air. | Hour at which Temperature taken. | Observations. |
|---|---|---|---|---|---|---|---|---|---|
| | A. At Sea | B. Near the Shore. | | | | | | | |
| **May.** | ° | ° | | Fathoms. | | | ° | | |
| 10 | – | 53 | ¼ mile | 2½ | Flood | N | 54 | Noon | Fresh breeze, cloudy. |
| 11 | – | 53 | 300 yards | 2½ | do. | N NW | 54 | 1 p.m. | Fresh breeze, rainy. |
| 12 | – | 53 | do. | 2½ | do. | N NW | 53 | 12 30 p.m. | Moderate do., cloudy |
| 13 | – | 54 | 440 yards | 2½ | do. | E S E | 56 | 11 a.m. | do. |
| 14 | – | 54 | 100 yards | 2½ | Low water | E S E | 56 | Noon | Strong breeze, cloudy |
| 15 | – | 52 | 200 yards | 2½ | Ebb | S E | 50 | do. | Strong breeze, rain. |
| 17 | – | 53 | 440 yards | 3 | do. | E S E | 52 | do. | Fresh breeze, rain. |
| 18 | – | 52 | 880 yards | 2½ | do. | E N E | 54 | 11 a.m. | Moderate breeze, do. |
| 19 | – | 51 | 440 yards | 3 | High water | N | 57 | 11 30 a.m. | Strong breeze, rain. |
| 20 | – | 53 | 300 yards | 2½ | do. | N | 56 | Noon | Moderate & cloudy. |
| 21 | – | 52 | 440 yards | 4 | Ebb | N E | 56 | 2 p.m. | do. |
| 22 | – | 53 | do. | 4 | Flood | N W | 55 | Noon | Light breeze, cloudy. |
| 24 | – | 53 | 300 yards | 3 | do. | S E | 55 | do. | Strong breeze, do. |
| 25 | – | 53 | do. | 3 | do. | S E | 56 | do. | Fresh breeze, rain. |
| 26 | – | 54 | do. | 3 | do. | E S E | 57 | do. | Fresh breeze, cloudy. |
| 27 | – | 52 | do. | 3 | Low water | E | 50 | do. | do. |
| 28 | – | 54 | do. | 3 | Ebb | E N E | 56 | do. | Moderate breeze, do. |
| 29 | – | 54 | do. | 3 | do. | N E | 67 | do. | Light breeze, do. |
| 31 | – | 52 | 440 yards | 5 | do. | N W | 59 | do. | Moderate breeze, do. |
| **June.** | | | Yards. | | | | | | |
| 1 | – | 53 | 440 | 5 | Ebb | W N W | 60 | Noon | Moderate and hazy. |
| 2 | – | 53 | 300 | 5 | High water | N | 59 | do. | Light breezes, rain. |
| 3 | – | 53 | 440 | 4 | do. | W | 59 | 12 40 p.m. | Strong breezes, do. |
| 4 | – | 55 | 300 | 3 | Flood | W | 60 | Noon | Light breezes, hazy. |
| 5 | – | 56 | 300 | 3 | do. | W S W | 68 | do. | Moderate and hazy. |
| 7 | – | 59 | 300 | 3 | do. | W S W | 66 | do. | Light breezes, rain. |
| 8 | – | 59 | 300 | 4 | do. | E | 66 | do. | Light breezes, cloudy |
| 9 | – | 59 | 440 | 4 | do. | N E | 62 | do. | Moderate breezes, do. |
| 10 | – | 59 | 300 | 3 | do. | N E | 66 | do. | do. |
| 11 | – | 60 | 440 | 4 | Low water | N E | 64 | do. | Moderate do., hazy |
| 12 | – | 60 | 300 | 3½ | do. | S W | 66 | do. | Fresh breezes, rain. |
| 14 | – | 58 | 300 | 3 | Ebb | S W | 63 | do. | do. |
| 15 | – | 58 | 400 | 4 | do. | N | 62 | do. | do. |
| 16 | – | 58 | 300 | 4 | do. | S W | 58 | do. | Fresh breezes, cloudy |
| 17 | – | 60 | 400 | 3 | do. | N | 60 | do. | Moderate breezes, do. |
| 18 | – | 60 | 300 | 3½ | do. | N W | 62 | do. | do. |
| 19 | – | 61 | 400 | 4 | Flood | N N E | 62 | do. | Fresh breezes, hazy. |
| 21 | – | 60 | 300 | 4 | do. | N | 62 | do. | Moderate breezes, do. |
| 22 | – | 58 | 300 | 3½ | do. | N | 62 | do. | do. |
| 23 | – | 58 | 400 | 4 | do. | W N W | 62 | 1 30 p.m. | do. |
| 24 | 58 | – | 440 | 7 | do. | W N W | 62 | 12 30 p.m. | do. |
| 25 | – | 60 | 300 | 5 | do. | N | 70 | 1 p.m. | do. cloudy. |
| 26 | – | 59 | 400 | 4 | Ebb | N | 70 | 11 a.m. | do. hazy. |
| 28 | – | 60 | 440 | 3½ | do. | E | 77 | Noon | Light breezes, cloudy |
| 29 | 59 | – | 880 | 7 | do. | N E | 78 | do. | do. |
| 30 | – | 60 | 300 | 3 | do. | E | 82 | do. | do. |

## WESTPORT DIVISION, &c.—*continued.*

| 1869. | Temperature. A. At Sea. | Temperature. B. Near the Shore. | Distance from Land. | Depth of Water. | State of Tide, &c. | Wind. | Temperature of Air. | Hour at which Temperature taken. | Observations. |
|---|---|---|---|---|---|---|---|---|---|
| **July.** | ° | ° | Yards. | Fathoms. | | | ° | | |
| 1 | – | 63 | 440 | 3½ | Ebb | N E | 84 | Noon | Light airs & cloudy. |
| 2 | – | 63 | 440 | 3½ | do. | N W | 84 | do. | do. |
| 3 | – | 62 | 300 | 3 | High water | W N W | 76 | do. | Fresh breezes, do. |
| 5 | – | 62 | 400 | 4 | Flood | S W | 66 | do. | Strong breezes, rain. |
| 6 | – | 62 | 400 | 3½ | do. | N W | 67 | do. | Moderate do. cloudy, |
| 7 | – | 63 | 300 | 3 | do. | S W | 74 | do. | Strong breezes, rain. |
| 8 | – | 62 | 400 | 3 | do. | W S W | 74 | do. | do. |
| 9 | – | 62 | 400 | 3 | do. | W S W | 78 | do. | Strong gales, cloudy. |
| 10 | – | 62 | 300 | 3½ | do. | W N W | 68 | do. | Moderate breezes, do. |
| 12 | – | 61 | 400 | 5 | Low water | N W | 67 | do. | Fresh breezes, cloudy |
| 13 | – | 61 | 400 | 5 | Flood | N W | 67 | 2 p. m. | Moderate do., rain. |
| 14 | – | 61 | 400 | 6 | Ebb | W | 66 | Noon | Fresh breezes, do. |
| 15 | – | 62 | 880 | 4 | do. | N W | 68 | do. | Moderate do., fog. |
| 16 | – | 63 | 400 | 5 | do. | N E | 78 | do. | Light airs, cloudy. |
| 17 | – | 63 | 400 | 3½ | do. | N W | 78 | do. | do. |
| 19 | – | 64 | 440 | 4 | Flood | S E | 84 | do. | do. |
| 20 | – | 64 | 440 | 4 | do. | S E | 88 | do. | do. |
| 21 | – | 64 | 400 | 3½ | do. | S | 84 | do. | Fresh airs, cloudy. |
| 22 | – | 64 | 400 | 4 | do. | S W | 78 | do. | Strong airs, rain. |
| 23 | – | 64 | 440 | 5 | do. | S W | 76 | do. | Fresh airs, rain. |
| 24 | – | 64 | 440 | 3½ | do. | S W | 78 | do. | Moderate do. cloudy. |
| 26 | – | 63 | 400 | 5 | Ebb | W N W | 72 | 11 20 a.m. | do. |
| 27 | – | 64 | 440 | 4 | do. | W N W | 78 | Noon | do. |
| 28 | – | 63 | 400 | 3½ | do. | W N W | 76 | do. | do. |
| 29 | – | 63 | 300 | 3 | do. | W S W | 76 | do. | Fresh gales, rain. |
| 30 | – | 63 | 400 | 4 | do. | S W | 76 | do. | Strong breezes, rain. |
| 31 | – | 62 | 400 | 3½ | do. | W S W | 60 | 12 30 p.m. | do. |

## WESTPORT DIVISION.—INNISGOWLA STATION, CO. MAYO.

Taken by WILLIAM BURR, Chief Boatman.

| | | | | | | | | | |
|---|---|---|---|---|---|---|---|---|---|
| **May.** | | | | Fathoms. | | | | | |
| 10 | 52 | 52 | ½ and ¼ mile | 1½ and 5 | Flood | NW | 59 | Noon | Temperature taken on the several oyster beds within the limits of this station. |
| 11 | 52 | 52 | do. | 2 ,, 5 | do. | N | 57 | do. | |
| 12 | 52 | 52 | ¼ & 200 yds. | 1½ ,, 11 | Low water | W | 58 | do. | |
| 13 | 52 | 52 | ¼ ,, 100 ,, | 10 ,, 1 | do. | E S E | 60 | 1 p.m. | |
| 14 | 52 | 53 | ½ ,, ¼ mile | 6 ,, 1 | Ebb | E S E | 59 | do. | |
| 15 | 52 | 52 | ¼ ,, 100 yds. | 7 ,, 1½ | do. | E | 54 | do. | |
| 17 | 52 | 51 | ½ ,, 100 ,, | 6 ,, 2 | do. | E | 53 | do. | |
| 18 | 52 | 52 | ¼ ,, 200 ,, | 6 ,, 2 | do. | N E | 59 | do. | |
| 19 | 52 | 51 | ¼ ,, 200 ,, | 5 ,, 1½ | High water | N N E | 50 | do. | |
| 20 | 52 | 52 | ¼ ,, 150 ,, | 6 ,, 3 | do. | NNW | 55 | do. | |
| 21 | 52 | 52 | ¼ ,, 200 ,, | 11 ,, 3 | Flood | NNE | 54 | do. | |
| 22 | 52 | 52 | ¼ ,, 150 ,, | 7 ,, 2½ | do. | N | 55 | do. | |
| 24 | 52 | 53 | ¼ ,, 200 ,, | 6 ,, 3 | do. | S E | 55 | do. | |
| 25 | 53 | 53 | ½ ,, ¼ mile | 7 ,, 3 | do. | E S E | 56 | do. | |
| 26 | 53 | 53 | do. | 6 ,, 2 | do. | S E | 54 | do. | |
| 27 | 52 | 51 | ¾ ,, ¼ mile | 7 ,, 2 | Low water | E N E | 49 | do. | |
| 28 | 52 | 52 | 3¼ ,, ¼ ,, | 6 ,, 3 | Ebb | N E | 55 | do. | |
| 29 | 52 | 52 | ½ ,, ¼ ,, | 10 ,, 2 | do. | N E | 60 | do. | |
| 31 | 53 | 54 | do. | 6 ,, 2 | do. | W | 64 | do. | |

## Westport Division, &c.—*continued.*

| 1869. | Temperature. A. At Sea. | Temperature. B. Near the Shore. | Distance from Land. | Depth of Water. | State of Tide, &c. | Wind. | Temperature of Air. | Hour at which Temperature taken. | Observations. |
|---|---|---|---|---|---|---|---|---|---|
| **June.** | ° | ° | | Fathoms. | | | ° | | |
| 1 | 54 | 54 | ½ and ¼ mile | 7 and 3 | Ebb | W | 60 | Noon | Temperature taken on the several oyster beds within the limits of this station. |
| 2 | 54 | 55 | do. | 8 ,, 3½ | do. | WNW | 57 | do. | |
| 3 | 55 | 56 | do. | 6 ,, 4 | High water | W | 59 | do. | |
| 4 | 55 | 55 | ¾ ,, ½ ,, | 10 ,, 4 | do. | WNW | 62 | do. | |
| 5 | 55 | 56 | ½ ,, ½ ,, | 7 ,, 3½ | Flood | WSW | 65 | do. | |
| 7 | 58 | 59 | do. | 6 ,, 3 | do. | W | 64 | do. | |
| 8 | 58 | 59 | ¾ ,, ¼ ,, | 13 ,, 4 | do. | E | 69 | do. | |
| 9 | 58 | 60 | do. | 8 ,, 4 | do. | E | 72 | do. | |
| 10 | 59 | 60 | ½ ,, ¼ ,, | 7 ,, 1½ | do. | E | 68 | do. | |
| 11 | 59 | 59 | ½ ,, 200 yds. | 9 ,, 1 | Low water | N E | 62 | do. | |
| 12 | 59 | 59 | ½ ,, ¼ mile | 6 ,, 2 | Ebb | W | 62 | do. | |
| 14 | 58 | 59 | do. | 5 ,, 1½ | do. | W | 58 | do. | |
| 15 | 58 | 58 | ¾ ,, ¼ ,, | 7 ,, 2 | do. | NW | 59 | do. | |
| 16 | 57 | 58 | ½ ,, ¼ ,, | 6 ,, 3 | do. | NW | 60 | do. | |
| 17 | 57 | 58 | ½ ,, ¾ ,, | 6 ,, 3½ | do. | NW | 59 | do. | |
| 18 | 57 | 58 | do. | 8 ,, 4 | High water | N | 62 | do. | |
| 19 | 56 | 57 | do. | 10 ,, 3 | Flood | N | 60 | do. | |
| 21 | 56 | 57 | ¾ ,, ¼ ,, | 9 ,, 2½ | do. | N E | 61 | do. | |
| 22 | 57 | 57 | ½ ,, ¼ ,, | 7 ,, 2 | do. | N E | 62 | do. | |
| 23 | 56 | 58 | ¾ ,, ¼ ,, | 8 ,, 1½ | do. | W | 63 | do. | |
| 24 | 57 | 59 | ¾ ,, ¼ ,, | 5 ,, 1 | do. | W | 65 | do. | |
| 25 | 57 | 59 | ½ ,, ¼ ,, | 6 ,, 1 | Low water | W | 72 | do. | |
| 26 | 58 | 60 | do. | 5 ,, 1 | do. | NW | 70 | do. | |
| 28 | 60 | 62 | ¾ ,, 200 yds. | 6 ,, 0¾ | Ebb | N | 71 | do. | |
| 29 | 60 | 61 | ½ ,, ¼ mile | 5 ,, 1 | do. | N E | 70 | do. | |
| 30 | 61 | 62 | ½ ,, ¼ ,, | 6 ,, 1 | do. | N E | 76 | do. | |
| **July.** | | | | | | | | | |
| 1 | 62 | 63 | ¾ and ¼ | 5 and 1½ | Ebb | E | 85 | Noon | Temperature taken on the several oyster beds within the limits of this station. |
| 2 | 62 | 63 | do. | 11 ,, 2 | do. | SW | 75 | do. | |
| 3 | 62 | 64 | ½ and ¼ | 9 ,, 3 | High water | N | 86 | do. | |
| 5 | 62 | 63 | ¾ ,, ¼ | 10 ,, 2 | Flood | WSW | 65 | do. | |
| 6 | 62 | 63 | ¾ ,, ¼ | 13 ,, 3½ | do. | SW | 64 | do. | |
| 7 | 62 | 63 | ½ ,, ¼ | 9 ,, 1½ | do. | SW | 68 | do. | |
| 8 | 62 | 63 | ½ ,, ¼ | 7 ,, 1 | do. | WSW | 67 | do. | |
| 9 | 62 | 63 | ¾ ,, ¼ | 5 ,, 1 | do. | WSW | 68 | do. | |
| 10 | 62 | 63 | ¾ ,, ¼ | 7 ,, ½ | do. | WSW | 68 | do. | |
| 12 | 62 | 62 | ½ ,, ¼ | 5 ,, 1 | Ebb | W | 66 | do. | |
| 13 | 62 | 62 | do. | 6 ,, 1 | do. | WNW | 65 | do. | |
| 14 | 62 | 62 | do. | 5 ,, 1 | do. | WSW | 63 | do. | |
| 15 | 62 | 62 | ¾ and ¼ | 7 ,, 1 | do. | W | 64 | do. | |
| 16 | 63 | 64 | ¾ ,, ¼ | 11 ,, 0½ | do. | E | 80 | do. | |
| 17 | 63 | 63 | ½ ,, ¼ | 7 ,, 2 | High water | N E | 74 | do. | |
| 19 | 63 | 63 | ½ ,, ¼ | 8 ,, 2½ | Flood | N E | 82 | do. | |
| 20 | 63 | 63 | ¾ ,, ¼ | 7 ,, 3 | do. | N | 81 | do. | |
| 21 | 64 | 65 | ½ ,, ¼ | 9 ,, 2 | do. | SW | 71 | do. | |
| 22 | 64 | 65 | ¾ ,, ¼ | 7 ,, 2 | do. | W | 66 | do. | |
| 23 | 64 | 64 | ½ ,, ¼ | 6 ,, 1½ | do. | W | 66 | do. | |
| 24 | 64 | 64 | ½ ,, ¼ | 5 ,, 1½ | Low water | WSW | 68 | do. | |
| 26 | 63 | 63 | ¾ ,, ¼ | 9 ,, 2 | Ebb | WNW | 66 | do. | |
| 27 | 63 | 63 | ¾ ,, ¼ | 6 ,, 1 | do. | WNW | 69 | do. | |
| 28 | 63 | 63 | ½ ,, ¼ | 7 ,, 1½ | do. | W | 67 | do. | |
| 29 | 62 | 62 | ½ ,, ¼ | 5 ,, 2 | do. | WSW | 65 | do. | |
| 30 | 62 | 62 | do. | 5 ,, 1 | do. | WSW | 63 | do. | |
| 31 | 62 | 62 | do. | 7 ,, 2½ | do. | W | 67 | do. | |

GALWAY DIVISION.—BALLYVAUGHAN STATION, CO. CLARE.

Taken by JOHN CONNELL, Chief Boatman.

| 1869. | Temperature. | | Distance from Land. | Depth of Water. | State of Tide, &c. | Wind. | Temperature of Air. | Hour at which Temperature taken. | Observations. |
|---|---|---|---|---|---|---|---|---|---|
| | A. At Sea. | B. Near the Shore. | | | | | | | |
| **May.** | ° | ° | | | | | ° | | |
| 10 | – | 50 | 500 yards | 7 feet | Flood | N | 53 | Noon | |
| 11 | – | 51 | 400 yards | 5 feet | do. | N W | 55 | do. | |
| 12 | – | 52 | 300 yards | 3 feet | do. | N W | 55 | do. | |
| 13 | – | 52 | 600 yards | 4 feet | do. | S S E | 59 | do. | |
| 14 | – | 53 | 550 yards | do. | Ebb | E | 58 | do. | |
| 15 | – | 52 | 250 yards | 5 feet | do. | S E | 53 | do. | |
| 17 | – | 52 | 400 yards | 6 feet | do. | S | 63 | do. | |
| 18 | – | 52 | 300 yards | do. | do. | N E | 50 | do. | |
| 19 | – | 54 | 200 yards | 5 feet | do. | N N E | 51 | do. | |
| 20 | – | 51 | 500 yards | 10 feet | do. | N N W | 53 | do. | |
| 21 | – | 52 | 400 yards | do. | High water | W N W | 57 | do. | |
| 22 | 52 | – | ½ mile | 9 fathoms | Flood | W | 57 | do. | |
| 24 | – | 52 | 300 yards | 6 feet | do. | S E | 57 | do. | |
| 25 | – | 52 | 400 yards | 5 feet | do. | E | 58 | do. | |
| 26 | – | 53 | 500 yards | 4 feet | do. | E by N | 54 | do. | |
| 27 | – | 50 | 200 yards | 3 feet | Low water | E | 48 | do. | |
| 28 | – | 51 | 250 yards | 4 feet | Ebb | E | 50 | do. | |
| 29 | – | 52 | 300 yards | 5 feet | do. | N N E | 53 | do. | |
| 31 | – | 53 | 400 yards | do. | do. | W | 58 | do. | |
| **June.** | | | | | | | | | |
| 1 | – | 54 | 400 yards | 6 feet | Ebb | W by S | 68 | Noon | |
| 2 | – | 55 | 500 yards | 8 feet | do. | W | 65 | do. | |
| 3 | – | 55 | 400 yards | do. | do. | W | 64 | do. | |
| 4 | – | 55 | 300 yards | 9 feet | High water | S W | 61 | do. | |
| 5 | – | 56 | 600 yards | 8 feet | Flood | W | 67 | do. | |
| 7 | – | 57 | 400 yards | 6 feet | do. | W | 68 | do. | |
| 8 | – | 58 | 500 yards | 7 feet | do. | N | 64 | do. | |
| 9 | – | 61 | do. | 5 feet | do. | N N E | 66 | do. | |
| 10 | – | 65 | 400 yards | 4 feet | do. | N E | 70 | do. | |
| 11 | – | 58 | 200 yards | 3 feet | do. | E N E | 55 | do. | |
| 12 | – | 57 | 150 yards | do. | Ebb | N | 60 | do. | |
| 14 | – | 56 | 500 yards | 5 feet | do. | W | 63½ | do. | |
| 15 | – | 55 | 600 yards | 6 feet | do. | N N W | 58 | do. | |
| 16 | – | 58 | 500 yards | 8 feet | do. | W N W | 68 | do. | |
| 17 | – | 57 | 400 yards | 10 feet | do. | W | 60 | do. | |
| 18 | – | 57 | do. | 11 feet | do. | N W | 64 | do. | |
| 19 | – | 58 | 350 yards | do. | Flood | N | 66 | do. | |
| 21 | – | 59 | 500 yards | 6 feet | do. | N W | 63 | do. | |
| 22 | – | 58 | 300 yards | 4 feet | do. | N | 61 | do. | |
| 23 | – | 58 | 250 yards | 2½ feet | do. | W by W | 68 | do. | |
| 24 | – | 61 | 300 yards | 3 feet | do. | N | 66 | do. | |
| 25 | – | 62 | 400 yards | do. | Low water | N | 70 | do. | |
| 26 | – | 64 | 300 yards | 3½ feet | Flood | N N E | 72 | do. | |
| 28 | – | 64 | 200 yards | 2 feet | Ebb | N | 76 | do. | |
| 29 | – | 64 | 250 yards | 4 feet | do. | N | 74 | do. | |
| 30 | – | 63 | 300 yards | 3 feet | do. | N E | 72 | do. | |

## GALWAY DIVISION, &c.—*continued.*

| 1869. | Temperature. A. At Sea. | Temperature. B. Near the Shore. | Distance from Land. | Depth of Water. | State of Tide, &c. | Wind. | Temperature of Air. | Hour at which Temperature taken. | Observations. |
|---|---|---|---|---|---|---|---|---|---|
| **July.** | ° | ° | | | | | ° | | |
| 1 | — | 64 | 400 yards | 6½ feet | Ebb | N E | 73 | Noon | |
| 2 | — | 65 | 350 yards | 7½ feet | do. | N | 73 | do. | |
| 3 | — | 66 | 400 yards | 9 feet | do. | N | 76 | do. | |
| 5 | — | 62 | 250 yards | 8 feet | Flood | S W | 70 | do. | |
| 6 | — | 62 | 500 yards | 7½ feet | do. | W | 72 | do. | |
| 7 | — | 65 | 400 yards | 6 feet | do. | S W | 76 | do. | |
| 8 | — | 64 | 250 yards | 4½ feet | do. | W S W | 71 | do. | |
| 9 | — | 66 | 350 yards | 2½ feet | do. | W | 66 | do. | |
| 10 | — | 63 | 450 yards | do. | do. | W S W | 74 | do. | |
| 12 | — | 64 | do. | 2 feet | Low water | W N W | 69 | do. | |
| 13 | — | 64 | do. | 3 feet | Ebb | W N W | 69 | do. | |
| 14 | — | 64 | 400 yards | 4 feet | do. | W | 76 | do. | |
| 15 | — | 64 | 300 yards | 5 feet | do. | W N W | 76 | do. | |
| 16 | — | 65 | 350 yards | 6 feet | do. | N | 76 | do. | |
| 17 | — | 65 | 400 yards | 7 feet | do. | N | 70 | do. | |
| 19 | — | 66 | 500 yards | 10 feet | High water | N E | 77 | do. | |
| 20 | — | 67 | 300 yards | 9 feet | Flood | N E | 84 | do. | |
| 21 | — | 66 | 350 yards | 8 feet | do. | S W | 74 | do. | |
| 22 | — | 64 | 450 yards | 6½ feet | do. | S W | 72 | do. | |
| 23 | — | 65 | 400 yards | 5 feet | do. | S W | 71 | do. | |
| 24 | — | 65 | 300 yards | 3 feet | do. | S W | 68 | do. | |
| 26 | — | 64 | 250 yards | 2½ feet | Low water | N W | 69 | do. | |
| 27 | — | 64 | 400 yards | 3 feet | Ebb | W | 70 | do. | |
| 28 | — | 64 | do. | 2 feet | do. | W | 70 | do. | |
| 29 | — | 63 | 300 yards | 4 feet | do. | W S W | 68 | do. | |
| 30 | — | 62 | 350 yards | 5½ feet | do. | W S W | 67 | do. | |
| 31 | — | 63 | 450 yards | 7 feet | do. | W by S | 67 | do. | |

## BALLYHEIGE DIVISION.—BALLYHEIGE STATION, Co. KERRY.

Taken by JOHN WILMOT, Chief Boatman.

| | A. At Sea. | B. Near the Shore. | Distance from Land. | Depth of Water. | State of Tide, &c. | Wind. | Temperature of Air. | Hour | Observations. |
|---|---|---|---|---|---|---|---|---|---|
| **May.** | | | | | | | | | |
| 10 | — | 52 | Taken from | 1 Foot | Flood. | S E | 48 | Noon | — |
| 11 | — | 56 | the shore. | do. | do. | N | 50 | do. | Light breeze. |
| 12 | — | 61 | do. | do. | Low water | N | 56 | do. | Moderate. |
| 13 | — | 59 | do. | do. | Ebb. | E S E | 54 | do. | Fresh. |
| 14 | — | 58 | do. | do. | do. | E | 53 | do. | Strong breeze. |
| 15 | — | 56 | do. | do. | do. | S E | 51 | do. | Moderate. |
| 17 | — | 57 | do. | do. | do. | W | 54 | do. | Light. |
| 18 | — | 58 | do. | do. | do. | N W | 53 | do. | Moderate. |
| 19 | — | 50 | do. | do. | do. | N W | 47 | do. | Fresh. |
| 20 | — | 55 | do. | do. | High water | N W | 52 | do. | Light. |
| 21 | — | 57 | do. | do. | Flood. | N W | 54 | do. | Moderate- |
| 22 | — | 60 | do. | do. | do. | N W | 56 | do. | do |
| 24 | — | 69 | do. | do. | do. | W | 55 | do. | do. |
| 25 | — | 59 | do. | do. | do. | S E | 53 | do. | Fresh. |
| 26 | — | 56 | do. | do. | do. | S E | 52 | do. | Strong. |
| 27 | — | 51 | do. | do. | do. | S E | 48 | do. | do. |
| 28 | — | 57 | do. | do. | Low water | E | 52 | do. | Light. |
| 29 | — | 57 | do. | do. | Ebb | N | 48 | do. | do. |
| 31 | — | 61 | do. | do. | do. | N | 59 | do. | Moderate. |

BALLYHEIGE DIVISION, &c.—*continued.*

| 1859. | Temperature. A. At Sea. | Temperature. B. Near the Shore. | Distance from Land. | Depth of Water. | State of Tide, &c. | Wind. | Temperature of Air. | Hour at which Temperature taken. | Observations. |
|---|---|---|---|---|---|---|---|---|---|
| **June.** | ° | ° | | | | | ° | | |
| 1 | – | 59 | On the | 1 Foot | Ebb | SW | 56 | Noon | Moderate. |
| 2 | – | 59 | shore off | do. | do. | W | 57 | do. | do. |
| 3 | – | 59 | the rocks. | do. | do. | NW | 56 | do. | do. |
| 4 | – | 59 | do. | do. | do. | W | 57 | do. | do. |
| 5 | – | 57 | do. | do. | High water | W | 55 | do. | do. |
| 7 | – | 59 | do. | do. | Flood | W | 55 | do. | do. |
| 8 | – | 65 | do. | do. | do. | E | 69 | do. | do. |
| 9 | – | 67 | do. | do. | do. | N | 64 | do. | Light. |
| 10 | – | 73 | do. | do. | Low water | N | 68 | do. | do. |
| 11 | – | 68 | do. | do. | Ebb | N | 65 | do. | do. |
| 12 | – | 65 | do. | do. | do. | WNW | 60 | do. | do. |
| 14 | – | 61 | do. | do. | do. | W | 59 | do. | do. |
| 15 | – | 59 | do. | do. | do. | NW | 57 | do. | Fresh. |
| 16 | – | 59 | do. | do. | do. | NW | 56 | do. | do. |
| 17 | – | 69 | do. | do. | do. | NW | 61 | do. | Strong. |
| 18 | – | 59 | do. | do. | High water | W | 59 | do. | Moderate. |
| 19 | – | 60 | do. | do. | Flood. | N | 57 | do. | do. |
| 21 | – | 65 | do. | do. | do. | NW | 61 | do. | do. |
| 22 | – | 64 | do. | do. | do. | N | 59 | do. | do. |
| 23 | – | 64 | do. | do. | do. | N | 60 | do. | Light. |
| 24 | – | 64 | do. | do. | do. | N | 61 | do. | Moderate. |
| 25 | – | 63 | do. | do. | do. | N | 60 | do. | Light. |
| 26 | – | 68 | do. | do. | do. | N | 66 | do. | do. |
| 28 | – | 73 | do. | do. | Ebb | N | 70 | do. | do. |
| 29 | – | 76 | do. | do. | do. | N | 73 | do. | do. |
| 30 | – | 70 | do. | do. | do. | N E | 70 | do. | do. |
| **July.** | | | | | | | | | |
| 1 | – | 68 | On the | 1 Foot | Ebb. | W | 68 | Noon | Light. |
| 2 | – | 73 | shore off | do. | do. | N | 71 | do. | do. |
| 3 | – | 74 | the rocks. | do. | do. | N | 71 | do. | do. |
| 5 | – | 70 | do. | do. | High water | SW | 69 | do. | Fresh. |
| 6 | – | 66 | do. | do. | Flood | SW | 65 | do. | do. |
| 7 | – | 66 | do. | do. | do. | WSW | 64 | do. | Strong. |
| 8 | – | 65 | do. | do. | do. | SW | 63 | do. | Fresh gale. |
| 9 | – | 65 | do. | do. | do. | NW | 62 | do. | Strong gale. |
| 10 | – | 67 | do. | do. | do. | W | 65 | do. | Moderate. |
| 12 | – | 70 | do. | do. | do. | W | 64 | do. | do. |
| 13 | – | 66 | do. | do. | Low water | WNW | 65 | do. | Light. |
| 14 | – | 67 | do. | do. | Ebb | WNW | 65 | do. | Moderate. |
| 15 | – | 68 | do. | do. | do. | W | 64 | do. | Light. |
| 16 | – | 70 | do. | do. | do. | SW | 66 | do. | do. |
| 17 | – | 69 | do. | do. | do. | S | 69 | do. | do. |
| 19 | – | 74 | do. | do. | do. | N | 68 | do. | do. |
| 20 | – | 76 | do. | do. | do. | W | 74 | do. | do. |
| 21 | – | 69 | do. | do. | High water | W | 75 | do. | Moderate. |
| 22 | – | 69 | do. | do. | Flood | SW | 70 | do. | Fresh. |
| 23 | – | 71 | do. | do. | do. | W | 69 | do. | Strong. |
| 24 | – | 71 | do. | do. | do. | SW | 70 | do. | do. |
| 26 | – | 68 | do. | do. | do. | SW | 65 | do. | do. |
| 27 | – | 69 | do. | do. | do. | W | 67 | do. | do. |
| 28 | – | 70 | do. | do. | do. | W | 67 | do. | do. |
| 29 | – | 67 | do. | do. | Low water | SW | 65 | do. | do. |
| 30 | – | 64 | do. | do. | Ebb | W | 65 | do. | do. |
| 31 | – | 68 | do. | do. | do. | W | 64 | do. | Fresh. |

## PULLENDIVA DIVISION.—PULLENDIVA STATION, Co. SLIGO.

### Taken by JAMES W. DARMODY, Chief Boatman.

| 1869. | Temperature. | | Distance from Land. | Depth of Water. | State of Tide, &c. | Wind. | Temperature of Air. | Hour at which Temperature taken. | Observations. |
|---|---|---|---|---|---|---|---|---|---|
| | A. At Sea. | B. Near the Shore. | | | | | | | |
| **May.** | ° | ° | | | | | ° | | |
| 10 | – | 53 | –––– | 5 feet | Flood | N | 51 | Noon | |
| 11 | – | 54 | –– | do. | do. | W | 51 | do. | |
| 12 | – | 53 | –– | do. | do. | WNW | 51 | do. | |
| 13 | – | 54 | –– | do. | do. | NNE | 52 | do. | |
| 14 | – | 53 | –– | do. | do. | E | 52 | do. | |
| 15 | – | 50 | –– | 4 feet | do. | E | 51 | do. | |
| 17 | – | 52 | –– | do. | High water | ENE | 51 | do. | |
| 18 | – | 52 | –– | do. | Flood | NE | 51 | do. | |
| 19 | – | 52 | –– | do. | do. | NE | 51 | do. | |
| 20 | – | 55 | –– | do. | do. | NNW | 52 | do. | |
| 21 | – | 55 | –– | do. | do. | NNW | 53 | do. | |
| 22 | – | 56 | –– | do. | do. | N | 55 | do. | |
| 24 | – | 53 | –– | do. | Low water | E | 54 | do. | |
| 25 | – | 53 | –– | do. | Ebb | E | 55 | do. | |
| 26 | – | 52 | –– | do. | do. | E | 52 | do. | |
| 27 | – | 49 | –– | do. | do. | NNE | 51 | do. | Cold easterly wind. |
| 28 | – | 51 | –– | do. | do. | N | 51 | do. | |
| 29 | – | 52 | –– | do. | do. | E | 53 | do. | |
| 31 | – | 54 | –– | do. | do. | NW | 55 | do. | |
| **June.** | | | | | | | | | |
| 1 | – | 54 | –– | 5 feet | Ebb | SW | 56 | Noon | |
| 2 | – | 54 | –– | do. | do. | SW | 59 | do. | |
| 3 | – | 54 | –– | do. | High water | SW | 60 | do. | |
| 4 | – | 55 | –– | do. | Flood | SW | 61 | do. | |
| 5 | – | 56 | –– | do. | do. | SW | 62 | do. | |
| 7 | – | 54 | –– | do. | do. | NW | 62 | do. | |
| 8 | – | 56 | –– | do. | do. | N | 61 | do. | |
| 9 | – | 53 | –– | do. | do. | N | 61 | do. | |
| 10 | – | 56 | –– | do. | do. | N | 61 | do. | |
| 11 | – | 54 | –– | do. | do. | NE | 62 | do. | |
| 12 | – | 56 | –– | do. | Low water | SW | 62 | do. | |
| 14 | – | 56 | –– | do. | Ebb | W | 62 | do. | |
| 15 | – | 56 | –– | do. | do. | N | 60 | do. | |
| 16 | – | 56 | –– | do. | do. | N | 60 | do. | |
| 17 | – | 56 | –– | do. | do. | WNW | 61 | do. | |
| 18 | – | 56 | –– | do. | do. | NW | 61 | do. | |
| 19 | – | 58 | –– | do. | do. | NW | 61 | do. | |
| 21 | – | 58 | –– | do. | do. | SW | 62 | do. | |
| 22 | – | 58 | –– | do. | do. | NW | 62 | do. | |
| 23 | – | 58 | –– | do. | High water | W | 63 | do. | |
| 24 | – | 59 | –– | do. | Flood | W | 64 | do. | |
| 25 | – | 61 | –– | do. | do. | NE | 64 | do. | |
| 26 | – | 61 | –– | do. | do. | N | 63 | do. | |
| 28 | – | 62 | –– | do. | do. | NE | 63 | do. | |
| 29 | – | 64 | –– | do. | do. | NE | 63 | do. | |
| 30 | – | 64 | –– | do. | do. | NE | 63 | do. | |

## PULLENDIVA DIVISION, &c.—*continued.*

| 1869. | Temperature. A. At Sea. | B. Near the Shore. | Distance from Land. | Depth of Water. | State of Tide, &c. | Wind. | Temperature of Air. | Hour at which Temperature taken. | Observations. |
|---|---|---|---|---|---|---|---|---|---|
| **July.** | ° | ° | | | . | | ° | | |
| 1 | – | 65 | — | 5 feet | Ebb | N E | 67 | Noon | |
| 2 | – | 66 | — | do. | do. | N E | 68 | do. | |
| 3 | – | 66 | — | do. | High water | N N E | 69 | do. | |
| 5 | – | 66 | — | do. | Flood | N N E | 69 | do. | |
| 6 | – | 66 | — | do. | do. | W | 68 | do. | |
| 7 | – | 66 | — | do. | do. | SSW | 70 | do. | |
| 8 | – | 64 | — | do. | do. | SW | 69 | do. | |
| 9 | – | 62 | — | do. | do. | SW | 68 | do. | |
| 10 | – | – | — | do. | — | – | – | do. | |
| 12 | – | – | — | do. | — | – | – | do. | |
| 13 | – | – | — | do. | — | – | – | do. | Glass broken by |
| 14 | – | – | — | do. | — | – | – | do. | accident. |
| 15 | – | – | — | do. | — | – | – | do. | |
| 16 | – | – | — | do. | — | – | – | do. | |
| 17 | – | 62 | — | do. | High water | SW | 67 | do. | |
| 19 | – | 62 | — | do. | Flood | NNW | 68 | do. | |
| 20 | – | 64 | — | do. | do. | S | 70 | do. | |
| 21 | – | 64 | — | do. | do. | S | 72 | do. | |
| 22 | – | 62 | — | do. | do. | SW | 74 | do. | |
| 23 | – | 62 | — | do. | do. | W | 73 | do. | |
| 24 | – | 61 | — | do. | do. | SW | 74 | do. | |
| 26 | – | 61 | — | do. | Low water | SSW | 75 | do. | |
| 27 | – | 62 | — | do. | Ebb | SW | 73 | do. | |
| 28 | – | 62 | — | do. | do. | SW | 71 | do. | |
| 29 | – | 62 | — | do. | do. | S | 74 | do. | |
| 30 | – | 62 | — | do. | do. | SSW | 74 | do. | |
| 31 | – | 62 | — | do. | do. | W | 76 | do. | |

## KENMARE DIVISION.—LACKEEN POINT, CO. KERRY.

Taken by THOMAS BROWN, Chief Boatman.

| **May.** | | | | | | | | | |
|---|---|---|---|---|---|---|---|---|---|
| 10 | 55 | – | 1¾ miles | 12 fathoms | Flowing | N | 57 | Noon | The nearest oyster |
| 11 | 55 | – | 2 miles | do. | Flood | NNW | 56 | do. | banks are at Dun- |
| 12 | 54 | – | 1½ miles | do. | do. | N N E | 58 | do. | kerrin, four miles |
| 13 | 55 | – | 1 mile | do. | do. | S E | 58 | do. | off, but there are |
| 14 | 52 | – | 1½ miles | do. | do. | E N E | 56 | do. | oysters scattered |
| 15 | 52 | – | 1½ miles | do. | do. | N N E | 51 | do. | about where these |
| 17 | 55 | – | 1½ miles | do. | do. | S W | 54 | do. | temperatures have |
| 18 | 55 | – | 1½ miles | do. | Ebb | N W | 58 | 1 p.m. | been taken. |
| 19 | 53 | – | 1½ miles | do. | do. | NNW | 53 | Noon | |
| 20 | 53 | – | do. | do. | do. | N W | 57 | do. | |
| 21 | 55 | – | do. | do. | do. | N W | 57 | do. | |
| 22 | 55 | – | do. | do. | Flood | WSW | 57 | do. | |
| 24 | 55 | – | do. | do. | do. | SW | 59 | do. | |
| 25 | 55 | – | do. | do. | do. | ESE | 58 | do. | |
| 26 | 52 | – | 1 mile | do. | do. | ENE | 54 | do. | |
| 27 | 53 | – | do. | do. | do. | N | 53 | do. | |
| 28 | 51 | – | do. | do. | Low water | E N E | 52 | do. | |
| 29 | 53 | – | 1½ miles | do. | Flood | NNW | 58 | 1 30 p.m. | |
| 31 | 54 | – | do. | do. | Ebb | WNW | 61 | Noon | |

KENMARE DIVISION, &c.—*continued.*

| 1869. | Temperature. A. At Sea. | Temperature. B. Near the Shore. | Distance from Land. | Depth of Water. | State of Tide, &c. | Wind. | Temperature of Air. | Hour at which Temperature taken. | Observations. |
|---|---|---|---|---|---|---|---|---|---|
| **June.** | ° | ° | | | | | ° | | |
| 1 | 54 | – | 1 mile | 12 fathoms | Ebb | WSW | 60 | Noon | |
| 2 | 54 | . | 1½ miles | do. | do. | WSW | 60 | do. | |
| 3 | 53 | – | 1 mile | do. | High water | W | 59 | do. | |
| 4 | 55 | – | 1½ miles | do. | Flood | S W | 60 | do. | |
| 5 | 54 | – | 1 mile | do. | do. | S W | 58 | do. | ⎰ Crew on duty at |
| 7 }8 | – | – | – | – | – | – | – | — | ⎱ District Ship, per order of District |
| 9 | 60 | – | 1½ miles | 12 fathoms | Flood | S W | 69 | Noon | ⎰ Captain. |
| 10 | 59 | – | do. | do. | do. | S E | 68 | do. | |
| 11 | 56 | – | do. | do. | do. | E | 58 | do. | |
| 12 | 58 | – | 1 mile | do. | do. | W | 55 | do. | |
| 14 | 58 | – | 1½ miles | do. | Ebb | W | 55 | do. | |
| 15 | 57 | – | 1 mile | do. | do. | N W | 56 | do. | |
| 16 | 51 | – | do. | do. | do. | N W | 58 | do. | |
| 17 | 57 | – | do. | do. | do. | N W | 58 | do. | |
| 18 | 57 | – | 1½ miles | do. | do. | W | 58 | do. | |
| 19 | 58 | – | 1 mile | do. | Flood | WNW | 60 | do. | |
| 21 | 57 | . | 1½ miles | do. | do. | NNW | 60 | do. | |
| 22 | 58 | – | do. | do. | do. | . S | 62 | do. | |
| 23 | 58 | – | do. | do. | do. | E | 62 | do. | |
| 24 | 58 | – | do. | do. | do. | – | 65 | do. | |
| 25 | 58 | – | do. | do. | do | – | 67 | do. | |
| 26 | 58 | – | do. | do. | Low water | – | 66 | do. | |
| 28 | 60 | – | 1 mile | do. | Ebb | – | 68 | do. | |
| 29 | 62 | – | 1½ miles | do. | do. | – | 70 | do. | |
| 30 | 62 | – | do. | do. | do. | – | 70 | do. | |
| **July.** | | | | | | | | | |
| 1 | 64 | – | 1½ miles | 12 fathoms | Ebb | W | 70 | Noon | ⎰ On board H.M. |
| 2 }3 | – | – | – | – | – | – | – | — | ⎱ Gunboat *Cromer*, for duty. |
| 5 | 62 | – | 1 mile | 12 fathoms | Flood | S W | 64 | Noon | ⎰ On duty, for In- |
| 6 | – | – | – | – | – | – | – | — | ⎱ spection by Dis- trict Captain. |
| 7 | 64 | – | 1½ miles | 12 fathoms | Flood | S W | 68 | Noon | |
| 8 | – | – | – | – | – | – | – | — | Impracticable. |
| 9 | 64 | – | 1 mile | 12 fathoms | Flood | WNW | 68 | 1 30 p.m. | |
| 10 | 64 | – | 1½ miles | do. | do. | S W | 67 | do. | |
| 12 | 65 | – | do. | do. | Low water | NNW | 66 | do. | |
| 13 | 65 | – | do. | do. | Ebb | N E | 67 | do. | |
| 14 | 65 | – | 1 mile | do. | do. | S W | 68 | do. | |
| 15 | 68 | – | 1½ miles | do. | do. | S W | 70 | do. | |
| 16 | 68 | – | 1 mile | do. | do. | S E | 70 | do. | |
| 17 | 68 | – | 4 miles | do. | do. | W | 70 | do. | |
| 19 | 68 | – | 1½ miles | do. | Flood | WNW | 72 | do. | |
| 20 | 68 | – | do. | do. | do. | WSW | 74 | do. | |
| 21 | 64 | – | do. | do. | do. | S W | 68 | do. | |
| 22 | 65 | – | 1 mile | do. | do. | WSW | 67 | do. | |
| 23 | 66 | – | 1½ miles | do. | do. | WSW | 67 | do. | |
| 24 | 64 | – | 1 mile | do. | Low water | WSW | 66 | do. | |
| 26 | 66 | – | 1½ miles | do. | Ebb | WSW | 68 | do. | |
| 27 | 66 | – | 1 mile | do. | do. | S W | 68 | do. | |
| 28 | 67 | – | do. | do. | do. | WSW | 69 | do. | |
| 29 | – | – | – | – | – | – | – | — | Impracticable. |
| 30 | 65 | – | 1 mile | 12 fathoms | Ebb | WNW | 68 | 1 30 p.m. | |
| 31 | 66 | – | do. | do. | do. | S W | 68 | do. | |

## Leith Division, Edinburgh.—North Berwick Station, Berwick.

Taken by the Commanding Officer of the Coast-guard.

| 1869. | Temperature. A. At Sea. | Temperature. B. Near the Shore. | Distance from Land. | Depth of Water. | State of Tide, &c. | Wind. | Temperature of Air. | Hour at which Temperature taken. | Observations. |
|---|---|---|---|---|---|---|---|---|---|
| **May.** | ° | ° | Miles. | Fathoms. | | | ° | | |
| 10 | 45 | 46 | ½ | 4 | Flood | N E | 47 | Noon | Cold, rain. |
| 11 | 46 | 47 | ½ | 6 | do. | W | 52 | do. | Fine. |
| 12 | 47 | 48 | ½ | 6 | do | W | 52 | do. | Cloudy. |
| 13 | 47 | 49 | ½ | 8 | do. | W S W | 55 | do. | Fine. |
| 14 | 47 | 48 | ½ | 9 | do. | E | 53 | do. | do. |
| 15 | 47 | 48 | ½ | 4 | do. | E by S | 49 | do. | Cloudy; strong breeze. |
| 17 | 47 | 48 | ½ | 9 | do. | E S E | 50 | 1 30 p.m. | do. |
| 18 | 46 | 47 | ½ | 8½ | Ebb | E | 48 | do. | do. |
| 19 | 46 | 47 | ½ | 8 | do. | N N E | 52 | do. | do. |
| 20 | 45 | 46 | ½ | 4¼ | do. | W by N | 47 | do. | do. |
| 21 | 46 | 48 | ½ | 8 | do. | E | 53 | do. | do. |
| 22 | 48 | 50 | ½ | 10 | do. | E | 55 | do. | do. |
| 24 | 48 | 50 | ½ | 10 | Flood | E | 54 | do. | Fine; moderate air. |
| 25 | 47 | 48 | ½ | 9¼ | do. | E S E | 49 | do. | Cloudy. |
| 26 | 48 | 49 | ½ | 6 | do. | E S E | 50 | do. | do. |
| 27 | — | 48 | — | — | do. | N E by E | 48 | do. | Stormy. |
| 28 | 48 | 48 | — | — | do. | E N E | 48 | do. | do. |
| 29 | 48 | 50 | ½ | 7½ | do. | E | 57 | do. | Hazy. |
| 31 | 49 | 50 | ¾ | 5 | Low water | Calm | 56 | do. | Fine. |
| **June.** | | | | | | | | | |
| 1 | 49 | 50 | ½ | 9 | Flood | E S E | 56 | 2 p.m. | Fine; gentle breeze. |
| 2 | 50 | 51 | ½ | 8 | Ebb | Calm | 58 | Noon | Cloudy. |
| 3 | 51 | 52 | ½ | 5 | do. | W | 57 | do. | do. strong breeze. |
| 4 | 57 | 52 | ½ | 9 | do. | W | 56 | do. | Squally. |
| 5 | 52 | 53 | ½ | 9 | do. | E | 57 | do. | Heavy rain; light airs. |
| 7 | 52 | 54 | ½ | 7 | Flood | W | 63 | do. | Hazy; moderate breeze. |
| 8 | 51 | 54 | ½ | 9 | do. | W by N | 61 | do. | Light breeze. |
| 9 | 52 | 53 | ½ | 8 | do. | W | 61 | do. | Cloudy; fresh breeze |
| 10 | 52 | 53 | ½ | 8 | do. | E | 57 | do. | Cloudy; light breeze |
| 11 | 52 | 52 | ½ | 8½ | do. | W | 59 | do. | do. |
| 12 | 52 | 52 | ½ | 8 | do. | W | 57 | do. | Cloudy; fresh breeze |
| 14 | 51 | 52 | ½ | 7½ | do. | E | 54 | do. | Light breeze; clear. |
| 15 | — | 47 | — | — | Low water | N E | 48 | do. | Rain; strong gale. |
| 16 | — | 50 | — | — | Ebb | N | 49 | do. | Light breeze; ground swell. |
| 17 | 51 | 50 | ½ | 5 | do. | W | 53 | do. | Light breeze; cloudy |
| 18 | 51 | 52 | ½ | 9½ | do. | E S E | 56 | do. | do. |
| 19 | 51 | 53 | ½ | 9½ | do. | E | 57 | do. | do. |
| 21 | 51 | 53 | ½ | 10 | High water | E | 56 | do. | do. |
| 22 | 51 | 53 | 1 | 14 | Flood | E | 57 | do. | Moderate breeze; clear. |
| 23 | 52 | 54 | ½ | 8½ | do. | N W | 65 | do. | do. |
| 24 | 52 | 54 | ½ | 8½ | do. | E | 66 | do. | Moderate breeze; cloudy. |
| 25 | 53 | 54 | ½ | 8½ | do. | E | 65 | do. | Light breeze; fine. |
| 26 | 53 | 55 | ½ | 8½ | do. | W | 67 | do. | Light breeze; hazy. |
| 28 | 53 | 55 | ½ | 8¼ | do. | E | 63 | do. | Light breeze; clear. |
| 29 | 53 | 55 | ½ | 8½ | do. | E | 63 | do. | Light breeze; fine. |
| 30 | 52 | 54 | ½ | 8 | Ebb | E | 62 | do. | do. |

LEITH DIVISION, &c.—*continued.*

| 1869. | Temperature. A. At Sea. | Temperature. B. Near the Shore. | Distance from Land. | Depth of Water. | State of Tide, &c. | Wind. | Temperature of Air. | Hour at which Temperature taken. | Observations. |
|---|---|---|---|---|---|---|---|---|---|
| **July.** | ° | ° | Miles. | Fathoms. | | | ° | | |
| 1 | 53 | 55 | ½ | 9 | Ebb | E | 64 | Noon | Light breeze; fine. |
| 2 | 54 | 55 | ½ | 8¾ | do. | E | 65 | do. | Light breeze; hazy. |
| 3 | 54 | 56 | ½ | 8½ | do. | N | 62 | do. | do. |
| 5 | 55 | 56 | ½ | 9 | do. | S S W | 66 | do. | Fresh breeze; cloudy |
| 6 | - | 57 | — | — | High water | W | 65 | do. | Strong breeze |
| 7 | 56 | 57 | ½ | 9 | Flood | W | 66 | do. | Light breeze; fine. |
| 8 | 56 | 58 | ½ | 9½ | do. | S W | 67 | do. | Strong do. cloudy. |
| 9 | - | 57 | — | — | do. | W | 67 | do. | Heavy gale. |
| 10 | 57 | 58 | ½ | 8½ | do. | W½N | 68 | do. | Strong breeze. |
| 12 | 56 | 58 | ½ | 9½ | do. | WNW | 66 | do. | do. |
| 13 | - | 57 | ½ | 8½ | do. | WNW | 65 | do. | do. |
| 14 | - | 57 | — | — | Low water | W | 65 | do. | do. |
| 15 | 55 | 57 | — | — | Ebb | W | 69 | do. | do. |
| 16 | 55 | 57 | ½ | 8¼ | do. | W | 69 | do. | do. |
| 17 | 56 | 58 | ½ | 8½ | do. | E | 67 | do. | Moderate breeze. |
| 19 | 55 | 56 | ½ | 9½ | do. | E | 68 | do. | do. |
| 20 | 54 | 55 | ½ | 9½ | do. | E | 66 | do. | do. |
| 21 | 55 | 56 | ½ | 10 | Flood | E | 68 | do. | do. |
| 22 | 58 | 57 | 1 | 12½ | do. | W | 64 | do. | do. |
| 23 | 57 | 58 | ½ | 10 | do. | NNW | 63 | do. | Fresh breeze. |
| 24 | 57 | 57 | ½ | 10 | do. | S | 68 | do. | Gentle breeze. |
| 26 | 56 | 57 | ½ | 8½ | do. | SSW | 67 | do. | Moderate breeze. |
| 27 | 57 | 58 | ½ | 8½ | do. | N W | 67 | do. | Light breeze. |
| 28 | 56 | 58 | ½ | 8 | do. | S E | 70 | do. | do. |
| 29 | 57 | 58 | ½ | 8 | Low water | S S E | 71 | do. | Fresh breeze. |
| 30 | 56 | 57 | ½ | 8½ | Ebb | W | 66 | do. | Strong breeze. |
| 31 | 56 | 57 | ½ | 9 | do. | W | 63 | do. | Fresh breeze. |

ABERDEEN DIVISION.—BRIDGE OF DON STATION, ABERDEENSHIRE.

Taken by JOHN BARNES, Staff Commander.

| | | | | | | | | | |
|---|---|---|---|---|---|---|---|---|---|
| **May.** | | | | | | | | | |
| 10 | - | 48 | — | — | — | N E | 48 | — | Heavy sea on the bar. |
| 11 | - | 48 | — | — | — | E | 48 | — | |
| 12 | 46 | 48 | ½ mile | 3 fathoms | Flood | S E | 48 | Noon | |
| 13 | 46 | 48 | do. | do. | do. | S S W | 48 | 11 30 a.m. | |
| 14 | 46 | 48 | do. | do. | do. | S E | 48 | Noon | |
| 15 | 46 | 48 | do. | do. | do. | S E | 48 | do. | |
| 17 | 46 | 48 | do. | do. | do. | - | 48 | do. | |
| 18 | 46 | 48 | do. | do. | do. | - | 48 | do. | |
| 19 | - | - | — | — | — | N E | 48 | — | Strong gales, with a heavy sea on; the bar not passable. |
| 20 | | | | | | N | 48 | | |
| 21 | | | | | | N | 48 | | |
| 22 | | | | | | N | 48 | | |
| 24 | | | | | | E | 48 | | |
| 25 | | | | | | E S E | 48 | | |
| 26 | | | | | | E | 48 | | |
| 27 | | | | | | N E | 48 | | |
| 28 | 46 | 48 | ½ mile | 3 fathoms | Flood | N E | 48 | Noon | |
| 29 | 46 | 48 | do. | do. | do. | N | 50 | do. | |
| 31 | 46 | 48 | do. | do. | do. | N | 50 | do. | |

## ABERDEEN DIVISION, &c.—continued.

| 1869. | Temperature. | | Distance from Land. | Depth of Water. | State of Tide, &c. | Wind. | Temperature of Air. | Hour at which Temperature taken. | Observations. |
|---|---|---|---|---|---|---|---|---|---|
| | A. At Sea. | B. Near the Shore. | | | | | | | |
| **June.** | ° | ° | | | | | ° | | |
| 1 | 50 | 52 | ½ mile | 3 fathoms | Low water | S E | 54 | Noon | |
| 2 | 50 | 52 | do. | do. | do. | S W | 54 | 11 30 a.m. | |
| 3 | 50 | 52 | do. | do. | Ebb | S W | 54 | Noon | |
| 4 | 50 | 52 | do. | do. | do. | – | 51 | do. | |
| 5 | 50 | 52 | do. | do. | do. | – | 54 | do. | |
| 7 | 50 | 52 | do. | do. | Flood | – | 54 | do. | |
| 8 | – | . | do. | do. | — | N W | 52 | — | |
| 9 | – | – | do. | do. | — | N | 52 | - - | Heavy gales; bar impassable. |
| 10 | – | .. | do. | do. | — | N | 52 | — | |
| 11 | – | – | do. | do. | — | N | 52 | — | |
| 12 | 52 | 52 | do. | do. | Flood | S W | 54 | Noon | |
| 14 | 51 | 52 | do. | do. | do. | E | 54 | do. | |
| 15 | 52 | 53 | do. | do. | do. | E | 54 | do. | |
| 16 | – | – | do. | do. | — | N | 54 | — | Heavy sea on the bar. |
| 17 | – | – | do. | do. | — | S W | 54 | — | |
| 18 | – | – | do. | do. | — | E | 54 | — | |
| 19 | 52 | 52 | do. | do. | Ebb | E | 54 | Noon | |
| 21 | 52 | 52 | do. | do. | do. | N E | 54 | do. | |
| 22 | 52 | 52 | do. | do. | do. | N E | 54 | do. | |
| 23 | 52 | 52 | do. | do. | High water | N N E | 54 | do. | |
| 24 | 52 | 54 | do. | do. | do. | N E | 54 | 11 30 a.m. | |
| 25 | 52 | 54 | do. | do. | do. | S | 56 | 11 45 a.m. | |
| 26 | 54 | 56 | do. | do. | Flood | – | 58 | Noon | |
| 28 | 54 | 56 | do. | do. | do. | – | 58 | do. | |
| 29 | 54 | 56 | do. | do. | do. | – | 58 | 11 15 a.m. | |
| 30 | 54 | 56 | do. | do. | do. | – | 58 | 11 a.m. | |
| **July.** | | | | | | | | | |
| 1 | 54 | 56 | ½ mile | 3 fathoms | Low water | – | 58 | Noon | |
| 2 | 54 | 56 | do. | do. | do. | – | 58 | 11 45 a.m. | |
| 3 | 54 | 56 | do. | do. | Ebb | – | 58 | Noon | |
| 5 | 54 | 56 | do. | do. | do. | S | 58 | do. | |
| 6 | 54 | 56 | do. | do. | do. | N W | 58 | do. | |
| 7 | 54 | 56 | do. | do. | do. | S W | 58 | do. | |
| 8 | 54 | 56 | do. | do. | High water | S W | 58 | do. | |
| 9 | 54 | 56 | do. | do. | do. | S W | 58 | do. | |
| 10 | 54 | 56 | do. | do. | Ebb | S W | 58 | do. | |
| 12 | 54 | 56 | do. | do. | do. | S W | 60 | do. | |
| 13 | 54 | 56 | do. | do. | Flood | W S W | 60 | do. | |
| 14 | 54 | 56 | do. | do. | do. | S W | 60 | do. | |
| 15 | 56 | 56 | do. | do. | do. | S | 60 | do. | |
| 16 | 56 | 56 | do. | do. | Low water | – | 60 | do. | |
| 17 | 56 | 58 | do. | do. | Ebb | – | 60 | do. | |
| 19 | 56 | 58 | do. | do. | do. | – | 60 | do. | |
| 20 | 56 | 58 | do. | do. | Flood | S | 60 | do. | |
| 21 | 56 | 56 | do. | do. | do. | S | 60 | do. | |
| 22 | 56 | 56 | do. | do. | High water | S E | 58 | do. | |
| 23 | 56 | 56 | do. | do. | do. | S W | 60 | do. | |
| 24 | 56 | 56 | do. | do. | Flood | S W | 60 | do. | |
| 26 | 56 | 56 | do. | do. | do. | S | 60 | do. | |
| 27 | 56 | 56 | do. | do. | do. | S | 58 | do. | |
| 28 | 56 | 56 | do. | do. | do. | S W | 58 | do. | |
| 29 | 56 | 56 | do. | do. | do. | S | 58 | do. | |
| 30 | 56 | 56 | do. | do. | do. | S | 58 | do. | |
| 31 | 56 | 56 | do. | do. | do. | S W | 58 | do. | |

ABERDEEN DIVISION.—LERWICK STATION, MAINLAND, SHETLAND ISLES.

Taken by THOMAS JOHNSTON, Chief Officer.

| 1860. | Temperature. | | Distance from Land. | Depth of Water. | State of Tide, &c. | Wind. | Temperature of Air. | Hour at which Temperature taken. | Observations. |
|---|---|---|---|---|---|---|---|---|---|
| | A. At Sea. | B. Near the Shore. | | | | | | | |
| **May.** | ° | ° | Miles. | Fathoms. | | | ° | | |
| 10 | 46 | 48 | 1 | 10 | Ebb | S S E | 50 | 11 45 a.m. | |
| 11 | 47 | 50 | ¾ | 9 | do. | N W | 55 | Noon | |
| 12 | 47 | 48 | 1½ | 11 | do. | N E | 50 | do. | |
| 13 | 47 | 48 | 3 | 12 | High water | N W | 49 | 11 45 a.m. | |
| 14 | 47 | 48 | 1 | 8 | do. | N N W | 50 | Noon | |
| 15 | 48 | 49 | 2½ | 10 | Flood | E N E | 50 | do. | |
| 17 | 48 | 48 | 2 | 10 | do. | N E | 49 | 11 45 a.m. | |
| 18 | 48 | 50 | 1½ | 9 | do. | Calm | 52 | 12 30 p.m. | |
| 19 | – | 47 | – | – | do. | N N E | 46 | 12 15 p.m. | Strong gale. |
| 20 | 47 | 49 | 2 | 10 | Low water | N E | 52 | 12 10 p.m. | |
| 21 | 48 | 49 | 2½ | 11 | Ebb | N N W | 50 | Noon | |
| 22 | 49 | 50 | 1½ | 8 | do. | N N E | 52 | 12 30 p.m. | |
| 24 | 48 | 50 | 3 | 12 | do. | N | 50 | 11 30 a.m. | |
| 25 | 47 | 48 | 2 | 10 | do. | S E | 49 | 11 45 a.m. | |
| 26 | 48 | 48 | 1 | 8 | do. | N N W | 47 | Noon | |
| 27 | 47 | 48 | 2 | 9 | High water | N N W | 47 | 11 45 a.m. | |
| 28 | 47 | 48 | 1½ | 8 | do. | E N E | 48 | 12 10 p.m. | |
| 29 | 48 | 50 | 2 | 9 | Flood | W | 54 | 11 45 a.m. | |
| 31 | 48 | 49 | 2½ | 10 | do. | N | 50 | 11 45 a.m. | |
| **June.** | | | | | | | | | |
| 1 | 48 | 48 | 2 | 10 | Flood | N N W | 49 | 12 15 p.m. | |
| 2 | 48 | 50 | 2 | 8 | do. | S W | 55 | do. | |
| 3 | 49 | 50 | 1½ | 6 | Low water | W | 58 | 11 30 a.m. | |
| 4 | 50 | 49 | 2 | 8 | do. | Calm | 54 | 12 15 p.m. | |
| 5 | 49 | 50 | 3 | 10 | Ebb | Calm | 57 | Noon | |
| 7 | 50 | 53 | 1 | 8 | do. | Calm | 57 | 11 30 a.m. | |
| 8 | 49 | 51 | 2 | 12 | do. | W | 54 | 12 30 p.m. | |
| 9 | – | 49 | – | – | do. | N W | 46 | Noon | Strong N W gale. |
| 10 | – | 48 | – | – | do. | N | 48 | do. | do. |
| 11 | 49 | 50 | 1½ | 10 | High water | W X W | 52 | 11 30 a.m. | |
| 12 | 49 | 50 | 1 | 8 | do. | W S W | 53 | Noon | |
| 14 | 49 | 50 | 1½ | 9 | Flood | E | 52 | do. | |
| 15 | 50 | 50 | 1 | 9 | do. | N W | 52 | 11 40 a.m. | |
| 16 | 50 | 52 | 2 | 8 | do. | N N W | 58 | Noon | |
| 17 | 50 | 51 | 2 | 8 | do. | N N W | 53 | 11 30 a.m. | |
| 18 | 51 | 53 | 2 | 9 | Low water | N N W | 56 | do. | |
| 19 | 52 | 54 | 2 | 9 | do. | E | 58 | 12 30 p.m. | |
| 21 | 50 | 50 | 1 | 8 | Ebb | N N E | 55 | Noon | |
| 22 | 50 | 53 | 3 | 10 | do. | N N W | 56 | 12 10 p.m. | |
| 23 | 50 | 54 | 1 | 8 | do. | W | 58 | 12 30 p.m. | |
| 24 | 52 | 55 | 2 | 8 | do. | Calm | 72 | 11 45 a.m. | |
| 25 | 53 | 54 | 2 | 9 | do. | W S W | 66 | 12 15 p.m. | |
| 26 | 52 | 54 | 2 | 9 | High water | W S W | 62 | Noon | |
| 28 | 51 | 52 | 2 | 8 | Flood | W | 64 | do. | |
| 29 | 51 | 52 | 2 | 8 | do. | W | 62 | do. | |
| 30 | 52 | 56 | 2½ | 10 | do. | W | 66 | 12 10 p.m. | |

ABERDEEN DIVISION, &c.—*continued.*

| 1869. | Temperature. | | Distance from Land. | Depth of Water. | State of Tide, &c. | Wind. | Temperature of Air. | Hour at which Temperature taken. | Observations. |
|---|---|---|---|---|---|---|---|---|---|
| | A. At Sea. | B. Near the Shore. | | | | | | | |
| **July.** | ° | ° | Miles. | Fathoms. | | | ° | | |
| 1 | 52 | 52 | 2 | 10 | Flood | WNW | 60 | 12 30 p.m. | |
| 2 | 51 | 53 | 2 | 8 | do. | E N E | 56 | Noon | |
| 3 | 52 | 54 | 1½ | 8 | Low water | E N E | 57 | 11 40 a.m. | |
| 5 | 52 | 54 | 1½ | 8 | Ebb | S | 57 | Noon | |
| 6 | 52 | 53 | 2 | 8 | do. | W | 57 | 11 45 a.m. | |
| 7 | 51 | 52 | 2 | 10 | do. | W | 54 | 12 10 p.m. | |
| 8 | 51 | 54 | 2 | 10 | do. | S | 60 | 12 30 p.m. | |
| 9 | 51 | 54 | 1½ | 8 | do. | SSW | 58 | 11 45 a.m. | |
| 10 | 52 | 54 | 2 | 8 | do. | WSW | 60 | 12 15 p.m. | |
| 12 | 51 | 53 | 2 | 9 | High water | WSW | 58 | Noon | |
| 13 | 51 | 53 | 1 | 8 | Flood | WNW | 56 | 11 40 a.m. | |
| 14 | 51 | 53 | 2 | 8 | do. | N E | 58 | 11 45 a.m. | |
| 15 | 51 | 53 | 2 | 9 | do. | WNW | 58 | Noon | |
| 16 | 51 | 52 | 1½ | 9 | do. | WNW | 56 | 12 30 p.m. | |
| 17 | 53 | 55 | 1½ | 9 | do. | W | 72 | Noon | |
| 19 | 52 | 54 | 2 | 10 | Low water | NW | 65 | 12 30 p.m. | |
| 20 | 52 | 53 | 1½ | 9 | Ebb | SW | 58 | do. | |
| 21 | 52 | 54 | 2 | 9 | do. | S | 58 | 12 15 p.m. | |
| 22 | 52 | 54 | 2 | 9 | do. | WSW | 63 | 11 30 a.m. | |
| 23 | 53 | 54 | 2 | 9 | do. | SSW | 61 | 12 20 p.m. | |
| 24 | 53 | 56 | 2 | 9 | do. | S W | 63 | Noon | |
| 26 | 53 | 55 | 1½ | 8 | High water | S | 60 | 12 15 p.m. | |
| 27 | 52 | 54 | 1 | 8 | Flood | NNW | 57 | 11 40 a.m. | |
| 28 | 53 | 54 | 2 | 10 | do. | SW | 62 | 12 30 p.m. | |
| 29 | 53 | 55 | 2 | 10 | do. | S | 60 | 11 45 a.m. | |
| 30 | 53 | 55 | 1½ | 9 | do. | W | 64 | Noon | |
| 31 | 54 | 55 | 1½ | 9 | do. | Calm | 62 | 11 40 a.m. | |

CROMARTY DIVISION.—CROMARTY STATION, ROSS-SHIRE.

Taken by THOMAS LAPÉNOTIÈRE, Divisional Officer.

| **May.** | | | | | | | | | |
|---|---|---|---|---|---|---|---|---|---|
| 10 | 47 | 47 | ½ | 23 | Ebb | Calm | 53 | Noon | Greenwich time observed with A, and 10″ to 15″ difference in time for B, *later.* |
| 11 | 47 | 47 | ¼ | 28 | do. | WNW | 50 | do. | |
| 12 | 48 | 48 | ¼ | 21 | Flood | W | 58 | do. | |
| 13 | 47 | 48 | ¼ | 20 | do. | W | 57 | do. | Cloudy. |
| 14 | 47 | 49 | ½ | 22 | do. | E | 54 | do. | Clear. |
| 15 | 47 | 48 | ¾ | 23 | do. | E | 50 | do. | do. |
| 17 | 49 | 49 | ¼ | 27 | do. | E | 52 | do. | do. |
| 18 | 49 | 50 | ½ | 22 | do. | E | 51 | do. | Cloudy. |
| 19 | 49 | 50 | ½ | 18 | Ebb | N | 52 | do. | Showery. |
| 20 | 49 | 49 | ½ | 25 | do. | N | 51 | do. | do. |
| 21 | 48 | 48 | ½ | 24 | do. | N | 50 | do. | Cloudy. |
| 22 | 48 | 48 | ½ | 25 | do. | Calm | 50 | do. | do. |
| 24 | 49 | 50 | ½ | 23 | do. | E | 49 | do. | Clear. |
| 25 | 49 | 50 | ½ | 22 | do. | E | 50 | do. | Cloudy. |
| 26 | 49 | 50 | ½ | 22 | Flood | E | 48 | do. | do. |
| 27 | 49 | 49 | ½ | 12 | do. | N E | 47 | do. | Showery, hail. |
| 28 | 49 | 50 | ½ | 24 | do. | E | 49 | do. | Clear. |
| 29 | 49 | 50 | ½ | 21 | do. | W | 52 | do. | Cloudy. |
| 31 | 49 | 50 | ½ | 24 | do. | NW | 50 | do. | do. |

CROMARTY DIVISION, &c.—*continued.*

| 1869. | Temperature. A. At Sea | Temperature. B. Near the Shore. | Distance from Land. (Miles) | Depth of Water. (Fathoms) | State of Tide, &c. | Wind. | Temperature of Air. | Hour at which Temperature taken. | Observations. |
|---|---|---|---|---|---|---|---|---|---|
| **June.** | | | | | | | | | |
| 1 | 49 | 51 | 1/2 | 21 | Flood | E | 49 | Noon | Cloudy. |
| 2 | 52 | 52 | 1/4 | 20 | do. | Calm | 60 | do. | Clear. |
| 3 | 50 | 52 | 1/4 | 24 | Ebb | W | 54 | do. | Cloudy, rain. |
| 4 | 50 | 52 | 1/2 | 25 | do. | NNW | 53 | do. | do. |
| 5 | 51 | 52 | 1/4 | 19 | do. | E | 57 | do. | do. |
| 7 | 51 | 53 | 1/2 | 20 | do. | Calm | 59 | do. | do. |
| 8 | 52 | 52 | 1/2 | 20 | do. | NW | 50 | do. | do. |
| 9 | 51 | 52 | 1/2 | 17 | do. | NNW | 54 | do. | do. |
| 10 | 50 | 51 | 1/2 | 20 | Flood | NNW | 53 | do. | do. |
| 11 | 49 | 51 | 1/2 | 24 | do. | NNW | 48 | do. | do. |
| 12 | 49 | 51 | 1/2 | 22 | do. | W | 52 | do. | Fine weather. |
| 14 | 50 | 51 | 1/2 | 22 | do. | E | 50 | do. | Rain. |
| 15 | 50 | 50 | 1/2 | 16 | do. | N E | 46 | do. | Clear. |
| 16 | 51 | 52 | 1/4 | 16 | do. | N N E | 50 | do. | Light rain. |
| 17 | 51 | 54 | 1/2 | 6 | do. | Calm | 56 | do. | Cloudy. |
| 18 | 53 | 53 | 1/2 | 15 | Ebb | E | 59 | do. | do. |
| 19 | 52 | 52 | 1/2 | 20 | do. | E | 57 | do. | do. |
| 21 | 52 | 53 | 3/4 | 27 | do. | E S E | 57 | 11 30 a.m. | do. |
| 22 | 52 | 52 | 3/4 | 17 | do. | NW | 58 | do. | do. |
| 23 | 51 | 54 | 1 | 18 | do. | Calm | 57 | do. | do. |
| 24 | 53 | 57 | 2 | 11 | Flood | Calm | 58 | do. | do. |
| 25 | 52 | 57 | 2 | 11 | Ebb | W | 64 | 2 p.m. | Clear. |
| 26 | 53 | 58 | 2 | 4 | Flood | NW | 64 | do. | Cloudy. |
| 28 | 54 | 59 | 3/4 | 25 | do. | E | 60 | do. | Fine. |
| 29 | 56 | 57 | 1/2 | 19 | do. | E | 62 | do. | Clear. |
| 30 | 56 | 58 | 1/2 | 4 | do. | E | 60 | do. | do. |
| **July.** | | | | | | | | | |
| 1 | 58 | 61 | | 24 | Flood | E | 70 | Noon | Clear. |
| 2 | 58 | 60 | | 21 | do. | E | 60 | do. | Hazy. |
| 3 | 57 | 58 | | 21 | Ebb | E | 60 | do. | Cloudy. |
| 5 | 58 | 59 | | 22 | do. | WSW | 62 | do. | Rain. |
| 6 | 56 | 58 | | 5 | do. | W by S | 59 | do. | Strong gales; clear. |
| 7 | 54 | 55 | | 24 | do. | E | 57 | do. | Hazy. |
| 8 | 54 | 55 | | 22 | do. | W | 61 | do. | Cloudy. |
| 9 | 56 | 57 | | 10 | do. | SW | 58 | do. | Cloudy; heavy gale. |
| 10 | 52 | 54 | | 19 | Flood | NNW | 58 | do. | Cloudy. |
| 12 | 54 | 57 | | 6 | do. | W | 59 | do. | Strong gales; fine. |
| 13 | 53 | 55 | | 12 | do. | NW | 58 | do. | do. |
| 14 | 53 | 55 | | 22 | do. | W | 59 | do. | Hazy. |
| 15 | 55 | 58 | | 24 | do. | W | 62 | do. | Cloudy. |
| 16 | 55 | 60 | | 5 | do. | W | 60 | do. | Clear. |
| 17 | 55 | 57 | | 10 | Ebb | E | 63 | do. | Cloudy. |
| 19 | 56 | 57 | | 9 | do. | E S E | 58 | do. | do. |
| 20 | 56 | 58 | | 23 | do. | E | 58 | do. | do. |
| 21 | 58 | 59 | | 7 | do. | S E | 68 | do. | Clear. |
| 22 | 54 | 56 | | 22 | do. | WSW | 62 | do. | Cloudy. |
| 23 | 58 | 59 | | 9 | do. | SW | 69 | do. | Squally. |
| 24 | 56 | 57 | | 17 | Flood | SW | 64 | do. | do. |
| 26 | 56 | 57 | | 16 | do. | S E | 62 | do. | Hazy. |
| 27 | 56 | 57 | | 24 | do. | E S E | 60 | do. | Cloudy. |
| 28 | 56 | 58 | | 23 | do. | W | 66 | do. | do. |
| 29 | 58 | 59 | | 13 | do. | SW | 62 | do. | do. |
| 30 | 56 | 58 | | 4 1/2 | do. | NNW | 59 | do. | Clear. |
| 31 | 57 | 58 | | 17 | do. | W | 62 | do. | Thick, with rain. |

GREENOCK DIVISION.—ARDROSSAN STATION, AYRSHIRE.

Taken by W. M'Millan, Chief Boatman.

| 1869 | Temperature. | | Distance from Land. | Depth of Water. | State of Tide, &c. | Wind. | Temperature of Air. | Hour at which Temperature taken. | Observations. |
|------|-----|-----|------|-----|-----|-----|-----|-----|-----|
| | A. At Sea. | B. Near the Shore. | | | | | | | |
| **May.** | ° | ° | | Feet. | | | ° | | |
| 10 | — | 45 | In the har- | 6 | Ebb | E | 48 | Noon | No oyster beds. |
| 11 | — | 45 | bour | 6 | do. | N W | 55 | do. | |
| 12 | — | 46 | do. | 8 | High water | N W | 55 | do. | |
| 13 | — | 47 | do. | 8 | Flood | S W | 60 | do. | |
| 14 | — | 47 | do. | 6 | do. | S | 59 | do. | |
| 15 | — | 47 | do. | 6 | do. | E | 57 | do. | |
| 17 | — | 48 | do. | 4½ | do. | E | 57 | do. | |
| 18 | — | 48 | do. | 3 | do. | E | 57 | do. | |
| 19 | — | 48 | do. | 2½ | do. | N | 57 | do. | |
| 20 | — | 46 | do. | 2 | Low water | N | 55 | do. | |
| 21 | — | 47 | do. | 3 | Ebb | N | 55 | do. | |
| 22 | — | 50 | do. | 4½ | do. | Var. | 59 | do. | |
| 24 | — | 49 | do. | 5 | do. | S E | 59 | do. | |
| 25 | — | 49 | do. | 6½ | do. | E | 57 | do. | |
| 26 | — | 49 | do. | 6½ | High water | E | 57 | do. | |
| 27 | — | 47 | do. | 6½ | Flood | E | 55 | do. | |
| 28 | — | 49 | do. | 6 | do. | E | 59 | do. | |
| 29 | — | 49 | do. | 5 | do. | N | 55 | do. | |
| 31 | — | 52 | do. | 4 | do. | N W | 55 | do. | |
| **July.** | | | | | | | | | |
| 1 | — | 60 | In the har- | 1 foot | Flood | Calm | 73 | Noon | |
| 2 | — | 60 | bour | do. | do. | Calm | 72 | do. | |
| 3 | — | 64 | do. | do. | Low water | S W | 75 | do. | |
| 5 | — | 60 | do. | do. | Ebb | S W | 66 | do. | |
| 6 | — | 63 | do. | do. | do. | N W | 65 | do. | |
| 7 | — | 64 | do. | do. | do. | S W | 67 | do. | |
| 8 | — | 63 | do. | do. | do. | S W | 67 | do. | |
| 9 | — | 61 | do. | do. | do. | W | 62 | do. | |
| 10 | — | 63 | do. | do. | High water | W | 64 | do. | |
| 12 | — | 59 | do. | do. | Flood | N W | 60 | do. | |
| 13 | — | 60 | do. | do. | do. | N W | 65 | do. | |
| 14 | — | 59 | do. | do. | do. | N W | 60 | do. | |
| 15 | — | 60 | do. | do. | do. | Ebb | 64 | do. | |
| 16 | — | 54 | do. | do. | Low water | N W | 69 | do. | |
| 17 | — | 65 | do. | do. | do. | Var. | 75 | do. | |
| 19 | — | 66 | do. | do. | Ebb | N W | 76 | do. | |
| 20 | — | 61 | do. | do. | do. | Calm | 77 | do. | |
| 21 | — | 60 | do. | do. | do. | Var. | 69 | do. | |
| 22 | — | 61 | do. | do. | do. | Calm | 69 | do. | |
| 23 | — | 62 | do. | do. | High water | S | 70 | do. | |
| 24 | — | 62 | do. | do. | do. | S S W | 68 | do. | |
| 26 | — | 62 | do. | do. | Flood | S W | 66 | do. | |
| 27 | — | 63 | do. | do. | do. | S W | 67 | do. | |
| 28 | — | 64 | do. | do. | do. | W | 74 | do. | |
| 29 | — | 60 | do. | do. | do. | N | 64 | do. | |
| 30 | — | 60 | do. | do. | do. | S W | 61 | do. | |
| 31 | — | 59 | do. | do. | do. | N W | 69 | do. | |

STRANRAER DIVISION.—PORT PATRICK STATION, WIGTONSHIRE.

Taken by DAVID M'INTOSH, Chief Boatman.

| 1869. | Temperature. | | Distance from Land. | Depth of Water. | State of Tide, &c. | Wind. | Temperature of Air. | Hour at which Temperature taken. | Observations. |
|---|---|---|---|---|---|---|---|---|---|
| | A. At Sea. | B. Near the Shore. | | | | | | | |
| **May.** | ° | ° | Yards. | | | | ° | | |
| 10 | – | 49 | 200 | 12 feet | Ebb | N E | 56 | Noon | No oyster beds at or |
| 11 | – | 50 | 100 | 10 feet | do. | NW | 58 | do. | near Port Patrick. |
| 12 | – | 50 | 150 | 12 feet | do. | NW | 56 | do. | |
| 13 | 50 | 51 | 300 | 6 fathoms | do. | NW | 60 | 12 30 p.m. | |
| 14 | – | 50 | 100 | 10 feet | Flood | S E | 58 | 11 30 a.m. | |
| 15 | – | 50 | 100 | 12 feet | do. | E S E | 59 | Noon | |
| 17 | – | 50 | 100 | 14 feet | do. | S E | 58 | do. | |
| 18 | – | 51 | 50 | 8 feet | do. | S E | 60 | do. | |
| 19 | – | 51 | 50 | 10 feet | do. | E | 59 | do. | |
| 20 | – | 50 | 100 | 12 feet | do. | N N E | 58 | do. | |
| 21 | – | 50 | 200 | 11 feet | Ebb | WNW | 61 | do. | |
| 22 | – | 52 | 40 | 6 feet | do. | NW | 63 | do. | |
| 24 | – | 52 | 40 | 5 feet | do. | S E | 62 | do. | |
| 25 | – | 51 | 100 | 10 feet | do. | S E | 60 | do. | |
| 26 | – | 51 | 100 | 8 feet | do. | E S E | 58 | do. | |
| 27 | – | 51 | 200 | 12 feet | do. | E | 58 | do. | |
| 28 | – | 51 | 200 | 12 feet | Flood | E | 58 | do. | |
| 29 | – | 52 | 50 | 8 feet | do. | NW | 60 | do. | |
| 31 | – | 50 | 200 | 10 feet | do. | NW | 57 | do. | |
| **June.** | | | | | | | | | |
| 1 | 52 | – | 300 yards | 6 fathoms | Flood | SW | 62 | Noon | |
| 2 | – | 53 | 200 yards | 12 feet | do. | S | 65 | do. | |
| 3 | – | 53 | do. | 13 feet | do. | WSW | 64 | do. | |
| 4 | – | 53 | 100 yards | 10 feet | Ebb | WNW | 64 | do. | |
| 5 | – | 53 | 200 yards | 12 feet | do. | S S W | 59 | do. | Thick rain. |
| 7 | – | 53 | do. | 10 feet | do. | S | 64 | do. | Thunder. |
| 8 | – | 53 | do. | 8 feet | do. | N N W | 60 | do. | |
| 9 | – | 54 | 100 yards | 6 feet | do. | N N W | 64 | do. | |
| 10 | – | 54 | do. | 5 feet | do. | NW | 62 | do. | |
| 11 | – | 53 | do. | 6½ feet | Flood | NW | 63 | do. | |
| 12 | – | 55 | 50 yards | 7 feet | do. | SW | 62 | do. | |
| 14 | – | 54 | 100 yards | 8 feet | do. | N N W | 60 | do. | |
| 15 | – | 54 | do. | 9 feet | do. | N N W | 58 | do. | Hail; showers. |
| 16 | – | 54 | do. | 12 feet | do. | N N W | 57 | do. | |
| 17 | – | 55 | 50 yards | 8 feet | do. | SW | 65 | 1 30 p.m. | |
| 18 | – | 54 | 200 yards | 10 feet | do. | NW | 62 | 12 30 p.m. | |
| 19 | – | 54 | do. | 12 feet | Ebb | S E | 64 | Noon | |
| 21 | – | 55 | do. | 10 feet | do. | NW | 62 | do. | |
| 22 | – | 55 | 100 yards | 8 feet | do. | NW | 62 | do. | |
| 23 | – | 54 | do. | 6½ feet | do. | N N W | 61 | do. | Hazy; thunder. |
| 24 | – | 55 | 200 yards | 8 feet | do. | WNW | 65 | do. | |
| 25 | – | 56 | ¼ mile | 10 fathoms | do. | Calm | 72 | 12 30 p.m. | |
| 26 | – | 57 | 50 yards | 10 feet | Flood | NW | 73 | Noon | |
| 28 | – | 58 | do. | 8½ feet | do. | NW | 65 | 1 p.m. | |
| 29 | – | 58 | ¼ mile | 11 fathoms | do. | NW | 65 | Noon | Hazy. |
| 30 | – | 58 | 200 yards | 12 feet | do. | Calm | 68 | do. | Calm and fine. |

STRANRAER DIVISION, &c.—*continued.*

| 1869. | Temperature. A. At Sea. | Temperature. B. Near the Shore. | Distance from Land. | Depth of Water. | State of Tide, &c. | Wind. | Temperature of Air. | Hour at which Temperature taken. | Observations. |
|---|---|---|---|---|---|---|---|---|---|
| **July.** | ° | ° | | | | | ° | | |
| 1 | − | 56 | 200 yards | 8 feet | Flood | N N W | 64 | Noon | No oyster beds at or |
| 2 | − | 56 | do. | 7 feet | do. | N N W | 64 | do. | near Port Patrick. |
| 3 | − | 56 | do. | 5½ feet | do. | Calm | 68 | do. | |
| 5 | − | 56 | 50 yards | 4 feet | Ebb | S S W | 64 | do. | |
| 6 | − | 57 | 200 yards | 10 feet | do. | N W | 65 | do. | Thick, with rain. |
| 7 | − | 56 | 50 yards | 8 feet | do. | S S W | 65 | do. | Thick fog. |
| 8 | − | 56 | do. | 9 feet | do. | S S E | 64 | do. | |
| 9 | − | 56 | do. | 10½ feet | do. | W S W | 64 | do. | |
| 10 | − | 58 | 200 yards | 12 feet | do. | W S W | 68 | do. | |
| 12 | − | 57 | do. | 11 feet | Flood | W N W | 64 | do. | |
| 13 | − | 57 | do. | 13 feet | do. | N W | 62 | do. | |
| 14 | − | 58 | do. | 10½ feet | do. | W N W | 62 | do. | |
| 15 | − | 58 | 50 yards | 8 feet | do. | Calm | 64 | do. | Hazy. |
| 16 | − | 58 | do. | 10 feet | do. | N N W | 60 | 1 30 p.m. | |
| 17 | − | 59 | ¼ mile | 14 fathoms | do. | Calm | 70 | Noon | |
| 19 | − | 58 | 200 yards | 12 feet | Ebb | N W | 66 | do. | |
| 20 | − | 59 | do. | 10½ feet | do. | Calm | 70 | do | |
| 21 | − | 58 | 50 yards | 8 feet | do. | S S W | 69 | do. | |
| 22 | − | 58 | do. | 7 feet | do. | S S E | 65 | do. | Thick fog. |
| 23 | − | 59 | do. | 6½ feet | do. | S S W | 67 | do. | Thunder. |
| 24 | − | 58 | 200 yards | 12 feet | do. | S S W | 67 | do. | |
| 26 | − | 58 | ½ mile | 12 fathoms | Flood | N W | 64 | do. | Thunder. |
| 27 | − | 59 | 200 yards | 10 feet | do. | W S W | 65 | do. | do. |
| 28 | − | 59 | do. | 8½ feet | do. | S W | 67 | do. | |
| 29 | − | 58 | do. | 7 feet | do. | S S W | 64 | do. | Fresh gale and rain. |
| 30 | − | 58 | do. | 6½ feet | do. | S W | 63 | do. | |
| 31 | − | 60 | ¼ mile | 11 fathoms | do. | S W | 64 | 12 30 p.m. | Sultry; thunder. |

# ABSTRACT

OF THE

## TABLES OF TEMPERATURE

FOR

MAY, JUNE, JULY, 1869.

ABSTRACT of the TABLES of TEMPERATURE

## MAY.

| Locality. | Situation. | Latitude. | 10. | | 11. | | 12. | | 13. | | 14. | |
|---|---|---|---|---|---|---|---|---|---|---|---|---|
| | | | A. | B. | A. | B. | A. | B. | A. | B. | A. | B. |
| Arcachon, . | W. C. F. | — | - | 62 | - | 62 | - | 62 | - | 62 | - | 63 |
| Cougre, . . | do. | — | - | - | - | - | - | - | - | - | - | - |
| Auray, . . | do. | — | - | - | - | - | - | - | 60 | 60 | 61 | 61 |
| Granville, . | do. | — | - | - | - | - | - | - | - | - | - | - |
| Jersey, . . | Channel | — | - | - | - | - | - | - | - | - | - | - |
| St. Catherine's, | S. C. E. | 50/50 | 52 | 53 | 52 | 53 | 52 | 54 | 52 | 54 | 52 | 53 |
| Eastbourne, . | do. | — | 52 | 53 | 51 | 52 | 51 | 51 | 52 | 52 | 51 | 51 |
| Ramsgate, . | S. E. C. E. | 50/75 | 54 | 56 | 52 | 56 | 52 | 54 | 54 | 55 | - | 54 |
| Cromer, . . | E. C. E. | 52/70 | - | 53 | - | 51 | - | 53 | - | 52 | - | 52 |
| Whitehaven, . | W. C. E. | 54/50 | 46 | 49 | 49 | 49 | 49 | 50 | 50 | 50½ | 50 | 50½ |
| Douglas, . . | E. C. Man | 54/20 | - | 46 | - | 47 | - | 48 | - | 48 | - | 48 |
| Bangor, . . | W. C. W. | 53/20 | - | 50 | - | 50 | - | 51 | - | 52 | - | 52 |
| Milford, . . | do. | 51/30 | - | 50 | - | 53 | - | 51 | - | 54 | - | 52 |
| Queenstown, . | S. C. I. | 51/50 | 53 | 53 | 53 | 53 | 53 | 53 | 52 | 55 | 52 | 55 |
| Waterford, . | do. | 52/10 | - | 52 | - | 54 | - | 54 | - | - | - | - |
| Arklow, . . | E. C. I. | — | - | - | - | - | - | - | - | - | - | - |
| Dublin, . . | do. | 53/20 | - | 49 | - | 49 | - | 48 | 48 | - | - | 50 |
| Carlingford. . | do. | 54/ | - | - | - | - | - | 55 | - | 55 | - | 55 |
| Carrickfergus. . | do. | 54/30 | - | 49 | - | 49 | - | 48 | - | 49 | - | 50 |
| Rathmullen, . | N. C. I. | 55/5 | - | 49 | - | 49 | - | 50 | - | 50 | - | 49 |
| Carn, . . | do. | 55/17 | - | 43 | - | 49 | - | 43 | - | 44 | - | 44 |
| Rutland, . . | do. | 54. 58 | - | 48 | - | 48 | - | 49 | - | 51 | - | 52 |
| Belmullet, . | W. C. I. | 54/10 | - | - | - | - | - | - | - | - | - | - |
| Westport, . | do. | 53/45 | - | 52 | - | 53 | - | 52 | - | 53 | - | 52 |
| Galway, . . | do. | 53/10 | - | 52 | - | 51 | - | 52 | - | 52 | - | 53 |
| Ballyheigh, . | do. | 52/20 | - | 52 | - | 56 | - | 61 | - | 59 | - | 58 |
| Pullendiva, . | do. | 54/20 | - | 53 | - | 54 | - | 53 | - | 54 | - | 53 |
| Kenmare, . | S. W. C. I. | 51/50 | 55 | - | 55 | - | 54 | - | 55 | - | 52 | - |
| North Berwick, | E. C. S. | — | 45 | 46 | 46 | 47 | 47 | 48 | 47 | 49 | 47 | 48 |
| Aberdeen, . | do. | — | - | - | - | - | 46 | 48 | 46 | 48 | 46 | 48 |
| Cromarty, . | N. E. C. S. | — | 47 | 47 | 47 | 47 | 48 | 48 | 47 | 48 | 47 | 48 |
| Greenock, . | W. C. S. | — | - | 45 | - | 45 | - | 46 | - | 47 | - | 47 |
| Portpatrick, . | do. | — | - | 49 | - | 50 | - | 50 | 50 | 51 | - | 50 |

EXPLANATIONS.

| | |
|---|---|
| A. column—Temperature at sea. | W.C.E.—West coast of England. |
| B. column—Temperature near shore. | W.C.I.—West coast of Ireland. |
| W.C.F.—West coast of France. | W.C.S.—West coast of Scotland. |

for month of MAY, 1869.

## MAY.

| 15. | | 16. | | 17. | | 18. | | 19. | | 20. | | Locality. |
|---|---|---|---|---|---|---|---|---|---|---|---|---|
| A. | B. | A. | B. | A. | B. | A. | B. | A. | B. | A. | B. | |
| – | 63 | – | 63 | – | 63 | – | 63 | – | 63 | – | 62 | Arcachon. |
| – | – | – | – | – | – | – | – | – | – | – | – | Cougre. |
| 61 | 61 | 61 | 61 | 62 | 62 | 61 | 61 | 61 | 61 | 61 | 61 | Auray. |
| – | – | – | – | – | – | – | – | – | – | – | – | Granville. |
| – | – | – | – | – | – | – | – | – | – | – | – | Jersey. |
| 52 | 52 | 52 | 52 | – | 52 | – | 52 | – | 52 | 52 | 53 | St. Catherine's. |
| 50 | 50 | 50 | 52 | 53 | 54 | 53 | 53 | 54 | 56 | 54 | 55 | Eastbourne. |
| – | 56 | – | – | 58 | 58 | – | 58 | – | 58 | 56 | 57 | Ramsgate. |
| – | 51 | – | – | – | 52 | – | 51 | 51 | 52 | – | 52 | Cromer. |
| 50 | 50½ | – | – | 50 | 51 | 49 | 50 | 49 | 50 | 49 | 50 | Whitehaven. |
| – | 48 | – | – | – | 47 | – | 48 | – | 46 | – | 49 | Douglas. |
| – | 52 | – | – | – | 52 | – | 53 | – | 51 | – | 53 | Bangor. |
| – | 52 | – | – | – | 53 | – | 52 | – | 49 | – | 54 | Milford. |
| 52 | 53 | 52 | 54 | 54 | 54 | 53 | 53 | 53 | 55 | 53 | 56 | Queenstown. |
| – | – | – | – | – | 55 | – | 55 | – | 53 | – | 54 | Waterford. |
| – | – | – | – | – | – | – | – | – | – | – | – | Arklow. |
| 50 | – | – | – | – | 50 | – | 50 | – | 50 | 48 | – | Dublin. |
| – | 54 | – | – | – | – | – | 56 | – | 56 | 57 | – | Carlingford. |
| – | 52 | – | – | – | 51 | – | 47 | – | 50 | – | 48 | Carrickfergus. |
| – | 49 | – | – | – | 49 | – | 49 | – | 49 | – | 49 | Rathmullen. |
| – | 44 | – | – | – | 44 | – | 44 | – | 44 | – | 44 | Carn. |
| – | 49 | – | – | – | 48 | – | 49 | – | 49 | – | 50 | Rutland. |
| – | – | – | – | – | – | – | – | – | – | – | – | Belmullet. |
| – | 51 | – | – | – | 52 | – | 52 | – | 52 | – | 53 | Westport. |
| – | 52 | – | – | – | 52 | – | 52 | – | 51 | – | 51 | Galway. |
| – | 56 | – | 57 | – | – | – | 50 | – | 50 | – | 55 | Ballyheigh. |
| – | 50 | – | – | – | 52 | – | 52 | – | 52 | – | 55 | Pullendiva. |
| 52 | – | – | – | 55 | – | 55 | – | 53 | – | 53 | – | Kenmare. |
| 47 | 48 | – | – | 47 | 48 | 46 | 47 | 46 | 47 | 45 | 46 | North Berwick. |
| 46 | 48 | – | – | 46 | 48 | – | – | – | 47 | 47 | 49 | Aberdeen. |
| 47 | 48 | – | – | 49 | 49 | 49 | 50 | 49 | 50 | 49 | 49 | Cromarty. |
| – | 47 | – | – | – | 48 | – | 48 | – | 48 | – | 46 | Greenock. |
| – | 50 | – | – | – | 50 | – | 50 | – | 51 | – | 50 | Portpatrick. |

EXPLANATIONS.

E.C.I.    S.C.I.    In like manner denote the east,
E.C.E.    N.C.I.    south, or north coasts of
S.C.E.    N.C.S    these countries.

[continued.

ABSTRACT of the TABLES of TEMPERATURE

## MAY.

| Locality. | Situation. | Latitude. | 21. | | 22. | | 23. | | 24. | | 25. | |
|---|---|---|---|---|---|---|---|---|---|---|---|---|
| | | | A. | B. | A. | B. | A. | B. | A. | B. | A. | B. |
| Arcachon, | W. C. F. | — | - | 61 | - | 61 | - | 61 | - | 61 | - | 62 |
| Cougre, | do. | — | - | - | - | - | - | - | - | - | - | - |
| Auray, | do. | — | 59 | 59 | 60 | 60 | 61 | 61 | 61 | 61 | 60 | 60 |
| Granville, | do. | — | - | - | - | - | - | - | - | 59 | 58 | 59 |
| Jersey, | Channel | — | - | - | - | - | - | - | - | - | - | - |
| St. Catherine's, | S. C. E. | 50/50 | 52 | 53 | 53 | 53 | - | - | 46 | 47 | 53 | 54 |
| Eastbourne, | do. | — | 51 | 51 | 55 | 56 | - | - | 55 | 56 | 56 | 56 |
| Ramsgate. | S. E. C. E. | 50 75 | 56 | 57 | 57 | 58 | - | - | 56 | 58 | 56 | 58 |
| Cromer, | E. C. E. | 52/70 | - | 58 | - | 53 | - | - | - | 52 | - | 53 |
| Whitehaven, | W. C. E. | 54/50 | 50 | 51 | 50 | 51 | - | - | 50 | 50½ | 50 | 50 |
| Douglas, | E. C. Man | 54/20 | - | 49 | - | 50 | | - | - | 50 | - | 49 |
| Bangor, | W. C W. | 53/20 | - | 51 | - | 52 | - | - | - | 53 | - | 53 |
| Milford, | do. | 51/30 | - | 54 | - | 55 | - | - | - | 53 | - | 55 |
| Queenstown, | S. C. I. | 51/50 | 53 | 56 | 53 | 56 | - | - | 53 | 56 | 53 | 57 |
| Waterford, | do. | 52/10 | - | 54 | - | 54 | - | - | - | 65 | - | 64 |
| Arklow, | E. C. I. | — | - | - | - | - | - | - | - | - | - | - |
| Dublin, | do. | 53/20 | - | 50 | - | 50 | - | - | - | 50½ | - | 50½ |
| Carlingford, | do. | 54/ | 58 | - | - | 56 | 54 | - | - | 55 | - | 65 |
| Carrickfergus, | do. | 54/30 | - | 52 | - | 53 | - | - | - | 63 | - | 62 |
| Rathmullen, | N. C. I. | 55/3 | - | 50 | - | 50 | - | - | - | 53 | - | 51 |
| Carn, | do. | 55/17 | - | 46 | - | 46 | - | - | - | 46 | - | 46 |
| Rutland, | do. | 54/58 | - | 50 | - | 49 | - | - | - | 50 | - | 51 |
| Belmullet, | W. C. I. | 54/10 | - | - | - | - | - | - | - | - | - | - |
| Westport, | do. | 53/45 | - | 53 | - | 53 | - | - | - | 55 | - | 54 |
| Galway, | do. | 53/10 | - | 52 | 52 | - | - | - | - | 52 | - | 52 |
| Ballyheigh, | do. | 52/20 | - | 57 | - | 60 | - | - | - | 60 | - | 59 |
| Pullendiva, | do. | 54/20 | - | 55 | - | 56 | - | - | - | 53 | - | 53 |
| Kenmare, | S. W. C. I. | 51/50 | 55 | - | 55 | - | - | - | 56 | - | 55 | - |
| North Berwick, | E. C. S. | — | 46 | 48 | 48 | 30 | - | - | 48 | 50 | 47 | 48 |
| Aberdeen, | do. | — | 48 | 49 | 49 | 50 | - | - | 48 | 50 | 47 | 48 |
| Cromarty, | N. E. C. S. | — | 48 | 48 | 48 | 48 | - | - | 49 | 50 | 49 | 50 |
| Greenock, | W. C. S. | — | - | 47 | - | 50 | - | - | - | 49 | - | 49 |
| Portpatrick, | do. | — | - | 50 | - | 52 | - | - | - | 52 | - | 51 |

for mouth of MAY, 1869—*continued.*

### MAY.

| 26. | | 27. | | 28. | | 29. | | 30. | | 31. | | Locality. |
|---|---|---|---|---|---|---|---|---|---|---|---|---|
| A. | B. | A. | B. | A. | B. | A. | B. | A. | B. | A. | B. | |
| – | 62 | – | 62 | – | 62 | – | 62 | – | 62 | – | 62 | Arcachon. |
| – | – | – | – | – | – | – | – | – | – | – | – | Cougre. |
| 61 | 62 | 61 | 61 | 61 | 62 | 61 | 61 | 60 | 60 | 61 | 61 | Auray. |
| 58 | 58 | 58 | 59 | 57 | 58 | 57 | 57 | 57 | 57 | 58 | 58 | Granville. |
| – | – | – | – | – | – | – | – | – | – | – | – | Jersey. |
| 54 | 55 | 53 | 55 | 52 | 53 | 51 | 50 | – | – | 52 | 54 | St. Catherine's. |
| 57 | 57 | 57 | 57 | 55 | 55 | 52 | 52 | – | – | 53 | 54 | Eastbourne. |
| 57 | 59 | 52 | 54 | – | 52 | – | 52 | – | – | 54 | 55 | Ramsgate. |
| – | 52 | – | 49 | – | 50 | – | 49 | – | – | . | 50 | Cromer. |
| 50 | 51 | 50 | 51 | 51 | 51½ | 51 | 51 | – | – | 51 | 51½ | Whitehaven. |
| – | 49 | – | 49 | – | 49 | – | 50 | – | – | – | 50 | Douglas. |
| – | 50 | – | 50 | – | 51 | – | 51 | – | – | – | 52 | Bangor. |
| – | 55 | – | 52 | – | 51 | – | 51 | – | – | – | 53 | Milford. |
| 51 | 54 | 51 | 53 | 50 | 52 | 52 | 54 | – | – | 54 | 56 | Queenstown. |
| – | 63 | – | 64 | – | 63 | – | 63 | – | – | – | 63 | Waterford. |
| – | – | – | – | – | – | – | – | – | – | – | – | Arklow. |
| 50 | – | 50 | – | – | 50 | – | 50 | – | – | 50½ | – | Dublin. |
| – | 57 | – | 56 | – | 56 | – | 57 | – | – | – | 56 | Carlingford. |
| – | 62 | – | 64 | – | 61 | – | 61 | – | – | – | 63 | Carrickfergus. |
| – | 50 | – | 48 | – | 49 | – | 51 | – | – | – | 52 | Rathmullen. |
| – | 41 | – | 45 | – | 39 | – | 50 | – | – | – | 45 | Carn. |
| – | 50 | – | 49 | – | 50 | – | 50 | – | – | – | 49 | Rutland. |
| – | – | – | – | – | – | – | – | – | – | – | – | Belmullet. |
| – | 53 | – | 50 | – | 53 | – | 54½ | – | – | – | 55 | Westport. |
| – | 53 | – | 50 | – | 51 | – | 50 | – | – | – | 53 | Galway. |
| – | 56 | – | 51 | – | 57 | – | 57 | – | – | – | 61 | Ballyheigh. |
| – | 52 | – | 49 | – | 51 | – | 52 | – | – | – | 54 | Pullendive. |
| 52 | – | 53 | – | 51 | – | 53 | – | – | – | 54 | – | Kenmare. |
| 48 | 49 | – | 48 | – | 48 | 48 | 50 | – | – | 49 | 50 | North Berwick. |
| 48 | 48 | 47 | 46 | 47 | 48 | 46 | 48 | – | – | 48 | 49 | Aberdeen. |
| 49 | 50 | 49 | 49 | 49 | 50 | 49 | 50 | – | – | 49 | 50 | Cromarty. |
| – | 47 | – | 49 | – | 49 | – | 49 | – | – | – | 52 | Greenock. |
| – | 51 | – | 51 | – | 51 | – | 52 | – | – | – | 50 | Portpatrick. |

ABSTRACT of the TABLES of TEMPERATURE

JUNE.

| Locality. | Situation. | Latitude. | 1. | | 2. | | 3. | | 4. | | 5. | | 6. | |
|---|---|---|---|---|---|---|---|---|---|---|---|---|---|---|
| | | | A. | B. | A. | B. | A. | B. | A. | B. | A. | B. | A. | B. |
| Arcachon, . . | W. C. F. | — | - | 62 | - | 62 | - | 63 | - | 63 | - | 64 | - | 64 |
| Cougre, . . | do. | — | - | - | - | - | - | - | - | - | - | - | - | - |
| Auray, . . . | do. | — | 60 | 60 | 60 | 61 | 61 | 61 | 60 | 61 | 62 | 63 | 63 | 64 |
| Gorvather, . | do. | — | 60 | 61 | 60 | 62 | 60 | 62 | 60 | 61 | 68 | 69 | 62 | 62 |
| Granville, . | do. | — | 58 | 58 | 58 | 58 | 59 | 59 | 59 | 59 | 60 | 60 | 60 | 61 |
| Jersey, . . | Channel | — | - | 56 | - | 58 | - | 59 | - | 57 | - | 59 | - | - |
| St. Catherine's, . . | E. C. E. | 50/50 | 53 | 55 | 53 | 55 | 53 | 55 | 54 | 55 | 64 | 54 | - | - |
| Eastbourne, . | do. | — | 55 | 56 | 55 | 56 | 56 | 56 | 55 | 57 | 56 | 55 | - | - |
| Ramsgate, . | S. E. C. E. | 50/75 | 56 | 57 | 55 | 57 | 55 | 57 | 56 | 53 | 58 | 59 | - | - |
| Cromer, . | E. C. E. | 52/70 | - | 52 | - | 53 | - | 54 | 52 | 55 | 53 | 55 | - | - |
| Whitehaven, | W. C. E. | 54/50 | 50 | 51 | 51 | 52 | 51 | 51 | 51 | 52 | 52 | 52 | - | - |
| Douglas, . | E. C. Man | 54/20 | - | 51 | - | 50 | - | 51 | - | 53 | - | 53 | - | - |
| Bangor, . | W. C. W. | 53/20 | - | 56 | - | 55 | - | 54 | - | 56 | - | 56 | - | - |
| Milford, . | do. | 51/30 | - | 55 | - | 54 | - | 55 | - | 57 | - | 60 | - | - |
| Queenstown, . | S. C. I. | 51/50 | 57 | 58 | 55 | 59 | 56 | 58 | 54 | 56 | 56 | 56 | - | - |
| Waterford, . | do. | 52/10 | - | 57 | - | 57 | - | 56 | - | 56 | - | 57 | - | - |
| Arklow, . | E. C. I. | — | 50 | 52 | 50 | 56 | 50 | 52 | 51 | 50 | 50 | 50 | - | - |
| Dublin, . | do. | 53/20 | - | 52 | - | 52 | - | 52 | - | 52 | - | 51 | - | - |
| Carlingford, . | do. | 54/ | - | 57 | 55 | - | 56 | - | 56 | - | 58 | - | - | - |
| Carrickfergus, | do. | 54/50. | - | 57 | - | 56 | - | 52 | - | 53 | - | 54 | - | - |
| Rathmullen, | N. C. I. | 55/5 | - | 52 | - | 52 | - | 53 | - | 54 | - | 54 | - | - |
| Carn, . . . | do. | 55/17 | - | 45 | - | 47 | - | 46 | - | 47 | - | 48 | - | - |
| Rutland, . | do. | 54/58 | - | 51 | - | 52 | - | 52 | - | 54 | - | 54 | - | - |
| Belmullet, . | W. C. I. | 54/10 | - | - | - | - | - | - | - | - | - | - | - | - |
| Westport, . | do. | 53/45 | - | 56 | - | 56 | - | 56 | - | 56 | - | 57 | - | - |
| Galway, . | do. | 53/10 | - | 54 | - | 55 | - | 55 | - | 55 | - | 56 | - | - |
| Ballyheigh, . | do. | 52/20 | - | 59 | - | 59 | - | 59 | - | 59 | - | 57 | - | - |
| Pullendiva, . | do. | 54/20 | - | 54 | - | 54 | - | 54 | - | 55 | - | 56 | - | - |
| Kenmare, . | S. W. C. I. | 51/30 | 54 | - | 54 | - | 53 | - | 55 | - | 54 | - | - | - |
| North Berwick, . . | E. C. S. | — | 49 | 50 | 50 | 51 | 51 | 52 | 51 | 52 | 52 | 53 | - | - |
| Aberdeen, . | do. | — | 48 | 48 | 48 | 50 | 49 | 50 | 50 | 49 | 49 | 50 | - | - |
| Cromarty, . | N. E. C. S. | — | 49 | 51 | 52 | 52 | 50 | 52 | 50 | 52 | 51 | 52 | - | - |
| Greenock, . | W. C. S. | — | - | 52 | - | 52 | - | 56 | - | 56 | - | 57 | - | - |
| Portpatrick, . . | do. | — | 52 | 53 | - | 53 | - | 53 | - | 53 | - | 53 | - | - |

for month of JUNE, 1869.

## JUNE.

| 7. | | 8. | | 9. | | 10. | | 11. | | 12. | | 13. | | 14. | | 15. | | Locality. |
|---|---|---|---|---|---|---|---|---|---|---|---|---|---|---|---|---|---|---|
| A. | B. | A. | B. | A. | B. | A. | B. | A. | B. | A. | B. | A. | B. | A. | B. | A. | B. | |
| – | 65 | – | 66 | – | 66 | – | 66 | – | 66 | – | 66 | – | 66 | – | 66 | – | 65 | Arcachon. |
| – | – | – | – | – | – | – | – | – | – | – | – | – | – | – | – | – | – | Congre. |
| 63 | 65 | 63 | 64 | 63 | 63 | 62 | 62 | 62 | 63 | 64 | 65 | 65 | 66 | 62 | 62 | 63 | 63 | Auray. |
| 60 | 67 | 67 | 69 | 67 | 68 | 65 | 66 | 62 | 63 | – | – | 61 | 62 | 61 | 62 | 61 | 61 | Gorvather. |
| 59 | 60 | 60 | 61 | 60 | 61 | 60 | 61 | 59 | 59 | 59 | 59 | 59 | 59 | 59 | 60 | 59 | 59 | Granville. |
| – | 59 | – | 61 | – | 60 | – | 58 | – | 58 | – | 59 | – | – | – | 58 | – | 56 | Jersey. |
| 55 | 56 | 55 | 57 | 55 | 57 | 55 | 57 | 56 | 57 | 56 | 57 | – | – | 57 | 58 | – | 58 | St. Catherine's. |
| 57 | 59 | 59 | 58 | 59 | 61 | 59 | 60 | 59 | 59 | 58 | 59 | – | – | 58 | 58 | 58 | 59 | Eastbourne. |
| 61 | 63 | 60 | 61 | 59 | 60 | 59 | 60 | 57 | 59 | 58 | 59 | – | – | 58 | 59 | – | 58 | Ramsgate. |
| – | 54 | – | 56 | – | 56 | – | 55 | – | 54 | – | 56 | – | – | – | 54 | – | 55 | Cromer. |
| 52 | 53 | 53 | 54 | 54 | 55 | 55 | 55 | 55 | 55 | 56 | 56 | – | – | 56 | 56 | 56 | 56 | Whitehaven. |
| – | 52 | – | 53 | – | 51 | – | 52 | – | 52 | – | 53 | – | – | – | 52 | 51 | 52 | Douglas. |
| – | 58 | – | 56 | – | 58 | – | 57 | – | 57 | – | 56 | – | – | – | 55 | – | 51 | Bangor. |
| – | 59 | – | 55 | – | 57 | – | 58 | – | 57 | – | 57 | – | – | – | 55 | – | 55 | Milford. |
| 56 | 58 | 59 | 62 | 60 | 64 | 62 | 64 | 62 | 64 | 61 | 62 | – | – | 59 | 60 | 57 | 59 | Queenstown. |
| – | 57 | – | 58 | – | 61 | – | 62 | – | 61 | – | 59 | – | – | – | 59 | – | 59 | Waterford. |
| 52 | 51 | 50 | 52 | 52 | 54 | – | – | 51 | 50 | – | – | – | – | 50 | 52 | – | – | Arklow. |
| – | 52 | – | 52 | 52 | 52 | 52 | 52 | – | 52 | – | 52 | – | – | – | 52 | – | 52 | Dublin. |
| – | 63 | 62 | – | 62 | – | – | 63 | 60 | – | – | 62 | – | – | – | 61 | – | 60 | Carlingford. |
| – | 58 | – | 55 | – | 57 | – | 55 | – | 56 | – | 55 | – | – | – | 57 | – | 51 | Carrickfergus. |
| – | 55 | – | 55 | – | 37 | – | 56 | – | 56 | – | 54 | – | – | – | 54 | – | 53 | Rathmullen. |
| – | 49 | – | 49 | – | 49 | – | 51 | – | 50 | – | 50 | – | – | – | 50 | – | 50 | Carn. |
| – | 54 | – | 55 | – | 55 | – | 54 | – | 56 | – | 54 | – | – | – | 53 | – | 53 | Rutland. |
| – | – | 55 | 58 | 58 | 58 | 58 | 58 | 55 | 56 | 55 | 56 | – | – | 54 | 56 | 56 | 56 | Belmullet. |
| – | 59 | – | 63 | – | 63 | – | 62 | – | 64 | – | 63 | – | – | – | 59 | – | 63 | Westport. |
| – | 57 | – | 58 | – | 61 | – | 65 | – | 58 | – | 57 | – | – | – | 56 | – | 55 | Galway. |
| – | 59 | – | 65 | – | 67 | – | 73 | – | 68 | – | 65 | – | – | – | 61 | – | 59 | Ballyheigh. |
| – | 54 | – | 56 | – | 53 | – | 56 | – | 54 | – | 56 | – | – | – | 56 | – | 56 | Pullendiva. |
| – | – | – | – | 60 | – | 59 | – | 56 | – | 58 | – | – | – | 58 | – | 57 | – | Kenmare. |
| 52 | 54 | 51 | 54 | 52 | 53 | 52 | 53 | 52 | 52 | 52 | 52 | – | – | 51 | 52 | – | 47 | North Berwick. |
| 50 | 53 | 49 | 51 | – | 49 | – | 48 | 49 | 50 | 49 | 50 | – | – | 50 | 50 | 50 | 50 | Aberdeen. |
| 52 | 52 | 51 | 52 | 50 | 51 | 49 | 51 | 49 | 51 | 50 | 50 | – | – | 51 | 52 | 51 | 54 | Cromarty. |
| – | 55 | – | 53 | – | 52 | – | 53 | – | 53 | – | 53 | – | – | – | 56 | – | 51 | Greenock. |
| – | 53 | – | 53 | – | 54 | – | 54 | – | 53 | – | 55 | – | – | – | 54 | – | 54 | Portpatrick. |

[continued.

I

ABSTRACT of the TABLES of TEMPERATURE

**JUNE.**

| Locality. | Situation. | Latitude. | 16. | | 17. | | 18. | | 19. | | 20. | | 21. | |
|---|---|---|---|---|---|---|---|---|---|---|---|---|---|---|
| | | | A. | B. | A. | B. | A. | B | A. | B. | A. | B. | A. | B. |
| Arcachon, | W. C. F. | — | – | 64 | – | 64 | – | 64 | – | 64 | – | 64 | – | 64 |
| Cougre, | do. | — | – | – | 61 | 62 | 62 | 63 | 62 | 63 | 62 | 63 | 61 | 62 |
| Auray, | do. | — | 61 | 61 | 61 | 61 | 61 | 61 | 61 | 61 | 62 | 62 | 62 | 63 |
| Gorvather, | do. | — | 61 | 62 | 61 | 61 | 61 | 61 | 61 | 62 | 62 | 62 | 60 | 62 |
| Granville, | do. | — | 59 | 59 | 59 | 59 | 59 | 59 | 59 | 59 | 59 | 59 | 59 | 59 |
| Jersey, | Channel | — | – | 57 | 56 | 58 | – | 58 | – | 58 | – | – | – | 58 |
| St. Catherine's, | E C. E. | 50/50 | – | 58 | 57 | 58 | 58 | 58 | 58 | 58 | – | – | 58 | 58 |
| Eastbourne, | do. | — | 57 | 56 | 57 | 57 | 57 | 57 | 57 | 58 | – | – | 57 | 57 |
| Ramsgate, | S. E. C. E. | 50/75 | – | 58 | 56 | 57 | 57 | 59 | 57 | 59 | – | – | 57 | 59 |
| Cromer, | E. C. E. | 52/70 | – | 53 | – | 54 | – | 52 | – | 52 | – | – | – | 53 |
| Whitehaven, | W. C. E. | 54/50 | 56 | 56 | 55 | 56 | 56 | 57 | 56 | 57 | – | – | 56 | 57 |
| Douglas, | E. C. Man | 54/20 | 51 | 53 | 52 | 54 | 52 | 54 | 53 | 55 | – | – | 53 | 55 |
| Bangor, | W. C. W. | 53/20 | – | 54 | – | 54 | – | 54 | – | 56 | – | – | – | 58 |
| Milford, | do. | 51/30 | – | 57 | – | 57 | – | 55 | – | 56 | – | – | – | 59 |
| Queenstown, | S. C. I. | 51/50 | 59 | 60 | 61 | 63 | 62 | 64 | 60 | 62 | – | – | 61 | 64 |
| Waterford, | do. | 52/10. | – | 60 | – | 57 | – | 57 | – | 57 | – | – | – | 59 |
| Arklow, | E. C. I. | — | 52 | 50 | 50 | 50 | 50 | 52 | 52 | 50 | – | – | 52 | 50 |
| Dublin, | do. | 53/20 | – | 52 | 52 | 52 | – | 52 | 53 | – | – | – | 52 | – |
| Carlingford, | do. | 54/ | – | 60 | – | 59 | – | 59 | 56 | – | 57 | – | – | 63 |
| Carrickfergus, | do. | 54/50 | – | 52 | – | 56 | – | 54 | – | 55 | – | – | – | 54 |
| Rathmullen, | N. C. I. | 55/5 | – | 56 | – | 58 | – | 55 | – | 58 | – | – | – | 59 |
| Carn, | do. | 55/17 | – | 48 | – | 50 | – | 50 | – | 50 | – | – | – | 50 |
| Rutland, | do. | 54/58 | – | 54 | – | 54 | – | 55 | – | 56 | – | – | – | 56 |
| Belmullet, | W. C. I. | 54/10 | 56 | 56 | 55 | 58 | 54 | 57 | 55 | 56 | – | – | 58 | 57 |
| Westport, | do. | 53/45 | – | 62 | – | 63 | – | 58 | – | 60 | – | – | – | 58 |
| Galway, | do. | 53/10 | – | 58 | – | 57 | – | 57 | – | 58 | – | – | – | 59 |
| Ballyheigh, | do. | 52/20 | – | 59 | – | 60 | – | 59 | – | 60 | – | – | – | 65 |
| Pullendiva, | do. | 54/20 | – | 56 | – | 56 | – | 56 | – | 58 | – | – | – | 58 |
| Kenmare, | S. W. C. I. | 51/50 | 57 | – | 57 | – | 57 | – | 58 | – | – | – | 57 | – |
| North Berwick, | E. C. S. | — | – | 50 | 51 | 50 | 51 | 52 | 51 | 53 | – | – | 51 | 53 |
| Aberdeen, | do. | — | 50 | 52 | 50 | 51 | 51 | 53 | 52 | 54 | – | – | 50 | 50 |
| Cromarty, | N. E. C. S. | — | 53 | 53 | 52 | 52 | 52 | 52 | 52 | 52 | – | – | 52 | 52 |
| Greenock, | W. C. S. | — | – | 52 | – | 53 | – | 56 | – | 55 | – | – | – | 55 |
| Portpatrick, | do. | — | – | 54 | – | 55 | – | 54 | – | 54 | – | – | – | 55 |

for month of JUNE, 1869—*continued.*

## JUNE.

| 22. | | 23. | | 24. | | 25. | | 26. | | 27. | | 28. | | 29. | | 30. | | Locality. |
|---|---|---|---|---|---|---|---|---|---|---|---|---|---|---|---|---|---|---|
| A. | B. | A. | B. | A. | B. | A. | B. | A. | B. | A. | B. | A. | B. | A. | B. | A. | B. | |
| - | 64 | - | 64 | - | 64 | - | 64 | - | 64 | - | 65 | - | 66 | - | 66 | - | 66 | Arcachon. |
| 61 | 62 | 63 | 64 | 65 | 66 | 65 | 65 | 64 | 65 | 65 | 67 | 64 | 67 | 64 | 65 | 61 | 63 | Cougre. |
| 62 | 62 | 62 | 62 | 62 | 62 | 62 | 62 | 62 | 62 | 62 | 62 | 62 | 63 | 62 | 62 | 62 | 62 | Auray. |
| 61 | 63 | 62 | 64 | 62 | 64 | 62 | 64 | 60 | 61 | 61 | 63 | 63 | 65 | 63 | 65 | 63 | 64 | Gorvather. |
| 59 | 60 | 60 | 60 | 60 | 60 | 60 | 60 | 60 | 60 | 60 | 60 | 60 | 60 | 60 | 60 | 60 | 60 | Granville. |
| - | 60 | - | 60 | - | 60 | - | 60 | - | 60 | - | - | - | 60 | 58 | 60 | - | 58 | Jersey. |
| - | - | - | - | 58 | 59 | 57 | 59 | 57 | 59 | 58 | 60 | 58 | 60 | 58 | 60 | 58 | 60 | St. Catherine's. |
| 57 | 57 | 58 | 58 | 57 | 58 | 57 | 58 | 58 | 59 | - | - | 60 | 61 | 60 | 60 | 61 | 61 | Eastbourne. |
| 58 | 59 | 58 | 59 | 59 | 60 | 58 | 59 | 59 | 60 | - | - | 59 | 60 | 59 | 60 | 58 | 59 | Ramsgate. |
| - | 56 | - | 57 | - | 58 | 59 | 56 | 59 | 56 | - | - | - | 59 | - | 58 | - | 58 | Cromer. |
| 57 | 57 | 57 | 57 | 57 | 58 | 58 | 59 | 58 | 59 | - | - | 59 | 59 | 59 | 59 | 59 | 60 | Whitehaven. |
| 53 | 54 | 53 | 53 | 53 | 53 | 53 | 55 | 53 | 55 | - | - | 55 | 56 | 55 | 56 | 56 | 57 | Douglas. |
| - | 61 | - | 59 | - | 59 | - | 60 | - | 60 | - | - | - | 63 | - | 63 | - | 62 | Bangor. |
| - | 55 | - | 56 | - | 57 | - | 58 | - | 60 | - | - | - | 62 | - | 59 | - | 59 | Milford. |
| 62 | 64 | 63 | 64 | 64 | 66 | 63 | 66 | 65 | 66 | - | - | 68 | 70 | 69 | 71 | 71 | 80 | Queenstown. |
| - | 59 | - | 58 | - | 65 | - | 64 | - | 63 | - | - | - | 63 | - | 63 | - | 63 | Waterford. |
| 52 | 50 | 52 | 50 | - | - | - | - | - | - | - | - | - | - | - | - | - | - | Arklow. |
| 53 | - | - | 53 | - | 53 | 53 | - | - | 53 | - | - | - | 53 | - | 54 | - | 54 | Dublin. |
| - | 63 | - | 64 | - | - | 60 | - | 62 | - | - | 1 | - | 63 | - | 63 | - | 65 | Carlingford. |
| - | 57 | - | 58 | - | 58 | - | 57 | - | 58 | - | - | - | 60 | - | 60 | - | 60 | Carrickfergus. |
| - | 61 | - | 62 | - | 64 | - | 66 | - | 66 | - | - | - | 67 | - | 68 | - | 68 | Rathmullen. |
| - | 51 | - | 51 | - | 52 | - | 52 | - | 52 | - | - | - | 59 | - | 53 | - | 58 | Carn. |
| - | 57 | - | 57 | - | 58 | - | 59 | - | 59 | - | - | - | 59 | - | 59 | - | 60 | Rutland. |
| 55 | 57 | 55 | 55 | 58 | 59 | 59 | 59 | 58 | 61 | - | - | 58 | 55 | 58 | 60 | 58 | 61 | Belmullet. |
| - | 57 | - | 59 | - | 61 | - | 67 | - | 67 | - | - | - | 65 | - | 66 | - | 66 | Westport. |
| - | 58 | - | 58 | - | 61 | - | 62 | - | 64 | - | - | - | 64 | - | 64 | - | 63 | Galway. |
| - | 64 | - | 64 | - | 63 | - | 63 | - | 68 | - | - | - | 73 | - | 76 | - | 70 | Ballyheigh. |
| - | 58 | - | 58 | - | 59 | - | 61 | - | 61 | - | - | - | 62 | - | 64 | - | 64 | Pullendiva. |
| 58 | - | 58 | - | 58 | - | 58 | - | 58 | - | - | - | 60 | - | 62 | - | 62 | - | Kenmare. |
| 51 | 43 | 52 | 54 | 52 | 54 | 53 | 54 | 53 | 55 | - | - | 53 | 55 | 53 | 55 | 52 | 54 | North Berwick. |
| 50 | 53 | 50 | 54 | 52 | 54 | 53 | 55 | 52 | 54 | - | - | 51 | 52 | 51 | 52 | 52 | 56 | Aberdeen. |
| 52 | 52 | 51 | 54 | 53 | 57 | 52 | 57 | 53 | 58 | - | - | 54 | 59 | 56 | 57 | 56 | 58 | Cromarty. |
| - | 56 | - | 57 | - | 58 | - | 60 | - | 58 | - | - | - | 58 | - | 59 | - | 59 | Greenock. |
| - | 55 | - | 54 | - | 55 | 54 | 56 | - | 57 | - | - | - | 58 | 53 | 58 | - | 58 | Portpatrick. |

ABSTRACT of the TABLES of TEMPERATURE

**JULY.**

| Locality. | Situation. | Latitude. | 1. | | 2. | | 3. | | 4. | | 5. | | 6. | |
|---|---|---|---|---|---|---|---|---|---|---|---|---|---|---|
| | | | A. | B. | A. | B. | A. | B. | A. | B. | A. | B. | A. | B. |
| Arcachon, | W. C. F. | — | - | 66 | - | 66 | - | 66 | - | 66 | - | 66 | - | 66 |
| Cougre, | do. | — | - | 63 | - | 63 | 64 | 66 | 65 | 67 | 65 | 67 | 66 | 67 |
| Auray, | do. | — | 62 | 62 | 62 | 62 | 62 | 62 | 62 | 62 | 62 | 62 | 64 | 65 |
| Granville, | do. | — | 59 | 60 | 60 | 60 | 60 | 61 | 61 | 61 | 60 | 61 | 61 | 61 |
| Jersey, | Channel | — | - | 59 | - | 58 | - | 59 | - | - | - | 62 | - | 62 |
| St. Catherine's, | E. C. E. | 50/50 | 57 | 58 | 57 | 59 | 57 | 59 | - | - | 59 | 60 | 59 | 60 |
| Eastbourne, | do. | — | 60 | 60 | 60 | 60 | 60 | 61 | - | - | 60 | 62 | - | - |
| Ramsgate, | S. E. C. E. | 50/75 | - | 59 | - | 59 | 60 | 61 | - | - | 61 | 62 | 61 | 62 |
| Cromer, | E. C. E. | 52/70 | 56 | 58 | 56 | 58 | 56 | 58 | - | - | - | 59 | - | 65 |
| Whitehaven, | W. C. E. | 54/50 | 59 | 59 | 60 | 60 | 60 | 60 | - | - | 59 | 60 | 60 | 60 |
| Douglas, | E. C. Man | 54/20 | 55 | 56 | 55 | 56 | 55 | 57 | - | - | 55 | 57 | 56 | 58 |
| Bangor, | W. C. W. | 53/20 | - | 62 | - | 64 | - | 62 | - | - | - | 62 | - | 63 |
| Milford, | do. | 51/30 | - | 62 | - | 60 | - | 62 | - | - | - | 60 | - | 62 |
| Queenstown, | S. C. I. | 51/50 | 71 | 79 | 71 | 80 | 70 | 78 | - | - | 68 | 76 | 66 | 71 |
| Waterford, | do. | 52/10 | - | - | - | 63 | - | 64 | - | - | - | 65 | - | 63 |
| Arklow, | E. C. I. | — | - | - | - | - | 58 | 54 | - | - | 58 | 54 | - | - |
| Dublin, | do. | 53/20 | 53 | - | 53 | - | 53 | - | - | - | 54 | - | 54 | - |
| Carlingford, | do. | 54/ | - | 66 | - | 67 | 65 | - | - | - | 66 | - | - | 66 |
| Carrickfergus, | do. | 54/50 | - | 61 | - | 61 | - | 64 | - | - | - | 63 | - | 62 |
| Rathmullen, | N. C. I. | 55/5 | - | 68 | - | 69 | - | 69 | - | - | - | 66 | - | 67 |
| Carn, | do. | 55/17 | - | 54 | - | 56 | - | 56 | - | - | - | 57 | - | 61 |
| Rutland, | do. | 54/58 | - | 60 | - | 61 | - | 61 | - | - | - | 62 | - | 61 |
| Belmullet, | W. C. I. | 54/10 | 58 | 57 | 58 | 57 | 63 | 62 | - | - | 61 | 60 | 58 | 65 |
| Westport, | do. | 53/45 | - | 65 | - | 66 | - | 66 | - | - | - | 65 | - | 65 |
| Galway. | do. | 53/10 | - | 64 | - | 65 | - | 66 | - | - | - | 62 | - | 62 |
| Ballyheigh, | do. | 52/20 | - | 68 | - | 73 | - | 74 | - | - | - | 70 | - | 68 |
| Pullendiva, | do. | 54/20 | - | 65 | - | 66 | - | 66 | - | - | - | 66 | - | 66 |
| Kenmare, | S. W. C. I. | 51/50 | 54 | - | 54 | - | 53 | - | - | - | 55 | - | 54 | - |
| North Berwick, | E. C. S. | — | 53 | 55 | 54 | 55 | 54 | 56 | - | - | 55 | 56 | - | 57 |
| Aberdeen, | do. | — | 52 | 52 | 51 | 53 | 52 | 54 | - | - | 52 | 54 | 52 | 53 |
| Cromarty, | N. E. C. S. | — | 58 | 61 | 58 | 60 | 57 | 58 | - | - | 58 | 59 | 56 | 58 |
| Greenock, | W. C. S. | — | - | 60 | - | 60 | - | 64 | - | - | - | 60 | - | 63 |
| Portpatrick, | do. | — | - | 56 | - | 56 | - | 56 | - | - | - | 56 | - | 57 |

for month of JULY, 1869.

**JULY.**

| 7. | | 8. | | 9. | | 10. | | 11. | | 12. | | 13. | | 14. | | 15. | | Locality. |
|---|---|---|---|---|---|---|---|---|---|---|---|---|---|---|---|---|---|---|
| A. | B. | A. | B. | A. | B. | A. | B. | A. | B. | A. | B. | A. | B. | A. | B. | A. | B. | |
| - | 66 | - | 66 | - | 66 | - | 66 | - | 66 | - | 66 | - | 67 | - | 67 | - | 67 | Arcachon. |
| 65 | 66 | 65 | 67 | 66 | 67 | 66 | 67 | 66 | 68 | 66 | 68 | 66 | 68 | 66 | 69 | 66 | 69 | Cougre. |
| 63 | 65 | 65 | 65 | 65 | 65 | 65 | 65 | 66 | 66 | 67 | 67 | 66 | 67 | 66 | 67 | 67 | 67 | Auray. |
| 60 | 61 | 61 | 61 | 61 | 61 | 61 | 61 | - | - | 61 | 61 | 61 | 61 | 61 | 62 | 61 | 62 | Granville. |
| - | 64 | - | 62 | - | 63 | - | 62 | - | - | - | 62 | - | 63 | - | 63 | - | 63 | Jersey. |
| 59 | 60 | 59 | 60 | 60 | 61 | 60 | 62 | 60 | 62 | 60 | 62 | 60 | 62 | 60 | 62 | 61 | 62 | St. Catherine's. |
| 58 | 60 | 60 | 60 | 60 | 61 | 61 | 62 | - | - | 65 | 66 | 64 | 65 | 64 | 65 | 63 | 64 | Eastbourne. |
| 61 | 62 | 62 | 63 | 62 | 63 | 61 | 62 | - | - | 61 | 62 | 62 | 63 | 62 | 63 | 62 | 63 | Ramsgate. |
| - | 66 | - | 66 | - | 62 | - | 62 | - | - | - | 64 | - | 61 | - | 62 | - | 62 | Cromer. |
| - | 60 | 59 | 60 | 60 | 60 | 61 | 62 | - | - | 62 | 63 | - | 61 | 61 | 61 | 62 | 62 | Whitehaven. |
| 56 | 57 | 56 | 58 | 56 | 58 | 56 | 58 | - | - | 57 | 58 | 57 | 59 | 57 | 60 | 57 | 60 | Douglas. |
| - | 62 | - | 61 | - | 61 | - | 61 | - | - | - | 62 | - | 59 | - | 61 | - | 62 | Bangor. |
| - | 60 | - | 60 | - | 62 | - | 61 | - | - | - | 61 | - | 59 | - | 62 | - | 63 | Milford. |
| 64 | 70 | 63 | 68 | 64 | 67 | 64 | 69 | - | - | 65 | 69 | 66 | 70 | 67 | 70 | 64 | 69 | Queenstown. |
| - | 63 | - | 63 | - | 65 | - | 65 | - | - | - | 66 | - | 66 | - | 64 | - | 62 | Waterford. |
| - | - | - | - | - | - | 60 | 50 | - | - | 58 | 50 | 60 | 52 | 58 | 54 | 58 | 54 | Arklow. |
| - | 53 | - | 54 | - | 54 | - | 54 | - | - | - | 54 | - | 54 | 54 | - | 54 | - | Dublin. |
| - | 66 | - | 66 | - | 65 | - | 66 | - | - | 64 | - | - | 66 | - | 65 | 65 | - | Carlingford. |
| - | 60 | - | 62 | - | 60 | - | 60 | - | - | - | 62 | - | 59 | - | 60 | - | 64 | Carrickfergus. |
| - | 68 | - | 70 | - | 70 | - | 68 | - | - | - | 67 | - | 66 | - | 65 | - | 67 | Rathmullen. |
| - | 57 | - | 63 | - | 54 | - | 56 | - | - | - | 59 | - | 52 | - | 52 | - | 54 | Carn. |
| - | 62 | - | 61 | - | 61 | - | 64 | - | - | - | 64 | - | 60 | - | 59 | - | 59 | Rutland. |
| - | - | - | - | - | - | 56 | 58 | - | - | 60 | 58 | 59 | 60 | 58 | 60 | 62 | 61 | Belmullet. |
| - | 65 | - | 65 | - | 63 | - | 63 | - | - | - | 65 | - | 63 | - | 62 | - | 62 | Westport. |
| - | 65 | - | 64 | - | 66 | - | 63 | - | - | - | 64 | - | 64 | - | 64 | - | 64 | Galway. |
| - | 66 | - | 65 | - | 67 | - | 70 | - | - | - | 70 | - | 66 | - | 67 | - | 68 | Ballyheigh. |
| - | 64 | - | 62 | - | - | - | - | - | - | - | - | - | - | - | - | - | - | Pullendiva. |
| - | - | - | - | 60 | - | 59 | - | - | - | 56 | - | 58 | - | 58 | - | 57 | - | Kenmare. |
| 56 | 57 | 56 | 58 | - | 57 | 57 | 58 | - | - | 56 | 58 | 56 | 58 | - | 57 | - | 57 | North Berwick. |
| 51 | 52 | 51 | 54 | 51 | 54 | 52 | 54 | - | - | 51 | 53 | 51 | 53 | 51 | 53 | 51 | 53 | Aberdeen. |
| 54 | 55 | 54 | 55 | 56 | 57 | 52 | 54 | - | - | 54 | 57 | 53 | 55 | 53 | 55 | 55 | 58 | Cromarty. |
| - | 64 | - | 63 | - | 61 | - | 63 | - | - | - | 59 | - | 60 | - | 59 | - | 60 | Greenock. |
| - | 56 | - | 56 | - | 56 | - | 58 | - | - | - | 57 | - | 57 | - | 58 | - | 58 | Portpatrick. |

[continued.

ABSTRACT of the TABLES of TEMPERATURE

**JULY.**

| Locality. | Situation. | Latitude. | 16. | | 17. | | 18. | | 19. | | 20. | | 21. | | 22. | |
|---|---|---|---|---|---|---|---|---|---|---|---|---|---|---|---|---|
| | | | A. | B. | A. | B. | A. | B. | A. | B. | A. | B. | A. | B. | A. | B. |
| Arcachon, | W. C. F. | — | - | 67 | - | 67 | - | 67 | - | 67 | - | 67 | - | 67 | - | 67 |
| Cougre, . | do. | — | 66 | 69 | - | - | 66 | 67 | 66 | 67 | 67 | 68 | 67 | 68 | 67 | 67 |
| Auray, . | do. | — | 66 | 66 | 66 | 66 | 66 | 67 | 67 | 67 | 67 | 67 | 68 | 69 | 67 | 68 |
| Granville, | do. | — | 62 | 63 | 62 | 64 | 63 | 64 | 62 | 64 | 62 | 64 | 63 | 64 | 63 | 64 |
| Jersey, . . | Channel | — | - | 65 | - | 66 | - | - | - | 66 | - | 65 | - | 65 | - | 66 |
| St. Catherine's, | E. C. E. | 50/50 | 61 | 62 | 61 | 63 | - | - | 62 | 64 | 62 | 64 | 62 | 64 | 62 | 64 |
| Eastbourne, . | do. | — | 65 | 66 | 67 | 68 | - | - | - | - | 67 | 67 | 65 | 66 | 66 | 67 |
| Ramsgate, . | S. E. C. E. | 50/75 | 63 | 64 | 63 | 65 | - | - | 62 | 63 | 62 | 63 | 62 | 63 | 63 | 64 |
| Cromer, . | E. C. E. | 52,70 | - | 66 | - | 67 | - | - | - | 62 | - | 64 | - | 66 | - | 66 |
| Whitehaven, . | W. C. E. | 54/50 | 62 | 62 | 63 | 64 | - | - | 64 | 65 | 64 | 65 | 64 | 65 | 63 | 64 |
| Douglas, . | E. C. Man | 54/20 | 58 | 61 | 59 | 61 | - | - | 59 | 62 | 59 | 60 | 59 | 60 | 59 | 60 |
| Bangor, . | W. C. W. | 53/20 | - | 61 | - | 65 | - | - | - | 64 | - | 65 | - | 64 | - | 63 |
| Milford, . | do. | 51/30 | - | 62 | - | 63 | - | - | - | 61 | - | 63 | - | 63 | - | 60 |
| Queenstown, | S. C. I. | 51/50 | 60 | 64 | 62 | 65 | - | - | 61 | 65 | 59 | 64 | 56 | 66 | 54 | 64 |
| Waterford, | do. | 52/10 | - | 64 | - | 66 | - | - | - | 66 | - | 65 | - | 64 | - | 65 |
| Arklow, . | E. C. I. | — | 60 | 56 | 58 | 54 | - | - | - | - | 60 | 56 | 58 | 54 | 60 | 52 |
| Dublin, . . | do. | 53/20 | 54 | - | 54 | - | - | - | 60 | - | 54 | - | - | 60 | 60 | - |
| Carlingford, . | do. | 54/ | 64 | - | - | 67 | - | - | 67 | - | - | 70 | - | 68 | - | 72 |
| Carrickfergus, | do. | 54/50 | - | 60 | - | 66 | - | - | - | 69 | - | - | - | 64 | - | - |
| Rathmullen, . | N. C. I. | 55/5 | - | 68 | - | 70 | - | - | - | 70 | - | 71 | - | 72 | - | 70 |
| Carn, . . | do. | 55/17 | - | 57 | - | 57 | - | - | - | 58 | - | 65 | - | 59 | - | 58 |
| Rutland, | do. | 54/58 | - | 62 | - | 64 | - | - | - | 65 | - | 65 | - | 64 | - | 65 |
| Belmullet, . | W. C. I. | 54/10 | 63 | 64 | 61 | 62 | - | - | 60 | 62 | 60 | 62 | 61 | 63 | 60 | 62 |
| Westport, . | do. | 53/45 | - | 64 | - | 64 | - | - | - | 67 | - | 67 | - | 68 | - | 66 |
| Galway, . | do. | 53/10 | - | 65 | - | 65 | - | - | - | 66 | - | 67 | - | 66 | - | 64 |
| Ballyheigh, . | do. | 52/20 | - | 70 | - | 69 | - | - | - | 74 | - | 76 | - | 69 | - | 69 |
| Pullendiva, . | do. | 54/20 | - | - | - | 62 | - | - | - | 62 | - | 64 | - | 64 | - | 62 |
| Kenmare, . | S. W. C. I. | 51/50 | 57 | - | 57 | - | - | .. | 58 | - | 57 | - | 58 | - | 58 | - |
| North Berwick, | E. C. S. | — | 55 | 57 | 56 | 58 | - | - | 55 | 56 | 54 | 55 | 55 | 56 | 58 | 57 |
| Aberdeen, . | do. | — | 51 | 52 | 53 | 52 | - | - | 52 | 54 | 52 | 53 | 52 | 54 | 52 | 54 |
| Cromarty, . | N. E. C. S. | — | 55 | 60 | 55 | 57 | - | - | 56 | 57 | 56 | 58 | 58 | 59 | 54 | 56 |
| Greenock, . | W. C. S. | — | - | 64 | - | 65 | - | - | - | 66 | - | 61 | - | 60 | - | 61 |
| Portpatrick, . | do. | — | - | 58 | 56 | 59 | - | - | - | 58 | - | 59 | - | 58 | - | 58 |

for month of July, 1869.

### JULY.

| 23. | | 24. | | 25. | | 26. | | 27. | | 28. | | 29. | | 30. | | 31. | | Locality. |
|---|---|---|---|---|---|---|---|---|---|---|---|---|---|---|---|---|---|---|
| A. | B. | A. | B. | A. | B. | A. | B. | A. | B. | A. | B. | A. | B. | A. | B. | A. | B. | |
| – | 67 | – | 67 | – | 67 | – | 68 | – | 68 | – | 68 | – | 68 | – | 68 | – | 68 | Arcachon. |
| 67 | 67 | 66 | 67 | 65 | 65 | 65 | 65 | 65 | 65 | – | – | – | – | – | – | – | – | Cougre. |
| 67 | 68 | 67 | 68 | 68 | 68 | 67 | 68 | 67 | 67 | 67 | 67 | 66 | 67 | 65 | 66 | 65 | 66 | Auray. |
| 63 | 64 | 63 | 64 | 63 | 64 | 64 | 65 | 63 | 64 | 64 | 65 | 63 | 64 | 64 | 65 | 64 | 65 | Granville. |
| – | 64 | – | 64 | – | – | – | 64 | – | 64 | – | 65 | – | 65 | – | 64 | – | 65 | Jersey. |
| 62 | 63 | 62 | 64 | – | – | 63 | 64 | 63 | 64 | 63 | 63 | 63 | 64 | – | 64 | – | 64 | St. Catherine's. |
| 65 | 66 | 65 | 66 | – | – | 65 | 66 | 65 | 66 | 65 | 66 | 66 | 67 | 65 | 66 | 65 | 66 | Eastbourne. |
| 63 | 64 | 64 | 65 | – | – | 63 | 64 | 63 | 64 | 63 | 64 | 64 | 65 | 64 | 65 | 64 | 65 | Ramsgate. |
| – | 66 | – | 65 | – | – | – | 65 | – | 65 | – | 62 | – | 64 | – | 65 | – | 65 | Cromer. |
| 63 | 64 | 63 | 64 | – | – | 63 | 64 | 64 | 64 | 64 | 65 | – | 63 | – | 63 | 64 | 64 | Whitehaven. |
| 59 | 60 | 59 | 60 | – | – | 59 | 61 | 59 | 61 | 59 | 61 | 60 | 61 | 60 | 62 | 60 | 62 | Douglas. |
| – | 63 | – | 62 | – | – | – | 61 | – | 62 | – | 63 | – | 61 | – | 62 | – | 62 | Bangor. |
| – | 63 | – | 63 | – | – | – | 62 | – | 62 | – | 60 | – | 60 | – | 62 | – | 62 | Milford. |
| 53 | 61 | 51 | 60 | – | – | 50 | 61 | 52 | 59 | 49 | 53 | 48 | 53 | 45 | 49 | 41 | 46 | Queenstown. |
| – | 64 | – | 64 | – | – | – | 64 | – | 64 | – | 64 | – | 63 | – | 63 | – | 63 | Waterford. |
| 60 | 52 | 60 | 52 | – | – | 60 | 52 | – | – | 60 | 52 | – | – | 60 | 50 | 61 | 52 | Arklow. |
| 60 | – | – | 60 | – | – | – | 60 | – | 60 | – | 60 | – | 54 | – | 54 | 54 | – | Dublin. |
| – | 70 | 66 | – | – | – | 64 | – | – | 67 | – | 66 | – | 60 | – | 60 | 65 | – | Carlingford. |
| – | 62 | – | 63 | – | – | – | 62 | – | 62 | – | 64 | – | 61 | – | 61 | – | 63 | Carrickfergus. |
| – | 69 | – | 71 | – | – | – | 63 | – | 63 | – | 62 | – | 70 | – | 69 | – | 66 | Rathmullen. |
| – | 59 | – | 57 | – | – | – | 57 | – | 55 | – | 56 | – | 61 | – | 55 | – | 54 | Carn. |
| – | 64 | – | 64 | – | – | – | 65 | – | 65 | – | 64 | – | 64 | – | 65 | – | 64 | Rutland. |
| 60 | 62 | 61 | 62 | – | – | 62 | 62 | 60 | 62 | 60 | 61 | 60 | 61 | 60 | 60 | 60 | 60 | Belmullet. |
| – | 65 | – | 64 | – | – | – | 64 | – | 64 | – | 61 | – | 62 | – | 62 | – | 63 | Westport. |
| – | 65 | – | 65 | – | – | – | 64 | – | 64 | – | 64 | – | 63 | – | 62 | – | 63 | Galway. |
| – | 71 | – | 71 | – | – | – | 68 | – | 69 | – | 70 | – | 67 | – | 64 | – | 68 | Ballybeigh. |
| – | 62 | – | 61 | – | – | – | 61 | – | 62 | – | 62 | – | 62 | – | 62 | – | 62 | Pullendiva. |
| 58 | – | 58 | – | – | – | 58 | – | 58 | – | 60 | – | 62 | – | 62 | – | 62 | – | Kenmare. |
| 57 | 58 | 57 | 58 | – | – | 56 | 57 | 57 | 58 | 56 | 58 | 57 | 58 | 56 | 57 | 56 | 57 | North Berwick. |
| 53 | 54 | 53 | 56 | – | – | 53 | 55 | 52 | 54 | 53 | 54 | 53 | 55 | 53 | 55 | 54 | 55 | Aberdeen. |
| 58 | 59 | 56 | 57 | – | – | 56 | 57 | 56 | 57 | 56 | 58 | 56 | 58 | 58 | 59 | 57 | 58 | Cromarty. |
| – | 62 | – | 62 | – | – | – | 62 | – | 63 | – | 64 | – | 60 | – | 60 | – | 59 | Greenock. |
| – | 59 | – | 58 | – | – | 57 | 58 | – | 59 | – | 59 | – | 58 | – | 58 | 57 | 61 | Portpatrick. |

# OBSERVATIONS ON THE TEMPERATURE OF THE SEA.

## SOUTH YARMOUTH DIVISION.—ST. CATHERINE'S POINT STATION, ISLE OF WIGHT.

Taken by JOHN PEPPER, Chief Officer.

| 1868. | Temperature. | | Distance from Land. | Depth of Water. | State of Tide, &c. | Wind. | Observations. |
|---|---|---|---|---|---|---|---|
| | A. At Sea. | B. Near the Shore. | | | | | |
| Oct. | ° | ° | | | | | |
| 13 | 59 | 59 | ½ mile | 3 fathoms | High | NNW 2 | This observation was taken at Brook. |
| 14 | 60 | 58 | ¾ mile | 11 fathoms | Ebb W. | NNE 4 | Sea smooth. |
| 15 | 60 | 59 | ½ mile | 10 fathoms | do. | SW 6 | Sea rough. |
| 16 | – | 58 | 20 yards | 5 feet | do. | WSW 7 | Heavy sea. |
| 17 | 59 | 58 | ¾ mile | 11 fathoms | do. | WNW 4 | Ground sea. |
| 19 | 57 | 58 | ¾ mile | 8 fathoms | Flood E. | N 4 | do. |
| 20 | 55 | 54 | do. | 9 fathoms | do. | N 4 | Sea smooth. |
| 21 | 55 | 54 | ½ mile | 8 fathoms | do. | WNW 5 | Heavy sea. |
| 22 | 56 | 55 | ¾ mile | 10 fathoms | do. | WNW 5 | Heavy ground sea. |
| 23 | – | 55 | 6 yards | 3 feet | do. | NW 6 | Very heavy sea. |
| 24 | – | 54 | do. | do. | do. | SW 8 | do. |
| 26 | 56 | 55 | ½ mile | 9 fathoms | Low water | NW 5 | Heavy ground sea. |
| 27 | 55 | 53 | do. | do. | Ebb W. | NW 5 | Ground sea. |
| 28 | 55 | 53 | ¾ mile | 10 fathoms | do. | W 4 | Sea smooth. |
| 29 | – | 53 | 2 yards | 2 feet | do. | NW 8 | Very heavy sea. |
| 30 | 54 | 53 | ½ mile | 9 fathoms | do. | NW 5 | Heavy ground sea. |
| 31 | 55 | 53 | do. | do. | do. | W 6 | Heavy sea. |

## EASTBOURNE DIVISION.—HOLYWELL STATION, SUSSEX.

Taken by WILLIAM SNOOK, Chief Boatman, off Beachy Head.

| | | | | | | | |
|---|---|---|---|---|---|---|---|
| Oct. | | | | Fathoms. | | | |
| 12 | 55 | 54 | ½ mile; 300 yds. | 3 and 2 | Ebb W. | S E | No oyster beds on this coast. |
| 13 | 55 | 54 | ¾ mile; ½ mile. | 5 " 3½ | do. | Calm | |
| 14 | 55 | 54 | 1 mile; ¼ mile. | 5 " 3 | do | N | |
| 15 | 54 | 53 | ½ mile; 300 yds. | 4 " 2 | Flood E. | SW | |
| 16 | 54 | 53 | ¾ mile; 300 yds. | 5 " 2 | Ebb W. | W | |
| 17 | 57 | 56 | ½ mile; 300 yds. | 4 " 3 | do. | NW | |
| 19 | 57 | 56 | 1 mile; 200 yds. | 5 " 2 | Flood E. | N | |
| 20 | 57 | 56 | 1 mile; 300 yds. | 5 " 2 | do. | N | |
| 21 | 57 | 56 | 1 mile; 400 yds. | 5 " 3 | Ebb W. | NW | |
| 22 | 57 | 56 | 1 mile; 200 yds. | 5 " 2 | Flood E. | W | |
| 23, 24 | – | – | — | — | — | — | Coast impracticable for launching boat. |
| 26 | – | 56 | 200 yards | 1½ | Ebb W. | W | From the 26th instant this coast was impracticable for taking a boat outside, the reef running parallel to shore. |
| 27 | – | 56 | do. | 2 | do. | W | |
| 28 | – | 56 | 300 yards | 2½ | do. | W | |
| 29 | – | 56 | do. | 3 | do. | SW | |
| 30 | – | 55 | do. | 2½ | do. | NW | |
| 31 | – | 55 | do. | 3 | do. | SW | |

## Ramsgate Division.—Kingsgate Station, Kent.

Taken by Navigating-Lieutenant Edward Mouribgan, R.N.

| 1868. | Temperature. A. At Sea. | Temperature. B. Near the Shore. | Distance from Land. | Depth of Water. | State of Tide, &c. | Wind. | Observations. |
|---|---|---|---|---|---|---|---|
| Oct. | ° | ° | | Fathoms. | | | |
| 12 | 58 | 57½ | $\frac{8}{15}$ of mile | 7 | ½ ebb, SSE | SSE 2 | Temperature at A taken in the same position each day at noon, $\frac{8}{15}$ of a sea mile from high water mark. No oyster banks in the vicinity. |
| 13 | 59 | 58½ | do. | 7½ | ½ ebb, SSE | W 1 | |
| 14 | 59 | 57 | do. | 8 | ¼ ebb, NNW | N 5 | |
| 15 | 57 | 55½ | do. | 8¼ | do. | SW 6 | |
| 16 | 59 | 57 | do. | 8½ | 1 hour ebb, NNW | SW 5 | |
| 17 | 59 | 56 | do. | 9 | High water, NNW | W 3 | |
| 19 | 58 | 52 | do. | 8½ | ¾ flood, NNW | NW 4 | |
| 20 | 57½ | 52 | do. | 8¼ | do. | NW 4 | |
| 21 | 58 | 52 | do. | 7½ | ½ flood, no current | NW 5 | |
| 22 | 56 | 51 | do. | 7¼ | ¼ flood, SSE | NW 3 | |
| 23 | 56 | 51 | do. | 7¼ | Low water, SSE | SSW 5 | |
| 24 | 56 | 51 | do. | 7 | ¾ ebb, SSE | SSW 6 | |
| 26 | 55½ | 54½ | do. | 7½ | ½ ebb, no current | W 3 | |
| 27 | 55 | 48 | do. | 8 | ¼ ebb, NNW | NW 5 | |
| 28 | 52 | 49 | do. | 8½ | do. | W 3 | |
| 29 | 52 | 50 | do. | 8½ | High water, NNW | NW 6 | |
| 30 | 53 | 49 | do. | 8¾ | do. | W 4 | |
| 31 | 53 | 50 | do. | 9 | ¾ flood, NNW | WSW 4 | |

## Cromer Division.—Cromer Station, Norfolk.

Taken by William Frederick Hurrell, Chief Officer.

| | | | | | | | |
|---|---|---|---|---|---|---|---|
| Oct. | | | | | | | |
| 13 | 54 | 53 | 2 miles | 5 fathoms | Low water | SW | |
| 14 | 54 | 53 | 1 mile | do. | Ebb tide | N | |
| 15 | 54 | 54 | ½ mile | 4 fathoms | Flood S E | SW | |
| 16 | 55 | 54 | 1 mile | 5 fathoms | Ebb W | W by S | |
| 17 | 53 | 52 | 2½ miles. | 6 fathoms | Ebb NW | WSW | |
| 19 | - | 48 | Taken from the end of jetty. | 1 fathom | — | WNW | Heavy surf, could not launch the boat. |
| 20 | - | 48 | | do. | — | N E | |
| 21 | - | 49 | | do. | — | WNW | |
| 22 | - | 48 | | do. | — | NW | |
| 23 | 48 | 47 | 1 mile | 5 fathoms | High water | SW | |
| 24 | 48 | 47 | 2 miles | 6 fathoms | Flood S E | SSW | |
| 26, 27, 28, 29 | - | - | — | — | — | — | Heavy sea on the coast, could not launch boat. |
| 30 | 48 | 47 | 1½ miles | 5 fathoms | Ebb NW | WNW | |
| 31 | 48 | 47 | 2 miles | 6 fathoms | Ebb NW | W | |

## Fleetwood Division.—Whitehaven Station, Cumberlandshire.

Taken by **Albourn Greenfield**, Chief Officer, Second-class.

| 1868. | Temperature | | Distance from Land. | Depth of Water. | State of Tide, &c. | Wind. | Observations. |
|---|---|---|---|---|---|---|---|
| | A. At Sea. | B. Near the Shore. | | | | | |
| **Oct.** | ° | ° | | | | | |
| 14 | 49 | 49 | 1 mile | 5½ fathoms | 5 hrs. ebb SW | SSW | 2 45 p.m. |
| 15 | 51 | 50 | 1½ mile | 10 fathoms | High water | WNW | 10 30 a.m. |
| 16 | 46 | 45½ | 1000 yards | 3½ fathoms | 5½ ho. fld. NE | SW | 10 45 a.m. |
| 17 | 46 | 48 | Inshore | 4 feet | ½ ebb SW | WNW | 3 p.m., heavy sea. |
| 19 | 49 | 49 | ½ mile | 4 fathoms | 4½ ho. fld. NE | N E | Noon. |
| 20 | 48 | 47 | 1000 yards | 3½ fathoms | 4 ho. fld. NE | S S E | do. |
| 21 | 45 | 44 | 900 yards | do. | 3¼ ho. fld. NE | NW | do. |
| 22 | 46 | 44 | 1½ mile | 6¼ fathoms | 2¾ ho. fld. NE | NNW | do. |
| 23 | 46 | 43 | Inshore | 4 feet | 1¾ ho. fld. NE | NW | Noon, heavy sea. |
| 24 | 46 | 44 | do. | do. | Low water | S | do. |
| 26 | 46 | 43 | do. | do. | 4½ ho. ebb SW | WNW | do. |
| 27 | 44 | 43 | 900 yards | 3½ fathoms | 3½ ho. ebb SW | N by W | do. |
| 28 | 44 | 43 | ¾ mile | 4 fathoms | 2¾ ho. ebb SW | SW | do. |
| 29 | 44 | 43 | Inshore | 4 feet | 2 ho. ebb SW | NW | do. |
| 30 | 43 | 43 | 900 yards | 3¼ fathoms | 1½ ho. ebbSW | WNW | do. |
| 31 | 45 | 43 | 1½ mile | 6¾ fathoms | 1 hour's ebb | SW | do. |

## Bangor Division, Carnarvon.—Holyhead Station, Isle of Anglesea.

| | | | | | | | |
|---|---|---|---|---|---|---|---|
| **Oct.** | | | | | | | |
| 12 | – | 54 | 100 yards | 2 fathoms | Ebb | SW 2 to 3 C | |
| 13 | – | 53½ | do. | do. | — | NW 3 C | |
| 14 | – | 54½ | do. | do. | — | SW 2 | |
| 15 | – | 53½ | do. | do. | — | W by N | Clear. |
| 16 | – | 53½ | do. | do. | — | WSW 4 to 5 | Cloudy. |
| 17 | – | 53 | do. | do. | — | WNW 5 C | |
| 19 | – | 52½ | do. | do. | High water | NNW 6 to 7 C | |
| 20 | – | 53 | do. | do. | Flood | S 3 to 4 C | |
| 21 | – | 53½ | do. | do. | — | NW 4 | Clear. |
| 22 | – | 54 | do. | do. | — | W 2 to 3 | |
| 23 | – | 53½ | do. | do. | — | WNW 5 | Cloudy. |
| 24 | – | 53½ | do. | do. | — | SW by 6 | Rain. |
| 26 | – | 52½ | do. | do. | Flood | WNW 4 | Cloudy. |
| 27 | – | 52½ | do. | do. | Low water | WNW 5 | do. |
| 28 | – | 52¼ | do. | do. | Ebb | W by S 4 | do. |
| 29 | – | 52½ | do. | do. | do. | WNW 6 | do. |
| 30 | – | 52½ | do. | do. | do. | W 4 | do. |
| 31 | – | 52¼ | do. | do. | do. | SW by W 5 | Rain. |

## MILFORD DIVISION.—GOODWICK STATION, PEMBROKESHIRE.

Taken by JOHN G. ANNAL, Chief Officer, Second-class.

| 1868 | Temperature. | | Distance from Land. | Depth of Water. | State of Tide, &c. | Wind. | Observations. |
|---|---|---|---|---|---|---|---|
| | A. At Sea. | B. Near the Shore. | | | | | |
| Oct. | ° | ° | | | | | |
| 19 | 55 | No | Taken at the | From 14 feet | 4½ hrs. flood | N 6 | Observations taken at Goodwick, being the nearest coast-guard station to St. Brides' Bay. |
| 20 | 55 | oyster | Pier. | at high water | 5¼ hrs. flood. | SW 4 | |
| 21 | 55 | banks. | do. | to 2 feet at | High water | NW 6 | |
| 22 | 54 | do. | do. | low water. | ¾ hours ebb | NW 5 | |
| 23 | 54 | do. | do. | do. | 1½ hours ebb | NW 6 | |
| 24 | 54 | do. | do. | do. | 2¼ hours ebb | WSW 6 | |
| 26 | 54 | do. | do. | do. | 3¼ hours ebb | WNW 5 | |
| 27 | 54 | do. | do. | do. | 4½ hours ebb | NW 5 | |
| 28 | 54 | do. | do. | do. | 5¼ hours ebb | WSW 5 | |
| 29 | 54 | do. | do. | do. | Low water | WNW 6 | |
| 30 | 54 | do. | do. | do. | do. | WNW 5 | |
| 31 | 54 | do. | do. | do. | do. | W 7 | |

## BRIDLINGTON DIVISION.—FILEY STATION, YORKSHIRE.

Taken by NICHOLAS SWEETMAN, Chief Officer.

| | | | | | | | |
|---|---|---|---|---|---|---|---|
| Oct. | | | Yards. | Fathoms. | | | |
| 16 | - | 50 | 200 | 2 | Near low water, N | SW 5 | Temperature taken at noon each day. |
| 17 | - | 50 | do. | 2 | Low water, N | W 4 | |
| 19 | - | 50 | 180 | 2 | Near low water, N | W 2 | No oyster banks in Filey Bay. |
| 20 | - | 50 | 150 | 3 | ¾ ebb, N | NNW 3 | |
| 21 | - | 50 | do. | 2½ | do. | W 3 | |
| 22 | - | 50 | 120 | 2 | ½ ebb, N | NW 4 | |
| 23 | - | 48 | 100 | 2 | ¼ ebb, N | S 6 | |
| 24 | - | 45 | do. | 2 | do. | S 6 | |
| 26 | - | 51 | 300 | 1½ | High water | W 3 | |
| 27 | - | 46 | 35 | 1½ | do. | NW 4 | |
| 28 | - | 46 | 50 | 2 | ¾ flood, S | WSW 3 | |
| 29 | - | 47 | 70 | 2½ | ½ flood, S | WNW 5 | |
| 30 | - | 48 | 90 | 2½ | do. | W 4 | |
| 31 | - | 52 | 120 | 2½ | ¼ flood, S | WSW 5 | |

## QUEENSTOWN DIVISION.—CROSSHAVEN STATION, CO. CORK.

Taken by W. H. WRIGHT, Lieutenant, R.N.

| 1868. | Temperature. A. At Sea. | Temperature. B. Near the Shore. | Distance from Land. | Depth of Water. | State of Tide, &c. | Wind. | Observations. |
|---|---|---|---|---|---|---|---|
| Oct. | ° | ° | | | | | |
| 12 | 57 | 58 | ½ mile; 30 yds. | 8 fath.; 9 ft. | Ebb, S; ½ ebb, E | SW | |
| 13 | 57 | 57 | ½ mile; 10 yds. | 15 fath.; 2 ft. | ½ flood, N; ½ flood, W | NW | |
| 14 | 57 | 57 | ½ mile; 6 yds. | 5½ fath.; 2 ft. | ¾ flood, NW | W | |
| 15 | 57 | 56 | 300 yds.; 3 yds. | 4 fath.; 2 ft. | N W | NW | |
| 16 | 57 | 55 | 400 yds.; 4 yds. | 4½ fath.; 3ft | ¾ flood, W | NW | |
| 17 | 56 | 54 | 300 yds.; 6 yds. | 4 fth.; 1 fth. | ½ flood, W | NW | |
| 19 | 53 | 53 | 200 yds.; 6 yds. | 3½ fath.; 3 ft. | ¼ ebb, E | NW | |
| 20 | 53 | 53 | 300 yds.; 6 yds. | 3½ fath.; 4 ft. | do. | SW | |
| 21 | 52 | 51 | 300 yds.; 6 yds. | 3½ fath.; 4 ft. | ½ ebb, E | NW | |
| 22 | 52 | 51 | 400 yds.; 8 yds. | 3½ fath.; 4 ft. | do. | SW | |
| 23 | 53 | 52 | 300 yds.; 6 yds. | 3 fath.; 3 ft. | do. | NW | |
| 24 | - | 56 | 3 yards | 2 feet. | ¼ ebb, E | NW, fresh gale | |
| 26 | 54 | 53 | 300 yds.; 6 ft. | 3½ fath.; 3 ft. | ¾ flood, W | W | |
| 27 | 53 | 53 | 300 yds.; 4 ft. | do. | ½ flood, W | NW | |
| 28 | 54 | 53 | 300 yds.; 3 ft. | do. | do. | SW | |
| 29 | 52 | 52 | 300 yds.; 4 ft. | 6 fath.; 3 ft. | ¼ flood, W | NW | |
| 30 | 53 | 53 | 300 yds., 4 ft. | 4½ fath.; 3 ft. | High water, W | W | |
| 31 | 56 | 56 | 300 yds.; 3 ft. | 4 fath.; 3 ft. | Low water | SW | |

## WATERFORD DIVISION.—TRAMORE STATION, CO. WATERFORD.

Taken by RICHARD JOHNS, Chief Boatman.

| | | | | | | | |
|---|---|---|---|---|---|---|---|
| Oct. | | | | | | | |
| 12, 13 | - | - | — | — | — | — | Not taken, in consequence of absence of Inspecting Commander when orders arrived. |
| 14 | 58 | 57 | From the pier at Lady's Cove. Mr. Malcomson's oyster beds joining the back strand. | 1 foot | 1st qr flood E | SSW | Cloudy. |
| 15 | 58 | 57 | | do. | ½ flood E | WSW | Squally. |
| 16 | 56 | 52 | | do. | do. | WNW | do. |
| 17 | 55 | 48 | | do. | 1st qr. flood E | NW | Cloudy. |
| 19 | 54 | 48 | | do. | Last qr. ebb W | N | Blue sky. |
| 20 | 55 | 46 | | do. | do. | WSW | Rain. |
| 21 | 54 | 48 | | do. | ½ ebb W | WNW | Cloudy. |
| 22 | 54 | 48 | | do. | do. | W | do. |
| 23 | 54 | 48 | | do. | do. | W | Squally. |
| 24 | 55 | 46 | | do. | — | NW | do. |
| 26 | 54 | 48 | | do. | ¼ flood E | WNW | do. |
| 27 | 53 | 47 | | do. | do. | NW | Blue sky. |
| 28 | 52 | 46 | | do. | do. | W | Rain. |
| 29 | 53 | 47 | | do. | 1st qr. flood E | WNW | Squally. |
| 30 | 54 | 48 | | do. | do. | WNW | Cloudy. |
| 31 | 53 | 47 | | do. | do. | WSW | Fog. |

## Arklow Division.—Arklow Station, Co. Wicklow.

Taken by Samuel Carr, Second-class Chief Officer.

| 1868. | Temperature. A. At Sea. | Temperature. B. Near the Shore. | Distance from Land. | Depth of Water. | State of Tide, &c. | Wind. | Observations. |
|---|---|---|---|---|---|---|---|
| Oct. | ° | ° | | | | | |
| 12 | – | – | — | — | — | – | |
| 13 | 54 | – | 1,000 yards | 8 fathoms | ¾ ebb | N E | |
| 14 | 54 | – | 1,500 yards | do. | ½ ebb | S S W | |
| 15 | 52 | – | 1 mile | do. | ¾ flood | S W by W | |
| 16 | 53 | – | 2 miles | 9 fathoms | High water | S S W | |
| 17 | 53 | – | 2½ miles | do. | ¼ ebb | S W | |
| 19 | 52 | – | 3 miles | do. | High water | N W | |
| 20 | 50 | – | 4 miles | do. | ¾ flood | S W | |
| 21 | 51 | – | 4½ miles | do. | ½ flood | W N W | |
| 22 | 52 | – | 5 miles | 10 fathoms | ¼ flood | S W | |
| 23 | – | – | — | — | — | – | |
| 24 | 50 | – | 5½ miles | 10 fathoms | Low water | W | |
| 26 | – | 48 | 100 yards | 2 fathoms | ¼ flood | N W | |
| 27 | – | 48 | 150 yards | do. | ½ flood | W | |
| 28 | – | 47 | 200 yards | 2½ fathoms | ¾ flood | S W | |
| 29 | – | 48 | do. | 3 fathoms | High water | W | |
| 30 | – | 50 | 250 yards | do. | ¼ ebb | W | |
| 31 | 50 | – | 300 yards | 3½ fathoms | ½ ebb | W S W | |

## Howth Division.—Howth Station, Co. Dublin.

Taken by Wm. Henry M'Kegg, Boatman.

| Oct. | | | | Fathoms. | | | |
|---|---|---|---|---|---|---|---|
| 12 | 55 | 55 | 300 yards N E of lighthouse | 4 | ¾ ebb N | S | Moderate breezes and cloudy. |
| 13 | 55 | 55 | do. | 4¼ | ½ ebb S | WNW | do. |
| 14 | 55 | 55 | do. | 5 | ¼ ebb S | S | Light breezes, and cloudy. |
| 15 | 55 | 55 | do. | 5½ | High wat. S | W | Fresh breezes and cloudy. |
| 16 | 54 | 54 | Pier head. | 3½ | do. | W | Fresh gales and squally. |
| 17 | 53 | 53 | do. | 3½ | do. | W | Strong breezes and cloudy. |
| 19 | 51 | 51 | do. | 3½ | do. | NW | Fresh gales and cloudy. |
| 20 | 52 | 52 | do. | 3 | ½ ebb S | SW | Fresh breezes and cloudy. |
| 21 | 51 | 51 | do. | 3 | do. | NW | Fresh gales and squally. |
| 22 | 51 | 51 | 300 yards of lighthouse | 4½ | ¼ flood N | W | Light breezes and hazy. |
| 23 | 51 | 51 | do. | 4 | Low water N | W | Strong breezes and squally. |
| 24 | 51 | 51 | Pier head | 3 | ¾ flood S | W | Strong gales and squally. |
| 26 | 51 | 51 | 100 yards of pier head | 3 | ½ ebb S | W | Fresh breezes and cloudy. |
| 27 | 51 | 51 | do. | 3 | do. | W | Moderate breezes and cloudy. |
| 28 | 50 | 50 | do. | 3 | do. | W | Fresh breezes and gloomy. |
| 29 | 49 | 49 | Pier head | 3¼ | ¼ ebb S | W | Fresh gales and cloudy. |
| 30 | 49 | 49 | do. | 3¼ | do. | W | Strong breezes and cloudy. |
| 31 | 51 | 51 | do. | 3½ | High wat. S | SW | Moderate breezes and cloudy. |

## Carlingford Division.—Cranfield Point Station, Co. Down.

Taken by Daniel Collins, Chief Officer, at noon each day.

| 1868. | Temperature. | | Distance from Land. | Depth of Water. | State of Tide, &c. | Wind. | Observations. |
|---|---|---|---|---|---|---|---|
| | A. At Sea. | B. Near the Shore. | | | | | |
| Oct. | ° ′ | ° ′ | | | | | |
| 14 | 56 5 | – | 100 yards | 8 feet | ½ ebb | S S W | There are no oyster beds near this station. |
| 15 | – | 56 | do. | 3 feet | 2 hours ebb | W N W | |
| 16 | – | 55 75 | do. | do. | 1 hour ebb | W N W | Fresh gales. |
| 17 | – | 51 5 | do. | 4 feet | ½ hour ebb | W N W | do. |
| 19 | 51 75 | – | ½ mile | 18 feet | High water | N W | Fresh breeze. |
| 20 | 53 25 | – | do. | 20 feet | do. | S S W | do. |
| 21 | 55 | – | ¼ mile | 16 feet | ¾ flood | W N W | do. |
| 22 | – | 53 5 | — | 4 feet | ½ flood | N W | do. |
| 23 | 53 | – | ½ mile | 18 feet | ½ hour flood | W N W | do. |
| 24 | 52 5 | – | — | 4 feet | Low water | N W | Strong gales. |
| 26 | 52 75 | – | ¼ mile | 2 fathoms | ¾ ebb | W N W | Fresh breezes. |
| 27 | – | 55 | do. | 5 feet | ½ ebb | W N W | do. |
| 28 | – | 50 | do. | 4 feet | 2½ hours ebb | N W | Fresh gales. |
| 29 | – | 52 | do. | 6 feet | 2 hours ebb | N W | do. |
| 30 | – | 52 5 | do. | do. | 1½ hours ebb | N W | Fresh breezes. |
| 31 | – | 55 5 | do. | do. | 1 hour ebb | S W | |

Received Thermometer on 14th October, 1868.

## Carlingford Division.—O'Meath Station, Co. Down.

Taken by William Gray, Chief Boatman, in charge.

| | | | | | | | |
|---|---|---|---|---|---|---|---|
| Oct. | | ° | Yards. | Feet. | | | |
| 14 | - | 53 | 250 | 9 | 2 hours ebb | S | Moderate and fine. |
| 15 | – | 53 | 400 | 14 | 1 hour ebb | W | Strong breezes and squally |
| 16 | – | 52 | 600 | 16 | ¾ hour ebb | W | Fresh breezes and cloudy. |
| 17 | – | 51 | 500 | 13 | High water | NW | Strong breezes and cloudy |
| 19 | – | 48 | 500 | 13 | 4¾ flood | N | do. |
| 20 | – | 48 | 600 | 13 | 4 flood | S | Strong breezes and overcast. |
| 21 | – | 48 | 400 | 11 | 3¼ flood | NW | Moderate and clear. |
| 22 | – | 48 | 300 | 9 | 2½ flood | SW | Light breezes and cloudy. |
| 23 | – | 48 | 150 | 7 | 1¾ flood | NW | Moderate and cloudy. |
| 24 | – | 48 | 150 | 5 | 1 flood | WNW | Fresh gales and heavy squalls. |
| 26 | – | 48 | 150 | 6 | 4 ebb | NW | Moderate breezes and cloudy |
| 27 | – | 48 | 20 | 4 | 3 ebb | NW | Moderate and cloudy. |
| 28 | – | 47 | 250 | 10 | 2½ ebb | W | Strong breezes and cloudy. |
| 29 | – | 46½ | 250 | 7 | 1¾ ebb | NW | Fresh breezes and squally. |
| 30 | – | 46½ | 250 | 10 | 1¼ ebb | NW | do. |
| 31 | – | 47 | 400 | 15 | ¾ ebb | W | Light breezes and light rain. |

## Carrickfergus Division.—Carrickfergus Station, Co. Antrim.

Taken by Richard Jenkins, Chief Officer, Second-class.

| 1868. | Temperature. | | Distance from Land. | Depth of Water. | State of Tide, &c. | Wind. | Observations. |
|---|---|---|---|---|---|---|---|
| | A. At Sea. | B. Near the Shore. | | | | | |
| Oct. | ° ′ | ° ′ | Mile. | Fathoms. | | | (Taken at Noon.) |
| 12 | 52 30 | 53 | 1¼ | 3¼ | Ebb E | WSW | Moderate. |
| 13 | 53 | 53 30 | 1⅛ | 3 | do. | NW | Fine. |
| 14 | 52 | 52 | 1½ | 3½ | do. | SW | Moderate. |
| 15 | 52 | 52 30 | 1 | 3 | Flood W | W | Strong breeze. |
| 16 | 51 | 50 | 1¼ | 3¼ | do. | SW | Rain. |
| 17 | 51 | 49 | 1 | 3 | do. | W | Squally. |
| 19 | 49 | 46 | 1¼ | 3¼ | do. | NNW | Windy. |
| 20 | 52 | 46 | 1½ | 3½ | do. | SW | Moderate. |
| 21 | 51 15 | 48 | 1¾ | 3¾ | do. | W | Squally. |
| 22 | 48 | 46 | 1½ | 3¼ | do. | W | Fine. |
| 23 | 49 30 | 48 | 1 | 3 | do. | W | Squally. |
| 24 | 49 30 | 48 | 1 | 3 | do. | W | Strong gale. |
| 26 | 49 | 47 30 | 1¼ | 3 | Ebb E | W | Fresh breeze. |
| 27 | 49 | 46 15 | 1⅛ | 3⅛ | do. | WSW | Strong breeze. |
| 28 | 48 | 47 | 1½ | 3½ | do. | SW | Rain. |
| 29 | 49 | 47 | 1¼ | 3 | do. | WSW | Strong breeze. |
| 30 | 48 | 48 30 | 1½ | 3½ | do. | SW | do. |
| 31 | 48 | 49 | 1¼ | 3 | do. | WSW | Moderate. |

Note.—Natural oyster beds exist in Belfast Lough, off Carrickfergus, about 1½ miles from the shore, and in or about 3 fathoms of water.

## Ballycastle A Division.—Ballycastle Station, Co. Antrim.

Taken by George Williams, Chief Boatman, in charge.

| | | | | | | | |
|---|---|---|---|---|---|---|---|
| Oct. | | | | Feet. | | | |
| 12 | – | 56 | — | 3½ | ½ flood S | S 4 | Overcast and hazy; air warm. |
| 13 | – | 56 | — | 3½ | ¼ flood S | NW 4 | Clear and fine; air warm. |
| 14 | – | 55 30 | — | 3½ | ¾ flood S | SSW 4 | Overcast; do. |
| 15 | – | 55 | — | 4 | High water | NW 6 | Overcast and showery; air cold. |
| 16 | – | 54 20 | — | 3½ | ¼ flood S | NW 6 | Cloudy and showery; air cold. |
| 17 | – | 54 15 | — | 3½ | ¾ ebb N | WSW 5 | Blue sky and clear; air cold. |
| 19 | – | 54 | — | 3½ | ½ ebb N | NNE 7 | do. do. |
| 20 | – | 54 | — | 3½ | ¼ ebb N | SW by S 4 | Overcast and hazy; do. |
| 21 | – | 54 | — | 4 | 1 hour ebb N | WNW 5 | Clear and fine; do. |
| 22 | – | 54 15 | — | 4 | High water | SSW 4 | Cloudy and fine; air warm. |
| 23 | – | 54 | — | 3½ | 5 hrs. fld. S | W 5 | Overcast; air cold. |
| 24 | – | 53 15 | — | do. | ¾ flood S | SW by S 7 | Overcast, with rain; temperate. |
| 26 | – | 53 | — | do. | ¼ flood S | W 5 | Cloudy and showery; air cold. |
| 27 | – | 53 | — | do. | ½ flood S | W 6 | do. do. |
| 28 | – | 51 | — | do. | ¼ flood S | SW 6 | do. do. |
| 29 | – | 51 | — | do. | 1 hr. flood S | NNW 7 | Cold and showery; do. |
| 30 | – | 53 | — | do. | ½ hour ebb | W 6 | Cloudy and hazy; do. |
| 31 | – | 53 15 | — | do. | Low water | WSW 6 | Cloudy and fine; air warm. |

## RATHMULLEN DIVISION.—SHEEPHAVEN STATION, CO. DONEGAL.

Taken by WILLIAM BOYD, Comd. Boatman.

| 1868. | Temperature. A. At Sea. | Temperature. B. Near the Shore. | Distance from Land. | Depth of Water. | State of Tide, &c. | Wind. | Observations. |
|---|---|---|---|---|---|---|---|
| Oct. | ° | ° | | Feet. | | | |
| 12 | – | 53 | — | 3 | ½ flood | SW | No oyster beds. |
| 13 | – | 52 | — | 4 | ¾ flood | N | |
| 14 | – | 52 | — | 3 | ½ ebb | W | |
| 15 | – | 52 | — | 2 | ½ ebb | W | |
| 16 | – | 52 | — | 2 | Low water | SW | |
| 17 | – | 52 | — | 3 | Ebb | N E | Observations commenced at noon from this date. |
| 19 | – | 52 | — | 2 | do. | S | |
| 20 | – | 51 | — | 3 | do. | W | |
| 21 | – | 51 | — | 3 | do. | NW | |
| 22 | – | 51 | — | 4 | do. | SW | |
| 23 | – | 50 | — | 4 | do. | WSW | |
| 24 | – | 50 | — | 2 | High water | W | |
| 26 | – | 50 | — | 3 | Flood | WNW | |
| 27 | – | 49 | — | 2 | do. | W | |
| 28 | – | 48 | — | 2 | do. | W | Gale; hail showers. |
| 29 | – | 46 | — | 2 | do. | NW | do. |
| 30 | – | 48 | — | 2 | do. | NW | |
| 31 | – | 50 | — | 2 | Low water | SW | |

## CARN DIVISION.—WATCH VESSEL MOORED OFF MOVILLE STATION, CO. DONEGAL.

Taken by JAMES BLYGH, Chief Boatman, in charge of Victoria Watch Vessel.

| 1868. | Temperature. B. Near the Shore. | | | Distance from Land. | Depth of Water. | State of Tide, &c. | Wind. | Observations. 1 foot below surface. |
|---|---|---|---|---|---|---|---|---|
| Oct. | ° | ° | ° | Yards. | Fathoms. | | | |
| 12 | 49 | 50 | – | 500 | 3½, 4 | F T, E T, | W by S W, N W | 50, 49 |
| 13 | 50 | 48½ | 50 | do. | 2, 2¼, 4½ | E T, E T, H W | N W, N W, N W | 49, 50, 49½ |
| 14 | 50 | 48 | 50 | do. | 4, 3, 3½ | E T, F T, F T | S W, S W, S W by W | 50, 50, 49½ |
| 15 | 49 | 48 | 49 | do. | 3½, 3, 4¼ | E T, F T, F T | W by N W, N W, N W by W | 50, 49, 49 |
| 16 | 48½ | 48 | 48 | do. | 4, 3½, 4½ | E T, E T, F T | W by S W, N W, W | 48, 48, 48 |
| 17 | 47½ | 45½ | 46 | do. | 4, 2½, 5½ | E T, E T, F T | W N W, W N W, W N by W | 48, 46, 46 |
| 19 | 46 | 46 | 44 | do. | 4, 3½, 3½ | F T, E T, F T | N W by N, N N W | 46, 46, 43½ |
| 20 | 44½ | 43½ | 42½ | do. | 4, 4, 4 | F T, E T, F T | S, S W, S S W | 43½, 44, 42 |
| 21 | 43½ | 45 | 43½ | do. | 4, 3½, 3 | F T, E T, L W | W, W, W N W | 43, 44½, 42½ |
| 22 | 42 | 44½ | 44 | do. | 3, 4, 3¼ | F T, E T, E T | W, W, S S W | 41, 45, 43½ |
| 23 | 43½ | 44 | 44 | do. | 2¾, 3¼, 3 | F T, E T, E T | W, N W, W, W | 43, 44, 43½ |
| 24 | 42 | 41 | 45 | do. | 3, 4, 3½ | F T, F T, E T | S, S W, W N W, N N W | 42, 44, 43½ |
| 26 | 44 | 42½ | 48½ | do. | 3, 3, 4 | E T, F T, H W | W N W, W N W, W N W | 43½, 42, 49 |
| 27 | 38½ | 42¼ | 44 | do. | 3½, 3½, 4 | E T, F T, F T | N W by W, N W, N W | 38, 42½, 44 |
| 28 | 43 | 42 | 43½ | do. | 3½, 3½, 4 | E T, F T, F T | W N W, S W, S W | 43, 42½, 44 |
| 29 | 43½ | 42½ | 43 | do. | 3½, 3, 3½ | E T, F T, F T | N W, N W, N W | 43½, 43, 43 |
| 30 | 43 | 42½ | 43½ | do. | 3¾, 3½, 4 | E T, S W, F T | W N W, W N W, W N W | 43, 43, 44 |
| 31 | 44 | 42½ | 43 | do. | 3¼, 3, 3½ | E T, E T, F T | W, W S W, W | 44, 42½, 43 |

## Carn Division.—Moville Station, Co. Donegal.

Taken by James Blygh, Chief Boatman, in charge of Victoria Watch Vessel, moored off Moville.

| 1868. | Temperature. | | | | | | Distance from Land. | Depth of Water. | | | State of Tide, &c. | | | Wind. | |
|---|---|---|---|---|---|---|---|---|---|---|---|---|---|---|---|
| | A. At Sea. | | | B. Near the Shore. | | | | | | | | | | | |
| | 1 foot from bottom. | | | 1 foot from surface. | | | | | | | | | | | |
| | 7 A.M. | Noon. | 5 P.M. | 7 A.M. | Noon. | 5 P.M. | | | | | | | | | |
| Oct. | ° | ° | ° | ° | ° | ° | Yards. | Fths. | Fths. | Fths. | | | | | |
| 12 | 49 | 50 | – | 50 | 49 | – | 50 | 3½ | 4 | – | F | E | – | W S | W N W |
| 13 | 50 | 48½ | 50 | 49 | 50 | 49½ | do. | 3 | 2¾ | 4½ | E | E | High | N W | N W |
| 14 | 50 | 48 | 50 | 50 | 50 | 49½ | do. | 4 | 3 | 3½ | E | F | F | S W | S W |
| 15 | 49 | 48 | 49 | 50 | 49 | 49 | do. | 3½ | 3 | 4½ | E | F | F | W to N | W N W |
| 16 | 48½ | 48 | 48 | 48 | 48 | 48 | do. | 4 | 3¼ | 4½ | E | E | F | W to S | W N W |
| 17 | 47½ | 45½ | 46 | 48 | 46 | 46 | do. | 4 | 2½ | 3¾ | E | E | F | W N W | W N W |
| 19 | 46 | 46 | 44 | 46 | 46 | 43½ | do. | 4 | 3½ | 3½ | F | E | F | W N W | N N W |
| 20 | 44½ | 43½ | 42½ | 43½ | 44 | 42 | do. | 4 | 4 | 4 | F | E | F | S S W | S S W |
| 21 | 43½ | 45 | 43½ | 43 | 44½ | 42½ | do. | 4 | 3½ | 3 | F | E | L W | W N W | W N W |
| 22 | 42 | 44½ | 44 | 41 | 45 | 43 | do. | 3 | 4 | 3½ | F | E | E | N W | S S W |
| 23 | 43½ | 44 | 44 | 43 | 44 | 43½ | do. | 2¾ | 3¼ | 3 | F | E | E | W N W | N W |
| 24 | 42 | 44 | 45 | 42 | 44 | 43½ | do. | 3 | 4 | 3½ | F | F | E | S S W | N N W |
| 26 | 44 | 42½ | 48½ | 43½ | 42 | 49 | do. | 3 | 3 | 4 | E | F | H W | W N W | W N W |
| 27 | 38½ | 42½ | 44 | 38 | 42½ | 44 | do. | 3½ | 3¼ | 4 | E | F | F | N W | N W |
| 28 | 43 | 42 | 43½ | 43 | 42½ | 44 | do. | 3½ | 3¼ | 4 | E | F | F | W N W | S W |
| 29 | 43½ | 42½ | 43 | 43½ | 43 | 43 | do. | 3½ | 3 | 3½ | E | F | F | N W | N W |
| 30 | 43 | 42½ | 43½ | 43 | 43 | 44 | do. | 3¼ | 3½ | 4 | E | L W | F | N N W | W N W |
| 31 | 44 | 42½ | 43 | 44 | 42½ | 43 | do. | 3¾ | 3 | 3½ | E | E | F | W | W S W |

### Standing Order.

311/10. Royal Commission, Irish Fisheries,
10th October, 1868.

No specified time being given to take the temperature of the water in the order of 10th October, I instructed the Commissioned Boatman to take the temperature at 7 A.M., noon, and 5 P.M., also to take the temperature of the atmosphere, which he continued to take throughout the month. There are oysters in the neighbourhood of the Watch Vessel; it was an old dredging ground but is now very foul. The men who have dredged brought up very few oysters, some six or seven young ones; many old and large oyster shells have been brought up. Sea urchins plentiful, many brought up in the dredge and scollops, specimens of which I have kept.

James D. Curtis, Inspecting Commander, Carn Division.

## RUTLAND DIVISION.—RUTLAND STATION, CO. DONEGAL.

Taken by EDWARD CODRINGTON BALL, D.O., and MICHAEL M'CARTHY, Chief Boatman.

| 1868. | Temperature. A. At Sea. | Temperature. B. Near the Shore. | Distance from Land. | Depth of Water. | State of Tide, &c. | Wind. | Observations. |
|---|---|---|---|---|---|---|---|
| Oct. | | ° | | Feet. | | | |
| 12 | – | 54 | Near Innisloo | 10 | Low water | S | |
| 13 | – | 52 | Island. | 12 | $\frac{1}{4}$ ebb | NW | |
| 14 | – | 52 | do. | 6 | $\frac{1}{4}$ ebb | SSW | |
| 15 | – | 52 | do. | 8 | High water | NW | |
| 16 | – | 51 | do. | 10 | $\frac{1}{2}$ ebb | WNW | |
| 17 | – | 51 | do. | 12 | $\frac{3}{4}$ ebb | NW | |
| 18 | – | 50 | do. | 8 | $\frac{1}{2}$ ebb | WNW | |
| 19 | – | 50 | do. | 10 | $\frac{3}{4}$ ebb | N E | |
| 20 | – | 50 | do. | 7 | $\frac{1}{3}$ ebb | N | |
| 21 | – | 49 | do. | 8 | do. | NW | |
| 22 | – | 48 | do. | 10 | $\frac{1}{4}$ ebb | N | |
| 23 | – | 48 | do. | 11 | $\frac{1}{2}$ ebb | NW | |
| 24 | – | 48 | do. | 14 | High water | W | |
| 25 | – | 48 | do. | 12 | $\frac{3}{4}$ flood | NW | |
| 26 | – | 48 | do. | 12 | do. | NW | |
| 27 | – | 49 | do. | 11 | do. | NW | |
| 28 | – | 48 | do. | 10 | $\frac{1}{2}$ flood | SW | |
| 29 | – | 49 | do. | 7 | $\frac{1}{4}$ flood | NW | |
| 30 | – | 50 | do. | 6 | Low water | W | |
| 31 | – | 50 | do. | 6 | do. | SW | |

## BELMULLET DIVISION.—BALLYGLASS STATION, CO. MAYO.

Taken by JAMES MORGAN, Chief Boatman, in charge.

| | | | | | | | |
|---|---|---|---|---|---|---|---|
| Oct. | ° | ° | | Fathoms. | | | |
| 12 | 55 | 53 | 1 mile; $\frac{1}{4}$ mile | 12 and $1\frac{1}{2}$ | Low; $\frac{1}{2}$ flood W | SW | Fresh breeze and cloudy. |
| 13 | 55 | 53 | $\frac{1}{4}$ mile; do. | 6 ,, 2 | 1st qr. flood; $\frac{1}{2}$ flood, W | SW | Light breezes and cloudy. |
| 14 | 55 | 53 | do. | 4 ,, 3 | Low: high | SSW | Fresh breezes and cloudy. |
| 15 | 55 | 53 | do. | 6 ,, $1\frac{3}{4}$ | Last qr. flood; $\frac{1}{2}$ flood, W | WNW | Strong winds and squally; showers of hail. |
| 16 | 55 | 53 | do. | 6 ,, $1\frac{1}{4}$ | do. do. | WNW | Do. do. |
| 17 | 52 | 48 | do. | 4 ,, 1 | Low; qr. fld. | NW | Do. do. |
| 19 | 54 At noon | 49 | do. | $6\frac{3}{4}$ ,, 1 | $\frac{1}{2}$ ebb; last qr. ebb, E | N | Strong winds and squally; passing showers of hail; heavy sea on coast. |
| 20 | 52 | 52 | do. do. | 6 ,, $1\frac{1}{4}$ | $\frac{1}{2}$ ebb; $\frac{1}{2}$ ebb, E | S E | Strong winds and squally; at noon fell to light airs and drizzling mist. |
| 21 | 53 | 50 | do. | 5 ,, $1\frac{1}{4}$ | do. do. | NW | Strong winds and squally; passing showers of hail. |
| 22 | 52 | 50 | do. | 7 ,, $1\frac{1}{2}$ | $\frac{1}{4}$ ebb; $\frac{1}{4}$ ebb, E | SW | Fresh breezes and cloudy. |
| 23 | 52 | 50 | do. | 6 ,, $1\frac{1}{2}$ | 1st qr. ebb; 1st qr. ebb, E | W | Strong winds and squally. |
| 24 | – | – | do. | — | — | W | Impracticable to go afloat. A whole gale and squally, with rain. |

## BELMULLET DIVISION, &c.—*continued.*

| 1868. | Temperature. A. At Sea. | Temperature. B. Near the Shore. | Distance from Land. | Depth of Water. | State of Tide, &c. | Wind. | Observations. |
|---|---|---|---|---|---|---|---|
| Oct.—con. | ° | ° | | Fathoms. | | | |
| 26 | 51 | 48 | $\frac{1}{4}$ mile | 7 and $1\frac{1}{2}$ | Last qr. flood; last qr. fld. W | NW | Strong winds and squally, with showers of hail. |
| 27 | 52 | 48 | do. | 6 „ $1\frac{1}{4}$ | $\frac{1}{2}$ flood; $\frac{1}{2}$ flood, W | NW | Moderate breezes and cloudy. |
| 28 | – | – | do. | — | — | SW | Impracticable to go afloat. Strong gales and squally, with rain. |
| 29 | 49 | 48 | do. | 6 „ $1\frac{1}{2}$ | 1st qr. flood; 1st qr. flood | WNW | Strong winds and squally. |
| 30 | 50 | 50 | do. | 5 „ 1 | do. do. | W by N | Strong winds and squally, with drizzling rain. |
| 31 | 52 | 51 | do. | 6 „ 1 | do. do. | SW | Do. do. |

NOTE.—Could not get outside of Cashel Point lighthouse, Broadhaven, in consequence of the boisterous weather and heavy sea. The temperature at sea was taken inside of Broadhaven, from 12 fathoms to 5 fathoms.

## WESTPORT DIVISION.—PIGEON POINT STATION, CO. MAYO.

Taken by WILLIAM JOHN, Chief Boatman, in charge.

| | | | | | | | |
|---|---|---|---|---|---|---|---|
| Oct. | ° | ° | | Fathoms. | | | |
| 12 | – | 53 | $\frac{1}{4}$ mile | 2 | $\frac{1}{2}$ flood SE | WSW | Fresh. |
| 13 | – | 53 | do. | 2 | $\frac{1}{4}$ flood S E | W | Fine. |
| 14 | – | 52 | do. | 2 | do. | S | Moderate. |
| 15 | – | 53 | 200 yards | 1 | 1 hr. flood SE | WNW | Strong. |
| 16 | – | 52 | $\frac{1}{2}$ mile | 2 | $\frac{1}{2}$ flood S E | N W | Stormy. |
| 17 | – | 51 | $\frac{1}{4}$ mile | 1 | do. | N W | Fresh. |
| 19 | – | 49 | $\frac{1}{2}$ mile | $1\frac{1}{2}$ | 1 hr. ebb NW | N W | Moderate. |
| 20 | – | 49 | $\frac{1}{4}$ mile | $1\frac{1}{2}$ | $2\frac{1}{2}$ do. N W | S | Moderate, with rain. |
| 21 | – | 48 | $\frac{1}{2}$ mile | 1 | 4 hrs. ebb NW | N NW | Fresh and squally. |
| 22 | – | 49 | do. | 2 | 3 hrs. ebb NW | WSW | Moderate. |
| 23 | – | 48 | $\frac{1}{4}$ mile | $2\frac{1}{2}$ | 2 hrs. ebb NW | W | Stormy. |
| 24 | – | 49 | 100 yards | 1 | $1\frac{1}{2}$ hours ebb NW | W | do. |
| 26 | – | 49 | $\frac{1}{2}$ mile | 2 | $1\frac{1}{2}$ flood S E | N W | do. |
| 27 | – | 48 | $\frac{1}{4}$ mile | $1\frac{1}{2}$ | $2\frac{1}{2}$ flood S E | N W | Fresh and squally. |
| 28 | – | 47 | $\frac{1}{2}$ mile | $2\frac{1}{2}$ | 3 hours flood S E | WSW | Stormy. |
| 29 | – | 48 | 300 yards | $1\frac{1}{2}$ | $3\frac{1}{2}$ last quarter S E | N W | do. |
| 30 | – | 48 | $\frac{1}{2}$ mile | 2 | $2\frac{1}{2}$ last quarter S E | WNW | do. |
| 31 | – | 52 | do. | $1\frac{1}{4}$ | 1 hour last quarter S E | W | Moderate. |

## Westport Division.—Innislyre Station, Co. Mayo.

Taken by Charles Thomas, Chief Boatman, in charge.

| 18[illegible]. | Temperature. | | Distance from Land. | Depth of Water. | State of Tide, &c. | Wind. | Observations. |
|---|---|---|---|---|---|---|---|
| | A. At Sea. | B. Near the Shore. | | | | | |
| Oct. | ° | ° | | Fathoms. | | | |
| 12 | – | 54 | ½ mile | 3½ | H. water, S E | SW | Moderate breeze with rain. |
| 13 | – | 53 | 600 yards | 3 | ½ flood S E | W to N W | Moderate breeze and cloudy. |
| 14 | – | 55 | do. | 3½ | ½ flood S E | SW | do. |
| 15 | – | 54 | do. | do. | Low water | N W | Strong gales with rain. |
| 16 | – | 53 | do. | do. | do. | N W | Fresh gales with rain. |
| 17 | – | 51½ | do. | 2½ | do. | N W | Strong breeze with hail showers. |
| 19 | – | 51 | 300 yards. | 1½ | 5 hours ebb to the N W | N W | Light breezes and cloudy. |
| 20 | – | 50 | do. | 2½ | ¾ ebb N W | N W | Strong breeze with hail showers. |
| 21 | – | 50 | 300 yards | 2½ | ¾ ebb N W | N N W | Strong breeze with rain. |
| 22 | – | 51 | 300 yards. | 3 | ½ ebb | SW | Moderate breezes with rain. |
| 23 | – | 48 | do. | 3 | 2 hours ebb | W N W | Strong gales with hail. |
| 24 | – | 50 | 50 yards | 1½ | ¾ ebb N W | W S W | Strong gales and cloudy. |
| 26 | – | 50 | 300 yards | 3½ | ½ flood SE | W N W | Strong gales with rain. |
| 27 | – | 50 | 600 yards | 3½ | 2 hrs. flood S E | N W | Fresh breeze with rain. |
| 28 | – | 50 | 300 yards | 3½ | ½ flood | SW | Strong gales with rain. |
| 29 | – | 49 | 200 yards | 3 | 2 hrs. flood S E | N W | do. |
| 30 | – | 50 | 500 yards | 4 | 1½ hrs. flood | W S W | Strong breezes with rain. |
| 31 | – | 50 | 800 yards | 4 | 1 hour flood | SW | do. |

## Westport Division.—Innisgowla Station, Co. Mayo.

Taken by William Burb, Chief Boatman, in charge.

| | | | | | | | |
|---|---|---|---|---|---|---|---|
| Oct. | | | | | | | |
| 26 | 49 | 49 | ½ and 1 mile | 3½ & 9 faths. | ½ S E | N W | Temperature taken each day on different oyster ground. Depth of water on oyster beds from one to five fathoms. |
| 27 | 48 | 48 | ¾ and 1 mile | 4 & 10 faths. | ¾ E | N W | |
| 28 | 47 | 47 | ¾ mile | 3½ & 8 faths. | ¼ E S E | S W | |
| 29 | 47 | 46 | ¾ and 1 mile | 4 & 11 faths. | ½ S E | N W | |
| 30 | 47 | 47 | 1½ and 2 miles | 5 & 10 faths. | ¾ S E | W | |
| 31 | 48 | 48 | ½ and 2 miles | 3 & 16 faths. | ½ E | W S W | |

The first Thermometer received was found broken. Second Thermometer received on 26th instant.

## Galway Division.—Ballyvaughan Station, Co. Clare.

Taken by George Bond, Chief Officer.

| | | | | | | | |
|---|---|---|---|---|---|---|---|
| Oct. | ° ′ | ° ′ | | | | | |
| 12 | 55 | 55 | 1 mile; ¼ mile | 8 fathoms; 10 feet | Ebb; do. | W S W<br>W S W | 2 15 p.m. at sea; 3 30 p.m. on oyster bank. |
| 13 | 55 | 53 45″ | 1½ mile; 40 yds. | 4 feet; 4 fath. | Flowing S.<br>Flowing E. | N E<br>Calm | 9 35 a.m. on oyster bed; 10 30 a.m. at sea. |
| 14 | 55 45 | 55 | 2 miles; 150 yards | 9½ fathoms; 2 fathoms | do.<br>Flowing S. | S S W<br>SW | 11 40 a.m. at sea; 3 5 p.m. on oyster bank at New Quay. |

### GALWAY DIVISION, &c.—continued.

| 1868. | Temperature. A. At Sea. | Temperature. B. Near the Shore. | Distance from Land. | Depth of Water. | State of Tide, &c. | Wind. | Observations. |
|---|---|---|---|---|---|---|---|
| Oct. —con. | ° ′ | ° ′ | | | | | |
| 15 | – | 54 50 | 30 yards | 8 feet | High water | W N W | 4 30 p.m. near shore at Ballyvaughan. |
| 16 | – | 54 30 | 500 yards | 11 feet | Flowing S. | N W | 3 10 p.m. on oyster bank, Ballyvaughan. |
| 17 | 52 30 | 52 | 1½ miles; 400 yards | 9½ fathoms; 4 feet | Ebb; flowing S | W N W; W N W | 10 15 a.m. at sea; at noon on oyster bank at Ballyvaughan. |
| 19 | – | 49 | 500 yards | do. | Ebb | N W | At noon on oyster bank. |
| 20 | – | 50 | 6 yards | 3 feet | do. | S | Noon, edge of bank at Muckniss. |
| 21 | – | 50 | 400 yards | 6 feet | do. | N W | Noon, on oyster bank at Ballyvaughan. |
| 22 | – | 51 | 500 yards | 7 feet | do. | S S W | do. |
| 23 | – | 50 | 600 yards | 8 feet | do. | N W | do. |
| 24 | – | 51 | 10 yards | 4 feet | do. | W S W | Noon, near shore, Ballyvaughan. |
| 26 | – | 50 45 | 20 yards | 6 feet | Flowing S | W | do. |
| 27 | – | 50 | 500 yards | 7 feet | do. | W N W | Noon, on oyster bed, Ballyvaughan. |
| 28 | – | 49 15 | 6 yards | 3 feet | do. | S W | Noon, edge of oyster bed, Muckniss. |
| 29 | – | 50 | 200 yards | 8 feet | do. | W S W | Noon, on oyster bank, Ballyvaughan. |
| 30 | – | 50 45 | 8 yards | 4 feet | do. | W | Noon, near shore, Ballyvaughan. |
| 31 | – | 52 | 7 yards | 3 feet | do. | W S W | do. |

### GALWAY DIVISION.—KINVARRA STATION, Co. GALWAY.

#### Taken by GEORGE BOND, Chief Officer.

| 1868. | Temperature. A. At Sea. | Temperature. B. Near the Shore. | Distance from Land. | Depth of Water. | State of Tide, &c. | Wind. | Observations. |
|---|---|---|---|---|---|---|---|
| Oct. | | | | | | | |
| 12 | – | – | – | – | – | – | Not receiving the order till 2 p.m., no observations taken. |
| 13 | 54 45 | 54 | 1½ miles; 30 yds | 4½ faths.; 8 ft. | Flowing E; flowing S. | Calm; E N E | 11 5 a.m. at sea; near the shore at Kinvarra. |
| 14 | 55 | 54 50 | 250 yds.; 1 mile | 3 faths.; 4½ fathoms | Flowing S E.; flowing E | S S W; S S W | 1 30 p.m. on oyster bank at Dorria; 2 p.m. at sea. |
| 15 | – | 52 50 | 10 yards | 7 feet | Flowing S E | W | 4 p.m. near shore, Kinvarra. |
| 16 | – | 52 45 | 7 yards | 6 feet | Ebb | W | 7 a.m. do. |
| 17 | 51 | 51 | 1 mile; 300 yds. | 3 faths.; 5 feet | Flowing E; flowing S E | W N W; W N W | 2 5 p.m. at sea; 4 p.m. on oyster banks at Tyrone. |
| 19 | – | 50 | 100 yards | 4 feet | Ebb | N W | Noon, on oyster bank. |
| 20 | – | 50 30 | 4 yards | 3 feet | do. | S | do. |
| 21 | – | 49 45 | 12 yards | do. | do. | N W | Noon, near oyster bed. |
| 22 | 50 | – | 2½ miles | 7 fathoms | do. | S W | Noon, at sea. |
| 23 | – | 49 | 250 yards | 6 feet | do. | N W | Noon, on oyster bed, Pauldoog. |
| 24 | – | 52 | 6 yards | 4 feet | do. | W S W | Noon, near shore, Kinvarra. |
| 26 | – | 48 30 | 20 yards | 7 feet | Flowing S | W | Noon, on edge of oyster bank, Kinvarra. |
| 27 | – | 48 50 | 400 yards | do. | do. | N W | Noon, on oyster bed. |
| 28 | – | 50 30 | 300 yards | 9 feet | Flowing S E | S W | Noon, on oyster bed, Doorus. |
| 29 | – | 47 50 | 10 yards | 3 feet | Flowing S | W S W | Noon, near shore, Kinvarra. |
| 30 | – | 48 30 | 8 yards | do. | do. | W | Noon, near shore, Cunneen. |
| 31 | – | 52 | 7 yards | 4 feet | do. | W S W | Noon, near shore, Kinvarra. |

## Clifden Division.—Roundstone Station, Co. Galway.

Taken by Charles M'Donald, Chief Officer, Second-class.

| 1868. | Temperature. A. At Sea. | Temperature. B. Near the Shore. | Distance from Land. | Depth of Water. | State of Tide, &c. | Wind. | Observations. |
|---|---|---|---|---|---|---|---|
| Oct. | ° ′ | ° ′ | | | | | |
| 19 | 54 | – | 4 miles | 10 fathoms | Low water | N W | |
| 20 | – | 52 30 | 500 yards | 2 fathoms | Ebb S W | N W | Taken on the oyster banks at Inniskneе. |
| 21 | 54 | – | 3 miles | 7 fathoms | do. | N N W | |
| 22 | – | 52 30 | 300 yards | 10 feet | do. | S W | do. |
| 23 | 53 30 | – | $2\frac{1}{2}$ miles | 6 fathoms | do. | S W | |
| 24 | – | 51 30 | 300 yards | 10 feet | do. | W | Oyster bank at Cashel. |
| 26 | 52 30 | – | 2 miles | $4\frac{1}{2}$ fathoms | Flood N E | W | |
| 27 | – | 50 30 | 500 yards | 4 fathoms | do. | W N W | Oyster bank at Inniskneе. |
| 28 | 52 30 | – | 3 miles | 11 fathoms | do. | S S W | |
| 29 | – | 50 | 400 yards | 3 fathoms | do. | N N W | Oyster bank at Cashel. |
| 30 | 52 30 | – | 4 miles | 9 fathoms | do. | W S W | |
| 31 | – | 50 | 20 yards | 9 feet | do. | W S W | Oyster bank at Inniskneе. Sea fresher than usual at present on both oyster banks, caused by the heavy rains during the month. |

Note.—Forms and Thermometer received at Station October 17.

## Ballyheige Division.—Ballyheige Station, Co. Kerry.

Taken by Chief Boatman of Station.

| Oct. | ° | ° | | | | | |
|---|---|---|---|---|---|---|---|
| 13 | – | 55 | Off the rocks. | 1 foot | $\frac{1}{4}$ flood | NW | Heavy sea. |
| 14 | – | $49\frac{1}{2}$ | do. | 2 feet | $\frac{3}{4}$ flood | W | Coast impracticable. |
| 15 | – | 50 | do. | 3 feet | $\frac{1}{4}$ flood | W | Heavy ground swell. |
| 16 | – | 49 | do. | 4 feet | High water | NW | Heavy sea. |
| 17 | – | 52 | do. | 5 feet | $\frac{1}{4}$ flood | NW | Heavy ground swell. |
| 19 | – | 54 | do. | 1 foot 6 in. | Low water | N | Calm sea. |
| 20 | – | 51 | do. | 2 feet | $\frac{3}{4}$ ebb | NW | Ground swell. |
| 21 | – | $51\frac{1}{2}$ | do. | 1 foot | $\frac{1}{2}$ ebb | NW | Heavy sea. |
| 22 | – | $51\frac{1}{2}$ | do. | 3 feet | $\frac{1}{4}$ ebb | SW | do. |
| 23 | – | 51 | do. | 1 foot 6 in. | High water | SW | do. |
| 24 | – | 51 | do. | 2 feet | $\frac{3}{4}$ flood | WSW | do. |
| 26 | – | 49 | do. | 1 foot | High water | NW | Heavy surf. |
| 27 | – | $51\frac{1}{2}$ | do. | do. | $\frac{1}{4}$ flood | NW | Heavy ground swell. |
| 28 | – | 50 | do. | 2 feet | $\frac{1}{2}$ flood | SW | Heavy sea. |
| 29 | – | 49 | do. | 1 foot | $\frac{1}{4}$ flood | NW | do. |
| 30 | – | 52 | do. | 2 feet | do. | NW | do. |
| 31 | – | 53 | do. | 1 foot | Low water | W | do. |

## PULLENDIVA DIVISION.—PULLENDIVA STATION, Co. MAYO.

Taken by Mr. GEORGE HORWOOD, I.O., and W. S. YEO, Chief Boatman.

| 1868. | Temperature. | | Distance from Land. | Depth of Water. | State of Tide, &c. | Wind. | Observations. |
|---|---|---|---|---|---|---|---|
| | A. At Sea. | B. Near the Shore. | | | | | |
| **Oct.** | ° | ° | | | | | |
| 12 | -- | 53 | ---- | ---- | 4½ hrs. flood E | SW | Taken at 10 50 a.m. |
| 13 | -- | 53 | ---- | ---- | 5 flood E | WNW | „  1 24 p.m. |
| 14 | -- | 53 | ---- | ---- | do. | SSW | „  2 10 p.m. |
| 15 | -- | 53 | ---- | ---- | 4 flood E | WSW | „  2  0 p.m. |
| 16 | -- | 51 | ---- | ---- | 3 flood E | W | „  1 40 p.m. |
| 17 | -- | 48 | ---- | ---- | 2 flood E | W | „  1 50 p.m. |
| 19 | -- | 52 | ---- | ---- | 5 ebb NW | NW | Taken at noon. |
| 20 | -- | 51 | ---- | ---- | 4 ebb NW | S | do. |
| 21 | -- | 50 | ---- | ---- | 3½ ebb NW | WSW | do. |
| 22 | -- | 50 | ---- | ---- | 3 ebb NW | SW | do. |
| 23 | -- | 50 | ---- | ---- | 2 ebb NW | SW | do. |
| 24 | -- | .. | ---- | ---- | —— | -- | A heavy sea on the coast made it impracticable to test the temperature this day. |
| 26 | -- | 50 | ---- | ---- | 4½ flood E | -- | Taken at noon. |
| 27 | -- | 50 | ---- | ---- | 3½ flood E | -- | do. |
| 28 | -- | 50 | ---- | ---- | 2¼ flood E | -- | do. |
| 29 | -- | 47 | ---- | ---- | 2 flood E | -- | do. |
| 30 | -- | 50 | ---- | ---- | 1½ flood E | -- | do. |
| 31 | -- | 54 | ---- | ---- | ¾ flood E | -- | do. |

## KENMARE DIVISION.—LACKEEN POINT STATION, Co. KERRY.

Taken by Lieut. BOILEAU (Divisional Officer).

| Oct. | A. | B. | Distance from Land. | Depth of Water. | State of Tide. | Wind. | Observations. |
|---|---|---|---|---|---|---|---|
| | ° | ° | | | | | |
| 24 | -- | 56 | Alongside rocks | 8 feet | Ebb tide to W | Gale from WSW | Water quite fresh from heavy rain. Boat could not stand sea |
| 26 | 54 | 54 | 1 mile | 12 fathoms | Flood tide to E | N W 4 | |
| 27 | 53 | 49 | do. | do. | do. | N W 4 | Too rough for boat.  Water |
| 28 | -- | 49 | Alongside rocks | 8 feet | do. | WSW 6 | nearly fresh from heavy |
| 29 | 52 | 50 | 1½ miles | 12 fathoms | do. | N W 5 | rains. |
| 30 | 56 | 51 | 1 mile | do. | do. | W  4 | The few oysters here are of |
| 31 | 56 | 50 | do. | do. | do. | W  4 | a fine description of rock oysters. |

The thermometer which arrived here on the 12th was broken in coming through the post-office, and was returned to coast-guard office.

Second thermometer came also broken and was returned to office.

Third thermometer came on 23rd in good condition.

P.S.—I never saw finer oysters produced than there are in this bay.  It is a pity more seed is not brought here.  The seed from Tralee laid last year on the Sneem oyster bed, about the size of half-a-crown, are now large—in perfect order—price 7s. 6d. per 120.

APPENDIX F.

LIST of LICENCES GRANTED to plant OYSTER BEDS up to 31st
December, 1869.

| No. | Date of Licence. | Person to whom granted. | Locality of Beds. | Area of Beds. | | |
|---|---|---|---|---|---|---|
| | **1846.** | | | **A.** | **R.** | **P.** |
| 1 | 5th November, | W. H. Carter, esq., . | Tramore Bay, county Mayo, . | 19 | 1 | 11 |
| 2 | 7th December, | Luke Lyons, esq., . | Monroughrouy, county Mayo, . | 17 | 0 | 0 |
| | **1848.** | | | | | |
| 3 | 9th June, . | F. H. Downing, . | Off Daurus Point, county Kerry, | 3 | 2 | 28 |
| | **1849.** | | | | | |
| 4 | 24th February, | R. T. Evanson, . | Dunmanus Bay, county Cork, | 19 | 0 | 10 |
| | **1851.** | | | | | |
| 5 | 5th February, | John Mahony, esq., . | Estuary of Kenmare River, county Kerry. | 165 | 2 | 0 |
| 6 | 5th February, | Rev. Denis Mahony, . | Estuary of Kenmare River, county Kerry. | 147 | 2 | 0 |
| | **1852.** | | | | | |
| 7 | 17th November, | Thomas White, esq., . | Ballisodare Bay, county Sligo, | 132 | 1 | 26 |
| 8 | 17th November, | John C. Garvey, esq., | Clew Bay, county Mayo, . | 108 | 3 | 33 |
| | **1853.** | | | | | |
| 9 | 22nd September, | J. O. Woodhouse, esq., | Mulroy Bay, county Donegal, | 63 | 0 | 26 |
| | **1854.** | | | | | |
| 10 | 1st July, . | Burton Bindon, esq., | Carlingford Lough, co. Louth, | 51 | 3 | 10 |
| 11 | 15th November, | Hon. David Plunkett, | Killary Harbour, county Mayo, | 288 | 0 | 0 |
| 12 | 15th November, | J. K. Boswell, esq., . | Ballyconnelly Bay, co. Galway, | 233 | 0 | 0 |
| | **1855.** | | | | | |
| 13 | 18th July, . | John Richards, esq., . | Blacksod Bay, county Mayo, . | 90 | 0 | |
| | **1856.** | | | | | |
| 14 | 30th July, . | Lord Chas. P. P. Clinton, | Bear Haven, county Cork. | 45 | 0 | 0 |
| 15 | 21st August, . | Wm. Foreman, esq., | Ardbear Bay, county Galway, | 90 | 2 | 0 |
| | **1857.** | | | | | |
| 16 | 7th August, . | Thomas Eccles, esq., | Glengariffe Harbour, co. Cork. | 9 | 1 | 0 |
| | **1858.** | | | | | |
| 17 | 15th February, | Rev. A. Magee, . | Streamstown and Cleggan Bays, county Galway. | 277 | 0 | 0 |
| 18 | 15th February, | A. C. Lambert, esq., | Killary Harbour, co. Galway, . | 114 | 0 | 0 |
| | **1860.** | | | | | |
| 19 | 3rd February, | Rev. R. H. Wall, . | Mannin and Ardbear Bays, co. Galway. | 348 | 0 | 0 |
| 20 | 3rd February, | Knight of Kerry, . | Valencia Harbour, co. Kerry, . | 78 | 0 | 0 |
| 21 | 3rd February, | Captain W. Houston, | Killary Harbour, county Mayo, | 43 | 0 | 0 |
| 22 | 13th February, | Wm. M'Cormick, esq., | Achill Sound, county Mayo, . | 149 | 0 | 0 |
| 23 | 11th May, . | Edward Browne, esq., | Ballinakill Harbour, co. Galway, | 223 | 0 | 0 |
| 24 | 4th October, . | M. C. Cramer, esq., . | Oyster Haven, county Cork, . | 20 | 0 | 0 |
| 25 | 9th October, . | Ebenezer Pike, esq., . | Lough Mahon, Estuary of Lee, county Cork. | 47 | 0 | 0 |
| 26 | 14th November, | William Pike, esq., . | Achill Sound, county Mayo, . | 1,676 | 0 | 0 |

LIST of LICENCES GRANTED to plant OYSTER BEDS up to 31st
December, 1869—*continued.*

| No. | Date of Licence. | Person to whom granted. | Locality of Beds. | Area of Beds. | | |
|---|---|---|---|---|---|---|
| | | | | A. | R. | P. |
| 27 | 1861. 10th January, . | William Forbes, esq., | Meenwish Bay, county Galway, | 225 | 0 | 0 |
| 28 | 1862. 14th February, | Robt. W.C.Reeves, esq., | Clonderlaw Bay, county Clare, | 112 | 0 | 0 |
| 29 | 3rd March, . | James Walker, esq., . | Belfast Lough, Carrickfergus, . | 137 | 0 | 0 |
| 30 | 6th March, . | Edmund Power, esq., | Tramore Bay, co. Waterford, . | 270 | 0 | 0 |
| 31 | 1863. 29th May, . | Geo. Clive, esq., M.P., | Achill Sound, county Mayo, . | 489 | 0 | 0 |
| 32 | 1864. 2nd February, | Lord Fortescue, . | Tramore Bay, co. Waterford, . | 83 | 0 | 0 |
| 33 | 5th April, . | Lord Wallscourt, . | Galway Bay, county Galway, . | 1,770 | 0 | 0 |
| 34 | 10th June, . | Col. C. M. Vandeleur, M.P. | Poulnasherry Bay, county Clare, | 190 | 0 | 0 |
| 35 | 10th June, . | A. W. Wyndham, esq., | Newport Bay, county Mayo, . | 80 | 0 | 0 |
| 36 | 30th September, | Capt. George Austin, | Westport Bay, county Mayo, . | 194 | 0 | 0 |
| 37 | 31st October, . | John Kendall, esq., . | Ardbear and Maunin Bays, county Galway. | 236 | 0 | 0 |
| 38 | 31st October, . | Robt. T. Atkins, esq., | Lough Hyne, county Cork, . | 25 | 0 | 0 |
| 39 | 31st October, . | R. E. L. Athy, esq., | Galway Bay, county Galway, . | 100 | 0 | 0 |
| 40 | 31st October, . | P. M. Lynch, esq., . | Galway Bay, county Galway, . | 320 | 0 | 0 |
| 41 | 11th November, | A. Boate, esq., . | Dungarvan Harbour, county Waterford. | 65 | 0 | 0 |
| 42 | 11th November, | J. R. Dower, esq., . | Dungarvan Harbour, county Waterford. | 27 | 0 | 0 |
| 43 | 31st December, | Captain W. F. Barry, | Glandore Harbour, co. Cork, . | 68 | 0 | 0 |
| 44 | 31st December, | C. P. Archer, esq., . | Ballinakill Harbour, county Galway. | 48 | 0 | 0 |
| 45 | 31st December, | T. Young Prior, esq., | Ballinakill Harbour, county Galway. | 90 | 0 | 0 |
| 46 | 31st December, | P. Macauley, esq., . | Ballinakill and Barnaderg Bays, county Galway. | 150 | 0 | 0 |
| 47 | 31st December, | Col. F. A. K. Gore, | Killala Bay, county Mayo, . | 375 | 0 | 0 |
| 48 | 1865. 13th April, | Marquess of Sligo, . | Clew Bay, county Mayo, | 190 | 0 | 0 |
| 49 | 13th April, . | Sir Robt. Gore Booth, | Drumcliffe Bay, county Sligo, | 148 | 3 | 0 |
| 50 | 29th April, . | Rt. Hon. John Wynne, | Sligo Bay, county Sligo, . | 190 | 0 | 0 |
| 51 | 12th May, . | Lord Baron Ventry, . | Dingle Harbour, co. Kerry, . | 130 | 0 | 0 |
| 52 | 2nd November, | Law Life Assurance Society. | Clew Bay, county Mayo, . | 118 | 0 | 0 |
| 53 | 2nd November, | Marquess of Sligo, . | Clew Bay, county Mayo, . | 25 | 0 | 0 |
| 54 | 1st December, | Most Rev. Dr. M'Hale, | Shores of Achill Island, county Mayo. | 125 | 0 | 0 |
| 55 | 1st December, | Thos. M'Carthy Collins, esq. | Roaringwater Bay, co. Cork, . | 75 | 0 | 0 |
| 56 | 1st December, | Marquess of Sligo, . | Clew Bay, county Mayo, . | 26 | 0 | 0 |
| 57 | 1st December, | John Obins Woodhouse, esq. | Carlingford Lough, co. Louth, | 54 | 0 | 0 |
| 58 | 1st December, | Captain Acheson, | Ballinakill Harbour, county Galway. | 18 | 0 | 0 |
| 59 | 1st December, | Rich. J. Verschoyle, esq. | Ballisodare Bay, county Sligo, | 54 | 0 | 0 |
| 60 | 1st December, | Richard Mahony, esq., | Kenmare Estuary, co. Kerry, . | 30 | 0 | 0 |
| 61 | 1st December, | Mr. Robert M'Keown, | Killary Harbour, . . | 61 | 0 | 0 |
| 62 | 1866. 20th April, | William Dargan, esq., | Wexford Harbour, . . | 70 | 0 | 0 |
| 63 | 20th April, . | Marquess of Sligo, . | Clew Bay, county Mayo, . | 270 | 0 | 0 |
| 64 | 21st April, . | Miss Anne Fowler, . | Blacksod Bay, county Mayo, . | 11 | 0 | 0 |
| 65 | 4th June, . | John Obins Woodhouse, esq. | Carlingford Lough, co. Louth, | 42 | 0 | 0 |

LIST of LICENCES GRANTED to plant OYSTER BEDS up to 31st
December, 1869—*continued.*

| No. | Date of Licence. | Person to whom granted. | Locality of Beds. | Area of Beds. | | |
|---|---|---|---|---|---|---|
| | **1867.** | | | A. | R. | P. |
| 66 | 15th June, | Sir Rbt. Gore Booth, bt. | Drumcliffe Bay, county Sligo, | 87 | 0 | 0 |
| 67 | 10th July, | Horatio Hamilton Townsend, esq., | Skull Harbour, county Cork, . | 230 | 0 | 0 |
| 68 | 10th July, | Thomas Sandes, esq., | River Shannon, county Kerry, | 780 | 0 | 0 |
| 69 | 10th July, | Mrs. Elizab. Atkinson. | Blacksod Bay, county Mayo, . | 100 | 0 | 0 |
| 70 | 10th July, | M. J. C. Longfield, esq. | Roaringwater Bay, co. Cork, . | 310 | 0 | 0 |
| 71 | 10th July, | Thos. Kirkwood, esq., | Saleen Harbour, co. Mayo, . | 17 | 0 | 0 |
| 72 | 10th July, | Richd. D. Kane, esq., | Howth Strand, county Dublin, | 36 | 0 | 0 |
| 73 | 10th July, | Wm. & J. St. George, esqrs. | Galway Bay, county Galway, . | 810 | 0 | 0 |
| 74 | 10th July, | Chris.T.Redington,esq. | Galway Bay, county Galway, . | 650 | 0 | 0 |
| 75 | 10th July, | Mrs. Elizabeth Bury, | Lough Mahon, county Cork, . | 70 | 0 | 0 |
| 76 | 10th July, | Rev. Nicholas Martin, | Trawbreaga Bay, co. Donegal, | 90 | 0 | 0 |
| 77 | 15th July, | John Smyth, esq., . | Midleton River, county Cork, . | 10 | 2 | 0 |
| 78 | 15th July, | Stephen E. Collis, esq. | River Shannon, county Kerry, | 212 | 0 | 0 |
| 79 | 15th July, | Thomas Hicks, esq., . | Roaringwater Bay, co. Cork, . | 45 | 0 | 0 |
| 80 | 16th July, | Rt. W. C. Reeves, esq., | River Shannon, county Clare, | 30 | 0 | 0 |
| 81 | 24th July, | Fras. J. Graham, esq., | Barnaderg Bay, county Galway, | 90 | 0 | 0 |
| | **1868.** | | | | | |
| 82 | 31st January, | William Hart, esq., . | Lough Swilly, county Donegal, | 790 | 0 | 0 |
| 83 | 11th February, | Richard Lyons, esq., | Midleton River, county Cork, . | 15 | 0 | 0 |
| 84 | 11th February, | Charles Sandes, esq., | River Shannon, county Kerry, | 56 | 0 | 0 |
| 85 | 13th March, | Stephen Browne, esq., | Dunmanus Bay, county Cork, . | 9 | 0 | 0 |
| 86 | 13th March, | Col. Edward Cooper, | Ballysodare Bay, county Sligo, | 190 | 0 | 0 |
| | **1869.** | | | | | |
| 87 | 13th February, | Henry Herbert, | Kenmare Bay, . . . | 20 | 0 | 0 |
| 88 | 13th February, | Earl of Bantry, . | Adrigole Harbour, . . . | 18 | 0 | 0 |
| 89 | 13th February, | Earl of Bantry, . | Glengariffe Harbour, . . | 60 | 0 | 0 |
| 90 | 4th March, | John P. Nolan, . | Ard Bay, . . . . | 290 | 0 | 0 |
| 91 | 11th March, | Richard J. Mahony, . | Kenmare Bay, . . . | 46 | 0 | 0 |
| 92 | 11th March, | Thomas K. Sullivan, . | Kenmare Bay, . . . | 195 | 0 | 0 |
| 93 | 15th March, | John W. Payne, . | Bantry Bay, . . . | 51 | 0 | 0 |
| 94 | 14th June, | John W. Stratford, . | Killala Bay, . . . | 31 | 0 | 0 |
| 95 | 14th June, | Mrs. Cath. Brown, . | Courtmacsherry Bay, . . | 60 | 0 | 0 |
| 96 | 14th June, | William Little, . | Killala Bay, . . . | 190 | 0 | 0 |
| 97 | 10th September, | Lord Clermont, . | Carlingford Lough, . . | 46 | 0 | 0 |
| 98 | 10th September, | Henry W. Meredith, | Sligo Bay, . . . | 20 | 0 | 0 |
| 99 | 10th September, | Owen Wynne, . . | Sligo Bay, . . . | 77 | 0 | 0 |
| 100 | 10th September, | Owen Wynne, . | Sligo Bay, . . . | 53 | 0 | 0 |
| | | | Total, . . . | 16,935 | 1 | 24 |

NOTE.—Licence No. 2 (Luke Lyons), merged into Licence No. 71, to Thomas Kirkwood. Licence
No. 50 withdrawn, and a new Licence with altered boundaries issued to Owen Wynne, No. 99.

## APPENDIX G.

DIGEST of the Acts of Parliament and the By-Laws at present in force in Ireland for the regulation of the Oyster Fisheries, to which is added an Abstract of the Law enabling certain persons to form or plant Bait Beds. Compiled by THOMAS F. BRADY, Inspector of Irish Fisheries.

The Legislation on the subject of the Oyster Fisheries of Ireland being scattered over so many Acts of Parliament (no less than ELEVEN in number), rendering it difficult, if not almost impossible, for any person not thoroughly conversant with them, to understand the actual laws in force regulating this branch of the Fisheries of the country, has induced me to extract the sections bearing on the subject, from the different Acts, and present them in the form of a Digest. The present work is therefore published for the guidance and information of all persons interested in the subject, and it is hoped may be found useful to owners of Oyster Beds, persons about to form or plant New Beds or Layings, and the public generally.

5 & 6 Vic., c. 106; 7 & 8 Vic., c. 108; 8 & 9 Vic., c. 108; 11 & 12 Vic., c. 92; 14 & 15 Vic., c. 92; 24 & 25 Vic., c. 96; 29 & 30 Vic., c. 88; 29 & 30 Vic., c. 97; 30 Vic., c. 18; and 32 & 33 Vic., c. 92.

1. Persons entitled to Licence to plant Oyster Beds above, or above and below low-watermark :—

*Who entitled to Licence to plant beds. 32 & 33 Vic., c. 92, s. 14.*

   *a.* The owner of any several fishery.

   *b.* Any person with the consent of such owner.

   *c.* The owner of the Soil and Bed of any estuary.

   *d.* Any person with the consent of such owner.

   *e.* The owner of any land bordering on the Sea, or any estuary.

   *f.* Any person with the consent of such owner, but the Licence shall only continue to be in force for such period as shall be named in such consent.

   *g.* The occupier of any land bordering on the Sea or any estuary; but such Licence shall only continue and be in force during the continuance in occupation of the person who was in occupation at the time of granting such Licence.

   *h.* Any person with the consent of the occupier of the land bordering on the Sea, or any estuary; but such Licence shall only continue and be in force during the continuance in occupation of the person who was in occupation at the time of granting such Licence.

2. Persons entitled to plant Oyster Beds exclusively below low-watermark.

    *i.* Any of the persons named before.

    *k.* Any person whatever, with the Licence in writing of the Inspectors of Irish Fisheries, save that such Licence cannot be granted within a Several Fishery, or on the soil and bed of any estuary being the private property of some person other than the applicant, without the consent in writing of the owner thereof.

Note.—Forms of application for Licences can be obtained at the Office of the Inspectors of Irish Fisheries, Dublin. Every application must be accompanied with a six-inch Ordnance Sheet on which the proposed bed is clearly delineated and marked out.

## LICENCES.

**Inspectors may grant Licences. 32 & 33 Vic., c. 92, ss. 8, 14, and 29, and 29 & 30 Vic., c. 97, s. 4.**
3. Inspectors of Irish Fisheries may grant Licences to form or plant Oyster Beds or Layings, whether above or below low-watermark.

**Licences to be in writing. 29 & 30 Vic., c. 97, s. 5.**
4. Licences to be in writing under the hands of any two of the Inspectors of Irish Fisheries, and to define by reference to map or otherwise the position and limits of Oyster Bed. Licences may be made subject to such conditions and limitations, and may be perpetual or terminable, as to the Inspectors shall seem proper.

**Where public rights exist. 29 & 30 Vic., c. 97, s. 6.**
5. No Licence can be granted in any place where the Inspectors shall be of opinion that the public exercise and enjoy *bona fide* a substantially profitable fishing for oysters, nor within the limits of any Oyster Bed or Oyster Fishery, the property of any private person.

**Licences to be approved by Lord Lieut. 32 & 33 Vic., c. 92, s. 14.**
6. Licences subject to the approval of the Lord Lieutenant.

**Notice to be given previously to the granting of Licence. 29 & 30 Vic., c. 97 s. 6.**
7. Previously to granting Licence, notice, stating application and the time and place (not sooner than three weeks from the date of such notice), when and where the Inspectors shall hold a public inquiry in the district, as to the expediency of granting Licence, to be inserted at least three times in some newspaper circulating in the district; and also to be posted at or near the nearest police station.

**Notice to be given of granting Licence. 29 & 30 Vic. c. 97, s. 7.**
8. After granting Licence, like notices to be given, and a true copy of every such Licence signed by the Secretary, to be lodged with the Clerk of the Peace of the County within which the Licence shall operate; and a copy certified under the hand of such Clerk of the Peace shall be admitted in evidence in the same manner as if the copy was the original Licence.

**Persons dissatisfied may appeal. 29 & 30 Vic., c. 97, s. 8.**
9. Any person feeling dissatisfied may appeal *within one month* after the granting of Licence by way of memorial to the Lord Lieutenant in Council, that Licence may be vacated; and notice of such appeal must be given to the Licencee and to the Inspectors. Lord Lieutenant in Council shall adjudicate thereon, and either confirm or vacate such Licence.

**Effect of Licence. 29 & 30 Vic., c. 97, s. 9.**
10. Licence, if unappealed from, or if confirmed on appeal, shall be binding and conclusive on all persons, including the Queen, and shall operate to vest in Licencee, and heirs, &c., such rights and privileges as shall be given thereby, free from all prior or other rights, titles, estates, or interests.

11. Production of copy of Licence certified under the hand of Clerk of Peace, to be evidence in all Courts that the Licence of which it purports to be a copy was duly granted, and that all matters and things required to be done previously to the granting of Licence had been duly done and performed.

*Copy of Licence certified by Clerk of Peace to be evidence. 29 & 30 Vic., c. 97, s. 12.*

12. Inspectors may alter any Licence *heretofore* granted, or grant a new Licence in lieu thereof, to Licencee or his representative, so as to give effect to any agreement or undertaking given or entered into by or on behalf of any such Licencee, with any person or body subsequently to the date of such Licence.

*Power to alter Licences. 29 & 30 Vic., c. 97, s. 15.*

13. Any Licence heretofore granted or hereafter to be granted, determinable by a certificate of the Inspectors, certifying that they are not satisfied that the Oyster Bed is properly cultivated; and on such certificate the Licence and all rights or privileges absolutely determined, and all provisions of Acts shall cease to operate in relation to such Licence as an Oyster Fishery.

*Licence determinable on Certificate of Inspectors. 29 & 30 Vic., c. 97, s. 10; 32 & 33 Vic., c. 92, ss. 8 & 20.*

14. Inspectors may from time to time make such inquiries and examinations with respect to such Oyster Fishery and require from Licencee such information as they may think necessary or proper. Licencee shall afford all facilities for such inquiries and examinations, and give such information accordingly.

*Inspectors empowered to make inquiries and examinations.—Ib.*

15. If within three years from the date of Licence, proper steps have not been taken, in the opinion of the Inspectors, to form the Oyster Bed, Inspectors may by order in writing under the hands of any two of them revoke Licence, and thereupon all rights and privileges thereunder shall cease and determine.

*Power to revoke Licences in certain cases. 29 & 30 Vic., c. 97, s. 14.*

16. Previously to making such order, Inspectors shall serve notice of their intention upon the person for the time being entitled to the Licence, or in case he cannot be found, to cause such notice to be inserted three times at least in some newspaper circulating in the district. Order of revocation not to be made till after the expiration of one month from service of notice or from date of last advertisement, which shall last happen.

*Notice to be served on Licencee previously to making Order of Revocation.—Ib. Orders not to be made till one month after notice.*

---

LICENCES GRANTED BEFORE PASSING OF ACT 29 & 30 VIC., c. 88, (1866).

17. Same provisions as to revoking Licences heretofore granted by the Commissioners of Public Works in Ireland.

*29 & 30 Vic., c. 88, s. 3.*

18. A copy of such Licences, certified by Inspectors or their Secretary, evidence of original Licence.

*29 & 30 Vic., c. 88, s. 4.*

19. And every such Licence deemed effectual to vest in such Licencee, his heirs and assigns, the exclusive right of laying and planting Oysters, and fishing for Oysters in the Oyster Bed authorized by such Licence, free from all prior or other rights, titles, estates, or interest whatsoever.

*Effect of such Licences. 29 & 30 Vic., c. 88, s. 1.*

## INJURING OYSTER BEDS.

Penalties for
injuring
Oyster Beds.
29 & 30 Vic.,
c. 89, s.2. and
29 & 30 Vic.,
c. 97, s. 13.

20. Any person other than the Licencees or their assigns, agents, servants, and workmen, within the limits of any Oyster Bed or Laying, knowingly doing any of the following things :—

Using any implement of fishing, except a Line and Hook or a Net adapted solely for catching floating fish, and so used as not to disturb or injure in any manner any Oyster Bed or Oysters, or the Oyster Fishery :

Dredging for any ballast or other substance except under a lawful authority for improving the navigation :

Depositing any (*stone*, 29 *& 30 Vic., c. 97*,) ballast, rubbish, or other substance :

Placing any implement, apparatus, or thing (*in the opinion of the Inspectors*, 29 *& 30 Vic., c. 88*,) prejudicial, or likely to be prejudicial, to any Oyster Bed or Oysters, or Brood or Spawn thereof, or to the Oyster Fishery, except for a lawful purpose of navigation or anchorage :

Disturbing or injuring in any manner, except as last aforesaid, any Oyster Bed or Oysters, or Brood or Spawn thereof, or the Oyster Fishery :

Interfering with or taking away any of the Oysters from such Bed without the consent of the Licencees or Owners or occupiers of such Bed :

Liable to a penalty not exceeding Two Pounds for first offence—not exceeding Five Pounds for second offence—and not exceeding Ten Pounds for Third and every subsequent offence ; and also liable to make full compensation to the Licencees for all damage sustained by them by reason of unlawful act, and in default of payment, same may be recovered by the grantees (*Licencees*, 29 *& 30 Vic., c. 97*,) by proceedings in any Court of competent Jurisdiction, whether offender has been prosecuted for or convicted of offence or not.   (See also 42–46.)

---

## CLOSE SEASON.

Close Season.
5 & 6 Vic., c.
106, s. 33.

21. The general Close Season for Oysters is between 1st May and 1st September, and unlawful to dredge for, take, catch, or destroy (*or have in possession*, s. 36,) any Oysters or Oyster Brood between those dates, except where the season may have been or may be altered.

5 & 6 Vic., c.
106, s. 36, and
11 & 12 Vic.,
c. 92, s. 42.

Penalty, Forfeiture of Oysters, and any sum not exceeding Five Pounds, and not less than Ten Shillings.

NOTE.—This season has been altered in the following localities, viz. :—In Tralee Bay from 1st April to 1st November ; in Carlingford Lough from 1st March to 1st November ; in Achill Sound, Clew Bay, and Blacksod Bay, from 1st April to 1st October; but between 1st and 15th April and 20th June and 1st October Oysters may be taken in Clew Bay from the natural public bed, lying below level of lowest water of spring tides, for purpose of replenishing private Oyster Beds in Clew Bay alone.—(*See Appendix* A.)

---

## ALTERATION OF CLOSE SEASON.

Inspectors
may alter
close season.
5 & 6 Vic., c.
106, s. 33.

22. Inspectors of Irish Fisheries empowered to alter close season. (*See Appendix* A.)

Notices and
Meeting pre-
vious to
alteration.
7 & 8 Vic., c.
108 s. 4.

23. Before alteration of Season, a meeting of the persons possessed of or interested in such Fishery to be called.   Notice of the day and place for such meeting to be given, not less than 14 days from the date of such notice by handbills and advertisement, twice at least, in some newspaper

published and circulating in the county or several counties, within which, or on the coast whereof, such Fishery is in whole or part situated.

24. Decision to be published in *Dublin Gazette*, and in some one newspaper circulating in the county or each of the counties within which such Fishery is in whole or part situated; and a copy lodged in the offices of the Clerks of Peace and Petty Sessions; and such other publicity, by posting of handbills or otherwise, as shall seem fit. Decision to be published. 5 & 6 Vic., c. 106, s. 34.

25. For the purpose of convicting any person offending against such decision, a copy of the *Gazette* containing such decision, or an attested copy of such decision, obtained from the office of the Clerk of the Peace (who is required to furnish same on payment of a sum not exceeding twopence for every seventy-two words) conclusive evidence of the existence of such decision and of the due publication thereof. Offences against such decision. 5 & 6 Vic., c. 106, s. 34.

26. Constabulary empowered to enforce the regulations for the observance of the Close Season. Constabulary 7 & 8 Vic., c. 108, s. 2.

27. Coast-guard empowered to enforce provisions of Act, or any Order, Regulation, or By-law. Coast Guard. 5 & 6 Vic., c. 106, s. 86.

28. Inspectors empowered to permit, for or in any district or place, the dredging for Oysters from any natural public Bed, lying below the level of the lowest water of Spring Tides, during such part of the Close Season as they may think fit to appoint, for the purpose of replenishing and supplying artificial Oyster Beds or Layings, or other Beds and Layings the exclusive property of any person, but for no other purpose whatsoever. Power to dredge during part of close time. 8 & 9 Vic., c. 108, s. 19.

29. If any Oysters so taken in the Close Season brought to shore, or sold or offered for sale, or found in the possession of any person on land, or used for any other purpose than the replenishing or supplying any such artificial or other Bed, the person offending shall forfeit such Oysters, and be liable to penalty not exceeding Five Pounds and not less than Ten Shillings. Penalty for bringing on shore, &c. 8 & 9 Vic., c. 108, s. 19. 5 & 6 Vic., c. 106, s. 36, and 11 & 12 Vic., c. 92, s. 42.

30. Inspectors empowered to prohibit, during any part of the Close Season, that any Boat shall have on board a Dredge or other implement for taking Oysters. Inspectors may prohibit Dredge on board during close season. 8 & 9 Vic., c. 108, s. 20.

## BY-LAWS, &c.

31. Inspectors empowered, upon the application of any person interested in any Oyster Fishery in any particular locality, to decide upon, fix, and appoint a period, not exceeding Three Years, within which it shall not be lawful to dredge for, take, catch, or destroy any Oyster or Oyster Brood in such locality. Before any such Order made, meeting to be called as in the case of altering Close Season (*see No. 23*), and decision published as directed (*see No. 24*). Inspectors may suspend for a fixed period Oyster Fishery in any locality. 7 & 8 Vic., c. 108, s. 5.

32. Inspectors empowered to make By-laws, Rules, and Regulations, as to them shall seem expedient, to prevent the destruction or removal from the Natural Beds of small unsizable Oysters, and to fix the size or dimensions of the smallest Oysters which may be removed; and to appoint such means to be adopted in dredging and culling Oysters on the fishing grounds as will secure the return to the sea of all Oysters of May make By-laws for improvement of Oyster Fisheries. 8 & 9 Vic. c. 108, s. 20.

less dimensions than those to be so fixed ; and during any part of the Close Season, or in places where dredging for Oysters shall be prohibited, to prohibit that any Boat shall have on board a Dredge or other implements for taking Oysters ; and to make such other Rules and Regulations as they think fit for the increase, improvement, and protection of the Oyster Fisheries.

Publication of intended By-laws.
5 & 6 Vic., c. 106, s. 92.
33. Copies of such By-laws to be lodged with Clerks of Peace and Petty Sessions, and notice thereof posted at the usual places for posting notices in each Petty Sessions District at least One Month before same laid before Lord Lieutenant in Council for approval

Appeal against.
5 & 6 Vic., c. 106, s. 92.
34. Any person aggrieved may appeal against same to Lord Lieutenant in Council.

Publication of. 5 & 6 Vic., c. 106, s. 93.
35. When approved by Lord Lieutenant in Council, to be lodged with Clerks of Peace and Petty Sessions, and with Coast-guard Officers, and in such places as to the Inspectors shall seem fit.   Printed copies to be provided and sold at a price not exceeding One Shilling for each copy ; and notice of publication, and place where same may be purchased, to be given for Three Months subsequent to publication in such of the Metropolitan and Provincial Papers as Inspectors shall appoint.

Evidence of.
5 & 6 Vic., c. 106, s. 93.
36. Printed copy of By-law, &c., obtained from Clerk of Peace or Petty or Quarter Sessions, and certified to be a true copy, evidence of existence of By-law, and of the due publication thereof.

(*For copies of By-laws, &c., in force, see Appendix* A.)

---

31 & 32 Vic., c. 45, s. 67.
37. Inspectors of Irish Fisheries may from time to time lay before Her Majesty in Council By-laws for restricting or regulating dredging for Oysters on any Oyster Beds or Banks within twenty miles, measured from a straight line drawn from the eastern point of Lambay Island to Carnsore Point.   And all such By-laws shall apply equally to all Boats and persons on whom they may be binding.   Her Majesty may, by Order in Council (*a*) direct such By-laws to be observed ; (*b*) impose penalties not exceeding Twenty Pounds for breach of any such By-law ; (*c*) apply to the breach of such By-laws, such (if any) of the enactments in force respecting the breach of the Regulations respecting Irish Oyster Fisheries within the exclusive Fishery Limits of the British Islands, and with such modifications and alterations as may be found desirable ; (*d*) revoke or alter any Order so made.

The Close Time, by any such Order, not to be shorter than that prescribed for the time being by the Inspectors of Irish Fisheries, in respect of Beds within the exclusive Fishery Limits of the British Islands.

Every such Order binding on all British Sea Fishing Boats, and on any other Sea Fishing Boats in that behalf specified in the Order, and on the Crews of such Boats.   (*See Appendix* A.)

---

## WATER BAILIFFS.

Proprietors, &c. of Oyster Bed may appoint Water Bailiffs.
6 & 9 Vic., c. 106, s. 21.
38. Proprietor or Tenant of any Oyster Bed or Laying, or any associated body of persons interested in the protection and improvement of any Oyster Fishery, may appoint Water Bailiffs for protection of Fishery, and for enforcement of provisions of Act, and of any By-laws, Rules, and Regulations.

39. Water Bailiffs so appointed may exercise and use all the powers *Powers of.* and authorities of a Constable, so far as the same may be necessary. *8 & 9 Vic., c. 108, s. 21.* (*For powers of Water Bailiffs—see also 5 & 6 Vic., c.* 106, *s.* 84, and impeding or obstructing, *ib.* s. 90.)

40. Appointment must be approved and confirmed by two or more *Appointment* Justices in Petty Sessions in the district within which Bailiff is to act, *of, to be confirmed by* and Justices shall indorse the Warrant, and may revoke appointment and *Justices.* dismiss such Bailiff, and approve and confirm appointment of some other *5 & 6 Vic., c. 106, s. 52.* person.

41. Warrant subject to Stamp Duty of Five Shillings. (*For form of* *Subject to* *Warrant—see Appendix* B.) *Stamp Duty. 8 & 9 Vic., c. 108, s. 13.*

<hr>

GENERAL PROVISIONS.

42. Any person stealing any Oysters or Oyster Brood from any *Stealing* Oyster Bed, Laying, or Fishery, the property of any other person, and *oysters, felony.* sufficiently marked out or known as such, guilty of Felony, and liable to *24 & 25 Vic., c. 96, s. 26.* be punished as in the case of Simple Larceny.

43. Any person unlawfully and wilfully using any Dredge, Net, *Using any* Instrument, or Engine whatsoever, within the limits of any Oyster *engine within limits of* Fishery, being the property of any other person, and sufficiently marked *Oyster* out or known as such, for the purpose of taking Oysters or Oyster Brood, *Fishery. 24 & 25 Vic.,* although none shall be actually taken, or unlawfully and wilfully, with *c. 96, s. 26.* any Engine dragging upon the ground or soil of such Fishery, guilty of a Misdemeanour, and liable to be imprisoned for a period not exceeding Three Months with hard labour, and with or without solitary confinement.

44. Nothing to prevent any person taking Floating Fish within the *Not to* limits of any Oyster Fishery with any Net or Engine adapted for *prevent the taking of* taking Floating Fish only. *floating fish. 24 & 25 Vic., c. 96, s. 26.*

45. All Oysters being in or on any Oyster Bed, Laying, or Fishery *Oysters in the* which is the property of any person, and is sufficiently marked out or *Oyster* known as such, shall be the absolute property of such person, and in *Grounds or Fishery to be* all Courts of Law and Equity and elsewhere, and for all purposes, civil, *Owner's* criminal, or other, shall be deemed to be in the actual possession of *property. 30 Vic., c. 18, s. 3.* such person.

46. All Oysters removed by any person from any such Oyster Bed, Lay- *Oysters* ing, or Fishery, and not either sold in market overt, or disposed of by or *removed from the Fishery* under the authority of the person to whom such Bed, Laying, or Fishery *to be Owner's* belongs as aforesaid, shall be the absolute property of such last-mentioned *property. 30 Vic., c. 18,* person, and in all Courts of Law and Equity and elsewhere, and for all *s. 4.* purposes, civil, criminal, or other, the absolute right to the possession thereof shall be deemed to be in such last-mentioned person.

47. If any person found offending, any Officer or person empowered *Offenders* to enforce provisions of Act, or any person interested in the Fishery, *may be apprehended* may require him to desist from such offence, and also to tell his Christian *if they refuse to tell their* name and surname and place of abode, and in case of refusal or giving *names. 5 & 6* a general description of his abode, so as to be illusory for the purpose *Vic., c. 106, s. 87.* of discovery, or continuing offence, lawful for the officer or person so requiring, and any person acting by his order and in his aid to apprehend such offender and convey him before a Justice of the Peace. Offender not to be detained longer than *Twelve* Hours. (See sec. 87 in Act.)

Using vio-
lence.
5 & 6 Vic., c.
106, s. 88.
48. Where any persons, to the number of Three or more together, shall by violence, intimidation, or menace, attempt to impede or obstruct any other person in the lawful prosecution of any Fishery, any Bailiff, Officer of Her Majesty's Navy or Coast-guard, or Peace Officer, and any person acting by their order or in their aid may apprehend such offenders and convey them before a Justice of the Peace. Offenders liable to a penalty of Twenty Pounds and costs, in addition to any other penalty to which they may be liable for any other offence against Act.

How offences
may be tried.
5 & 6 Vic., c.
106, s. 94.
49. Offences may be tried and adjudged and determined on in a summary way by one or more Justices of the Peace, on the complaint, verbal or otherwise, of any person.

Proceedings
under Petty
Sessions Acts.
29 & 30 Vic.,
c. 97, s. 11.
50. Proceedings to be under Petty Sessions and Summary Jurisdiction Acts (1851).

Evidence of
Informers,
Owners, &c.
admissible.
5 & 6 Vic., c.
106, s. 104.
51. Evidence of Informers, Owners, or Occupiers of or persons interested in the Fishery, or any person, though entitled to a proportion of the penalty, admissible.

### BAIT BEDS.

Bait beds
may be made.
5 & 6 Vic., c.
106, s. 13.
53. Inspectors empowered to grant to any Owners or Occupiers of land bordering on the Sea or any estuary, or to any person, with the consent of such Owner or Occupier, Licences for the formation of Bait Beds between high and low water marks, and in all other places adjacent to their respective portions of lands, as shall be suitable for the purpose. Such Beds to be held as private property, and the Licencees to hold exclusive control over them so long as they shall be Owners or Occupiers of such land. Licence to be granted only where no public Banks or Beds at present exist.

Interfering
with or
taking away
bait from
such.
5 & 6 Vic., c.
106, s. 13.
54. Any person interfering with or taking away Bait from such Bed after its formation, without consent of Owner or Occupier, liable to a penalty of Five Pounds.

### APPENDIX A.—ABSTRACT OF BY-LAWS, ORDERS, &c., IN FORCE TO 31ST DECEMBER, 1869.

#### SOUTH-EAST COAST OF IRELAND, FROM WICKLOW HEAD TO CARNSORE POINT.—(1st September, 1868.)

That the Close Time, during which it shall not be lawful to dredge for, take, catch, or destroy any Oysters or Oyster Brood, on or off the South-east coast of Ireland, between Wicklow Head and Carnsore Point, shall be between the 30th April and the 1st September in each year.

#### COASTS OF DUBLIN, WICKLOW, AND WEXFORD.—(23rd April, 1869.)
*Approved by Her Majesty in Council, 29th April, 1869.*

Prohibiting between the 30th April and 1st September in each year the dredging for, taking, catching, or destroying any Oyster or Oyster Brood on or off any part of the East and South-East Coast of Ireland, within the distance of Twenty miles measured from a straight line drawn from the Eastern point of Lambay Island in the county Dublin to Carnsore Point in the county Wexford, outside the exclusive Fishery Limits of the British Islands.

#### WEXFORD COAST.—(8th April, 1862.)

First—All persons engaged in fishing for or taking Oysters off the Wexford Coast, south of Raven Point, shall cull all such Oysters as may be taken or caught; and shall not remove from any Fishing Ground or Oyster Bed any Oyster of less dimensions than three inches, at the greatest diameter thereof, and shall immediately throw back into the Sea all Oysters of less dimensions than aforesaid, as well as all gravel and fragments of shells as shall be raised or taken while engaged in such fishing ; and no person shall take from any Oyster Bed, Rock, Strand, or Shore, off said Wexford Coast, south of Raven Point, any Oyster of less dimensions than three inches, at the greatest diameter thereof ; and any person offending in any respect against this By-Law, Rule, or Regulation shall, for each offence, forfeit and pay a sum of Two Pounds.

Second—All persons are hereby prohibited from throwing into the Sea, on any Oyster Bed, or Oyster Fishing Ground off the said Wexford Coast, the ballast of any boat, or any other matter or thing injurious or detrimental to the Oyster Fishery ; and all persons acting contrary hereto shall, for each offence, forfeit and pay a sum of Two Pounds.

### CORK HARBOUR.—(28th October, 1853.)

First—That between the 1st May and the 1st September, no boat shall have on board any dredge or other implement for taking Oysters. Penalty, Two Pounds.

Second—Every fisherman shall, on the fishing ground, cull all Oysters, and shall not remove any Oyster of less dimensions than two and a-half inches at the greatest diameter thereof ; and shall throw back into the Sea all gravel and fragments of shells as he shall raise while engaged in such fishing. Penalty, Two Pounds.

Third—All persons are prohibited from throwing into the Sea, on any Oyster Bed or Oyster Fishing Ground, the ballast of any boat, or any other matter or thing injurious to the Oyster Fishery. Penalty, Two Pounds.

Fourth—No person shall, between Sunset and Sunrise, dredge for, take, or catch any Oysters within the Harbour of Cork. Penalty, Five Pounds.

### TRALEE BAY.—(28th September, 1860.)

First—That between the 1st day of April and the 1st day of November in any year, being the Close Season for Oysters in the said Bay of Tralee, no boat, in the said Bay of Tralee, shall have on board any dredge or other implement for the taking of Oysters ; and if, between the periods aforesaid, there shall be on board any boat any such dredge or other implement for the taking of Oysters, the master or owner of such boat shall, for each such offence, forfeit and pay a sum of Five Pounds.

Second—All persons engaged in fishing for or taking Oysters in said Bay of Tralee, shall cull all such Oysters as may be taken or caught ; and shall not remove from any fishing ground or Oyster Bed any Oyster of less dimensions than two inches and one-half, at the greatest diameter thereof, and shall immediately throw back into the Sea all Oysters of less dimensions than aforesaid, as well as all gravel and fragments of shells as shall be raised or taken while engaged in such fishing ; and no person shall take from any rock, strand, or shore of said Bay of Tralee, any Oyster of less dimensions than two inches and one-half, at the greatest diameter thereof ; and any person offending in any respect against this By-Law, Rule, or Regulation shall, for each offence, forfeit and pay a sum of Two Pounds.

Third—All persons are hereby prohibited from throwing into the Sea, on any Oyster Bed, or Oyster Fishing Ground in the said Bay of Tralee, the ballast of any boat, or any other matter or thing injurious or detrimental to the Oyster Fishery ; and all persons acting contrary hereto shall, for each offence, forfeit and pay a sum of Two Pounds.

L. 2

### GALWAY BAY.—(18th March, 1868.)

First—All persons engaged in fishing for or taking Oysters in Galway Bay shall, on the Fishing Ground, cull all such Oysters as may be taken or caught, and shall not remove from any Fishing Ground or Oyster Bed any Oyster of less dimensions than two inches and one-half at the greatest diameter thereof, and shall immediately throw back into the Sea all Oysters of less dimensions than aforesaid, and all such gravel and fragments of shells as shall be raised or taken while engaged in such fishing ; and any person offending in any respect against this By-Law, Rule, or Regulation shall, for each offence, forfeit and pay a sum of Two Pounds.

Second—All persons are hereby prohibited from throwing into the Sea on any Oyster Bed, or Oyster Fishing Ground, the ballast of any boat, or any other matter or thing injurious or detrimental to the Oyster Fishery ; and all persons acting contrary hereto shall, for each such offence, forfeit and pay a sum of Two Pounds.

Third—No person shall, between Sunset and Sunrise, dredge for, take, or catch any Oysters within said Bay, or any of the Estuaries of the Rivers flowing into the same ; and every person acting contrary hereto shall, for each offence, forfeit and pay a sum of Five Pounds.

Fourth—That between Nine o'clock in the evening of any day and Six o'clock in the morning of the following day, no boat shall have on board any dredge or other implement for the taking of Oysters ; and if, between the hours aforesaid, there shall be on board any boat any such dredge or other implement for the taking of Oysters, the Master or Owner of such boat shall, for each such offence, forfeit and pay a sum of Five Pounds.

### ACHILL SOUND, CLEW BAY, AND BLACKSOD BAY—
### (15th December, 1860.)

First—That between the 1st day of April and the 1st day of October in any year, being the Close Season for Oysters in said Clew Bay, Achill Sound, and Blacksod Bay, no boat, in the said Clew Bay, Achill Sound, and Blacksod Bay, shall have on board any dredge or other implement for the taking of Oysters ; and if between the periods aforesaid there shall be on board any boat any such dredge or other implement for the taking of Oysters, the master or owner of such boat shall for each such offence, forfeit and pay a sum of Five Pounds.

Second—All persons engaged in fishing for or taking Oysters in said Clew Bay, Achill Sound, and Blacksod Bay, shall cull all such Oysters as may be taken or caught ; and shall not remove from any Fishing Ground or Oyster Bed any Oyster of less dimensions than two inches and one-half, at the greatest diameter thereof, and shall immediately throw back into the Sea all Oysters of less dimensions than aforesaid, as well as all gravel and fragments of shells as shall be raised or taken while engaged in such fishing ; and no person shall take from any rock, strand, bed, or shore of said Clew Bay, Achill Sound, and Blacksod Bay, any Oyster of less dimensions than two inches and one-half, at the greatest diameter thereof ; and any person offending in any respect against this By-Law, Rule, or Regulation shall, for each offence, forfeit and pay a sum of Two Pounds.

Third—All persons are hereby prohibited from throwing into the Sea, on any Oyster Bed, or Oyster Fishing Ground in said Clew Bay, Achill Sound, and Blacksod Bay, the ballast of any boat, or any other matter or thing injurious or detrimental to the Oyster Fishery ; and all persons acting contrary hereto shall, for each offence, forfeit and pay a sum of Two Pounds.

Fourth—No person shall, between Sunset and Sunrise, dredge for, take, or catch, any Oysters within said Clew Bay, Achill Sound, and Blacksod Bay ; and every person acting contrary hereto shall, for each offence, forfeit and pay a sum of Five Pounds.

### CLEW BAY, COUNTY MAYO.—(1st April, 1865.)

That for the sole purpose of replenishing and supplying licensed Oyster Beds and other Oyster Beds, the exclusive property of any person or persons within Clew Bay alone, in the County of Mayo, and for no other purpose whatever, it may be lawful for any person to dredge for and take Oysters from any natural Public Bed in the said Clew Bay lying below the level of the lowest water of Spring Tides, between the 1st and 15th April, and the 20th June and 1st October in each year, such periods being respectively included within the Close Time at present fixed for the Oyster Fisheries within the said Clew Bay : Provided always, that if any Oysters dredged or taken during such part of the Close Season shall be brought to shore, or sold or offered for sale, or be found in the possession of any person on land, or be used for any other purpose than the replenishing or supplying any such artificial or other Bed as aforesaid, every person so offending shall forfeit all such Oysters, and be subject and liable to the same penalties and forfeitures as by said first-recited Act (5 & 6 Vic.) prescribed in cases of offences against the provisions of the said first-recited Act for the observance of the Close Season in respect of Oysters.

### CARLINGFORD LOUGH.—(17th April, 1860.)

First—That between the 1st day of March and 1st day of November in any year, it shall not be lawful for any person to dredge for, take, catch, or destroy any Oysters or Oyster Brood within the said Lough of Carlingford, or off or from any of the shores or rocks of said Lough, and any person offending against this By-Law shall, for each such offence, forfeit and pay a sum of Five Pounds.

Second—That between the 1st day of March and the 1st day of November in any year, no boat, in the said Lough of Carlingford, shall have on board any dredge or other implement for the taking of Oysters ; and if, between the periods aforesaid, there shall be on board any boat any such dredge or other implement for the taking of Oysters, the master or owner of such boat shall, for each such offence, forfeit and pay a sum of Five Pounds.

Third—All persons engaged in fishing for or taking Oysters in said Lough of Carlingford, shall cull all such Oysters as may be taken or caught ; and shall not remove from any Fishing Ground or Oyster Bed any Oyster of less dimensions than two inches and one-half, at the greatest diameter thereof, and shall immediately throw back into the Sea all Oysters of less dimensions than aforesaid, as well as all gravel and fragments of shells as shall be raised or taken while engaged in such fishing, and no person shall take from any rock, strand, or shore of said Lough of Carlingford, any Oyster of less dimensions than two inches and one-half, at the greatest diameter thereof ; and any person offending in any respect against this By-Law, Rule, or Regulation shall, for each offence, forfeit and a pay sum of Two Pounds.

Fourth—All persons are hereby prohibited from throwing into the Sea, on any Oyster Bed, or Oyster Fishing Ground in the said Lough of Carlingford, the ballast of any boat, or any other matter or thing injurious or detrimental to the Oyster Fishery ; and all persons acting contrary hereto shall, for each offence, forfeit and pay a sum of Two Pounds.

## APPENDIX H.

REPORT on the COMPOSITION of the SOILS of OYSTER GROUNDS; and on the QUALITIES which exert most INFLUENCE on OYSTER CULTIVATION, by W. K. SULLIVAN, PH.D., Professor of Chemistry to the Catholic University and the Royal College of Science, and Secretary of the Royal Irish Academy.

The circumstances which influence the production and growth of the animals which inhabit the sea-shore are :—

1. Temperature;
2. Depth of water at high and low water,
3. Comparative amount of sunshine, especially the relative amount which falls during low water in the spawning season;
4. Saltness of the water, in connexion with great rainfalls, and the influx of fresh water from rivers and brooks;
5. Currents;
6. Suspended matter;
7. Nature of the shore and sea bottom.

Temperature may be considered from three points of view :—the mean annual temperature of the water, the maxima and minima temperatures during the season of spawning, and the mixture of currents of cold and warm waters which is very destructive to some kinds of animals, especially if it occurs during spawning.

The depth of water influences the amount of light which penetrates the water, the aeration of the water, and the temperature.

The amount of sunshine influences the amount of oxygen in the water, and consequently the greater or lesser activity of all forms of animal life. When high water occurs about noon, during the time of reproduction of the animals and plants which live in the intertidal zone, the action of the sun is greatest, and the development of life most active. It is the reverse in the zone beyond low water-mark. The young of those animals which spawn in shallow water, beyond low water-mark, when the tide is low, and when low water occurs in the middle of the day in summer, develop more rapidly than when the spawning takes place in very deep water, and when low water occurs in the evening or morning. The height to which the tide rises is otherwise also of importance, not only to the zone between low and high water, but to the zone beyond low water-mark. The alternation of deep and shallow water exposes the plants and sedentary animals to successive alternations of temperature, and to great variations in the amount of gases in the water.

Great falls of rain sometimes suddenly add such quantities of fresh water to the inner zone of sea water as to materially alter, often for many hours, the character of the water. Such a change must seriously affect young animals if it takes place during spawning. The same effect is permanently produced in estuaries and bays into which rivers flow. In this case the marine fauna differs from that along the shores of the open sea. Even here the production of certain forms of animal life may be greatly affected by a sudden accession of fresh water brought into the estuary by floods. Fresh water also brings down large quantities of organic matter in solution and in suspension; the drainage of cities and towns, which helps the development of certain kinds of infusoriæ, favours the growth of certain plants and animals, and retards that of others.

Strong currents and waves exert very great influence on animal life, especially on its distribution. Animals and plants do not thrive, as a rule, where the water is agitated very much; indeed shingle shores, over which the waves break with violence, are notoriously barren of life,

especially of plants and sedentary animals. Strong currents also act
in another way, they carry along a quantity of suspended matter which
is injurious to sedentary animals.

The nature of the soil of the shore and sea bottom is intimately connected with currents and the moving power of water. The suspended
matter brought down by rivers, and the matter derived from the gradual
eating away of the coasts are deposited in accordance with three causes:
size of the suspended matter, its specific gravity, and its form; that is,
the largest, densest, and roundest particles are those first deposited. Loose
matter is lifted up by moving water in accordance with similar laws;
namely, the smallest, least dense, and roundest fragments are first moved;
the largest, densest, and flatest last. The effect of these laws is that the
loose matter of shores is sifted and sorted, and the same thing happens with
the suspended matter of rivers. In one place we find, according to the
velocity of the currents, the shingle, in another the sand, and in a third
the mud. But not only is gravel separated from the sand, and the latter
from the mud, the round rolled gravel is not mingled with the flat
shingle, or the granular mud with the highly hydrated unctuous clay,
provided the motion of the water has been sufficient to permit of the
loose materials being thoroughly sifted. By the action of the variable force
of tidal currents, this kind of perpetual sifting of the loose materials of sea
coasts and sea bottoms is always going on. Each kind of material thus
sifted out has its own fauna and flora. Submarine rocks sheltered from the
violence of the waves and the force of currents, and favourably circumstanced as to temperature and sunlight, are always covered with a rich
vegetation and peopled with varied forms of animal life. Mud when
sheltered from the disturbing action of the waves, or when sufficiently
consolidated not to be moved at every rise and fall of the tide, becomes
covered with vegetation and sedentary animals. On the other hand, no
vegetation fixes itself on fine mud which is continually being moved by
the rise and fall of the tide. The only animals which can live on such a
mud bank are annelides, and other creatures which bury themselves in
it. This is also the case where the suspended matter of rivers continually
deposit fresh layers of mud, even though the deposited mud may not be
again disturbed. Those mollusca and annelides which can bury themselves
below the line of tidal disturbance of the sand, can live on sandy shores
even in shallow waters; but scarcely any form of animal life can exist
on a shingle shore. Even the slightest change in the angle of declivity
of a sandy beach alters the conditions of animal life, and consequently
more or less affects the fauna.

Independent of this general effect which the *mechanical constitution* of
the shore and littoral sea bottom has on marine plants and sedentary
animals inhabiting it, the *nature* of the soil, conjointly with the other
causes above enumerated, by the influence which they exert on the food
of plants and animals, produce a marked action on the character of the
flora and fauna, that is, upon the association of species.

Even upon the individuals of the same species of animal the soil is
found to exert so great an influence that fishermen can often distinguish
the individuals from different localities, even from places not far removed
from each other. This is especially the case with oysters, the shape,
size, colour, and flavour of which are almost as various as those of fruit
or tobacco grown on different soils. Were we able to determine the
specific qualities of the soil which produce those differences in the qualities of oysters it would be an important step in their cultivation. Again,
soils favourable for the reproduction of the oyster are not always equally
favourable for their subsequent development; and again, there are
many places where oysters thrive, but where they cannot breed. This

problem of the specific influence of the soil is, however, a very difficult and complicated one. First, because it is almost impossible to separate the specific action of the soil from those of the other causes enumerated ; and next, because, though much has been written on the subject of oysters, I do not know of any systematic series of experiments carried out upon different soils and for a sufficient length of time to enable accidental causes to be eliminated, which could afford a clue to the determination of the relative importance of the action of the several causes above enumerated, at the different stages of development of the oyster.

In the absence of such experiments it is clearly worth while to give the results of a comparative analysis of muds from well-known oyster localities, made with a view of determining whether the chemical composition, or rather, the mineralogical character of the soil exercised any, and if any, what influence upon the growth of oysters. For this purpose the Royal Commissioners placed at my disposal a considerable number of specimens of soils from natural oyster beds, and from places where artificial oyster cultivation had been tried either successfully or unsuccessfully.

The remains of plants and animals mixed up with the sand or mud in the small samples sent to me for examination could not, save in exceptional cases, be in such a state of preservation as to enable me to determine with certainty the species to which they belonged. But even were it otherwise, the small number of individuals, and the necessarily very limited examples of different genera and species which such small samples could contain, would give but a very inadequate idea of the flora and fauna of each oyster bed, and of the adjoining littoral sea bottom. In describing the character of each sand or mud I have, nevertheless, noted the plants and animals present (with the exception of the microscopical ones), wherever the remains were sufficiently preserved to enable me to do so. Generally the species observed were those which seem to exist abundantly in most oyster grounds.

I believe the character and abundance of Diatomacea and Rhizopoda, and other microscopic animals, in oyster grounds, is of primary importance in connexion with oyster cultivation. The green colour of the Colchester and Marennes oyster shows how much the quality may be affected by such organisms. It is probable that the action or influence of the soil of oyster grounds upon the oyster at the various stages of its growth depends mainly upon the nature and comparative abundance of the Diatomacea, Rhizopoda, Infusoria, and other microscopical organisms which inhabit the ground. I have accordingly always noted where the mud appeared to be rich in Diatomacea, Foraminifera, and other microscopic organisms. A thorough study of a few differently situated oyster grounds exhibiting well-marked differences in the character of the oyster from this point of view by a competent microscopist acquainted with the classes of plants and animals just mentioned would be of great scientific interest and practical importance.

As the green colour of the mantle of oysters from certain localities just referred to is commonly attributed to copper, and as such oysters are consequently believed very generally to be poisonous, and their value therefore greatly depreciated, I made the most careful search for traces of that metal in the muds which I had received from grounds known to produce green-bearded oysters. Oysters and other mollusca placed in solutions containing copper and other metals absorb them, and retain them in their tissues. I have had two or three opportunities of examining oysters which had assimilated copper owing to mine-water containing it being allowed to flow into estuaries at places close to oyster beds. In every case the copper was found in the body only of the oyster, which it coloured blueish green, and not in the mantle or beard, *which was not green*. In the green-bearded oysters which I have had an opportunity of examining, the body was not green, and no trace of copper could be detected in any part of the animal. The colour, too, was not the same as that of the true copper oysters, but rather that which would result from the deposition of chlorophyl or other similar chloroid vegetable body in the cells.

The sands and muds examined were from the following localities :—

FRANCE.
1. The River La Trinite, or Crach Auray, Department of Morbihan.
2. Marennes, Department of Charente.
3. Arcachon, Department of Gironde.*

ENGLAND.
1. The River Crouch, Essex.
2. The River Roach, Ditto.
3. Hayling Island, Hampshire.

IRELAND.
1. Lough Swilly, county of Donegal.
2. Ballysadare, county of Sligo.
3. Aughinish Bay, county of Galway.
4. Roundstone Bay,     Ditto.
5. Traroe, county of Clare.
6. Ballyvaughan, Ditto.
7. Besborough, north shore of the Estuary of the Shannon, county of Clare.
8. Carrig Island, south shore of the Estuary of the Shannon, county of Kerry.
9. Valentia, county of Kerry.
10. Sneem,     Ditto.
11. Foaty Island, county of Cork.
12. Tramore, county of Waterford.

I shall follow the same order in describing the several specimens.

## FRANCE.

1. *River La Trinité, Auray, Department of Morbihan.*—Sample of mud from the best oyster ground, furnished by the Baron de Wolbock.

*Description.*—Loamy alluvial mud, free from gravel, of a yellowish-gray colour when dry. Grayish-blue externally, when fresh and moist; but of an intense black colour internally. Oxydized readily to a yellowish-gray when exposed to air and light. When dry it formed a brittle, friable, porous mass, not at all like plastic clay. When washed it left a good deal of sand, consisting of quartz, minute fragments of felspar, fluor, and spangles of mica, mixed with abundance of comminuted shells. The washed clay was free from carbonates. The vegetable fragments and plants intermixed with the clay belonged to : Zostera marina, Chordina flagelliformis, Litosiphon pusilus, and, apparently, to a species of Carpomitra. The remains of mollusca belonged chiefly to : Cerithium reticulatum, Buccinum undatum, a species of Dentalium, apparently D. tarentinum, a species of Astarte (A. Sulcata?), and young oysters. The mud contained abundance of Diatomacea, Rhizopoda, and, apparently, other microscopical organisms.

The rocks along this part of the coast of France are granite, gneiss, and lower palæozoic slates and grits, a good deal altered. The sand, gravel, and shingle of the coast are derived from these rocks. The fine mud which serves to hold the sand together is a highly hydrated alluvial mud,

* Some doubt having arisen as to the specimen from Arcachon being from that locality at all, the description has been omitted.

originally derived from the decomposition of felspar and slate rocks, and mixed with, more or less, organic matter, most of it being derived from microscopic plants and animals.

2. *Marennes, Department of Charente.*—Specimen of shelly sand (*Sable Vazal Coquillé*) from a locality suitable for breeding, sent by M. Coste.

*Description.*—Fine quartzose sand, containing spangles of mica, mixed with a fine bluish highly hydrated mud, which was of a yellow colour when exposed to sunlight. It was full of whole and broken fragments of shells (chiefly Cerithium reticulatum in great abundance, Adeorbis subcarinatus, Buccinum (probably B. undatum), Cardium edule (?), and young oysters). The centre of the mass was very black, and contained Diatomacea, Foraminifera, and Infusoria. Bits of Ulva latissima were also mixed up with this and No. 3 mud from the same locality. The coast of France, in the neighbourhood of Marennes, consists of the chalk marl, or Turonian series of cretaceous rocks, Eocene sandstones and clays, drift gravels, and alluvium. The sand and mud of the shore and littoral sea-bottom is derived chiefly from the tertiary rocks.

3. *Marennes.*—Specimen of fine sedimentary mud (*Terre Glaise*) from a locality which has proved successful both for breeding and fattening, sent by M. Coste.

*Description.*—This specimen consisted of the same sand and clay as No. 2, but in different proportions, the clay predominating in this specimen, the sand in No. 2. Owing to the abundance of clay, the colour was more bluish than that of No. 2, and the centre of the mass much blacker when not exposed to air and light. The intermixed shells were also abundant, but the microscopical organisms were especially abundant. The clay free from shells did not effervesce.

No trace of copper could be detected in either of the preceding muds from Marennes.

### ENGLAND.

4. *River Roach, Essex.*—Sample of mud from oyster ground.

*Description.*—Alluvial mud, consisting of blueish-black slightly calcareous plastic clay, and much quartzose sand. It was free from pebbles, except some fragments of comminuted shells. The sample examined contained no remains of plants except a pine shaving. The centre of the mass excluded from the air was quite black from the decomposition of organic matter, derived chiefly from microscopical animal organisms, Diatomaceæ, &c. No trace of copper was detected in this mud. A copper nail, a pin, or other object of copper or brass, dropped on the shore, or from a boat, may give rise to accidental traces of copper, but otherwise it is not likely that any copper occurs naturally in solution in the water of this river.

5. *River Crouch, Essex.*—Sample of mud from oyster ground.

*Description.*—A yellowish gray mixture of quartzose sandy clay, and fine gravel, chiefly made up of comminuted bivalve shells, and some pebbles of yellowish and brownish cherty quartz, and chalk flints. The clay separated from the gravel and quartz sand was slightly calcareous. The only remains of plants noticed were bits of Zostera. The fine mud freed from sand like that from the river Roach was highly hydrated, and contained Diatomaceæ and Infusoria in comparative abundance. The decomposition of these microscopical organisms, and of other vegetable and animal matter, caused the moist mass to blacken when air was excluded. No trace of copper could be detected in this sample also.

6. *Hayling Island, Hampshire.*—Sample of mud from *Cockle Rythe.*

*Description.*—Grayish blue, highly unctuous plastic clay, with intermixed fine white sand like that produced by the denudation of certain chalk rocks. The sand was not uniformly distributed through the mud, as if the latter rested on a deposit of sand, or that currents brought sand in from time to time. It also contained fragments of chalk flints, bits of coal and cinders, probably part of the ashes, &c., thrown over board by steamers, fragments of woody matter, twigs, reeds, and what appeared to be Zostera marina. The interior of the moist mass was very black from decomposing microscopic animal and vegetable matter. Like most blue clays, it oxydized to a yellow colour when exposed in a moist state to the sun and air. The fine mud is not calcareous.

7. *Hayling Island.*—Sample of mud from *Menghan Rythe.*

*Description.*—Very similar to that from Cockle Rythe. It had less sand, however, and was more plastic. It contained fragments of plants like reeds, and a species seemingly of Chordaria. The centre of the mass was very black, from decomposing microscopic organisms. On exposing the moist mass to sun and air, it oxydized and assumed a yellow colour. The fine mud is not calcareous.

8. *Hayling Island.*—Sample of mud from *Langston Channel.*

*Description.*—Blueish-black, and in the centre of mass intensely black, unctuous plastic clay, which oxydizes, and assumes a yellow colour when exposed in a moist state to sun and air. It did not effervesce with acid. When washed it left a small quantity of fine white quartz sand. Bits of Zostera marina, fragments of apparently a Chordaria, and fine root-like filaments. Abundant evidence of microscopic organisms.

9. *Hayling Island.*—Sample of mud marked A².

*Description.*—Grayish blue, and in centre, black unctuous plastic clay, which oxydizes, and assumes a yellow colour when exposed to the sun and air. It gave, when washed, some quartz sand, fragments of black chalk flints, rounded fragments of white chalk, and white limestone; several leaves of dicotyledonous trees were also found.

10. *Hayling Island.*—Sample of clay marked "Bed B., marl from high ground, mud at bottom from deep water."

*Description.*—Very unctuous blue clay, intensely black in the centre of the mass. When exposed to the sun and air it oxydizes, and assumes a yellow colour. When washed it yielded a little fine sand, comminuted shells, fragments of more or less indurated chalk and of vegetable matter, like sea weeds. The amount of sand and gravel was very small.

The whole of the Hayling muds are derived from the Lower Eocene dark blue clays and sands of the Hampshire Basin, which represent the London Clay of the London Basin. The descriptions above given apply equally well to the true "London Clay" muds of the estuary of the Thames. The Langston Channel mud appeared to be the one richest in microscopic life.

### IRELAND.

11. *Lough Swilly, co. of Donegal.*—Sample of sand from a bed formerly successful.

*Description.* — Fine clay slate mud, mixed with quartz sand, a little slate debris, and a large proportion of comminuted shells. The interior of the mass was very black. This mud resembled very much the mud from Marennes, described under No. 3, and which was from a locality where oysters are both bred and fattened.

12. *Lough Swilly.*—Sample from cleaned bottom of Mr. Hart's enclosed pond at Fahan.

*Description.*—Coarse gravel of blue and greenish schists, intermingled with stiff very plastic clay of a gray colour where it is sandy.

13. *Lough Swilly.*—Sample of the fine silt which deposits on the cleaned bottom of Mr. Hart's enclosed pond at Fahan.

*Description.*—Blue, highly hydrated silty clay, intensely black in the interior of the mass from the decomposition of organic matter, chiefly derived from microscopic animal organisms, intermixed with sand of local rocks, chiefly green and gray schists and grits, vein quartz, and with broken shells.

Mr. Hart describes the cleaned bottom of his pond as follows:—" It has a basis of strong clay; on this a dark shelly sand (left when the soft mud [No. 13] was scraped off), and on the sand a thick coating of gravel, which is now slightly coated with silt" [No. 13]. This silt covers the bottom of the uncleaned portion of the pond, and " finds its way to the cleaned part of the pond where the oysters are laid down, and appears to have very nutritive properties."

14. *Lough Swilly.*—Specimen of sand, gravel, &c., of the outer shore, near Mr. Hart's pond.

*Description.*—Sand and gravel: beach sand with intermingled pebbles of various sizes, chiefly of schists, grits, vein quartz, melaphyre, a good-sized pebble of limestone. Clay: Amber-coloured stiff clay, containing no organic matter, and not flocculent like the deposited muds rich in microscopical animal matter.

Mr. Hart thus describes No. 14:—"Samples of the different sorts of soil found in a spadeful of stuff dug from the open foreshore. In most places the clay is further from the surface, the deposit of sandy mud and gravel on it being deeper the greater is the distance from high water mark. Shells, principally those of the Anomia or saddle oyster, are plentifully scattered on the shore."

The shores of Lough Swilly and the surrounding district consist of gneiss, mica schist, quartz rock, and Lower Silurian altered limestone. Greenstone dykes also occur in the slates. The soils, 11, 12, 13, and 14, are derived from these rocks.

15. *Ballysadare Bay, county of Sligo.*—Three samples of mud from one of the best beds belonging to Mr. Creighton.

*Description.*—*a.* Beach sand composed of comminuted shells, quartz sand, and brownish grits fragments. Bits of bright green sea-weed—apparently an Ulva—were mixed up with the sand.

*b.* Beach sand somewhat coarser than *a*, containing fragments of chert, and small pebbles of grits.

*c.* Sand of fine comminuted shells, worn fragments of shells, and brownish grit pebbles. The latter and some of the shell fragments were coated with patches of brownish red lichen-like sea-weed.

There was very little clay-silt in either of the specimens, which were however small in quantity. Diatomaceæ and Rhizopoda could however be detected in it when separated as well as possible from the sand.

16. *Rosmuck, near Ballinahinch, county of Galway.*—Sand from Mr. Robinson's oyster grounds.

*Description.*—White coral sand like that of Roundstone and other bays on the coast of Galway, containing a few oyster shells and Lucina Spinifera (?). The local rocks are granitoid and quartz rock, but the coral sand contained no gravel or fragments of them.

17. Sample of an oyster bed from the same district as No. 16.

*Description.*—A mass of oyster shells resting on coral sand intermixed with a fine dark grayish, very hydrated silt, rich in animal matter. No trace of local gravel.

18. *Aughinish Bay, south shore of Galway Bay.*—Sample of soil suitable for fattening oysters, said to be similar to the Red Bank of Burren.

*Description.*—Fine porous calcareous sand, intermixed with a highly hydrated silty clay, comminuted shells, and quartzose sand. There were also many large fragments of univalve and bivalve shells, and fragments of chert covered with Litosiphon pusilus.    The local rock is Carboniferous limestone, from which the whole of the mud is evidently derived.

19. *Burren, county of Clare.*—Sample of bottom of the Red Bank, the property of John C. Singleton, esq., well known for its fattening properties.

*Description.*—Gray sand, composed of chert, quartz, comminuted shells (chiefly bivalve and Cerithium reticulatum (?), &c.), and spines of Echinus. The mass was held together by a small quantity of fine hydrated silty mud derived from the denudation of limestone (which is the local rock), and very rich in vegetable and animal matter derived from microscopical organisms.

At the Aughinish side of the bay, there is a bed owned by Mr. James Hynes, the ground of which is very similar.

20. *Burren, county of Clare.*—Sample of experimental bed of Mr. Henry O'Connell, of Limerick, which has been successful to a certain extent.

*Description.*—A sand composed of comminuted shells, forms of Cerithium, apparently C. reticulatum, spines of Echinus, young bivalve shells, apparently Cardium edule, held together by a fine highly hydrated silty mud, rich in animal matter.    The Cerithium formed the greater part of the mass; the mud was not at all so abundant as in No. 18.

21 and 22. *Traroe, Burren, county of Clare.*—Two samples from the part of the Bay from Traroe to Mucknish, upon which are the fattening oyster beds of Mr. Michael Hynes, Mr. Michael Curtin, and Mr. Fergus Curtin.    The samples are so much alike that the one description will answer for both.

*Description.*—Coarse coral sand—partly cemented together by calc sinter—small univalve shells, fragments of bivalves, spines of Echinus, and limestone pebbles covered with Litosiphon pusilus.

The celebrated Poldoody Beds are further in-shore, near Bell Harbour.

23. *Ballyvaughan, county of Clare.*—Sample of bottom of oyster beds belonging to the representatives of the late James Hickey, esq.

*Description.*—Fine quartzose beach sand, intermixed with abundance of comminuted shells, a few pebbles of red grits, fragments of oyster shells, and a little hydrated silt abounding in animal matter. The mass was black in the centre when not exposed to air and sunshine.    The beds of Curranroe, Burren, and Ballyvaughan are all fattening beds, the young oysters for stocking them being brought from the Law Life Assurance Company's oyster beds at Rossmuck, near Ballinahinch, and Berturbay in Galway, and Westport in Mayo.

24. *Besborough, Knock, north shore of Estuary of Shannon, county of Clare.*

*a.* Mud from the fattening bed of Mr. R. W. C. Reeves, where the oysters become green-bearded.

*Description.*—Rich dark blue clay marl, drying dark whitish gray, containing scarcely any quartzose sand, but full of fragments of marine plants.    Not a trace of copper could be detected in this mud.    Mr. Reeves says that a green weed grows on the mud, but that he does not think the colour of the beard is due to it.    He also says that the Poldoody oyster is green-bearded ; and that the soil is the same as that just described, but that the water is deep, and the oysters never exposed, even at low water of spring tides.

*b.* Mud taken from the river out from the shore where trials had been made with hurdles and flags as spat collectors.

*Description.*—Blackish blue very unctuous rich clay marl, oxydizing yellow.

These muds contained Diatomaceæ (some of the forms being freshwater ones), Foraminifera, &c.

25. *Carrig Island, in the Estuary of the Shannon, near Ballylongford,*

*county of Kerry.*—Sample of soil of enclosed pond or tank constructed by Charles Saunders, esq. This mud appears to represent also the soil of the fattening beds at the outer end of the island.

*Description.*—Unctuous highly hydrated blackish-brown silty clay, free from pebbles, but full of minute fragments of grits and gritty shales. The mud did not effervesce. It is apparently derived from the calcareous and other shales of the Coal Measures.

26. *Carrig Island, southern shore of the Estuary of the Shannon, near Ballylongford, county of Kerry.*—Sample of the mud now deposited in the tank, after a quantity of the old bottom had been thrown up on the bank. This tank has been hitherto a failure, but apparently from causes not connected with the soil.

*Description.*—Blackish-blue or grayish mud, drying hard, and breaking into fragments like some kinds of shale-clay. It did not effervesce, and contained very little animal matter. It is only a somewhat more sandy variety of No. 23, and, like it, full of fragments of plants.

27. *Valentia, county of Kerry.*—Sample of the soil of the Knight of Kerry's oyster ground.

*Description.*—Blue and greenish clay-slate debris, with fragments of red grits imbedded in a clay mud of a dark colour, which became very black in the interior when kept moist, and air and light excluded. There was also a great abundance of Cerithium reticulatum, Cardium edule, a species of Cœcum, a species of Astarte, Buccinum undatum, Adeorbis subcarinatus, a species of Trochus, probably T. cinerarius. The gravel was rather abundant, and was derived from the local rocks—Silurian slates and sandstones. This soil resembled in many ways the mud of Auray (No. 1).

28. *Sneem, Kenmare River, county of Kerry.*—Sample of soil from an oyster pond of about one statute acre in area, belonging to Mr. Bland. This pond has proved a failure.

*Description.*—A mass of finely comminuted bivalve shells intermixed with some yellowish fine mud, consisting of fine silt and extremely fine quartz sand. The mud was highly hydrated and contained some animal matter, so that the mass blackened slightly here and there wherever there was any mud. The mud freed from the shells did not effervesce. The rocks of the district consist of Silurian slates and grits, and Carboniferous limestone.

29. *Foaty Island, Cork Harbour.*—Sample of mud from the oyster bed of A. H. Smith Barry, esq., M.P.

*Description.*—Fine plastic dark-blue clay marl, containing some red grit pebbles coated with Confervæ, and comminuted oyster shells. The interior of the moist mass was of a most intense black. When exposed to air and light it rapidly oxydized and became of a rusty colour. This mud abounded in microscopic animal matter, Diatomaceæ, &c., and was one of the most unctuous of all the muds examined. The quantity of carbonate of lime in it made it, however, sufficiently porous. This mud is derived from the denudation of Silurian grits, and shales, and Carboniferous limestone. It is also, no doubt, affected by the sewage of the city of Cork.

30. *Tramore, county of Waterford.*—Sample of soil of Mr. Malcolmson's ponds.

*Description.*—Brownish yellow sands and gravel, consisting of fragments of local rocks (slates, grits, felstones, greenstones, and limestone of the Cambro-Silurian or Lower Silurian formation), intermixed with a little clay. This clay was not flocculent, and contained scarcely any organic matter; indeed, with the exception of a periwinkle shell and some fragments of other shells, there was no evidence of animal life in the soil.

31. *Tramore.*—Mr. E. Power's oyster beds and tank at Kilmacleague. Sample (No. 1, Beach Park) of the bottom of the first parc (park) or bed formed by Edmund Power, esq., several years ago, out of the beach, as at Isle Ré, for breeding on fascines. It failed as a breeding parc, though oysters improve somewhat in it.

*Description.*—Stiff yellow clay containing pebbles of the local Lower Silurian grits, slates, felstones, greenstones, and limestones, and with streaks of brownish manganiferous ferric hydrate through it, deposited by the water as the specimen dried. Here and there the clay was light coloured—the iron having been reduced from the state of ferric compounds to ferrous, and dissolved out. When air and light were excluded the interior of the moist mass blackened somewhat. The clay contained very little organic matter however.

32. *Tramore.*—Mr. E. Power's oyster beds and tank at Kilmacleague. Sample (No. 2, Wark's Gap) of bottom of natural pond where there is a large quantity of fresh water and consequently much mud. Oysters improve more in this mud than on any other part of Mr. E. Power's licensed grounds. He believes the oysters spawn, but that the spat is carried away by currents and lost in the mud.

*Description.*—Fine beach sand of quartz, felstone, and other local rocks, intermixed with a small quantity of very fine silty mud, which blackened when air and light were excluded from the moist mass. The mass also contained Confervæ in abundance, tubes of agglutinated sand formed by Annelides (Hermellæ), and comminuted periwinkles.

33. *Tramore.*—Sample of soil from the bottom of one of the tanks formed inside Mr. E. Power's embankment. The experiment with these tanks failed.

*Description.*—Coarse gravel of local rocks (slates, grits, vein quartz, felstone, &c.) with a little intermixed sandy clay and fragments of shells. The clay was not flocculent, and did not contain much organic matter. It blackened, however, here and there when air and light were excluded from the moist mass.

From the preceding descriptions, as well as from the nature of the local rocks in the neighbourhood of prolific natural oyster beds, it is evident that oyster cultivation may thrive upon shores and sea bottoms formed of granitoid rocks, schistose rocks, clay-slate, grits, shales, sandstones, limestone, chalk, clays—in fact, of rocks of all kinds. Consequently so far as the nature of the rock is concerned, oysters may be cultivated on any part of the Irish coast. Again, that while the gravel, sand, and clay of the sea-shore are, as a rule, formed from local rocks, in some places, as along the coasts of Wexford and Wicklow, they are derived from drift gravel, a good deal of which has been formed by the denudation of existing local rocks, but part also from limestone and other rocks not now found on the coast, or only here and there. In some places the sands and gravels derived from local rocks may be so covered over by deposits of coral sand or comminuted shells as to have no influence on the actual soil of the oyster ground, as is the case on parts of the west coast of Ireland (see descriptions of Nos. 16 and 17, p. 172). It further appears that the soil of all places successful as fattening stations contains more or less of a fine flocculent highly hydrated silty clay, abounding in vegetable and animal matter derived chiefly from Diatomacea, Rhizopoda, and other microscopical organisms; and that the soils of those places which have proved successful as breeding stations always contain some of it, but not necessarily as much as those which fatten; and lastly, that in those places which have proved failures, this peculiar kind of mud is either wholly absent, or inferior in quality and quantity.

In conclusion, I may sum up briefly the principal conclusions to which the study of the soil of oyster grounds has led me.

1. That the influence of the soil upon the breeding and growth of oysters is complicated by : temperature, especially during the spawning season ; sudden alternations of heat and cold, due to currents ; alternation of depth of water, especially as regards whether the maximum of sun-heat and light concords with low water during the spawning season ; velocity of tide, angle of inclination of shore, &c.

2. That the soil of oyster ground may be made up of materials of any of the great classes of rocks, arenaceous, argillaceous, or calcareous, provided they contain—

3. More or less of a fine flocculent highly hydrated silt, rich in organic matter, which indicates that Diatomacea, Rhizopoda, Infusoria, and other minute creatures abound.

4. That the character and abundance of such small organisms in a locality seems to be the true test of a successful oyster ground.

5. And lastly, that although oysters do undoubtedly assimilate copper from water where mine-water containing traces of that metal flow into the sea in the neighbourhood of the oyster beds, the copper is chiefly, if not exclusively, confined to the body of the oyster, and does not appear to reach the mantle or beard. That the so-called green oysters of Essex, Marennes, and other places, on the other hand, are green-bearded and contain no copper, nor can the most minute trace of copper be detected in the soil of the oyster grounds where such green-bearded oysters are produced.

---

## APPENDIX I.

ROYAL COMMISSION IRISH OYSTER FISHERIES—12th May, 1869.

### QUERIES.

1. Are there any, and if so, what description of oyster beds in this division?

2. Where are the natural public beds situated?

3. Are there any, and if so, what regulations enforced for throwing back undersized oysters, or otherwise protecting the beds? and are any means adopted to re-stock the public beds?

4. How many boats on an average in the year dredge on these public beds—distinguishing the number of smacks and row boats?

5. How many men in each boat or smack?

6. How many dredges?

7. Is dredging carried on all the year round; and if not during what months do the fishermen generally dredge?

8. What is the nature of the directions you received with regard to the observance of close time, &c.?

9. When does close time commence and terminate in your locality?

10. Are the public beds in a declining or prosperous state? If the former, when did the decline commence?

11. What, in your opinion, is the cause of the decline?

12. Are there any oyster grounds in your locality used only for fattening purposes? If so, state where situated?

13. What *private* beds are in your district—distinguishing those that are natural and artificial?

14. State situation of each private bed, and the names and addresses of the owners.

15. Are there any, and if so, what means adopted to stock the *private* natural beds?

16. Are there any natural beds in the neighbourhood of the artificial ones?

17. State the nature of the artificial cultivation—whether on the foreshore or below it, and about the area actually taken up with artificial cultivation?

18. If the artificial cultivation has not proved successful, to what is it generally attributed?

19. What private beds have been formed in your district? Give names and addresses of owners, and locality of each bed?

20. Any general observations.

To be returned with Replies to the Commissioners of Irish Oyster Fisheries, Dublin.

## APPENDIX K.

### EXTRACT from the COMMISSIONERS' REPORT.

" III. Reviewing the oyster fisheries which have been thus briefly described under these two heads, it will be seen that the difference of the systems pursued in them consists firstly, in the maintenance of a close-season ; secondly, in a restriction as to the size of the oysters permitted to be taken.

" With respect to both of these points, in the estuary of the Thames the witnesses examined by us all agree in deprecating any interference by legislation ; they maintain that no benefit would result from such measures to the public grounds, while the private grounds would be all but ruined, and that the average supply of oysters to the market would be greatly diminished ; and though their grounds have been without any spat for some years they do not attribute this in any way to over-dredging, but solely to natural causes over which they have as yet no control. They confidently expect that when a favourable season recurs their grounds will again be supplied with brood.

" On the other hand, the local fishermen who dredge the beds in shallow water and in bays on all other parts of the coast are, with few exceptions, in favour of the maintenance of a close-season ; they are also opposed to the taking of small oysters for the purpose of laying them down on beds distant from their own neighbourhood, though they are not generally opposed to moving them for the purpose of laying them down on beds of their own.

" IV. We may now proceed to discuss these questions in detail.

" We conceive it to be satisfactorily proved that any interference with the working of the private oyster beds during the close-time would be highly injurious. It is conclusively shown that it is only by very careful working and superintendence that the injury resulting from the deposit of mud and the growth of weeds can be repaired, and that the destruction of the oysters on the great scale by inroads of mussels which choke them, or of five-fingers which devour them, can be prevented. Some of the evidence which has been laid before us in these heads is worthy of the most careful attention.

" 58,397. Do the mussels on the ground interfere with the oysters?—If we got mussels among the oysters, they would very soon smother them.

M

"58,617. Do you agree with Mr. Nichols, that if the spat were left on the flats it would never arrive at maturity, but would be strangled by the five-fingers?—Yes, I am very strongly of that opinion, and we have had it proved.

"58,618. What ground have you for thinking so?—That has been the case when any of the spat has been left there. In 1860, when we had our last spat, some portion of it was left there in the winter time, when we could not go to work upon it, because if we had taken it away and laid it upon our grounds it would have been killed by the frost; we therefore left it lying upon the flats, and when we went for the purpose of taking it in the spring of the year following, we found that it had all been destroyed by five-fingers.

"58,619. Did you upon that occasion find many five-fingers upon the ground?—Yes, they came in like swarms of bees, completely filling the ground in a day. I never saw anything like it; we saw all the water filled with them.

"61,561. I should like now, with your permission, to say a few words with regard to the necessity of maintaining a close-season. I think there can be no question of this, that if the close-season were enforced upon the Whitstable ground it would ruin the fishery altogether. There is no question at all about that. I quite agree with what Mr. Smith said, namely, that the ground upon which freshets are constantly coming and bringing sullage with them require to be continuously cleaned. Then again a heavy gale of wind will come on, and roll up the oysters in a ridge three feet deep. Great injury would be done to the oysters unless they were worked, and by working them in the course of a day or two they would all be spread over again. When they are spread the mud all goes away, but if they were left on that ridge the mud would settle all round them and kill them very rapidly. In the next place, that ridge, if allowed to remain, would cause an eddy and a fresh deposit of mud all round it for many yards. In the next place, it is just at that time of year that we want to work on account of the five-fingers coming upon the beds. They come like a flock of gulls, and unless they were well dredged they would soon destroy the spat. There is one kind that will eat an oyster itself; yet it is a singular thing with regard to them that after they have been dredged for a time they roll themselves up and float away. So much is that the case that in places where the fishermen have caught ten bushels of five-fingers one day they will go out the next day and not catch one. If during the close months the fishermen were unable to dredge, of course it would follow that the five-fingers would soon clear the oysters off the beds. To show the advantage of working the beds in the summer time, I may say that about four years ago, some time after the great spat in 1858, the Whitstable Company, when the oysters came, wanted more ground. There was a piece of ground about half a mile in extent lying on the east side of the regular ground, which had not been worked by the company, because they thought it was useless to work it. Well, they took it into their heads to work upon it and clean it, and it was said last year by two of the jury that since the time they had cleaned it they had sold off that piece of ground alone more than 150,000 bushels of oysters. Indeed that ground now is one of the best pieces of ground they have, and upon that half mile they lay their brood."

" It is impossible to study this evidence without being struck by the great complexity of the conditions upon which the prosperity of an oyster bed depends, even if we look at the action and interaction of mussels and starfish alone, without considering any other of the numerous active and passive enemies of the oyster. Nor is it possible to be other than impressed by the necessity of extreme caution in concluding that any observed increase or diminution in the supply of oysters has arisen from any one cause.

"The consideration of such facts as those here detailed leads us to attach very great weight to the opinion expressed by many competent witnesses, that the enforcement of a close-time in the open grounds is not only unnecessary but may be positively injurious, by allowing the accumulation of mud and weeds, and by permitting the five-fingers to commit their ravages without check. At the same time it can hardly be admitted that open-sea oyster beds must perish if not dredged, as some of the witnesses maintained. How could the beds ever grow to a sufficient size to be worth dredging if their very existence depended upon their being dredged?

" In favour of the existing system of close-time it is urged :

  a. That during close-time the oysters are unfit for food.
  b. That dredging over the beds will crush and destroy the young spat.
  c. That if the oysters are taken while breeding the supply must soon come to an end.

" But to all these allegations very forcible replies are given :

*a.* It is generally agreed that not more than 20 per cent. or thereabouts of the oysters are ever spawning at once, at least 80 per cent. even at the worst of times being eatable and in good condition. The celebrated naturalist, Kröyer, who undertook an official examination of the Danish oyster beds, found not more than one oyster in ten spatting, even in July and August.

*b.* Those who have been in the habit of dredging for marine animals, and of bringing up the most delicately-organized creatures in great abundance alive, will not be disposed to attach much weight to this objection. Every naturalist is aware that the most delicate Corallines and Ascidians may be dredged up roughly, placed in a bucket of sea water, and examined in full health and vigour after an hour's sail homeward under such circumstances.

" The evidence of practical oyster cultivators whom we have examined on this point is worthy of careful attention.

" According to the opinions expressed by this and other witnesses, not only is no harm done by dredging over the young spat, but positive injury is the result of not dredging over the ground before the spat is deposited.

" But it is rare for the spatting to take place early in May, and if it does, as the young oysters swim about for 22 to 27 days, dredging over the beds cannot possibly do them harm for the greater part, if not the whole month of May ; while if, as is more usual, the spatting does not occur until June, July, or even August or September, not only may dredging during these months be totally innocuous to the spat on account of its not having settled ; but, on the theory that dredging over the spat is injurious, great damage may be done in the two first of the open months.

" Even admitting a certain amount of destruction from dredging over the spat, the question arises whether this destruction is likely to be greater than that which will result from leaving the oyster to the undisputed sway of mussels, star-fishes, weeds, and mud ? This is a question which can only be decided by experience. In the present state of our information it can only be said that legislative interference is just as likely to do harm as good ; and that so far as the present close-time is concerned, dredging in May must certainly have less effect upon the brood than dredging in September."

---

## APPENDIX L.

### TO THE INSPECTOR-GENERAL OF FISHERIES IN FRANCE.

Sir,—I have the honour to acknowledge the receipt of your letter of the 27th June.

In my last letter, of the 27th June, I had the honour of showing you compendiously the state of the oyster culture in the basins of Arcachon, and I explained to you the difficulties I experienced in collecting the necessary information. My journey to Bordeaux to vote at the Plebiscite, the repairs required by the vessel, and the works urgently required to be done on the beds at this time of the year, prevented me seeing the *parqueurs*, to converse with them, to revisit their beds—in a word, to study the question of the artificial reproduction of oysters in the basin of Arcachon in a complete manner.

I cannot to-day enter into the large details or give the necessary figures. It is, however, possible for me to show the great traits of the position of the beds of Arcachon at this moment ; this rapid sketch will suffice, sir, to make you appreciate the actual state and the brilliant future that will repay the intelligent work of the parkers.

On the 6th April I took the command of the "Sylphe." My predecessor, M. Le Commandant Marchand, explained to me the manner of cultivating the parks, trials attempted, sudden disasters, &c. He showed me the Imperial Parks, the ponds in process of construction, &c.

From the first moment I understood the importance of this culture I was astounded at the greatness of the idea, at its happy application, and from that day I vowed to develop it, and to spread it. It is under your high direction, sir, that I have taken the first steps ; you have been good enough to give me the benefit of your experience ; I, on my part have worked, reflected, consulted the oldest fishermen of the basin ; each day my task appeared greater, and more useful.

What is it in effect ? To put under cultivation the earth that the low water leaves uncovered, and to spread ease in the midst of a poor population of fishermen and sailors, who are the born servants of the state—women and children can work on the beds, a largely remunerative work.

The 1,000 tiles covered with hydraulic lime, put in their place on the beds, cost £3 12s. 6d. ; it will be necessary also to clean the park, and get rid of crabs and *bigorneaux perceurs*, to get the tiles removed to the ponds when the winter sets in, and later on to detach the young brood ; a continuous work is necessary to keep the beds in a good state, but at the end of the year what will be the worth of the 1,000 tiles? If there has been a good spat, they will be worth from one to two thousand francs. This is the price I saw paid to two fishermen at Arcachon for their oysters. What were then the expenses? I will inform you. There are about 120 days' work each year, which represents from 200 to 250 francs ; the parkers will then have an easy and immediate return. Before these magnificent results, obtained at little cost, everybody is prepared to work. Last year about 500,000 tiles were put in the basin, this year there are at least two millions extra ; 300,000 at Meitros, 720,000 at Arcachon. I am not certain of the number of people employed at La Teste, Arès, Audenge, &c., &c. ; however, I am certain from having seen it, that there are a very large number, each one following his inclination and his means to march with enthusiasm in the new path, worked to increase his trade ; great and small are rivals with ardour. Here one finds Monsieur Bethurius, the large proprietor, who puts down 150,000 tiles on his parks, there is seen the poor fisherman who puts down his few hundred tiles on his small bed. All then have understood the use and the great advantages of this culture ; but whence comes this knowledge? It is without doubt from the establishment of the Imperial Parks that they derive it. They are in fact model parks in which the best methods of culture are sought out, studied, perfected, and then made common. They preach with example what is without contradiction a sort of eloquence in the grasp of all. The most ordinary men, from the facts that pass under their eyes, hurry to imitate us. What can say more, or be so convincing as these figures? 1,300 tiles placed on the beds of L'Ahilon in June last (1869), from which the spat was detached in April, produced a million oysters from three to five and six centimetres. I will have the honour to inform you in my next letter to what size these oysters have arrived.

These Imperial Parks have fulfilled to the utmost their rôle of model farm, they have supplied oysters to necessitous *parqueurs*, sold them to those richer, who undertake the culture of oysters on a larger scale. Such is the importance of these model farms, that I had the honour of proposing to you, sir, in one of my previous letters, that a return should be published each year of the works done on the Imperial Parks, of the methods employed, and the results obtained. Many people in effect have asked me for information and advice. I have received letters from parkers at Auray, La Trinité, the River Crach, from England, Holland, and Belgium, asking for advice.

This rôle is then of use, it is well marked out, well filled under the inspiration of your high abilities, and your great experience. It is necessary to continue in that way, and especially to work in the Basin of Arcachon. A few words will suffice to show that it is *there* especially that the Imperial Parks should be kept and cultivated with care.

At low tide the basin offers a great abundance of banks of mud, or gravel, or shells, separated by narrow but deep channels. What comes to pass at the spatting time, when the tide rises? The oyster that was lowest on the bed, dry from one to two hours, will open as soon as it feels the pleasant freshness of the waves, it will send forth its spat, the current will carry them on and will place them on these beds covered with shells, and collectors placed there by the hand of man; for the pass is narrow, and the basin is large; but when the tide is full in, it divides in several branches, it flows then more slowly, and with far less violence, the waves are broken and the water is less agitated. The microscopic oyster will then have every chance of attaching itself to a shell or a tile placed in the vicinity, whilst in open bays the troubled waters will not allow it to rest on any fixed point, and many are lost in this manner.

The Basin of Arcachon we see is then admirably constructed by nature to serve as a nursery for the growth of oysters, to produce millions, then to spread them on the coast of France, or to sell them to other nations. Your great experience, sir, had well understood the importance of this point, and time has justified your choice and labour. Still, some years of patience, of work, and of foresight, and we will have arrived at a splendid result.

Last year 18,000 tiles were placed on the Imperial beds, this year I put down 68,000. The 1,300 tiles at Arcachon produced a million of oysters; if the harvest of 1870 be as good as that of 1869, we will collect from four to five millions of oysters. Monday last, the 27th June, I saw* on the greater part of the tiles, by tens, twenties, and thirties; on several I even counted as many as fifty. In some days I will be able to say how many oysters we may expect this year.

It will not be as great as I would have expected, but the *vote du plebiscite* at Bordeaux, and the mending of the vessel, kept me from Arcachon during the month of May; then again, I have been short of hands, and considering the number of tiles that had to be put down, I was obliged to commence to place the collectors on the 15th of May. The tiles, although I took the precaution to place them where they would be well washed by the current, are a little soiled by the deposit of mud, and do not give the same return as those put down in the beginning of June, and even from the 12th to the 21st June. But I had a great number of *appareils* to put down; this year, on account of the unaccustomed heat, promised to be exceptional; I had not sufficient money to hire labourers, so I had to act as I did.

We have this year unusual expenses to go to, viz., two large boats for

* Number left out in original.

the service of the parks, one of them for the purpose of carrying tiles, wood, lime, &c., &c., the other a light boat for the watching of the beds, and to chase poachers, &c.; they will cost about £24; 55,000 tiles, together with wood, and iron wire, necessary for the erection of stacks of tiles—lime (£24), wood and stakes, wicker, broom, for the large ponds on Crastorbe; shovels, picks, hatchets, skates, coal-tar, straw-hats, baskets, knives for detaching, different tools, &c., &c. If we wish to reap the price of our labours, the same sum of 10,000 francs will be necessary for the year 1871. If I ask for the same sum, it is because I will require a second lot of tiles, in order to be free to detach the spat later on in the year, so as not to be compelled to do this in a hurry, to put the old tiles back again on the beds, and consequently to do it more slowly and more carefully, and to injure fewer oysters, then to pick out the injured oysters, to construct boxes, covered with wire gauze, and to place them inside to heal.

On these conditions what can we hope for? In 1870, four to five millions of oysters, let us only say three millions. In 1871 at least as many. The beds have to-day five millions, this will be at least twelve millions in 1872, and the beds will be self-supporting, at least they will cost very much less, possessing already the tiles. To come to the help of the small *parqueurs*, and to sell a part of the product for the profit of the Treasury.

Such are, sir, the actual state of things, and the results that a wise and prudent administration of the Imperial Parks will bring about.

I dare not, having that object in view, sell any oysters this year, or at least if any were sold, they should only be a very small quantity, until the beds were thickly enough sown to be able to furnish a production *normal and regular*.

I have the honour to be, sir,

Your most obedient servant,

A. De Rochebrune.

---

REPORT of the COMMANDANT of the steam vessel, the "SYLPHE," to M. COSTE, Inspector-General of Fisheries.

Arcachon,
On board the "Sylphe,"
16th September, 1870.

I returned to Arcachon on the 12th of this month, and on the same day I visited L'Ahilon.

The spat last year was good, but this year it is splendid—I then visited several parks and conversed with the parkers; all are delighted at the results obtained. *There are oysters in abundance everywhere.* The *gardes maritimes*, and the Inspector of Fisheries have both confirmed me in this statement. Never was there ever such a sight seen in the basin. The old residents here say that not since 1859 has there been a similar abundance, but at that time they had not such an important number of collectors (at the lowest calculation two millions of tiles), as were put down this year; this is the reason I can state for saying that *never* has there been such a harvest. It is a very *manna*, sent down from heaven, which ought to guarantee the prosperity of the basin for ever, if the parkers know how to be prudent. There has already been some outlay—work for women and children—the future will be still better, and will give comfort to the people of Arcachon. I cannot as yet say what amount of young brood there is, but I will give a modest approximation which will certainly be under the truth. However, I give you the figures, sir, and will leave you to judge. There are, *at the lowest computation*, two millions of tiles; I believe there are more, but I will take this amount. I take on an average twenty-five oysters per tile (all those I examined had fully that amount, and I even do not take into account all that the parkers state that there are). We then have *fifty* millions of young oysters on the collectors. The shells of the cockles thrown on the natural beds, have also collected the spat. In certain places, on Le Cès, for example, the oysters are in bunches of four and five. I will put down, however, this quantity of spat at a less figure than that on the tiles—about thirty millions, and I can state without fear of exaggeration, that there are at least *eighty millions* of young oysters, perhaps more, even from 100 to 150 millions. The visit to the parks and natural beds next month will enable me to give you more exact information. In a word, sir, our parks all present a beautiful and interesting sight. The pilot of Marennes, who accompanied me here, and who knows all the works of this description undertaken at Oleron and along the coast, was perfectly amazed at such results. *He saw and was convinced.* Incredibility has become enthusiasm. I would much wish that events would permit you coming here, sir, to judge for yourself what our works have produced. They are the result of your observations, and your long and patient labours have to-day been crowned with the most brilliant success. All you predicted is realized. The basin of Arcachon is constructed by nature to reap the spat of the oyster. I beg you will excuse the unconnectedness of this report. I am writing in a hurry, under the impression of what I have seen in the last few days. *I saw in haste, but I am positive I saw well,* and that I am *below* the truth.

(Signed)     DE ROCHEBRUNE,
Captain of the Steam Vessel
the "Sylphe," at Arcachon.

REPORT to the INSPECTOR-GENERAL of FISHERIES, on the situation of the IMPERIAL PARK of the BASIN of ARCACHON. By M. MARCHAND, Captain of the *Sylphe*.

### GENERAL CONDITIONS.

The Imperial Parks have been kept up and managed by a special grant of £140.

The expenses consist in the purchase of cockles, shells, tiles, hydraulic lime, boats for the transport of materials, people, planks for tiles, shovels, different tools, spars for beacons, hatchets, nails, &c., and various things required for the parks.

We placed 20,000 tiles covered with a coating of water lime, in ruches of 45 tiles each, forming about 444 ruches, all resting on a deal flooring We have ascertained that there are on an average 100 spat per tile; 150 *cubic* yards of shells have been scattered about over the different parks, and the show of spat there is remarkably good. The old shells and the shells of live oysters are covered with spat, we cannot actually fix the number, but there is a very fine production.

### ESTABLISHMENT of CLAIRES.

The determination to construct claires for tiles covered with spat is excellent, and in time will prove very beneficial; it is a very good plan, the young oysters will thus be protected from the ravages of parasites, and the inclemency of the weather.

The tables with fascines have a large quantity of spat on them, but on the 2,000 fascines there are not so many, owing to the great heat. The drainage pipes that form the boundary of L'Ahilon have all spat on them.

### LOSS OWING TO THE GREAT HEAT.

This loss will be recovered; the spatting of part of the oysters, at a time when the weather was warm and fine, has tended to cover the old oyster shells, the cultch, and the large oysters, in an extraordinary manner. The rubble of L'Ahilon has very little spat except on the lower part of the blocks.

### TEMPEST of the 20th and 21st SEPTEMBER.

The tempest of the 20th and 21st September has cleaned the parks, washed away the mud and the seaweeds, but the parks of Cès and L'Ahilon lost many oysters which were thrown upon the neighbouring foreshores and into the channels, they will be found later on in the public fishing. It is a description of forced sowing.

### PARK DU CÈS.

The park of Cès is in a good state of natural reproduction, which is shown most on the cockle shells; we owe this result to the great care which has been bestowed on it, in management, and in keeping it clean. The spat on 5,000 tiles there is superb. This park will have to be rendered "healthy," as it were, by means of channels cut with a fall, by having it raked, and by having the weeds taken away. The park of Cès has suffered by the great heat, and by the tempest of September, but it is a very reproductive and precious bed. In 1870 it will be necessary to put down 100 cubic yards of cockle shells, and 2,000 tiles.

### CRASTORBE.

A good park, well kept, sixty cubic yards of cockle shells were put down; the channels for the improvement of the park and to allow the water to run in work well. Natural reproduction is good. The cultch put down at a suitable time shows a good spat. Walking must be prevented on this park as the soil is very soft; people after ducks and *courtines* must be prevented from going on to it; even supposing that each person does not gather some oysters, the way in which they have to follow their calling destroys the young oysters, not only on Crastorbe, but especially on its borders, which are rich, and naturally derive benefit from the works and the spat on the park.

The watchfulness of the guards and of *la Goalette la Loubine* is very active and efficacious, but very fatiguing.

### CLAIRES DE CRASTORBE.

The claires ordered to be undertaken by the Minister of the Marine are in course of construction on the first hectare of the Sud and Crastorbe.

A special report with plans will be furnished, but it is best to wait until the works are completed, as there might have to be some modification of the original plan, considering the clayey and soft nature of the soil.

The oysters will be well preserved there, in shelter from mud, and all dead sea-weed. Two claires nearly finished answer already very well; the weeds and anything else that float towards the entrance of the water into the claires are all removed with rakes. The parkers will find here a subject for serious consideration.

## L'Ahilon.

This park, established on the foreshore of L'Ahilon, is very well managed. The claires require mending, and the centre dyke should be filled up; 19,000 tiles covered with hydraulic lime have been placed there; a good spat has taken place; more than 100 oysters on each tile; the soil is excellent and covered with spat; many have fallen from off the tiles; at the time of the tempest of the 21st September the average was taken after this storm. The debris of tiles, the posts and drainage pipes, are all covered with spat. Thirty cubic yards of cultch were put on the bed; the spat was very abundant; the storm of September carried a portion of them into the channels. The thirty-two tables with fascines have some spat. The fascines themselves very few. L'Ahilon is specially fitted for the production of oysters, which grow with a remarkable rapidity here; the mud was an objection, but since its establishment as an Imperial Park the works that have been executed have made it a superior oyster park; there is not such another in the whole basin. The experiments in the time of putting up the hutches give the following results:

| Date of erection. | Average of oysters per tile. |
|---|---|
| 23 June, | 106 |
| 10 July, | 68 |
| 24  „ | 22 |
| 10 August, | 33 |
| 23  „ | 22 |
| Tides of September, | from 1 to 5 |
| The 22nd of September, after the storm, | — |
| After, | — |

The "Loubine" watches this park very zealously; the duty is very fatiguing considering the proximity of the small grants of oyster parks.

### Use of the Imperial Parks.

For several years, the results obtained by the Imperial Parks have borne their fruit, many of the persons holding concessions having adopted the same methods of culture as those in use on the Imperial Parks.

This year more than 600,000 tiles coated with a preparation of hydraulic lime, have been placed in the basin, which have all received a good quantity of spat, with the exception of 8,000 tiles of the Syndicat du Trou du Sud, placed in a bad position.

According to the ground selected and the height of the collectors above the level of the low water mark, the other undertakings have obtained results varying from 35 to 100 spat per tile; for the different parks the average is about 75 oysters per tile; so the parkers say, and I think it must be very nearly exact.

Already sales have taken place between the cultivators and parkers, the oysters from the tiles of 1869 are quoted at £800 per million, these oysters, from their size, naturally will remain in the basin of Arcachon.

### Cultivators.

The cultivators of oysters with tiles are not very well pleased with their position; they naturally desire to realize their profits as soon as possible, as their expenses are considerable. I think it would be desirable, even necessary, to give them permission to sell immediately a portion of their spat; by this means they would have the requisite funds and would be able to increase their operations, the future prosperity of the basin would be more quickly assured than by restrictive measures, and later on full liberty of action for the sale of the product of their tiles, either detached from, or with the tiles, might be allowed them.

The surveillance would be very easily managed—the oyster grown on a tile, in a measure, preserves indelibly its mark of origin, the lower shell has a light flattened appearance near the hinge, and a small quantity of the lime, during at least two years (and that without giving the oyster an unsightly or unpleasant shape).

## USEFUL RESTRICTION.

But, as compensation, the deep sea oysters and the oysters from the cultch and shells, for the future, should not be allowed to be sold for the market or for export, until they had attained the size of seven centimetres.

The Imperial Parks, well managed, are the natural sources from which the basin will be restocked ; they can support themselves.

The quantity of oysters sold to the Inscription Maritime has allowed of the productive foreshores being cultivated ; they have been furnished with cultch to enable the necessary works to be done, so that thus the Imperial Parks contribute to their own maintenance by the sale of their oysters ; the natural beds opposed to them, as producing as much per hectare as the others ; this year the storms of September have given them a large quantity of their small oysters, and spat ; as I mentioned before, it is to the Imperial Parks they owe this stock.

The 100,000 oysters from the imperial beds, sold to the Inscription Maritime was a lucky stroke for the purchasers, for during the interval between the buying of them in March and their being sold actually, they were covered with spat.    Before selling other oysters, either to individuals or to the Inscription Maritime, it would be well to establish a minimum for the Imperial parks, about ten millions of oysters, which appears to be the normal amount during 1870.    It would be disastrous for the future prosperity of the beds to even sell one of them later ; on the contrary, by a regular sale, varying in extent according to the amount produced, the basin itself would not only be restocked, but would be capable of furnishing oysters to others.

I consider that the granting of oysters to individuals is bad, causing jealousy ; for the most part, these gifts are turned into money, the persons to whom they have been given, selling them even before they get them themselves ; we have often also seen complaints in regard to the good or bad appearance of the oysters.

## WORKS to be undertaken in 1870.

To continue the ordinary methods of culture, shown by the experiences of many years, and the experiments that have proved successful in 1869.

Firstly.—To complete the claires of Crastorbe.

Secondly.—Remake the claires of L'Ahilon.

Thirdly.—To throw down the centre ditch of L'Ahilon.

Fourthly.—To spread cultch on Cès and Crastorbe.    During the *mortes eaux* to prepare the collectors of all sorts, and to coat the tiles with hydraulic lime.

To purchase from 20,000 to 100,000 more tiles, and to suppress the tables with fascines as being too costly for the amount produced.

To place large fascines where they won't be left uncovered.

Here is what, for the first year, this increase in material would cost, afterwards we would only have to pay for the cultivating.

If the tiles off L'Ahilon had not been given away, we would now have 40,000, and our production for the year would be doubled.

|  | Francs. |
|---|---|
| 1,000 tiles cost . . . . . | 60 |
| Hydraulic lime for 1,000 tiles costs . | 6 |
| The wood for 1,000 tiles costs . . | 10 |
| Thus the expense for 80,000 tiles, . | 4,800 |
| Lime for 100,000 tiles, . . . | 600 |
| For the *plateaux*, . . . . | 1,000 |
| About 200 cubic yards of cultch, . | 1,500 |
|  | 7,900 |
| Cost of working, purchase of nails, sprigs, skates, boats, tools, coal-tar, &c., . . . . . . . . | 2,500* |
| Total, | 10,400 |
| For the first year, . . . . . . | 10,400 |
| Cost for the future, . . . . ˙ . . | 4,100 |

The older the tiles are, the better they can be coated with the lime, which thus becoming thicker, they are less liable to be broken than the new ones, which often arrive cracked; indeed the loss for breakage is put down at one per cent.

Supposing even that the spat for 1870 is only at the rate of fifty oysters per tile, that would amount to five millions of oysters, which, in the month of October of the same year, would be worth 100,000 francs, for six months only, that is, it would pay for the station and more than double the cost of the material for a year.

The stock and the cultch remaining as benefice.

In the event of these propositions meeting with your approval, the material should be purchased at the latest, towards the 15th of February, 1870, in order to have the necessary time for preparation.

It would also be as well to obtain officially from the administration of bridges and ways, or domains, a grant of about 1,000 metres of the island called " L'Ile aux Oiseaux," in order to be able to place our materials for cultivation on it; the thing exists at present on sufferance.

On board the *Sylphe*, the 14th December, 1869.

The Lieutenant of the vessel,

˙ MARCHAND.

---

## APPENDIX M.

### SOCIETY for affording RELIEF to the SAILORS of CONCARNEAU.

#### RULES OF THE SOCIETY.

CHAPTER I.—*Formation of the Society—its aim—constitution.*

1. A society has been formed for affording relief to the sailors of the maritime circonscription of the sub-division of Concarneau.

2. This society will be called " A Society for affording Relief to the Sailors of Concarneau."

3. It will have for its object :—

    1. To meet the pressing wants of the wives, children, fathers, mothers, brothers, sisters, orphans, and minors of sailors drowned at sea.

    2. To assist sailors who by accident or loss at sea, are reduced to poverty.

    3. To procure medical aid and medicine for sailors that have become sick at sea.

* According to the number of collectors.

4. Medical aid and medicine will be procured for the members of this society and their families, both at Concarneau and Lauriec, until the society has no resources wherewith to assist the whole circonscription maritime.

5. The society is composed of members participating, and honorary members.

6. The members participating are all the sailors in the quarter of Concarneau. They are admitted from sixteen years of age, and partake of the advantages of the society.

7. Honorary members are those who contribute to the prosperity of the society. Honorary members are admitted on their simply applying at the office of the society.

8. Honorary members do not participate in the advantages of the society.

9. Every sailor desirous of becoming a participating member, will be admitted without right of entrance during the two first years, after which, if he is over twenty-six years of age, he will pay a sum fixed by the council of administration.

## Chapter II.—*Administration.*

10. The administration is composed of a president, elected by the Emperor, and fourteen members selected by the general assembly, half from the honorary members, and the others from the participating members, who will meet together to name their office.

11. The president watches over and assures the execution of the laws ; he makes the return each year in conformity with the 20th article of the decree regulating relief societies.

The duties of the secretary are to attend to the correspondence, and to keep the archives.

The treasurer takes the receipts, and makes the payments of the society upon a visé by the president, or a member with powers for that purpose.

12. There is every year a general assembly, at which all the honorary members attend, and those of the participating members, as hold any office in the society.

At this meeting the report of the state of the society is read, and the members pronounce upon any questions submitted to them.

13. The council of administration meets whenever summoned by the president.

14. Half of the council of administration is elected anew each year.

Those with the majority of votes are elected.

## Chapter III.—*Obligations of its Members.*

15. Each member shall, each year, at the close of the Sardine Fishery, pay as follows :—Skippers, 5 francs ; men, 4 francs.

16. Fishermen that follow any other fishing, or who are engaged in trading as sailors, if they desire to partake of the advantages of the society, must pay the above mentioned sum at the same time.

17. Any sailors engaged in the navy, will, upon their return to their quarter, have to pay—if they wish to continue as members of the society—the same amount of money as was paid by the other members in their absence.

18. Honorary members will have to pay as a subscription to the society a sum not less than 5 francs.

Any member not paying his subscription will be declared as having resigned.

19. The subscriptions of honorary members will be paid to the treasurer in July of each year.

### CHAPTER IV.—*Obligations of the Society to its Members.*

20. The council of administration will be called upon to decide the amount of money to be distributed as help, and that within the limits of the resources of the society.

21. Independently of the care stated in articles 3 and 4, participating members *alone*, will be allowed 1 franc a day whenever sickness will have prevented their working during four consecutive days. This payment will cease when the doctor thinks it no longer required.

22. Help in either money or kind can be equally given in certain cases, viz., in case of death or loss.

23. As soon as a participating member or one of his family is taken sick, or has met with an accident, he is to inform the doctor accordingly, as also the treasurer, who should immediately give the sick person a card with their name on it, upon which the name of the sickness, and the prescriptions given by the doctor should be written.

24. The doctors will be chosen by the administration, and their fees will be paid by subscription.

25. The administration will make arrangements with one or several apothecaries, for the furnishing of medicines, or with the doctor, if there be no apothecary in the locality.

26. No medicines at the expense of the society will be allowed to be delivered unless accompanied with a voucher signed by the doctor.

27. No help is allowed for sickness caused by debauchery or intemperance, nor for any injuries received by a member in a fight, when it is proved that he was the aggressor; nor for injuries received in public rows, in which he has voluntarily taken a part.

28. In case of death, indigent participating members will be buried at the expense of the society.

29. Every year a funeral service will be said for those dead. The administration and all the members will be invited to take part in this religious ceremony.

30. The president will name, according as the society requires it, a certain number of members, taken in turn from the roll of participating members, who shall be called "visitors," and whose duty it will be to see the sick, to watch that they receive exactly the help due to them, and to give them their own help if it is required by the sick persons or their families.

### CHAPTER V.—*Social Funds, and their placing of Fund.*

31. The social fund is composed of:—

1. Subscriptions of members participating.
2. Subscriptions of members honorary.
3. Help of the State Department and Commune.
4. Gifts and private legacies.

32. When the funds of the society exceed 1,000 francs, the surplus will be placed in the reserve fund of Quimper.

33. Any change in the foregoing rules must be submitted to the administration before it becomes valid.

No change can take place without the majority of votes in the general assembly, and shall be approved by the Government.

Made at Concarneau, this 24th day of January, 1864.

The members of the council of administration—
(Signed,)

PENANROS DUPPONT, BALERTRIE, GUILLON, SAUBAN, BRISSON, HENU, QUELLENEC, GUILLIRME, SAUBAN.

The president of the society (signed), ALIX.

True copy—The president of the society,
(Signed), ALIX.

---

## APPENDIX N.

INFORMATION relative to the OYSTER BREEDING ESTABLISHMENTS at ILE DE RÉ.

| QUESTION. | ANSWER. |
|---|---|
| 1. Number of ponds and fattening beds ? | 3,044 | 932 } 3,936 |
| 2. Extent in hectares ? | 202 hectares, 47 ares, 72 centares. |
| 3. Number of owners of parks ? | About 2,450. |
| 4. Number of owners of fattening beds ? | About 578. |
| 5. Number of persons employed ? | About 5,000. |
| 6. Does the Government exact payment from, or does it impose conditions upon those obtaining grants ? | The concessions are free and are capable of being revoked at any time and without any compensation being given ? |
| 7. What is the extent of the public or natural beds in the sea ? | There are none at the Ile de Ré. |
| 8. During how many days last year were the public or natural beds allowed to be dredged ? | See Question No. 7. |
| 9. During what months may oysters be dredged ? | In the parks, from the 1st September to the 30th April following. In the fattening beds, during the whole year. |
| 10. What was the quantity of oysters sold last year? | 879,713. |
| 11. What was the value of that quantity ? | 31,145 francs. |
| 12. What quantity is there at present on the Island. | In the parks, 2,250,000 In the fattening ponds, 286,000 Total, 2,536,000 |
| 13. At what age is the young oyster transferred from the cultch to the beds ? | A year after birth. |

| QUESTION. | ANSWER. |
|---|---|
| 14. When they are moved are they taken from their place of birth? | They are moved to places where they grow, fatten, and green. They are left where they were spatted if the ground is suitable. |
| 15. What is about the loss incurred in moving them from the tiles? | It is insignificant, probably about 20 per cent. |
| 16. At what age as a rule are the young oysters sold at the Ile de Ré. | At two years old they are sold for the market; at one year, they are sold to stock beds. |

| YEARS. | Number of Concessions made during so many years. | Number of Oysters Sold and Gathered. | | Extent of Ground given each Year. | Extent of Ground under Cultivation each Year. |
|---|---|---|---|---|---|
| | | Number of Oysters. | Amount in Francs. | | |
| | | | | hr. ar. c. | |
| 1857 | 121 | -- | — | 6 05 00 | — |
| 1858 | 444 | — | -- | 22 20 00 | — |
| 1859 | 835 | 157,900 | 3,150 | 46 51 86 | 4 54 00 |
| 1860 | 843 | 401,350 | 8,027 | 44 48 86 | 7 90 50 |
| 1861 | 322 | 1,615,000 | 32,892 | 16 10 00 | 20 05 00 |
| 1862 | 439 | 2,780,740 | 53,000 | 21 95 00 | 27 04 00 |
| 1863 | 498 | 5,650,230 | 113,382 | 24 90 00 | 55 03 00 |
| 1864 | 298 | 2,376,440 | 45,456 | 14 90 00 | 30 50 50 |
| 1865 | 72 | 1,919,900 | 50,500 | 3 61 40 | 31 95 00 |
| 1866 | 3 | 1,181,000 | 37,912 | 13 60 | 25 00 00 |
| 1867 | 51 | 879,713 | 31,145 | 1 62 00 | 22 59 50 |
| | 3,976 | 16,961,893 | 375,464 | 202 47 72 | — |

## APPENDIX O.

### WHITSTABLE OYSTER FISHERY.

| Year. | Quantity of Brood obtained from the Flats. | Total Cost. | Average Cost per Wash. | Quantity of Brood obtained from Essex. | Total Cost. | Average Cost per Wash. | Grand Totals. | |
|---|---|---|---|---|---|---|---|---|
| | | | | | | | Quantities of Brood from Flats and Essex. | Total Cost. |
| | Wash. | £ s. d. | s. d. | Wash. | £ s. d. | s. d. | Wash. | £ s. d. |
| From July, 1852, to July, 1853, | — | — | — | — | — | — | 63,853½ | 15,240 0 5 |
| 1853–4, | — | — | — | — | — | — | 55,937 | 16,200 4 0 |
| 1854–5, | 3,018 | 905 8 1 | 6 0 | 41,083½ | 15,064 0 2 | 7 4 | 44,101½ | 15,969 8 3 |
| 1855–6, | — | — | — | — | — | — | 30,004 | 10,322 8 11 |
| 1856–7, | 11,040 | 3,000 3 10 | 5 6 | 29,664 | 8,250 1 8 | 5 6 | 40,704 | 11,250 5 6 |
| 1857–8, | 30,070 | 6,914 13 7 | 3 10 | 41,774 | 14,142 10 8 | 6 9 | 77,844 | 21,057 4 3 |
| 1858–9, | 49,319 | 8,574 17 7½ | — | 85,559½ | 20,136 2 7 | — | 134,878½ | 28,711 0 2½ |
| 1859–60, | 48,058 | 8,319 7 9 | — | 35,423 | 11,519 13 4 | — | 83,481 | 19,839 1 1 |
| 1860–1, | 11,851 | 2,761 4 11 | — | 37,858½ | 13,271 19 6 | — | 49,709½ | 16,033 4 5 |
| 1861–2, | 5,131 | 1,520 15 7 | — | 79,803 | 35,192 6 1 | — | 84,937 | 36,713 1 8 |
| 1862–3, | 2,419 | 858 17 11 | — | 20,080½ | 12,563 11 11½ | — | 22,499½ | 13,389 9 10½ |
| 1863–4, | 2,398 | Prices varying from 9s. to 16s. | | 12,836 | Prices varying from 13s. 8d. to 16s. | | 15,234 | 14,553 19 2 |
| 1864 to March, 1865, | 914 | 483 3 7 | 0 11 | 1,769½ | 1,462 5 3 | 17 0 | 2,683½ | 1,945 8 10 |
| Do. . . | — | — | — | 2,500 | 2,625 0 0 | 21 0 | 2,500 | 2,625 0 0 |

## WHITSTABLE OYSTER COMPANY—*continued.*

| Year. | Quantity of Oysters obtained from Ireland. | Quantity of Oysters from Scotland. | Quantity of Oysters from Falmouth, Jersey, Channel, and Hamble. | Total Cost of the same. | Value of Natives and Commons sold in London and Home Markets from August to May in each year. | Value of Natives sold in Foreign Markets. | Price paid for Labour from August each year to May in the next year. | Total Expenses for each year, from August in each year to May in the next year. |
|---|---|---|---|---|---|---|---|---|
| | Barrels. | Barrels. | Tubs. | £ s. d. | £ s. d. | £ s. d. | £ s. d. | £ s. d. |
| 1852, | None. | None. | 11,645½ | | 47,413 19 1 | 2,258 14 11 | 1852–3, 16,793 9 9 | 48,484 11 1 |
| 1853, | Do. | Do. | 9,809 | 2,254 9 8 | 31,700 16 8 | — | 1853–4, 17,822 5 2 | 45,427 1 5½ |
| 1854, | Do. | Do. | — | 2,115 7 7 | 31,449 12 10 | — | 1854–5, 14,154 15 0 | 43,994 1 11 |
| 1855, | Do. | Do. | — | — | 31,449 12 10 | — | 1855–6, 14,166 11 6 | 36,715 9 3½ |
| 1856, | Do. | Do. | — | — | 30,964 19 7 | — | 1856–7, 14,131 8 8 | 42,335 13 4 |
| 1857, | Do. | Do. | — | 2,261 19 10½ | 30,986 7 7 | — | 1857–8, 19,415 6 11 | 58,887 2 11½ |
| 1858, | Do. | Do. | — | 3,803 8 10½ | 11,484 6 10½ | 985 10 0 | 1858–9, 20,445 13 9½ | 65,948 10 9½ |
| 1859, | Do. | Do. | — | 3,543 17 4 | 51,588 2 7½ | 6,385 3 3 | 1859–60, 20,531 18 6 | 64,286 12 7½ |
| 1860, | Do. | Do. | — | 1,046 11 2½ | 43,173 6 8½ | 4,481 15 0 | 1860–1, 16,713 4 4 | 45,745 1 6 |
| 1861, | Do. | Do. | — | 2,135 3 11 | 22,117 1 10 | 11,429 3 6 | 1861–2, 27,641 18 9 | 74,354 18 1 |
| 1862, | Do. | Do. | — | 5,473 6 7 | 58,911 12 7½ | 13,216 0 0 | 1862–3, 43,731 14 4 | 97,794 2 1 |
| 1863, | Do. | Do. | — | 9,442 10 8 | 74,778 19 3½ | 25,556 19 10 | 1863–4, 46,609 10 8½ | 79,860 0 7½ |
| 1864, | 2,654 | 2,838 | 1,183 | 4,917 7 8½ | 55,217 3 5 | 19,660 2 0 | | |
| 1865, | 1,933 | 1,009 | — | 1,422 12 0 | Returns for this year not yet sent in. | | | |

The above Returns show :—
1. The amount received by the Company for natives and commons included.
2. An account of the natives sold in the foreign markets.
3. The amount paid for labour on the ground.
4. The total expenses of the Company during each year.

A tub of oysters is about 26 gals.   A barrel do. is about 28 do.

---

PRICES of NATIVE OYSTERS (WHITSTABLE) from the year 1825 to 1870.

| | Average price per Bushel for the year. | | Average price per Bushel for the year. |
|---|---|---|---|
| | £ s. d. | | £ s. d. |
| From August, 1825, to May, 1826, | 0 19 0 | 1846–7, | 2 7 0 |
| 1826–7, | 1 0 0 | 1847–8, | 2 1 0 |
| 1827–8, | 1 8 0 | 1848–9, | 2 1 0 |
| 1828–9, | 1 16 0 | 1849–50, | 2 0 6 |
| 1829–30, | 1 13 0 | 1850–1, | 1 11 0 |
| 1830–1, | 1 10 0 | 1851–2, | 1 16 0 |
| 1831–2, | 1 11 0 | 1852–3, | 2 2 0 |
| 1832–3, | 1 10 0 | 1853–4, | 2 7 0 |
| 1833–4, | 1 16 0 | 1854–5, | 2 9 0 |
| 1834–5, | 1 19 0 | 1855–6, | 2 1 0 |
| 1835–6, | 1 12 0 | 1856–7, | 1 18 0 |
| 1836–7, | 1 13 0 | 1857–8, | 2 2 0 |
| 1837–8, | 1 12 0 | 1858–9, | 2 2 0 |
| 1838–9, | 1 12 0 | 1859–60, | 2 2 0 |
| 1839–40, | 1 17 0 | 1860–1, | 2 2 0 |
| 1840–1, | 2 2 0 | 1861–2, | 2 2 0 |
| 1841–2, | 2 0 0 | 1862–3, | 2 8 0 |
| 1842–3, | 2 10 0 | 1863–4, | 3 8 0 |
| 1843–4, | 2 18 0 | 1864–5, Prices varied from 80s. to 90s. | 4 10 0 |
| 1844–5, | 3 0 0 | 1869–70, | 10 2 0 |
| 1845–6, | 2 18 0 | | |

DUBLIN: Printed by ALEXANDER THOM, 87 & 88, Abbey-street,
For Her Majesty's Stationery Office.

www.ingramcontent.com/pod-product-compliance
Lightning Source LLC
Chambersburg PA
CBHW031059280326
41928CB00049B/1109